Jane's

Special
Forces
Recognition Guide

Jane's Recognition Guides

Aircraft
Guns
Special Forces
Tanks and Combat Vehicles
Trains
Vintage Aircraft
Warships

Special Forces
Recognition Guide

Ewen Southby-Tailyour

HARPER

NEW YORK • LONDON • TORONTO • SYDNEY

HARPER

First published in 2005 by **Collins**

HarperCollins Publishers
77-85 Fulham Palace Road
Hammersmith
London w6 8jb
UK
www.collins.co.uk

HarperCollins Publishers Inc
10 East 53rd Street
New York
NY 10022
USA
www.harpercollins.com

www.janes.com

ISBN-13: 978-0-00-718329-6

HarperCollins books may be purchased for
educational, business or sales promotional
use. For information in the United States,
please write to: Special Markets
Department, HarperCollins Publishers Inc.,
10 East 53rd Street, New York, NY 10022.

The name of the 'Smithsonian',
'Smithsonian Institution' and the sunburst
logo are registered trademarks of the
Smithsonian Institution.

Printed in China

11 12 13   10 9 8 7 6 5 4 3

Contents

Introduction

One accepted definition of modern Special Forces is 'a military unit trained for unconventional operations and especially counter-insurgency'. It might now be argued that with the general proliferation of worldwide terrorism all military forces and most police forces should be trained for unconventional operations: certainly there should be considerably more awareness of, and training for, asymmetric warfare.

By their nature Special Forces are ideally suited to combat asymmetric warfare: indeed, because of their capability of operating in small numbers or even alone – yet with an array of weapons that would normally be deployed by rather larger units – they are able to conduct their own versions of asymmetric warfare against terrorist cells: a case of 'the biter bit' perhaps. In the opposite direction as it were, a point to be remembered is that military Special Forces of the more powerful countries tend to be (but by no means always are) employed in strategic operations rather than tactical.

Throughout history there have been forces temporarily raised for a special operation but the First and Second World Wars saw a marked proliferation of such units: units which were often disbanded once the aim had been accomplished. However, a few survived to mature into permanent formations within today's armed forces while retaining their original *raison d'etre*: commando units and parachute regiments (airborne as opposed to airmobile or airportable which, for the purposes of this publication, are generally considered to be neither special nor elite – although there are exceptions) that had not existed before 1939 now remain in many countries as regular, elite – if not always special – forces. Now, almost all special forces select men and women for training from both their regular and reserve forces: after which selection, incidentally, the worldwide pass rate for such trainees is estimated to be as low as between 10 and 15 per cent.

The dividing line between military, police, customs and government-sponsored, special and elite forces, secret forces, intelligence gathering forces, counter-insurgency, anti-terrorist, and anti-piracy forces (and, now, forces aimed at biological terrorism) plus those employed in the fight against the illegal trafficking of drugs, weapons and humans, is often blurred. This is especially so in the military where elite organisations tend to contain Special Forces within their Order of Battle. These elite troops include those whose duties might involve raiding and intelligence gathering (two reasons for the formation of Special Forces in the first place), deep-reconnaissance and the conduct of 'amphibious, advanced force operations' (which could include submarine, helicopter and minesweeping operations). Elite forces are often needed to cover and protect Special Forces and, in the context of this publication, the specialist skills required for these tasks may well be every bit as special as those required by the forces they are supporting: hence the inclusion of them and their equipment in the following lists.

Units whose personnel are 'prone to capture' by the nature of their support for Special Forces' operations also deserve a place in the following lists for, again, most Special Forces rely on these units to insert and extract them from the theatre of operations. These 'insertion' organisations may include submarine, fixed wing aircraft and helicopter crews as well as the coxswains of small, fast, surface craft and even the drivers of fast, all-terrain vehicles. The training and change in philosophical outlook of these 'insertion' crews (and the authorities that command them) is crucial and is well demonstrated by the reply of the captain of one country's Special Forces, fast-insertion craft: when asked what would happen if he put his craft ashore, unintentionally, while in support of a Special Forces attack, he replied that he would be court-martialled. That concern at the back of his mind did not allow him to take perfectly acceptable risks in support of those whose risks were far greater.

Troops especially – and, of importance to this publication, permanently – trained to operate in particularly harsh environments are also included: although not automatically, for some formations may boast impressive titles but little else beyond the norm – the USA's 10th Mountain Division is one such as, to quote from an unnamed source during the Afghanistan Campaign, 'the

Division doesn't do mountains!' Mountain, jungle, desert and high latitude operations require skills for their success not usually found in regular infantry and artillery units; no matter how well trained those units may otherwise be.

Organisations which in both World Wars might have been regarded as useful only in unconventional warfare will find that much of yesterday's unconventional warfare is today's regular warfare: this is becoming particularly so with the developing threat of asymmetric terrorism and is a statement equally true of modern equipment and transport.

All Special Forces units receive their share of criticism and are often derided, through jealousy perhaps, as 'private armies' composed of arrogant, military misfits: in the case of the UK's wartime Coastal Forces of Motor Torpedo Boats, Motor Gun Boats and Motor Launches, these august and brave men even earned the sobriquet, 'Costly Farces'. While it is true that some Special Forces units attract men and women who regard the norms of military discipline as an unnecessary impediment to their art, it is equally true that those units which do harbour people with this attitude are less successful. It also has to be accepted that standards of Special Forces differ from country to country and it is certainly true that one country's elite or Special Forces may be another's mundane formation. Equally true is the fact that a certain kudos is attached to the possession of a 'Special Force' even if that 'Special Force' is, in reality, pretty conventional and basic by the standards of others. Thus, while some nations may claim the possession of a Special Force, in reality the declared unit may be far from worthy of this title – if it exists at all!

On paper, special or elite forces may be costly to train and maintain but, once their efforts are seen against a wider backdrop, this criticism often becomes muted. For instance, in the Second World War's North African campaign one man commanding small, motorized, desert patrols was credited with destroying more enemy aircraft than the whole of his country's airforce in that theatre.

Some Presidential Guards – or their equivalent – are included for the simple reason that, in a country that has such formations, they are regarded as elite if not special, with particular trust placed in their abilities and loyalties. This is not, though, always the case, for some 'guard formations' may be little more than gangs of loyal thugs.

This publication merely lists equipment and Special Forces units with sparse details and thus is of a size to be easily pocketed while travelling. For a fuller, in-depth, study of the equipment used – and by whom – the relevant Jane's publications should be studied, starting, perhaps, with *Jane's Amphibious and Special Forces*.

Finally, it should be pointed out that, by their very nature, Special Forces should remain in the background and court no publicity: thus, in theory, it should not be easy to obtain information of their very existence let alone their equipment, organisation and modus operandi. Therefore this publication can never be up-to-date nor, perhaps, wholly accurate nor complete as some information has had to be gained through unconventional and not always very reliable routes and sources!

One thing is certain: not everything used by the world's Special Forces is listed here because details (and especially photographs, without which an entry is disbarred) are simply not available other than that an item or piece of equipment is in use. Additionally, some lists are not complete because so much similar equipment is in use that there is only room for a few samples: this is especially true of the surveillance sections.

Ewen Southby-Tailyour

Combat
Equipment

Browning P302 Vest BELGIUM

The P302 vests have a wide belt and self-gripping closures that ensure fast and comfortable adjustment. They can be worn under a shirt or uniform. Available either with sixteen layers of protective Z2 fibre (Model P302/16) or with twenty-four layers (Model P302/24), depending on the protective level required.

SPECIFICATION:

USED BY:
Widespread service worldwide

CONTRACTOR:
Browning SA, Herstal, Belgium

FEATURES:
- 16 or 24 layers of Z2 fibre
- P303 has side protection
- P304 has side, groin and dorsal protection

PSP M31 Assault Vest CANADA

M31 external assault vests

SPECIFICATION:

USED BY:
In use with several Special Forces

CONTRACTOR:
Pacific Safety Products Inc, Canada

FEATURES:
- With or without AK-47 magazine pockets
- Removable ballistic panels
- 1000 denier Cordura fabric
- Colours: olive-drab, tan, navy, black, US woodland camo, US desert camo and Australian camo

Designed to provide basic protection in situations where a large number of vests need to be bought on a limited budget. The vest is available in two configurations. The fully outfitted version has hard armour plate pockets both on the front and the back. The front plate pocket is on the inside of the carrier allowing space on the outside for two AK-47 magazine pockets. The rear plate pocket is an external design, featuring a flap with hook-and-loop closure and drainage grommets. Optionally the vest can be be supplied without pockets.

Acton ECW Mukluk Boot CANADA

This Extreme Cold Weather (ECW) boot is issued to the Canadian armed forces and includes a double-walled wool duffel sock combined with a 12 mm (1/2 in) thick removable felt insole and a plastic insole for air circulation which provides excellent thermal insulation. The boot is rated for use at temperatures of -54°C (-65°F). The outsole allows the boot to be used with both skis and snowshoes, and an interior urethane coating provides water resistance on the bottom of 150 mm (6 in). The boot incorporates a long lace, a D-ring closure to ensure a snug fit and a top 'snow-guard' lace to keep snow out and warm air in.

SPECIFICATION:

USED BY:
Canadian armed forces in extreme weather operations

CONTRACTOR:
Acton International Inc, Quebec, Canada

FEATURES:
• Full double-walled wool duffel sock
• Rated for use at temperatures of -54°C (-65°F)
• For use with skis and snowshoes
• D-ring closures

Acton ECW Thermo Boot CANADA

This Extreme Cold Weather (ECW) boot is
constructed on an outsole of 100 per cent natural
rubber. The proprietary Tractor outsole is self-
cleaning and is designed for a good grip and a sure
footing. The 9 mm Thermo insulation surrounds
the foot, and the removable Thermo liner and
insole keep the foot warm even in extreme
temperatures. The upper is further insulated with a
spun layer and has a Cordura nylon outer. The
insulation is completed with an embedded
polypropylene midsole that prevents transfer of
heat from foot to cold ground. All the materials
retain their resilience and flexibility in low
temperatures.

SPECIFICATION:

USED BY:
Canadian armed forces

CONTRACTOR:
Acton International Inc, Quebec,
Canada

FEATURES:
• Self-cleaning Tractor outsole
• Spun insulation on upper
• Fabric outer
• Embedded polypropylene
  midsole
• Thermo liner and insole

The Thermo liner incorporates
three layers:
• An external layer of Radiantex,
  which allows dampness to
  evaporate while keeping body
  heat close to the foot
• A layer of wool and polypro,
  which breathes with the body and
  passes damp away
• A hydrophobic polypropylene
  inner layer, which evaporates
  dampness away from the foot

Mustang Rescue Swimmer Drysuit CANADA

A tri-laminate nylon and butyl suit developed for surface swimmers.

SPECIFICATION:

USED BY:
us Navy and Coast Guard

CONTRACTOR:
Mustang, Canada

FEATURES:
• Double sealed and sewn seams
• Lightweight and flexible
• Exhaust valve on right forearm
• Dry weight, 3.2 kg (7 lb)

Marck Special Forces Boot FRANCE

SPECIFICATION:

USED BY:
French Special Forces

CONTRACTOR:
Marck, Argenteuil, France

FEATURES:
• Leather upper
• Gore-Tex lining
• Six pairs of metal lacing rings
• Rubber outsole
• Padded collar

Marck Desert Boot FRANCE

SPECIFICATION:

USED BY:
French Special Forces

CONTRACTOR:
Marck, Argenteuil, France

FEATURES:
- Leather and fabric upper
- Two pairs of lacing eyelets
- Six pairs of speedlace hooks
- Panama outsole

Marck High Desert Boot FRANCE

SPECIFICATION:

USED BY:
French Special Forces

CONTRACTOR:
Marck, Argenteuil, France

FEATURES:
- Leather and fabric upper
- Two pairs of lacing eyelets
- Six pairs of speedlace hooks
- Panama outsole

Marck Jungle Boot FRANCE

SPECIFICATION:

USED BY:
French Special Forces

CONTRACTOR:
Marck, Argenteuil, France

FEATURES:
• Leather and fabric upper
• Seven pairs of lacing eyelets
• Panama outsole

Marck Paratroop Boots FRANCE

SPECIFICATION:

USED BY:
French airborne forces

CONTRACTOR:
Marck, Argenteuil, France

FEATURES:
• Leather upper
• Five pairs of lacing eyelets
• Five pairs of speedlace hooks
• Full-train leather

Marck Special Forces Combat Suit FRANCE

This Special Forces suit has both breast and leg pockets, wrist cuffs with hook-and-loop adjustment and elasticised ankle cuffs. The suit has two vertical zips from near the neck to the ankle cuffs for ease of donning and removal.

SPECIFICATION:

USED BY:
French Special Forces

CONTRACTOR:
Marck, Argenteuil, France

Marck Airborne-Troops Suit FRANCE

SPECIFICATION:

USED BY:
French airborne forces

CONTRACTOR:
Marck, Argenteuil, France

FEATURES:
- Elasticised wrist and ankle cuffs
- Zip front opening with storm flap
- Two breast pockets
- Two hip pockets
- Two bellows leg pockets

Bolle Goggles FRANCE

Attacker tactical goggles

These goggles feature a polymer frame for flexibility and fit. The design includes slots to accommodate most eyeglasses. The large contour of the frame allows for increased peripheral vision, and the design is foam-free. The lens arrangement is a double polycarbonate design with anti-scratch and anti-fog treatment. The outside lens is 1.4 mm, and the inside lens is 0.7 mm, providing 2.1 mm of total protection. The lens can also be supplied as a 2.2 mm polycarbonate single lens. The outside of the lenses has Carbo Glass anti-scratch coating. There are options for clear or grey lenses, and other colours are available on request.

The adjustable black nylon fibre strap is 45 mm wide and 470 mm long. The strap can be treated with silicone on the inside as an option for better grip on the helmet. The face foam is 8 – 10 mm thick and is moisture-proof on the contact side; it is also washable, so that face paint can be completely removed. The top foam is 3 mm thick and is both dust-proof and moisture-proof. Bottom aerators of bulprene foam (2.5 mm) allow for even air flow.

SPECIFICATION:

USED BY:
French Special Forces

CONTRACTOR:
Bollé SAS, Arbent-Oyonnax, France

Commando Tactical Goggles FRANCE

These goggles feature a polymer frame for flexibility and fit. The large contour of the frame allows for increased peripheral vision, and the design is foam free. The lens is a double polycarbonate design with anti-scratch and anti-fog treatment. The outside lens is 1.4 mm, and the inside lens is 0.7 mm, providing 2.1 mm of total protection. The lens can also be supplied as a 2.2 mm polycarbonate single lens. There is Carbo Glass anti-scratch coating on the outside of the lens. Colour options for lenses are clear or grey, with other colours available on request. The night-vision training lens option allows for simulated night-time training.

The adjustable black nylon fibre strap is 45 mm wide and 470 mm long. An optional removable prescription adapter is available.

SPECIFICATION:

USED BY:
French Special Forces

CONTRACTOR:
Bollé sas, Arbent-Oyonnax, France

Airborne Troops Haversack FRANCE

Camouflage version

SPECIFICATION:

USED BY:
French airborne forces

CONTRACTOR:
Marck, Argenteuil, France

FEATURES:
• One main compartment
• Two side pouches
• Two adjustable shoulder straps

FBA Frogman Rucksack GERMANY

SPECIFICATION:

USED BY:
German combat swimmers and others

CONTRACTOR:
Ballonfabrik (FBA), Germany

FEATURES:
• Watertight and airtight
• Abrasion-resistant and tear-resistant
• NBC protection
• Buoyancy inflated approx 48 kg
• Weight empty approx 2.1 kg
• Stowage capacity approx 45 litres

This bag has been developed for frogmen and Special Forces who have to keep their equipment completely dry. A special pressure-control valve either allows air to be forced out of the bag to decrease buoyancy or allows inflation to increase buoyancy.

Schuberth Helme Type 828 Airborne Helmet   GERMANY

The Airborne 828 is a high-performance ballistic protection system developed to meet the specific demands of airborne forces. The head-hugging shell was designed to reduce the risk of line catch and entanglements. It has High Altitude Low Opening and High Altitude High Opening (HALO, HAHO) suitability, un-impaired visibility even in prone shooting positions and high ballistic protection and low weight.

SPECIFICATION:

USED BY:
German airborne forces and others

CONTRACTOR:
Schuberth Helme GmbH, Germany

FEATURES:
• Head-hugging compact shell
• HALO, HAHO suitability
• Low weight
• Three point chinstrap
• Chinstrap quick-release system
• Weight 1450 g
• Colours: olive-green or black
• Two sizes: 51 and 62 cm

Proteas Tactical Bullet Vest (PTBV)   GREECE

SPECIFICATION:

USED BY:
Greek Special Forces

CONTRACTOR:
Armadillo, Athens, Greece

FEATURES:
• Fulfills both operational and ballistic protection requirements
• Vest can be changed by addition of panels
• Incorporates lightweight impact-resistant plates

This vest is designed to fulfill both operational and ballistic protection requirements by offering an adaptable platform which can be easily changed according to the needs of the wearer. The vest provides a number of options which can be achieved by adding a different panel. Armadillo uses lightweight impact-resistant plates which provide protection against all known personal weapons while allowing a weight reduction over traditional armour of up to 70 per cent.

Christos J Kourtoglou Military Socks GREECE

Selection of military socks (see below)

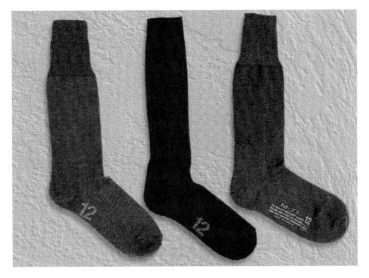

Left: C.N. M-72 men's socks with split terry foot bottom knitting (wool 80 per cent, nylon 20 per cent)

Centre: C.N. M-72 NE men's socks with split terry foot bottom Derby knitting (wool 70 per cent, nylon 30 per cent)

Right: C.N. M-71 men's socks with additional terry foot bottom plain knitting (wool 50 per cent, cotton 35 per cent, nylon 15 per cent)

These socks have been developed to withstand severe conditions and come in a variety of styles and mixtures of wool, cotton and nylon.

SPECIFICATION:

USED BY:
Greek armed forces and Special Forces

CONTRACTOR:
Christos J Kourtoglou, Athens, Greece

FEATURES:
SIZES: 11, 12, 13
COLOURS: olive drab, black, blue or air-force blue

Endymatotexniki END 200 Combat Harness and 201 Commando Harness GREECE

Endymatotexniki END 200 combat harness (1) and 201 commando harness (2)

This infantry/paratroop 200 combat harness is designed to fit over a flak jacket, allowing the user optimum freedom of movement and comfort. The 201 commando harness is designed to fit over a bullet-proof vest. It is padded and balanced to distribute the weight of the equipment proportionately over the body.

SPECIFICATION:

USED BY:
Greek Special Forces

CONTRACTOR:
Endymatotexniki, Athens, Greece

FEATURES:
- Four twin-magazine pouches
- Two single-hand grenade pouches
- One single-smoke grenade pouch
- One personal dressing pouch
- Two detachable canteen holders
- One pouch for binoculars or night-vision equipment
- 201: additional pockets for radio, flare, flashlight and so on

Shemagh ARABIA

SPECIFICATION:

USED BY:
Individuals, internationally

CONTRACTOR:
Privately purchased from a wide
variety of outlets

FEATURES:
• 100 per cent, lightly-woven
  cotton
• Approx 3 ft sq
• Various colours

This ubiquitous head-dress is worn by Special
Forces and others from the arctic to the desert.

Calzaturiera Mastromarco 3098 Paratroop Boot ITALY

SPECIFICATION:

USED BY:
Italian Special Forces

CONTRACTOR:
Calzaturiera Mastromarco, Italy

FEATURES:
• Water-resistant heavy calf leather
• Full calf lining
• Norwegian Goodyear welt
  construction
• Solid one-piece rubber outsole

Norge Army Shirt NORWAY

The fabric helps to disperse sweat.

SPECIFICATION:

USED BY:
Not an issued item outside
Norway but purchased privately
by many military and Special
Forces personnel

CONTRACTOR:
Norge, Norway

FEATURES:
• Very warm
• Half zip to neck

Norge Sweater NORWAY

Made of oiled wool with a v-neck kept closed by a hook-and-loop fastening. Hand warmer holes in the cuffs.

SPECIFICATION:

USED BY:
Not an issued item outside
Norway but purchased privately
by many military personnel

CONTRACTOR:
Norge, Norway

FEATURES:
• 100% wool
• Thumb-cuff feature

Granqvists P1013 Cover Mitt SWEDEN

SPECIFICATION:

USED BY:
Scandinavian and UK arctic forces

CONTRACTOR:
Granqvists AB, Karsltad, Sweden

FEATURES:
- For use outside finger gloves
- Polyester/canvas construction
- Dot-print surface for improved grip

Armourshield SBA – Standard Body Armour UK

The SBA series can be considered as general issue body armour, though this armour can be tailored to individual customer requirements. The series spans a wide range of protection levels and is available in numerous outer cover materials and camouflage patterns. The option to add ceramic/composite insert plates allows the SBA to be worn in most combat scenarios.

SPECIFICATION:

USED BY:
Used by peacekeeping organisations and national troops. Over 100,000 SBA units and insert plates in worldwide operational use

CONTRACTOR:
Armourshield Ltd, Manchester, UK

FEATURES:
- Wide range of protection levels
- Various outer cover materials and camouflage patterns
- Ceramic/composite insert plates can be added

Arktis Marine Battle Vest UK

SPECIFICATION:

USED BY:
In use with several Special Forces

CONTRACTOR:
Arktis Ltd, Exeter, UK

FEATURES:
- Cordura construction
- ABS plastic buckles
- Adjustable shoulder straps
- 12 magazine carrying capacity
- Two large utility pouches
- Snow-lock closures on water-
  bottle pouches
- D-rings for respirator attachment
- Dividers in ammo pouches
- Individual pouches for compass,
  FFD, multi-tool and bayonet
- One-finger closure clips
- Comes in any Cordura colour

Altberg Mk II Desert Boot UK

SPECIFICATION:

USED BY:
UK. Purchased privately by Special
Forces personnel for desert
operations

CONTRACTOR:
Altberg Boot Manufacturing
Company, Richmond, UK

FEATURES:
- Skywalk 1190 Trek dual-density
  rubber outsole
- Stilflex 883 Blake-stitched
  mid-flex midsole
- Soft calf leather on ankles and
  heel
- Cordura 1000 denier fabric upper
  with anti-fray treatment on inside
- Charles F Stead Tannery
  2.2-2.4 mm suede leather
- Colour: light sand suede
  leather/sand fabric

A lightweight hot-weather boot constructed to provide good underfoot support, the Mk II desert boot has an upper manufactured to minimise moisture retention.

BCB Jungle Boot UK

This boot has a canvas and nylon upper, a leather toe and heel and a Panama sole unit.

SPECIFICATION:

USED BY:
UK Special Forces

CONTRACTOR:
BCB International Ltd, Cardiff, UK

FEATURES:
- Canvas and nylon upper
- Leather toe and heel
- Panama sole unit
- Sizes: 5-13
- Colours: green and black

GB40 Desert Combat Boot UK

SPECIFICATION:

USED BY:
UK Special Forces

CONTRACTOR:
GB Britton Ltd, Bristol, UK

FEATURES:
- Moss-backed suede leather with drill canvas fabric tongue and legs
- Full bellows tongue
- Speedlacing system with locking device
- Direct vulcanised nitrile rubber outsole
- Deep-cleated tread
- Two-ply Cambrelle® vamp lining
- Rot-resistant polyester/cotton threads
- Tri-laminate woven insole
- Full-length contoured removable footbed

GB2 Combat Assault Boot UK

SPECIFICATION:

USED BY:
UK Special Forces

CONTRACTOR:
GB Britton Ltd, Bristol, UK

FEATURES:
- Black water-repellent full-grain combat leather
- Kip-leather lining
- Padded full bellows
- Softee combat leather tongue
- Backstrap with pull-on loop
- Minimal downward-facing seams
- Polyester/cotton threads
- Three eyelets and four speed loops on each side
- Direct-moulded dual-density PU outsole
- Deep-cleated tread
- Reinforced fluted steel for rigidity in waist
- Kip-leather sock

GB37 Desert Combat Boot (quick-release) UK

SPECIFICATION:

USED BY:
UK Special Forces

CONTRACTOR:
GB Britton Ltd, Bristol, UK

FEATURES:
- Beige moss-backed suede with 1000 denier Cordura fabric tongue
- Vamp lining
- Rot-resistant polyester/cotton threads
- Five speed-lacing loops and two eyelets on each side
- Heavy-duty nylon side zip on inside leg
- 2.5 mm leatherboard insole
- Direct vulcanised nitrile rubber outsole
- Deep-cleated tread
- PVC-coated paper seat sock

GB7 Lightweight Desert Boot UK

SPECIFICATION:

USED BY:
UK Special Forces

CONTRACTOR:
GB Britton Ltd, Bristol, UK

FEATURES:
- Moss-backed suede with 1000 denier Cordura fabric tongue, legs and collar
- Vamp lining
- Brushed Aqualine counter lining
- Rot-resistant polyester/cotton threads
- Seven beige round eyelets on each side
- 2.5 mm cellulose board insole
- Direct-moulded dual-density Ni-trax sole
- Low-density lightweight PU midsole
- Hard-wearing nitrile rubber outsole
- Deep-cleated tread
- PVC-coated paper seat sock

Arktis Severe-weather Gear UK

SPECIFICATION:

USED BY:
UK. Non-issue but purchased privately by arctic specialist personnel

CONTRACTOR:
Arktis Ltd, Exeter, UK

FEATURES:
- Full-length zip
- Two hand-warmer pockets
- Hem drawcord
- Bag for stowage
- Sizes: S, M, L, XL, XXL

This jacket was designed as a mid-layer, but, depending on the conditions, it can also be used as an outer layer. It is made from wind-resistant and shower-resistant nylon and is lined with low-bulk, high-insulation.

Silverman's DPM Para Smock UK

The pattern DPM para smock has knitted cuffs, a paratroopers strap between the legs and a flap under the legs to keep the smock in place during a jump.

SPECIFICATION:

WORN BY:
UK airborne forces

CONTRACTOR:
Silverman's Ltd, London, UK

FEATURES:
- Four bellows press stud pockets
- Dressing pouch on sleeve
- Colour: DPM

Silverman's DPM Sniper Smock UK

This Special Forces issue smock offers the hard-wearing properties the users demand.

SPECIFICATION:

USED BY:
UK Special Forces

CONTRACTOR:
Silverman's Ltd, London, UK

FEATURES:
- Bellows pockets
- Knitted cuffs
- Colour: DPM

Silverman's SAS DPM Windproof Smock UK

This SAS issue smock is made of gabardine windproof material and is designed to dry very quickly.

SPECIFICATION:

USED BY:
UK Special Forces

CONTRACTOR:
Silverman's Ltd, London, UK

FEATURES:
- Four bellows pockets
- Full zip with covering flap
- Colour: DPM

Divex Individual Waterproof Bergen UK

This bag has been ergonomically designed to provide ease of use and maximum carrying potential.

SPECIFICATION:

USED BY:
Combat swimmers of various countries

CONTRACTOR:
Divex Ltd, UK

FEATURES:
- Watertight and airtight
- Heavy duty construction
- Heavy duty, full length zip

Divex Special Operations Waterproof Rucksack UK

SPECIFICATION:

USED BY:
Combat swimmers of various
countries

CONTRACTOR:
Divex Ltd, UK

FEATURES:
• Ideal for combat swimming
• 50-litre waterproof volume
  capacity
• Adjustable buoyancy control, air-
  supply cylinder and oral inflator
• Air-supply hose, filling adapter
  and repair kit

This special operations waterproof rucksack will
remain waterproof at any depth providing air is
supplied during descent and internal pressure is
kept at or slightly above the ambient water
pressure.

Divex Combat Polyurethane Drysuit UK

This suit is designed to
maximise swimming
efficiency through the
use of easy glide
material. The high
level of durability
required for
parachuting or other
rapid water entry is
provided by the high
frequency of welded
seams that fuse the suit
to one piece of material
throughout.

SPECIFICATION:

USED BY:
In use with several maritime
Special Forces

CONTRACTOR:
Divex Ltd, UK

FEATURES:
• Maximum durability through use
  of high frequency welded seams
• Highly resistant to chemicals and
  abrasion
• Heavy duty non-magnetic zip
• Internal support straps ensure
  support in crotch area
• Direct fitting neck seal and
  integral ankle straps
• Inlet and exhaust valve ports
• Optional 6 mm (0.23 in) integral
  hood

BCB Arctic Glove UK

SPECIFICATION:

USED BY:
UK. Non-issue but purchased
privately by Royal Marines
Commando Forces and Special
Forces

CONTRACTOR:
BCB International Ltd, Cardiff, UK

FEATURES:
• Waterproof and breathable
• Made of Gore Tex
• Warm insulation
• Double leather palms

BCB Arctic Mitt UK

SPECIFICATION:

USED BY:
UK. Non-issue but purchased
privately by arctic-trained
personnel

CONTRACTOR:
BCB International Ltd, Cardiff, UK

FEATURES:
• Two mittens in one: the outer is
  waterproof; the inner is thick
  fleece
• Elasticated cuffs
• Trigger fingers

BCB Combat Glove UK

SPECIFICATION:

USED BY:
UK. Non-issue but widely used by
military including Special Forces

CONTRACTOR:
BCB International Ltd, Cardiff, UK

FEATURES:
• Soft pliable leather suitable for
  weapon handling
• Close-fitting
• MVP waterproof lining
• Internal knitted cuff and wrist
  strap

LBA Paratroop Helmet UK

SPECIFICATION:

USED BY:
Airborne forces worldwide

CONTRACTOR:
Lightweight Body Armour (LBA),
UK

FEATURES:
• Liner meets EN (European
  Standard) 966 requirements
• Fully adjustable three-point
  harness

LBA's paratroop helmet is available in either combat or PAS-TAC (Personal
Armour System – Tactical) helmet style and incorporates a shock-absorber
system which meets the standards of Euro Norm (EN) 966. This requires a
maximum residual acceleration of 250 g when impacted in a moving-head
mode with head energy (excluding helmet weight) of 75 J onto a variety of anvil
shapes. Although the shell and shape remain the same as the combat PAS-TAC
styles the liner and harness systems have been upgraded to improve the shock
attenuation and impact resistance of the helmet. The harness allows for
adjustment to the crown, headband and chinstrap to ensure that the optimum
gap between the head and the helmet shell is maintained. The helmets are
ruggedly constructed to meet the requirements of airborne forces.

BCB **Goggles** UK

SPECIFICATION:

USED BY:
UK. Non-issue but purchased privately by Special Forces personnel in arctic, desert and maritime conditions

CONTRACTOR:
BCB International Ltd, Cardiff, UK

FEATURES:
• Eye protection against dust, sunlight and wind
• 100% ultra-violet resistant
• Eye ventilation
• Elasticated adjustable strap
• Spare smoke glass supplied
• Weight: 100 g

These goggles have been designed for protection against sun, wind and dust. They incorporate eye ventilation and are said to be 100 per cent resistant to ultra-violet rays. The band is elasticated and adjustable. Spare smoke glass is also supplied.

WL **Gore Soldier '95 Gloves** UK

SPECIFICATION:

USED BY:
UK. Issued to all military personnel including Special Forces

CONTRACTOR:
WL Gore & Associates, UK

FEATURES:
• Approved by UK Ministry of Defence
• Part of Soldier '95 clothing
• Glove inserts made from tough three-layer laminate
• Designed especially for dexterity when handling weapons

NP Aerospace Para Helmet UK

This combat-proven helmet has a ballistic-protective shell which incorporates Natplas pre-forming technology. It also offers impact and fragmentation protection and is said to have an almost unlimited life expectancy.

SPECIFICATION:

USED BY:
UK airborne forces

CONTRACTOR:
NP Aerospace Ltd, UK

FEATURES:
- Ballistic protection
- Energy absorbent liner
- Resin-sealed edge
- 'Breakout' housing for ear defenders and communications equipment
- Natural fibres in all skin-contact areas
- Weight: 1.1 kg (2.4 lb)
- Sizes: S, M, L

Beaufort Mk 10 Immersion Suit UK

A one-piece garment with conventional wrist and neck seals. Particular attention at the design stage was give to reduce dressing time.

SPECIFICATION:

USED BY:
UK maritime Special Forces, especially air crew

CONTRACTOR:
Beaufort, UK

FEATURES:
- Breathable or impermeable fabric
- One-piece garment
- Urination tube fitted
- Waterproof slide from right shoulder to left hip
- Nine sizes

Typhoon Immersion Suit for Boating Operations UK

This immersion suit is designed for boating operations and can be adapted to suit individual customers.

SPECIFICATION:

USED BY:
In use with several maritime Special Forces

CONTRACTOR:
Typhoon Ltd, Cleveland, UK

FEATURES:
• Light but hard-wearing
• Can be worn over full combat dress and boots

CQC 90 Pattern Infantry Rucksack UK

SPECIFICATION:

USED BY:
UK armed forces

CONTRACTOR:
CQC Ltd, Barnstable, UK

FEATURES:
- Long: 360 x 580 x 280 mm
- Short: 360 x 490 x 330 mm
- Weight with yoke and two side pouches: 3 kg

The main body of this multipurpose rucksack set is available in two sizes, short or long; both have the same capacity but are designed to suit short or long backs. The light aluminium alloy frame is built into internal pockets of the rucksack and moulds to the individual body shape for improved comfort. An integral harness gives support over the shoulders and is adjusted by buckles and straps attached to the rucksack base. The buckles are quick-release, allowing the rucksack to be discarded quickly in an emergency. The main rucksack body carries a separate pocket at the front, an external pocket on the main lid and a map and document pocket built into the inside of the lid. Straps on the side enable the carriage of skis. The rucksack has a handle at the top and various load-carrying attachment points on the lid, sides and base as an aid when parachuting or to secure items such as sleeping bags. The lid is elasticated and has a shroud to prevent water from coming in. The two side pouches are attached to the main body by heavy-duty zips, supplemented for emergency by plastic clips. The lid of each pouch has a heavy-duty zip opening. The rucksack also has detachable side pockets, an adjustable padded waistbelt, two utility straps and a separate yoke with extension straps. This rucksack can stand alone as a conventional backpack, or it can be integrated into the overall 90 Pattern web equipment. Both side pockets can be detached from the main body of the rucksack and can be used singly or zipped together.

Hawkmoor Sabre Sacks UK

Sabre 80-130 sack

Hawkmoor researched and developed the Sabre load-bearing systems for the UK Ministry of Defence and overseas governments' Special Forces. The sacks in the Sabre range are compatible with the Personal Light Carrying Equipment system. The colour options include a Disruptive Pattern Material for camouflage.

SPECIFICATION:

USED BY:
UK armed forces, Special Forces

CONTRACTOR:
Hawkmoor Ltd/Karrimor SF,
Newton Abbot, UK

FEATURES:
• Capacity 80-130 litres
• Detachable pockets
• Zoom body zip
• SA SuperCool back

Silverman's Marines' Arctic Bergen UK

Similar to the UK Special Forces issue bergen, this water-resistant bergen has an external frame.

SPECIFICATION:

USED BY:
UK Royal Marines and others

CONTRACTOR:
Silverman's Ltd, London, UK

FEATURES:
• Colour: olive-green
• Capacity: 100 litres

Silverman's PLCE Bergen   UK

Part of the Soldier '95 issue equipment and used by Special Forces, this waterproof bergen has an internal alloy frame, a waist belt and side pouches. The detachable side pouches can be used to form a day patrol pack, with a yoke that is included.

SPECIFICATION:

USED BY:
UK armed forces and Special Forces

CONTRACTOR:
Silverman's Ltd, London, UK

FEATURES:
• Colour: DPM, green, black
• Capacity: 125 litres

Silverman's SAS Para Bergen   UK

Issued by the UK Ministry of Defence to UK Special Forces, this waterproof bergen consists of an external metal frame and an extremely hard-wearing butyl nylon pack.

SPECIFICATION:

USED BY:
UK Special Forces

CONTRACTOR:
Silverman's Ltd, London, UK

FEATURES:
• Colour: green
• Capacity: 125 litres

Arktis Patrol Pack UK

The Arktis patrol pack is a 40-litre pack which incorporates features that are common to most Arktis packs, such as high-quality Cordura construction, ABS plastic buckles, cotton duck fabric for comfort, a 10 mm closed-cell foam back pad for support, snow-lock closures round the main compartment, a grab handle, fully padded shoulder straps and a waist belt for stability. The pack comes in two sizes. In addition to the above, the patrol pack has a 50 mm waist belt, an external lid pocket, an internal lid pocket, D-rings for strap attachments and side zips to facilitate Arktis side pockets or PLCE-issue side pockets.

SPECIFICATION:

USED BY:
Widely used by Special Forces worldwide

CONTRACTOR:
Arktis Ltd, Exeter, UK

FEATURES:
- High-quality Cordura construction
- ABS plastic buckles
- Cotton duck fabric for comfort
- 10 mm closed-cell foam back pad for support
- Snow-lock closures round main compartment
- Grab handle
- Fully padded shoulder straps
- 50 mm waist belt for stability
- External lid pocket
- Internal lid pocket
- D-rings for strap attachment
- Side zips for Arktis or PLCE issue side pockets
- Two sizes available
- Capacity: 40 litres

Hawkmoor Sabre Patrol Packs UK

These packs allow the wearer to distribute the load more evenly while interacting with Personnel Load-Carrying Equipment. Hydration systems can also be incorporated and the vests can be used in conjunction with body armour. The Sabre 30 Hydro is a 30 – 40 litre pack with water-resistant zips and variable-capacity utility pouches. It is for use with fast-fill hydration systems. The Victory is a 25-litre patrol pack which is based on the civilian model and is expandable to 35 litres. The pack features water-resistant zips, volume adjusters and helmet straps. It is also designed to take a hydration system. Small versatile packs like the Victory and Hydro have evolved to meet the needs of rapid intervention forces or patrols, where mobility and fast-fill hydration have a higher priority than sheer load-carrying capacity.

SPECIFICATION:

USED BY:
UK armed forces, other Special Forces

CONTRACTOR:
Hawkmoor Ltd/Karrimor SF, Newton Abbot, UK

FEATURES:
- Compact front-reveal patrol pack:
  Sabre 30 capacity is 30 litres
  Sabre 35 capacity is 35 litres
  Sabre 35 has radio pocket
  Sabre 35 is compatible with Sabre hydration pack
- Sabre 30 Hydro patrol pack:
  Capacity is 30-40 litres
  Water-resistant zips
  Compatible with fast-fill hydration systems
- Sabre Victory patrol pack:
  Capacity expands from 25 to 35 litres
  Water-resistant zips
  Volume adjusters
  Helmet straps
  Large external net pouches

Irvin-GQ LLRP (Low Level Reserve Parachute) UK

SPECIFICATION:

USED BY:
UK airborne forces

CONTRACTOR:
Irvin-GQ Ltd, Bridgend, UK

FEATURES:
MINIMUM DEPLOYMENT ALTITUDE:
76 m (250 ft) AGL
MAXIMUM DEPLOYMENT SPEED:
278 km/h (150 kts)
ALL-UP SUSPENDED WEIGHT (AUW):
160 kg (350 lb)
RATE OF DESCENT AT 160 KG AUW:
6.9 m/s (22.6 f/s)
ASSEMBLY WEIGHT: 6.9 kg (15.2 lb)

The LLRP (Low Level Reserve Parachute) is a low profile, chest-mounted reserve assembly designed as a back-up system for use with troop parachutes that are cleared for drops from altitudes as low as 76m (250 ft). The LLRP incorporates a 20-gore, block constructed aeroconical canopy with a flying diameter of 6.2 m. Enhancements enable the improved extraction and faster inflation required for use at low level. The deployment is controlled for a successful opening either with a working main parachute, a partial malfunction or a high speed 'total malfunction'. A kicker spring is used to aid initial canopy deployment. A drogue with a frangible attachment to the canopy facilitates extraction at low speed deployments. At high speed, where the rapid extraction might be detrimental, the frangible attachment breaks leaving four integral assister pockets on the apex of the canopy to align the canopy during inflation. The apex vent of the canopy is closed by a break-tie. This prevents loss of pressure during the early stages of a low speed inflation whilst allowing the vent to open when required. Skirt assist lines are fitted around the peripheral hem of the canopy. They attach each rigging line to a point inside the canopy so that the rigging points at the peripheral hem are not under tension until the canopy is partially inflated. This has the effect of promoting initial canopy inflation to reduce height loss on deployment.

Irvin-GQ LLP Mk 1 Low Level Parachute UK

SPECIFICATION:

USED BY:
UK airborne forces

CONTRACTOR:
Irvin-GQ Ltd, Bridgend, UK

FEATURES:
MINIMUM DEPLOYMENT ALTITUDE:
76 m (250 ft) AGL
MAXIMUM DEPLOYMENT SPEED:
260 km/h (140 kts)
ALL-UP SUSPENDED WEIGHT (AUW):
160 kg (350 lb)
RATE OF DESCENT AT 115 KG AUW:
5.0 m/s (16.5 f/s)
RATE OF DESCENT AT 160 KG AUW:
5.9 m/s (19.5 f/s)
ASSEMBLY WEIGHT: 18.5 kg (41 lb)

The LLP Mk 1 Low Level Parachute is a static line operated paratroop parachute assembly that allows fully equipped airborne troops to carry out massed tactical parachute assaults from jump heights as low as 76m (250 ft). The H124 low level parachute canopy incorporates a number of proven features to meet the performance requirements. These include a shaped canopy, internal rigging lines, inflation pockets on the periphery of the canopy and an internal parachute. These features ensure fast and consistent openings, comfortable 'nine' levels during canopy inflation, rapid damping of canopy oscillation, a low rate of descent and a high tolerance to twisting of the rigging lines. The three-point closure harness is of the split-saddle type and is fully adjustable to provide a correct fit for all sizes of paratrooper. The harness incorporates canopy ground disconnects, two sets of D-ring anchorage points for the attachment of a reserve parachute assembly and the weapons/equipment container, a central equipment sling for suspension of the deployed weapons/equipment container. An integral carrying bag is fitted to the side of the outer pack. The outer pack fully encloses the deployment bag. The harness has been designed for maximum comfort and the minimum restriction to the paratrooper's mobility on the ground. The static line is stowed externally on the top of the outer pack and is fully covered by a flap.

Irvin-GQ Low Level Parachute Assembly UK

SPECIFICATION:

USED BY:
UK airborne forces

CONTRACTOR:
Irvin-GQ Ltd, Bridgend, UK

FEATURES:
CANOPY FLYING DIAMETER: 8 m
(26.25 ft)
ALL-UP SUSPENDED WEIGHT (AUW):
160 kg (350 lb)
MAXIMUM DEPLOYMENT SPEED:
260 km/h (140 kts)
MINIMUM DEPLOYMENT ALTITUDE:
76 m (250 ft) AGL
HEIGHT LOSS TO FULL CANOPY
INFLATION AT 160 KG AUW AND
140 KTS: less than 40 m (131 ft)
RATE OF DESCENT AT 160 KG AUW:
6 m/s (19.6 f/s)
ASSEMBLY WEIGHT: 13.6 kg (30 lb)

The Irvin-GQ 8m Low Level Parachute Assembly is a combination of the 8m
Low Level Conical Canopy with the pack/harness assembly of the in-service
LLP Mk1. This is a static line operated parachute assembly that allows fully
equipped airborne troops to carry out massed tactical parachute assaults from
jump heights as low as 76m (250 ft). The assembly can be deployed at speeds up
to 140 knots (260 km/h) from tactical transport aircraft. The 8m Low Level
Canopy is a highly developed conical canopy fitted with air scoops to give
positive opening characteristics and resistance to line twisting which ensures
repeatable inflation and height loss performance. In addition, the conical
canopy does not suffer from post inflation collapse thus further reducing
height loss performance. Four mesh covered stability slots ensure rapid
damping of canopy oscillation, a critical feature in a low level parachute. A net
skirt is incorporated to eliminate blown peripheries. Canopy control is via the
lift webs. The three-point closure harness is of the split-saddle type and is
fully adjustable to provide a correct fit for all sizes of paratrooper. The harness
incorporates canopy ground disconnects, two sets of D-ring anchorage points
for the attachment of a reserve parachute assembly and the weapons/
equipment container, a central equipment sling for suspension of the
deployed weapons/equipment container. The outer pack fully encloses the
deployment bag.

WL Gore Military Rainsuits UK

The Gore-Tex fabric two-piece rainsuit was designed in conjunction with the Trials and Development units of the UK Ministry of Defence (MOD), the Stores and Clothing Research and Development Establishment as well as the Defence Clothing and Textiles Agency. The fabric was first developed in the laboratory and then underwent rigorous testing in the field. It was approved by the MOD and now forms part of the Soldier '95 clothing system. The emphasis was on breathability, ease of movement and light weight. Gore-Tex allows sweat to escape, keeping the soldier dry and reducing the risk of heat stress. This in turn reduces the risk of hypothermia or stress-related errors of judgement.

SPECIFICATION:

USED BY:
UK, UA and German armies

CONTRACTOR:
WL Gore & Associates, UK

FEATURES:
- Made of Gore-Tex
- Infra-red-suppression finish
- Made to MOD specifications and approved for use by NATO forces

Marines' Arctic Bergen UK

SPECIFICATION:

USED BY:
UK Royal Marines, SAS, Parachute Regiment

MANUFACTURER:
Silverman's Ltd, London, UK

FEATURES:
COLOUR: Marines: olive green; SAS/Para: green
CAPACITY: Marines: 100 litres; SAS/Para: 125 litres
FRAME: external metal frame

BCB Commando Socks UK

SPECIFICATION:

USED BY:
UK. Non-issue but purchased privately by forces involved in severe weather operations

CONTRACTOR:
BCB International Ltd, Cardiff, UK

FEATURES:
• Fully cushioned sole
• 60% wool
• Sizes: large (6-11 boot size) and extra large (11.5-13 boot size)
• Colours: various

Many lessons were learned in the Falklands War, not least being the importance of keeping a soldier's feet healthy. Afflictions such as trench foot can have a disproportionate effect on the fighting ability of troops. These socks are designed to improve foot comfort and resistance to moisture. They feature 60 per cent wool and a fully cushioned sole.

Arktis Yoke UK

SPECIFICATION:

USED BY:
UK, various units

CONTRACTOR:
Arktis Ltd, Exeter, UK

FEATURES:
• Foam in shoulders
• Mesh back panel
• D-rings on back panel
• Colours: any Cordura colours
• One size

The Arktis yoke is a support system for webbing and can be used with Arktis webbing or with any other webbing. The yoke is made from Cordura fabric and features foam in the shoulders, as well as a mesh back panel for breathability and D-rings on the back panel and the shoulders for extra attachment. A strap enables the attachment of the 1713 side pockets.

Arktis 1724 Advanced Rig UK

SPECIFICATION:

USED BY:
UK Special Forces

CONTRACTOR:
Arktis Ltd, Exeter, UK

FEATURES:
• 1000 denier nylon
• added straps
• Four ammunition pouches
• Two slanted utility pouches
• Two first field dressing pouches
• Internal zip pockets

The advanced rig is designed to provide maximum ventilation and to be as comfortable as a vest. The straps are padded with 5 mm closed cell foam. The rig includes four ammunition pouches, two slanted utility pouches, two first field dressing pouches and internal zip pockets.

WL Gore Second Generation Extended Cold-Weather Clothing System USA

This second generation clothing system, consisting of a parka and trousers, has been designed for the temperature range of -51ºc – -56ºc (-60ºF – -70ºF). The trousers have seat and knee patches for abrasion resistance, cargo pockets and loops for a belt and braces, large cargo pockets with hand-warmer pockets behind them, a two-way full front zip, hook and loop closures on the wrists, underarm ventilation, reinforced elbows and a rank tab in the centre chest.

SPECIFICATION:

USED BY:
us Marine Corps

MANUFACTURER:
WL Gore & Associates Inc, USA

FEATURES:
• Gore-Tex membrane in combat trousers and coat
• Breathable
• Windproof

Armor of America TP-1E/TP-2E vest   USA

The TP-1E ballistic vest is a proven veteran of Naval
Special Warfare combat in the Gulf War. It has been
tested by special-operations military personnel
while scuba diving, parachuting, rappelling, rock
climbing, using boarding-nets and firing weapons
from all over the world. The TP-1E ballistic vest is
provided with a coccyx extension that works in
conjunction with the four nylon tension bands to
provide lower-back support as well as ballistic
protection. The neck tab extends up the spine to
protect against trauma impacts and fragmentation
when the wearer is in the prone position. The back
hard armour rifle insert pocket is a bellows design
that permits full movement of the shoulder blades
when the arms are extended, climbing or firing a
shoulder-mounted weapon. The Kevlar TP-1E and
the Spectra TP-2E afford the same level of ballistic
protection: steel-jacketed lead-core 9 mm
sub-machine gun fire.

SPECIFICATION:

USED BY:
US armed forces and Special
Forces

CONTRACTOR:
Armor of America Inc, California,
USA

FEATURES:
• TP-1E uses Kevlar
• TP-2E uses Spectra
• Ballistic protection against
steel-jacketed lead-core 9 mm
sub-machine gun fire

Armor of America τ-series Armor USA

The τ-panel ballistic vest was designed to meet the requirements of police and paramilitary operations in urban, desert or jungle environments. The vest is resistant to water and mildew. The shoulder straps are reinforced to support the weight of the front and back hard armour insert plates for rifle fire. Wide belly bands keep the hard armour insert snug to the body when running and climbing. The double overlocking hook-and-loop pile closure on the belly bands prevents them from opening accidentally when using load-bearing equipment or on a jungle patrol. Hook-and-loop pile attachment points on the lower edge of the waist closure are used to connect the optional removable groin panels. External carriers permit the τ-panel vest to serve as a load-bearing outer garment. The τ-series can be custom designed according to requirements.

SPECIFICATION:

USED BY:
Government, police and military personnel in South American anti-drug operations

CONTRACTOR:
Armor of America Inc, California, USA

FEATURES:
- Reinforced shoulder straps
- Wide belly bands
- Removable or permanent ID on front and back

DuPont Ranger Vest USA

This vest incorporates Kevlar KM27 fibre, to provide both fragmentation and bullet protection. The Ranger vest is slightly lighter than the army-issue Personal Armour System Ground Troops (PASGT) vest and provides 25 per cent higher fragmentation resistance as well as protection against the most common bullet threats such as the 9 mm and the 0.44 magnum. An optional chest plate provides multiple-hit protection against 7.62 mm rifle rounds. The vest is rated at NIJ Level IIIA without the plate and at Level III with the plate.

SPECIFICATION:

USED BY:
UK armed forces

CONTRACTOR:
DuPont Inc, USA

FEATURES:
- Kevlar KM27 fibre
- Fragmentation and bullet protection
- 25 per cent higher fragmentation resistance than PASGT vest for lighter weight
- Optional chest plate
- Rated at NIJ Level IIIA without plate
- Rated at NIJ Level III with plate

Altama 4155 Jungle Boot USA

A new development, in response to demand from us forces' personnel, has been the introduction of the Ripple Sole boot. The sole unit features a PolyUrethane (PU) removable insole with a Cambrelle® top lining, a three-layered Foamex thermal barrier, a rubber midsole, a PU cushioned midsole and a Ripple outsole.

SPECIFICATION

USED BY:
us armed forces

CONTRACTOR:
Altama Footwear, Georgia, USA

FEATURES:
- 156 g (5.5 oz) corrected cowhide
- 1000 denier Cordura upper
- Padded collar
- Reinforced ankle support
- Removable PU insole
- TruFit TF33 glass-fibre shank
- Nylon thread stitching
- One-piece vulcanised Panama tread

Altama 4156 Desert Boot USA

Altama has been a prime contractor to the US Department of Defense for over 30 years and supplied boots to the armed services during the Vietnam War and the 1991 Gulf War. It supplies products to a number of units in over 70 countries. A new development, in response to demand from US forces' personnel, has been the introduction of the Ripple Sole boot. The sole unit features a PolyUrethane (PU) removable insole with a Cambrelle® top lining, a three-layered Foamex thermal barrier, a rubber midsole, a PU cushioned midsole and a Ripple outsole.

SPECIFICATION:

USED BY:
US armed forces

CONTRACTOR:
Altama Footwear, Georgia, USA

FEATURES:
- 156 g (5.5 oz) tan suede leather
- Tan 1000 denier Cordura nylon with reinforced nylon ankle support
- Padded collar
- Tan DuPont Coolmax lining
- Mil-spec twill vamp lining
- Tan nylon-coated brass speedlace (five sets) and eyelets (two sets)
- Removable PU cushion inner sole with Cambrelle® cover
- Tan one-piece vulcanised rubber outsole
- Panama tread design
- Nylon thread stitching
- TruFit TF33 glass-fibre shank

Altama 5850 Desert Boot USA

Altama boots are supplied to the United States Department of Defense as well as to a number of other military and police forces. The boots have been worn on active service in Vietnam and the Persian Gulf.

SPECIFICATION:

USED BY:
us armed forces and others

CONTRACTOR:
Altama Footwear, Georgia, USA

FEATURES:
- Part tan suede leather and part Cordura fabric upper
- Reinforced nylon ankle support
- No. 9 natural cotton twill lining
- Hooks and eyelets of tan-coated aluminium
- Removable cushioned Bon-Foam insole
- Injection moulded PVC/polyurethane Panama tread outsole
- Nylon thread stitching
- TruFit TF33 glass-fibre shank

WL Gore Boots with Gore-Tex Membrane USA

Infantry combat boots

SPECIFICATION:

USED BY:
us Marine Corps

CONTRACTOR:
WL Gore & Associates Inc, Maryland, USA

FEATURES:
- Standard issue
- Nylon side panels
- Polyurethane midsole
- Rubber lug outsole

These boots have a membrane made of WL Gore's patented Gore-Tex fabric to make them waterproof yet breathable. The fabric is shaped into a bootie and is then steam-sealed with Gore-Seam tape that completely surrounds the foot, providing a barrier to water penetration while allowing perspiration vapour to escape. Removal of moisture facilitates cooling, improving the functional performance and reducing the likelihood of foot-related injury. The idea is that these boots provide long-wearing comfort and protection so that military personnel can focus on their mission.

Bates Enforcer Series Special-Ops Men's Amphibious Shoe E02114 USA

SPECIFICATION:

USED BY:
US maritime Special Forces

CONTRACTOR:
Bates, Michigan, USA

FEATURES:
- Quick-drying, synthetic upper
- Moulded, dual-density rubber outsole
- Removable EVA insole

Arctic Snow Camouflage Parka and Trousers USA

SPECIFICATION:

USED BY:
US armed forces and Special Forces

MANUFACTURER:
Military Logistics, Florida, USA

FEATURES:
- For camouflage in snow
- Parka has draw strings at waist, skirt and face
- Sizes: XS, S, M, L, XL

Developed to fit over a wet-weather parka and not as a substitute outer layer. Made of cotton warp and nylon filling Oxford, quarpel treated.

Military Logistics Desert Night Camouflage Parka and Trousers with Liners USA

SPECIFICATION:

USED BY:
us armed forces

CONTRACTOR:
Military Logistics, Florida, USA

FEATURES:
- For camouflage and warmth at night in desert conditions
- Parka has hood and drawcords at neck, hood, waist and hemline
- Sizes: XS, S, M, L, XL
- Colour: light green with dark and green grid pattern

Designed for the desert where temperatures can fall dramatically. Worn over daytime clothes. Buttons on inside for extra liners of quilted polyester.

WL Gore Intermediate Cold-Wet Gloves with Inserts

USA

SPECIFICATION:

USED BY:
us armed forces

CONTRACTOR:
WL Gore & Associates Inc, Maryland, USA

FEATURES:
- Cowhide outer shell
- Waterproof, windproof and breathable
- Polyester brush knit lining
- Flexor design
- Insert exceeds US military specification

Gentex EPS-21 Goggle System USA

The EPS-21 goggle system can be worn with a helmet

These goggles were originally developed for the rigorous specifications of the Israeli Defence Force. They are designed for protection against sun, wind, dust, ballistic fragmentation and laser radiation. The system consists of a goggle frame, a choice of straps, a clear ballistic lens, a wide range of easily installed outsert lenses, an optional corrective lens insert and a nylon carrying case for stowing the goggle and accessory lenses on personal load-bearing equipment. They are compatible with a variety of military and police helmet systems and sighting devices.

SPECIFICATION:

USED BY:
Standard issue to Israeli Defence
Forces

CONTRACTOR:
Gentex Corporation,
Pennsylvania, USA

FEATURES:
• Overall low profile allowing wide
  range of view
• Optically moulded 4 mm ballistic
  lens
• Revolutionary outsert lens design
• Easily interchangeable self-
  locking strapping designs
• Lightweight frame
• Corrective lenses can be easily
  inserted

Military Logistics M-1944 Sun, Wind and Dust Goggles

USA

These goggles are designed for ground troops and armoured-vehicle crewmen to protect against sun, wind and dust and also to provide ballistic protection. The goggles consist of an injection-moulded rubber frame with a polyurethane foam backing, covered with a skin where it is in contact with the face. There is an adjustable elastic headband. The frame is designed to be compatible with eyeglasses and has flannel-covered vent holes to keep out dust particles. The class 1 and 2 lenses are a single-piece, flat cellulose acetate or cellulose acetate butyral material of a nominal 0.8 mm thickness and are issued in both clear and neutral grey. The class 3 and 4 lenses are a single-piece, injection-moulded polycarbonate lens, curved with abrasion-resistant coating, in a nominal thickness of 2 mm. Ballistic lenses are procured separately. Snap fasteners incorporated in the foam layer facilitate lens replacement.

SPECIFICATION:

USED BY:
US armed forces

CONTRACTOR:
Military Logistics, Florida, USA

FEATURES:
- Ballistic protection
- Frame compatible with eyeglasses
- Adjustable elastic headband
- One size
- Colour: black with clear and neutral-grey lenses

A-III Large Airborne Rucksack USA

Eagle manufactures a range of rucksacks with different load capacities and designed for different mission scenarios. The products include the A-III large airborne rucksack, the large A-III pack and a variety of patrol packs.

SPECIFICATION:

USED BY:
US airborne forces

CONTRACTOR:
Eagle Industries Inc, Missouri, USA

FEATURES:
- Expanded cargo compartment
- Closed-cell foam padding
- Interior load-securing straps
- Night identification feature
- Compression loops
- ALICE attachment points
- Outside pockets for pop flares, antennae or miscellaneous items
- Optional extra pouches can be attached to the sides and a compression sack to the bottom
- Attachment point for lowering line
- Pack-to-harness straps under side pockets
- Shoulder straps double as leg straps
- Main compartment: 46 litres (2,855 in³)
- Front bellow pocket: 12 litres (735 in³)
- Upper left side pocket: 1.1 litres (68 in³)
- Lower left side pocket: 0.8 litres (52 in³)
- Right side pocket: 2 litres (120 in³)

Parachutist's Drop Bag USA

The parachutist's drop bag is designed to carry all necessary equipment and to meet full certification for paratroops.

SPECIFICATION:

USED BY:
Airborne forces

MANUFACTURER:
Eagle Industries Inc, Missouri, USA

FEATURES:
- 518 x 450 x 270 mm main compartment with 90 litres (5,520 in³) of storage space
- Lowering line with storage pocket for 2-4 m (7-15 ft) of line
- Vertical and horizontal compression straps
- Parachute grade hardware
- 1000 denier water-resistant and abrasion-resistant Cordura fabric
- Heavy-duty large number-10 YKK zips with paracord pulls on all zip sides

Eagle Airborne Assault Pack USA

The Eagle airborne assault pack is for 'demanding' operations.

SPECIFICATION:

USED BY:
US airborne forces

CONTRACTOR:
Eagle Industries Inc, Missouri, USA

FEATURES:
- 1000 denier abrasion-resistant and water-resistant Cordura fabric body and exterior pockets
- Pockets feature 22.5 mm Mil-Spec Cordura webbing and side-release buckles
- 39 mm 3175 kg tensile-strength Mil-Spec Type 13 webbing handle
- Handle/connector straps sewn to top and round the sides with five-cord thread on a class 7 machine
- Connector straps sewn under the side pockets with a webbing flap and side-release buckle
- Main compartment fitted with number-10 YKK zip that runs round the top of the bag and down both sides
- Top of the pack has reinforced holes with a Cordura and velcro flap, for radio antennas and wire routing
- Hook-and-loop mesh on top to hold side-release buckles out of the way when not in use
- Two horizontal and two vertical cinch straps inside Cordura bottom patch
- Lowering-line storage pocket (2.16-4.33 m lowering line)
- Webbing loops on the back to guide the lowering line with rubber bands
- Double metal D-rings and webbing loops on shoulder straps
- Fully adjustable sternum strap
- Main compartment: 33 litres (2,020 in³)
- Large side pocket: 1.4 litre (85 in³)

Eagle A-III Medical Pack USA

Airborne medical pack

The A-III medical pack is a mid-size frameless pack which opens to provide a full display of medical equipment for quick access.

SPECIFICATION:

USED BY:
US airborne forces

CONTRACTOR:
Eagle Industries Inc, Missouri, USA

FEATURES:
- Six 152 mm long x 101 mm high internal urethane-coated mesh pouches with velcro and pull-tab opening
- Pull-out 180 mm long x 230 mm wide x 225 mm deep pouch with centre divider
- Cloth-covered inner tri-fold flap that can be secured with a snap
- Pouches for splints
- Slots for body armour and clipboard
- Top drag handle
- Outer cinch straps
- Individual medical-gear placement patterns
- Extra elastic for medical tools
- Accepts all standard hydration systems including CamelBack
- Heavy-duty number-10 YKK zip
- Dimensions: 293 mm wide x 406 mm high x 192 mm deep
- Capacity: 33 litres (1989 in³)

Eagle Load-bearing Pack USA

Airborne assault pack

SPECIFICATION:

USED BY:
us airborne forces

CONTRACTOR:
Eagle Industries Inc, Missouri,
USA

FEATURES:
- Two horizontal compression
  straps
- 50 mm webbing on both sides
  and on bottom of pack for
  attaching extra gear
- Designed to be worn with the
  Eagle load-bearing vest
- Optional connector straps so
  pack can be used with TAC V1
  N/NU

The load-bearing pack is designed for stealth
operations and features two horizontal
compression straps to reduce load movement and
a clean exterior to reduce the risk of snagging.

Gentex HALO Lightweight Paratroop Helmet USA

SPECIFICATION:

USED BY:
us airborne forces

CONTRACTOR:
Gentex Corporation,
Pennsylvania, USA

FEATURES:
- Provides head, eye and facial
  protection
- Incorporates oxygen mask
  retention devices
- Lightweight aramid composite
  construction
- Liner, fitting pads and earpads all
  covered with cabretta leather
- Bayonet receivers
- Separate adjustable chin and
  nape straps
- Left-side and right-side earphone
  elements and external dynamic
  boom microphone
- Clear goggle assembly
- Sizes: M, L and XL

The Gentex High Altitude Low Opening
lightweight paratroop helmet is designed to
provide head, eye and facial protection and is
equipped with additional components to facilitate
communications. Oxygen mask retention devices
are installed so that various mask options can be
worn during military operations.

SPP Paratrooper Conversion Kit for PASGT Combat Helmet USA

SPECIFICATION:

USED BY:
Standard US military issue

CONTRACTOR:
Speciality Plastic Products of PA Inc, USA

FEATURES:
- Easy installation
- Protective foam neck pad
- Retention strap assures stability
- Fits all size PASGT helmets
- Colour: olive-green

The Paratrooper Conversion Kit is US military standard issue for all Personal Armour System Ground Troops (PASGT)-style combat helmets. It consists of a foam neck pad for the rear and a retention strap which assembles to the existing chin straps for extra helmet stability. Assembly is quick; a single screw at the rear of the helmet is loosened for assembly of the pad and strap. The free ends of the retention strap are attached to the chin strap with hook-and-loop fasteners.

WL Gore Lightweight Rainsuit USA

SPECIFICATION:

USED BY:
US Special Forces and Rangers

CONTRACTOR:
WL Gore & Associates Inc, Maryland, USA

FEATURES:
- Meets Gore's waterproof and performance standards
- Reinforced shoulders, elbows, knees and seat
- Infra-red reduction

Consists of a parka and trousers. Designed to stuff into the pockets of each of the garments.

Military Logistics Magnesium Snowshoes USA

SPECIFICATION:

USED BY:
us armed forces

CONTRACTOR:
Military Logistics, Florida, USA

FEATURES:
• Magnesium frame
• Nylon-coated steel cable
• White nylon webbing bindings
• 4 buckle adjustments
• One size
• Colour: white

These snowshoes consist of a magnesium frame laced with nylon-coated steel cable. The bindings are 25 mm (1 in) white nylon webbing with four buckle adjustments for attaching the snowshoe to the boot.

Military Logistics Men's Winter Socks USA

SPECIFICATION:

USED BY:
us armed forces in cold-weather
operations

CONTRACTOR:
Military Logistics, Florida, USA

FEATURES:
• Terry/tuff stitches
• Compatible with ski mountain
  boots and mukluks
• Sizes: 7 – 14
• Colour: natural

These socks are for wear with ski mountain boots or mukluks. They are seamless knitted socks with terry/tuff stitches throughout the inside. The materials used are 75 per cent merino wool and 25 per cent cotton.

TechSpun Environmental Sock System USA

This is a multisock system consisting of a Coolmax liner sock and two reversed terry nap US wool and polypropylene blend boot socks. The liner and outer sock must be worn together for the system to function. The Coolmax liner wicks away moisture from the foot, keeping it dry and also reducing the risk of bacterial infection.

The Extreme-Weather boot sock is made from high-density terry nap, which is designed to withstand maximum load conditions and provide first-rate insulation.

The All-Weather boot sock is a lighter version for less extreme conditions. The way the sock system works, according to the manufacturers, means that fewer socks need to be carried in the rucksack. All that is required is three pairs of the Coolmax inner sock and two pairs of the outer socks.

SPECIFICATION:

USED BY:
US navy and Marine Corps

CONTRACTOR:
TechSpun Inc, Pennsylvania, USA

FEATURES:
• Extreme-Weather (EW) boot sock:
  For temperatures from -40°C to 49°C (-40°F to +120°F)
  47% wool, 47% polypropylene, 6% nylon
  High-density knit construction

• All-Weather (AW) boot sock:
  For temperatures from -17°C to 37°C (0°F to +100°F)
  45% wool, 45% polypropylene, 10% nylon yarn

Foil Force Fin USA

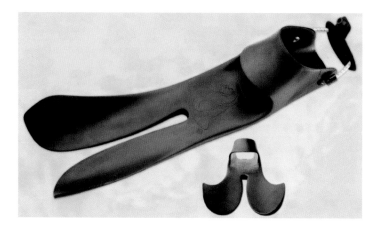

The fin is designed to channel water through a split in the fin and drive the diver forward. The design of the fin eradicates toe squeeze and calf fatigue, minimises cramping and maximises the effectiveness of the strongest kicking muscles. The clean edges of the fin cut through the water and the independently moving wingtips allow divers to fine tune their position in the water with small foot and leg movements. Vortex Generators, or bumps on the underside of the fin, keep water fast-flowing. The snap of the Force Fin blade flaps the foils behind the diver to channel the water through the blade's deep split for quick acceleration. Force Fin's patented up-curved blade enhances natural and aerobic kicking and is made from polyurethane with a stiffness of 87 and a rebound of 78. Buoyancy is negative at -10 per cent. The fin is fitted with a parachute webbing strap and ladder-lock buckle. There is a strap upgrade option of an Elastic Bungie heel strap with a Comfort Heel Pad and easy grip knob. The fin can also be fitted with an optional Comfort Instep cushion.

SPECIFICATION:

USED BY:
The Foil Force Fin was developed in response to a personal request from a Commander of US Military Diving Operations for an extended-range diving and surface-kicking fin

CONTRACTOR:
Foil Force, USA

FEATURES:
• Split fin for maximum efficiency
• Vortex Generators on underside of fin
• Patented upcurved blade
• Polyurethane construction (stiffness 87; rebound 78)
• Negative buoyancy -10 per cent
• Parachute webbing strap and ladder-lock buckle
• Elastic Bungie Heel Strap with Comfort Heel Pad and easy grip knob
• Optional Comfort Instep cushion
• Sizes: ML, L, XL, XXL

BlackHawk Industries Commando Chest Harness USA

front (1) and back (2)

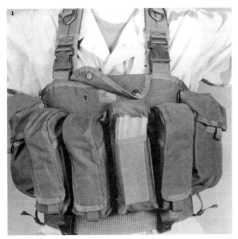

SPECIFICATION:

USED BY:
US Special Forces

CONTRACTOR:
BlackHawk Industries, Virginia,
USA

FEATURES:
• Four pouches
• Each pouch holds three AK-47
  magazines or three M16
  magazines or two M14 magazines
• Each pouch has a divider to
  separate magazines
• Inside back portion is padded
  with 1/4 in closed-cell foam
• Large utility or map pouch with
  its own Durasnap securing flap
• Made from Nytaneon materials

BlackHawk Industries Solar Harness USA

This harness is constructed with Mil-Spec Type 13 and Type 8 webbing.

SPECIFICATION:

USED BY:
US Special Forces

CONTRACTOR:
BlackHawk Industries, Virginia, USA

FEATURES:
• Compact and lightweight
• Adjustable
• Accessory loop

Communications

PSP-320 350 MHZ Hand-held Transceiver CHINA

This PSP-320 is a 350 MHZ hand-held transceiver
employing MPT1327 signalling. There are police-
function and trunking modes with advanced
frequency synthesiser, dot matrix display and
microprocessor used for channel management and
signalling control. The transceiver features
compact size, light weight plus an enhanced
battery capacity.

SPECIFICATION:

USED BY:
Chinese Special Forces

CONTRACTOR:
First Research Unit of the
Ministry of Public Security, China

FEATURES:
FREQUENCY RANGE: 336-370 MHZ
MODULATION: 16F3E
CHANNEL SPACING: 12.5-25 kHZ
OPERATING TEMPERATURE: -30°C
to +60°C
ANTENNA IMPEDANCE: 50
DIMENSIONS: 64 x 27.5 x 144 mm
(600 mAh battery); 64 x 27.5 x
144mm (1,200 mAh battery)
WEIGHT: 400 g (600 mAh battery);
550 g (1,200 mAh battery)

S9130 Mobile Radio CHINA

This is a mobile vehicle station using a direct PLL synthesiser, providing wideband or narrowband channels. An EPROM stores eight channels and sixteen groups, giving 128 available channels. Selection of channels is microprocessor-controlled which allows automatic identification and alarm as well as additional functions for police service. Channel management permits two channels to be continuously watched, eight channels to be directly scanned, and a priority channel to be set up. Programme and programme-priority scanning is available either automatically or manually.

SPECIFICATION:

USED BY:
Chinese Special Forces

CONTRACTOR:
First Research Institute of the Ministry of Public Security, China

FEATURES:
FREQUENCY COVERAGE:
146-174 MHz or 330-370 MHz
CHANNELS: 128
FREQUENCY STABILITY: +-3 ppm
MAX FREQUENCY DEVIATION:
+-5 kHz (wideband); 2.5 kHz (narrowband)
RECEIVER SENSITIVITY: <0.25 μV
(12 dB SINAD)

Nokia DA8522 Patrol Message Terminal FINLAND

The DA8522 is a rugged, digital microprocessor-based terminal for sending and receiving data by radio. The unit connects to an HF or VHF/UHF radio set. The built-in data modem uses a 1100 – 2300 HZ frequency band and is especially designed for HF transmissions. Transmission takes place in short bursts making it difficult to locate or jam.

SPECIFICATION:

USED BY:
In service worldwide

CONTRACTOR:
Nokia Telecommunications,
Finland

FEATURES:
DISPLAY: 16-character LED
KEYBOARD: 33 key, silicone rubber
MEMORY: Output memory 2000.
Input memory eight messages or
2000 characters
INTERFACES: Communications
equipment: voice grade 150 and
600 bits/s
POWER SUPPLY: six AA cells or
external 10-30 V DC
POWER CONSUMPTION: Receiving
mode 90mmw; edit/transmit
mode 100 mw to 1 w depending
on the characters in the display
DIMENSIONS: 185 x 100 x 53 mm
WEIGHT: 1.0 kg

Nokia M85050 Short Burst Message Terminal FINLAND

Nokia short burst message terminal with printer

The Nokia M85050 is a microprocessor hand-held unit for tactical communication by Defence and Special Forces and is intended for the editing, transmission and reception of messages in hostile environments. The transmission takes place via radio, satellite link or telephone line and always in encrypted form. With its accessories it fits into a small briefcase.

SPECIFICATION:

USED BY:
In service worldwide

CONTRACTOR:
Nokia Telcommunications, Finland

Confidence 500 FRANCE

Confidence 500 is a crypto telephone unit, compatible with any type of telephone (PSTN, ISDN, digital proprietary system). Placed under the telephone set, it is simply connected to the set's wire, between the handset and the telephone. Confidence 500 ensures total protection of communications between phone subscribers and/or between phone subscribers and secure GSM subscribers. It provides confidentiality through digital encryption of the voice and the data and authentication of users (the identity of the caller transmitted ciphered is displayed on the screen). Keys are loaded through a PC connected to the key introduction connector or introduced via the keyboard. Confidence 500 works in plain or in crypto mode; to shift from one mode to the other, it is only required to press one button. Due to the use of latest generation decoders, the system features excellent voice quality and speaker recognition both in plain and crypto modes. The length of the 128-bit keys ensures total security. Standard algorithms, already published, are also available. A customisation station enables the user to generate and manage his or her own encryption keys, therefore providing encryption autonomy.

SPECIFICATION:

USED BY:
In service

CONTRACTOR:
SAGEM Defence and Security Division SA, Paris, France

RM 520/540 **Radio Transceivers** FRANCE

The RM 500 range is a new generation of mobile transceivers designed for professional radio communication users, such as police and security forces, taxis and ambulances. These radios are particularly reliable, user-friendly and provide highly secure communications. They can integrate a GPS receiver and thus offer automatic positioning of the platform vehicle on a cartographic display. There is also an ERMES paging receiver and a digital answering/recording machine. Available in UHF and VHF, these mobile transceivers can be fully integrated into most PMR and trunk radio networks. Based on the latest technologies, they offer innovative functions such as: coded voice for higher communication privacy; data transmission via the built-in modem, with serial port and double-control protocol, for direct access to a PC; and programming of the transceivers by PC and software uploading offer flexibility for network design and future expansion.

SPECIFICATION:

USED BY:
In service

CONTRACTOR:
SAGEM Defence and Security Division, Paris, France

FEATURES:
FREQUENCIES: VHF 68/88, 146/174 MHZ, UHF 406/470 MHZ
CHANNEL SPACING: 12.5, 20, 25 KHZ
RF POWER: 25 W (adjustable)
AUDIO POWER: 10 W/8 ohms and double loudspeaker
ADJACENT CHANNEL PROTECTION: >70 dB / 25 KHZ
INTERMODULATION PROTECTION: >65 dB (according to ETS 300 086)
SENSITIVITY: <0.5 μV DDP
DIMENSIONS: RM 520: 150 X 175 X 33 mm; RM 540: 182 X 177 X 57 mm
WEIGHT: RM 520: 1 kg; RM 540: 1.2 kg

EL/S-8811 Vehicular Tactical Video Receiving Terminal

ISRAEL

Designed for use by highly mobile units and
suitable for installation in light vehicles, tanks, APCS
and other vehicles. The receiver/processor unit is
carried on a standard mounting. The monitor
comes in two versions: a 5 in (127 mm) fully
militarised monitor for vehicular installation or a
4 in (102 mm) flat monitor with a strap for chest
carrying. The display unit may be customised to
any monitor size.

SPECIFICATION:

USED BY:
Israeli forces

CONTRACTOR:
ELTA Electronics Industries Ltd,
Israel

Tadiran HF-2000 HF Radio System   ISRAEL

Tadiran HF-2000 HF radio system (manpack version)

By covering the full military band (1.5-30 MHZ) and
incorporating unique proprietary adaptive features
in the common transceiver unit (RT-2001), the
HF-2000 overcomes the traditional HF communication problems. Automatic link establishment
provides reliable long-range communication under
changing ionospheric conditions while active
squelch prevents false alarms and assures noise-free
communications. Embedded full-band frequency-
hopping, voice and data security and internal data
modem further expand the HF-2000 capabilities.
Features include: 1.5–30 MHZ military HF band; three
power output levels for manpack configurations
(5, 10, 20 W) and for vehicular/fixed configuration
(10, 50, 100 W); built-in active digital squelch; built-in
Tadiran ALE (Autocall); ALE per MIL-STD-141A
(optional); built-in encryption (COMSEC) and
Frequency Hopping (ECCM) for voice and data; and
built-in Burst (Flash) transmission. The PRC-2200
transmits 20 W of RF power and features full
HF-2000 capabilities in a manpack configuration.
For optimal power transfer to the whip antenna,
under all operational conditions, the PRC-2200
includes a fast, automatic antenna matching unit.

SPECIFICATION:

USED BY:
In widespread service with the
Israeli Defence Force, Border and
Civil Police

CONTRACTOR:
Tadiran Communications Ltd,
Israel

Diveguard Mk 2 Distress System for Special Forces

ISRAEL

Diveguard Mk 2 is a personal safety device for Special Forces. The system enables a team of divers to communicate SOS or OK messages within the team as well as home on a diver in distress. Furthermore, the system has a unique 'remote SOS' feature which enables a diver to provoke SOS signals on a missing diver and then to home on the signals, all within the team and with no need for outside help. This enables precious time to be gained in case of emergency. The system can be operated in darkness and in low temperature environments down to a depth of 50 m. Diveguard Mk 2 weighs about 600 g in air and is slightly buoyant in water.

SPECIFICATION:

USED BY:
Various maritime Special Forces

CONTRACTOR:
Rafael Armament Development Authority Ltd, Israel

Alinco DJ-X10 Scanning Receiver UK

This is a new top-of-the-range scanner with extra wideband coverage up to 2000 MHz. It has an especially sensitive receiver and a large 36-digit dot matrix plus a 22-segment illuminated display. There are 1200 memory channels and a channel scope spectrum analyser. Advanced scanning features include: programmed scan (up to 10 groups); programmed memory scan; any memory scan; mode scan; VFO search; dual VFO search; priority scan and band incursion scan. The DJ-X10 includes facilities for cloning another set and there is a selectable control beep tone with keypad lock control.

SPECIFICATION:

USED BY:
In service

CONTRACTOR:
Nevada Communications, UK

FEATURES:
FREQUENCY: 100 kHz – 2,000 MHz
SCAN SPEED: 25 channels p/s
SCAN STEPS: selectable
(50 Hz – 500 kHz) in 20 fixed steps
RECEIVER: triple superheterodyne
SIZE: 57 x 150 x 25.5 mm
WEIGHT: 320 g

Caracal (PRM 4740A) Frequency-hopping Hand-held Transceiver UK

Introduced in 1987, the Caracal claims to be the world's first frequency-hopping hand-held VHF/FM transceiver to meet full military specifications. The Caracal covers the 30 – 87.975 MHz frequency range. It also has ten programmable simplex or half-duplex channels out of its repertoire of 2320. Hopping in narrowband (6.4 MHz) and wideband (30 – 87.975 MHz) orthogonal modes, Caracal contains high-grade internal digital encryption and has an output of 1 W. Insertion of frequency and security codes is accomplished using the MA 4073B programmer or MA 4083B fill gun. A zeroise switch on each radio is used to erase codes rapidly. The synchronisation function is broadcast, requiring about six seconds. Other features include receive-only selective calling, frequency barring and 'hailing' by fixed-frequency radios when in the hopping mode.

SPECIFICATION:

USED BY:
Sold to a Middle East country and believed to have been bought by US Special Forces

CONTRACTOR:
Thales Communications, Crawley, UK

FEATURES:
The standard Caracal measures 247 x 75 x 38 mm and weighs 1 kg. It uses a variety of whip antennas and a handset or speaker microphone. The PRM 4740B has an integral speaker microphone. Both meet the general requirements of MIL-STD-810C and are compatible with the Jaguar range of systems.

Cougar-2000 Secure Radio UK

Cougar-2000 secure radio (1) and Cougar-2000 network radio unit (2)

Power output is variable from 1.5 – 5 w based on individual channel requirements. Cougar-2000 also offers complete scanning modes for reception and transmission of signals. The radios use 'intelligent' batteries with time/power displays of remaining battery life. Battery management has also been improved by developing battery chargers able to store and analyse the complete history of individual batteries and condition them automatically as necessary. Algorithms used for encryption by Racal in Cougar-2000 and the original Cougar radio will remain unpublished to ensure security. Cougar-2000 is designed to be adapted to provide a high-level secure communications network for military, paramilitary and civil security uses.

SPECIFICATION:

USED BY:
UK army and covert variant with a European security agency

CONTRACTOR:
Thales Communications, Crawley, UK

Cougarnet Communication System UK

Cougarnet communication system (1) and Cougar talk-through station (2)

Cougarnet is a secure radio system operating over the full FM band. It consists of various configurations of Cougar hand-held sets and the Cougarnet base station. The Cougar personal radio is the heart of the system and can be used or adapted for use in Static, Mobile or Transportable (SMT) roles. It provides analogue and secure digital voice communications by using in-built encryption modules. Security is further enhanced by two code combinations and a zeroise position. Channel frequencies and crypto codes can be changed by using a programmer or keyfill unit. A range of audio warning tones for transceiver malfunctions is incorporated. Area coverage or link-ups are possible using single- or two-frequency simplex operation.

SPECIFICATION:

USED BY:
UK navy and army, Sri Lankan navy, army, air force and VIP protection unit plus a number of other forces including an undisclosed customer on the Indian sub-continent

CONTRACTOR:
Thales Communications, Crawley, UK

FEATURES:
MODE: single- or two-frequency simplex
FREQUENCY RANGE: VHF: 68-88 and 132-174 MHZ;
UHF: 403-470 MHZ
NUMBER OF CHANNELS: ten programmable
ENCRYPTION: digital
POWER OUTPUT: 2, 10 or 20 W
POWER SUPPLY: 13.6 V DC
HEIGHT: 107 mm
WIDTH: 345 mm
DEPTH: 414 mm
WEIGHT: 16.5 kg

Davies Communications Systems UK

CT400 assault communications system

This company designs and manufactures specialised communications equipment and audio ancillaries to work in conjunction with the world's latest digital radio systems.

Special Forces and SWAT Teams: CT400 Assault Communications System. Swimmers/Divers: OSK and ODK Subsurface Swimmers' Audio Comset. Boats: RIBS 201 Boat Radio Intercom System. Vehicles: VIS 100 Military Fast Attack/Light Support Vehicle Radio Intercom System. Police: TACMIC CT & FAST Specialist Tactical Firearms Units/SWAT Teams. Covert Communications: Covert 500 Body Worn Covert Communications Range.

Covert Car Fit incorporates a microphone system which provides ambient noise suppression in order to reduce the transmission of background noise and enhance speech.

SPECIFICATION:

USED BY:
UK forces

CONTRACTOR:
Davies Industrial
Communications Ltd, UK

Digital Global Listening Post (DiGLiPo) UK

The Digital Global Listening Post provides instant international access to recorded intelligence via public telephone lines, satellite or cellular telephones. It has built-in receiver boards for VHF, UHF and microwave covert transmitters and an interface for voice, data and all telecom sources. The system records up to fifteen channels simultaneously and has the ability to simultaneously receive and store for later retrieval, 1500 hours of intelligence from RF telecom or data sources.

SPECIFICATION:

USED BY:
In service

CONTRACTOR:
VASCON, UK

Elite2000 XC UK

The SignalGuard Elite2000 XC Cellphone encryptor is a lightweight, low-profile unit that slides easily onto the Motorola MicroTAC cellphone to provide powerful encryption security during calls. The unit sits between the phone and the battery, adding less than an inch to the thickness of the phone, and less than 113.4 g to the weight. No phone modification is required. The Elite2000 XC is compatible with the other members of the Elite2000 Series, the Elite2000 XT Secure Telephone, and the Elite2000 XL Phone and Fax encryptor. The cellphone encryptor features selectable levels of security, as well as voice reconstruction using CES safe technology. The voice encryption utilises a global key for international compatibility, with a corporate key available for users in a single company or group. Personal identification numbers may also be used for enhanced security and, as with other members of the Elite2000 Series, the Elite2000 XC may be used for secure conference calls.

SPECIFICATION:

USED BY:
In service

CONTRACTOR:
Whiterock Communications Limited, UK

FEATURES:
SECURE MODE: users' voices transmitted full duplex encrypted
SPEECH DELAY: 250 ms when encrypted
POWER SUPPLY: cellphone battery
CONNECTOR: battery slide connector
SIGNAL BANDWIDTH: 50 HZ – 3,500 HZ
HOUSING: slicej casing
SIZE: increases cellphone depth by 20 mm
WEIGHT: approx 110 g

PTAC Secure Terminal Rugged Data Terminal UK

PTAC is a standard PC that can be configured to a specific tactical application (such as a data terminal) simply by downloading the appropriate PC compatible software. The prime elements are the keyboard and the display: their size has been maximised for use under NBC threat or arctic conditions and for readability in poor light yet minimised for convenience and safety in hostile conditions. The design allows the PTAC to fold so that the display screen and keyboard protect each other when the terminal is closed when the unit may be carried in a pocket. The equipment is sealed and desiccated to offer protection against immersion, driving rain, humidity and exposure to dust and sand. With the strength of the case, armoured display window and hinge seals, the PTAC will withstand an excess of one atmosphere in either direction and is thus able to accept both high altitudes – such as those experienced in parachuting – and a water depth of 6 feet (2 m).

SPECIFICATION:

USED BY:
In service with a number of undisclosed units in the UK and Eastern Europe

CONTRACTOR:
Redifon MEL Ltd, UK

PTR349 VHF/FM Radio UK

The PTR349 is a lightweight VHF/FM transceiver for short-range tactical communications in combat conditions. It is designed specifically for communications within the squad or infantry section or from squad to platoon headquarters. It is claimed to be inconspicuous in use and special provision is made for silent operation, thus making it suitable for patrol and ambush communications, convoy and river crossing control, amphibious landings, parachute drop zone communications and internal security operations.

SPECIFICATION:

USED BY:
In production and in service with armies in Africa, Europe and the Middle East in the early 1990s

CONTRACTOR:
BAE Systems, Christchurch, UK

FEATURES:
MODE: F3E narrowband FM at 5 kHz deviation by speech or 1.5 kHz tone
FREQUENCY RANGE: PTR349A, PTR349E and PTR349G: 37-49.975 MHZ PTR349B, PTR349F and PTR349H: 47-56.975 MHZ
NUMBER OF CHANNELS: 400
CHANNEL SPACING: 25 kHz
POWER OUTPUT: PTR349A and 349B: 0.5 W; PTR349E and 349F: 1 W; PTR349G and 349H: 3 W
ANTENNAS: 0.5 m whip, 1 m tape whip, 2 m wire
POWER SUPPLY: 12 V nominal from battery pack
BATTERY LIFE: 12 hours for 1:9 tx/rx ratio when using rechargeable battery with 0.5 and 1 W radios; slightly less with 3 W version

Radio-Controlled Explosive Initiator UK

SPECIFICATION:

USED BY:
In service

CONTRACTOR:
BDL Systems Ltd, UK

Based on the successful range of RS68 radio-controlled explosive initiators, this latest system allows the user to programme their own external code plugs for confidentiality and interchangeability.

Sonic Scrambler UK

Sonic Scrambler attached to a commercial telephone

SPECIFICATION:

USED BY:
In service worldwide

CONTRACTOR:
Sonic Communications
(International) Ltd, UK

The Sonic Scrambler is a practical means of ensuring that private conversations remain secure with a scrambler that simply attaches to an ordinary telephone. This scrambler has a fixed-spectrum inversion technique which is digitally controlled by the unit code select switch concealed in the battery compartment. With over 13,000 user-selected codes the Sonic Scrambler can operate over local, long-distance and international calls, protecting the user from all kinds of unauthorised interference. The unit is battery operated and no separate wires or special connectors are required. Completely self-contained, it is fixed to the existing telephone by a finger-grip strap and is compatible with most styles of telephone including cordless and cellular.

KY-189 Intelligent Secure Handset USA

The KY-189 handset is a tactical level, high-security scrambler in an intelligent handset designed to operate directly with the US Army's standard PRC-77 and VRC-12 radios, as well as most other tactical VHF radios, as a direct replacement for the existing audiophonics. The high-level tactical scrambler in NAPCO's KY-189 employs a microprocessor-controlled, pseudo-random rolling code, combined with random timing, audio frequency shift and synchronisation. The encryption algorithm provides over 100 million user-programmable security codes. Every time the PTT is pressed, the scrambler code changes to a new pseudo-random sequence for even higher security. The net also resynchronises with each transmission. As this scrambler is an analogue device it can be integrated into existing radio networks using standard repeaters and without any reduction in the radio's operating range. Added security features include the ability of the control terminal to change the code key of all the radios on its network remotely by radio and the ability to call selectively a captured or stolen radio and remotely destroy its memory so that the captured scrambler becomes inoperative.

SPECIFICATION:

USED BY:
US Special Forces

CONTRACTOR:
NAPCO International Inc, USA

The Boomerang4 USA

SPECIFICATION:

USED BY:
In service worldwide

CONTRACTOR:
ISA, Information Security
Associates, USA

The Boomerang4 locates eavesdropping devices hidden in walls and ceilings, plants and room furnishings. The Boomerang4 is the latest in a long line of non-linear Junction Detectors that have been in production since 1983. The Boomerang emits a low power microwave signal. It detects changes to the signal that are caused by transistors, diodes and other semi-conductors used in clandestine listening devices. The Boomerang4 can discern between the true electronic devices and metallic junctions that act like semi-conductors, eliminating 95 per cent of false alarms.

Active Ear-Defender ED200K USA

Active Ear-Defender ED200K fits over LITE headsets

SPECIFICATION:

USED BY:
US Special Forces

CONTRACTOR:
Television Equipment Associates,
USA

The Active Ear-Defender ED200k was developed to enable entry team access to a room during explosion of flash bangs and stun grenades. It provides whisper communications before entry plus hearing protection from concussion without compromising radio communications. The electronic design will not shut down during explosions but will limit the level of sound passing through the electronic hear-through to a comfortable 90 dB. The Active Ear-Defender will interface with LITE or LASH headsets to maintain radio communications.

Invisible Communications for Surveillance

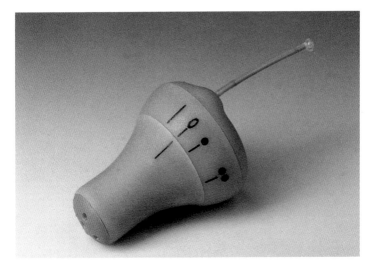

Collarset-II, a wireless earphone/concealed microphone with a press-to-talk switch, enables the user to transmit and receive radio signals with total secrecy. The system is almost impossible to detect even at distances of 609.6 mm. The Collarset series attaches to any portable radio. An optional shoulder harness will conceal the radio in the user's armpit. The microphone is located under the user's clothing, near the collarbone, and the press-to-talk switch can be in the hand, pocket or belt. The wireless induction earphone is hidden inside the user's ear and receives the radio signals magnetically from the inductor on the shoulder. The wireless earphone has a battery life of 60 – 100 hours and contains an automatic squelch circuit eliminating magnetic buzz when a voice signal is not present on the carrier. To transmit a message, the user depresses the push-to-talk button and speaks naturally; it is, of course, not necessary to talk directly into the microphone which is located under the user's clothing.

SPECIFICATION:

USED BY:
US Special Forces

CONTRACTOR:
Television Equipment Associates, USA

LASH Headset USA

LASH headset with moulded earplug

The LASH throat microphone and headset provides superior radio communication because the microphone picks up only voice box vibrations and, as a result, it makes better transmissions when the user is in a noisy environment. The throat microphone does not interfere with respirators, balaclavas, flash hoods or helmets and works with all portable radios. LASH will not slip and slide during vigorous Special Forces operations or police work. Because the chest-mounted press-to-talk switch has a front surface action, users with thick heavy gloves need only depress the front of the switch to transmit. LASH is weatherproof and heat resistant.

SPECIFICATION:

USED BY:
US Special Forces and police

CONTRACTOR:
Television Equipment Associates, USA

LITE Headset USA

The new LITE headset has been designed for Special Forces and police SWAT applications. The LITE headset comes with two microphones, a boom microphone for most transmissions and a throat or mask microphone for optimum communications when gas is deployed. The LITE headset has first-class peripheral hearing with gaps around the earphone that let the user hear ambient sound as though there is no obstruction, a requirement for close-quarter battle. It fits comfortably under most ballistic helmets and a foam cushion with fabric/elastic straps provides a secure fit which is comfortable under the helmet liner. For explosive entry, the headset accommodates any passive or active ear-defenders to protect the user's hearing from concussion. There is a chest-mounted press switch and to key the radio all the operator has to do is touch the front of the switch with anything, a finger, back of the hand, or even underarm.

SPECIFICATION:

USED BY:
US Special Forces and police

CONTRACTOR:
Television Equipment Associate, USA

Small Boat Intercom System USA

This new small boats intercom system provides duplex communication between a crew of four and is suited for Special Force and SWAT team applications. Normal conversation is possible between all four crew members even in noisy environments. While two of the crew send radio transmissions, all four can monitor the signals. To suit individual user requirements, operating conditions and radio equipment, a variety of submersible headsets or headset/helmets are available. An additional safety feature is the use of snatch connectors.

SPECIFICATION:

USED BY:
US Maritime Special Forces

CONTRACTOR:
Television Equipment Associates, USA

Secrette Headsets USA

Secrette headsets with throat microphone

These are single-earphone headsets for use by firefighting, security and SWAT units and come in two forms. The Secrette SEC5357GP consists of one shallow rubber ear cup with earphone and retaining ring to hold web headstraps. These straps connect with a touch fastener in such a manner that the headset is firmly secured and will not fall off during activity. A throat microphone has leather pads which are secured to the neck by an adjustable elastic breakaway strap. The complete headset is showerproof and is not affected by heavy dousing with water. The Secrette SEC5352GP uses the same earphone but is provided with a sturdy, adjustable, noise-cancelling boom-arm microphone which locates in a convenient position at the corner of the mouth. Both units are provided with a weatherproof spring-activated PTT switch in the main cable, which is terminated with a suitable plug for any specified radio set.

SPECIFICATION:

USED BY:
US forces

CONTRACTOR:
Television Equipment Associates, USA

20-Metre Submersible Miniature Secure Hand-held Radio (MSHR) USA

Designed for use by Special Forces, Air-Sea rescue, small boat crews and specialist law enforcement teams, the 20 m MSHR is one of the smallest, lightest and most secure 20 m submersible radios in the world. Weighing only 695 g with battery and antenna, the 20 m MSHR is housed in a rugged metal case and is submersible to 20 m of salt water. The radio transmits both voice and data (clear or encrypted) over 100 channels and provides full 136 – 174 MHz frequency coverage, embedded US type 1 COMSEC or optional exportable COMSEC, 5 W RF power output, Night-Vision Goggle (NVG) compatible 32 x 80 backlit LCD and 12 and 16 kbps secure voice and data modes. The radio uses advanced digital signal processing and microprocessor control allowing the addition of advanced features and software upgrades through a flash port.

SPECIFICATION:

USED BY:
US Maritime Special Forces

CONTRACTOR:
Thales Communications Inc, USA

Occasional Swimmer's Kit (OSK-1) USA

Occasional Swimmer's Kit (OSK-1) with radio container

The Occasional Swimmer's Kit OSK-1 provides submerisible communications to a depth of 20 m (66 ft). Three soft radio containers accommodate any portable or manpack radio with antenna attached; access to the radio for the manipulation of controls is via a waterproof zipper. A single- or double-earphone submersible headset can be supplied with either boom or throat microphone. A chest-mounted PTT switch contains a knob to control the radio volume or, alternatively, a hand-operated PTT switch can be supplied. These products can be interfaced to aircraft intercom systems for briefing purposes. Adaptors are available to accommodate any radio.

SPECIFICATION:

USED BY:
US Maritime Special Forces

CONTRACTOR:
Television Equipment Associates, USA

VL5000 Counter-Surveillance Receiver USA

The VL5000 is a lightweight and compact system for detection of covert radio frequency emissions. It will detect, locate and verify both AM and FM bugs operating between 2 MHz and 1.5 GHz. When a bug is detected, LEDs illuminate and confirm the presence of RF energy; when the verifier is operated the room noise generated at the start of the sweep will be heard in the headphone. At the same time the signal strength meter will indicate the strength of the signal.

SPECIFICATION:

USED BY:
In service

CONTRACTOR:
CCS International Ltd, USA

Walker's Tactical Ear USA

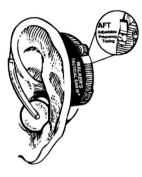

Walker's Tactical Ear is a hearing enhancement device that amplifies sound nearly nine times normal hearing, enough to hear even the slightest noise during stakeouts, surveillance and SWAT interventions. The device fits comfortably in the back of the ear and weighs only 3.3 g. The technology allows for omni-directional (360° range) hearing with emphasis on high-frequency sounds such as muted or low-level conversations between law enforcement officers or suspects; the loading of a gun chamber; the clicking of gun's safety catch and footsteps on abrasive surfaces. In addition, the Tactical Ear provides maximum hearing protection and its specially designed earplug delivers a noise-reduction rating of 29 – 33 dBs. A special safety circuit shuts off the Tactical Ear when a firearm is discharged, further protecting hearing. The device fits in only one ear, allowing the second ear to receive broadcasts from commanders via a radio earplug. Walker's Tactical Ear I and II are designed for law enforcement to be used by officers in both stealth (amplify) and dynamic (protect) situations. The model III features all of the specifications of the I and II in addition to Ultra Frequency Broadcast, which allows wireless voice communications when used with a personal radio.

SPECIFICATION:

USED BY:
In service

CONTRACTOR:
Walker's Game Ear Inc, USA

Ghost Series Transmitters USA

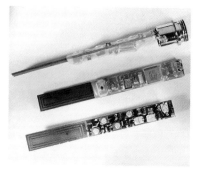

The CCS Ghost Series provides a powerful wireless microphone and tracking transmitter capable of delivering crystal-clear audio, pulse signals and emergency alarm to thwart kidnappers and cargo thieves. The advanced surface mount micro-board phone can fit in the barrel of a working pen and comes laminated for custom applications. As thin as a credit card and shorter than a cigarette, the WMTX 4400 is a wireless microphone with audio transmission. The WMTX 4200 is the same but includes voice activation. The WMTX 4500 adds a tracking pulse which can be followed using a field intensity directive receiver or can be picked up by a helicopter with a radius of one mile. The WMTX 4700 MD wireless microphone with tracking transmitter features a Man-Down switch to alarm the command station when immediate help is needed.

SPECIFICATION:

USED BY:
In worldwide service

CONTRACTOR:
CCS International Ltd, USA

FEATURES:
FREQUENCY: 395 – 410 MHz crystal controlled
MODULATION: narrowband
POWER OUTPUT: 20mW
ANTENNA: internal
POWER SUPPLY: 3 x 1.5 v No 392 batteries (standard)
DIMENSIONS: 69.5 x 7.5 x 4.5 mm
WEIGHT: 12 g
BATTERY LIFE: from 15 hours to one year depending on usage and vox operation
TESTED RANGE: up to 305 metres under ideal conditions; by helicopter up to 1.6 kilometres

Surveillance: Air

Codarra Avatar AUSTRALIA

A man-portable tactical surveillance UAV intended as a low-cost system for real-time imagery acquisition. It has high-wing, T-tailed powered sailplane configuration and no landing gear. It features composites (GFRP) construction and can be carried (dismantled) in a standard Australian Army backpack; assembly time is less than 15 minutes. It has an expected life of about 100 flights. Other features include a small CCD video camera in with 2.434 or 2.411 GHZ real-time downlink, improved, high-resolution digital camera, hand launch and belly landing under operator control.

SPECIFICATION:

USED BY:
Royal Australian Army

CONTRACTOR:
Codarra Advanced Systems,
Canberra, Australia

FEATURES:
POWERPLANT: Electric motor
(Ni/Cd batteries); two-blade
propeller
DIMENSIONS: Wingspan: 2.50 m
(8 ft 2.4 in)
WEIGHTS: Max payload: Approx
2.0 kg (4.4 lb); max launching
weight: <3.5 kg (7.7 lb)
PERFORMANCE: Cruising speed:
27 kts (50 km/h; 31 mph); typical
operating altitude: 120 m (400 ft),
180 m (600 ft)
MISSION RADIUS: 13.5 n miles
(25 km; 15.5 miles)
VIDEO TRANSMISSION RANGE:
2.7 n miles (5 km; 3.1 miles)
ENDURANCE: 1 hour

Schiebel Camcopter AUSTRIA

Camcopter 5.1 close-range helicopter

The Camcopter can be used for: ground and aerial surveillance; target acquisition and designation; minefield and surface ordnance survey; day/night traffic; border patrol and observation; NBC survey; and environmental monitoring. Small size and stealth characteristics minimise the risk of detection.

SPECIFICATION:

USED BY:
Austrian army, Egyptian navy, French army, German army and US army. Also evaluated by British army and US Naval Surface Warfare Centre

CONTRACTOR:
Schiebel Elektronische Gerate GmbH, Vienna, Austria

FEATURES:
POWERPLANT: One 11.2 kw (15 hp) Minarelli two-stroke engine with remote start. Fuel capacity 12.5 litres (3.3 US gallons; 2.75 Imp gallons), expandable to 30 litres (7.9 US gallons; 6.6 Imp gallons)
MAIN ROTOR DIAMETER: 3.09 m (10 ft 1.7 in)
TAIL ROTOR DIAMETER: 0.50 m (1 ft 7.7 in)
FUSELAGE: Length: 2.68 m (8 ft 9.5 in); max width: 0.82 m (2 ft 8.3 in)
HEIGHT OVERALL: 0.80 m (2 ft 7.5 in)
WEIGHT EMPTY: 43 kg (94.8 lb)
FUEL WEIGHT (STANDARD): 17.4 kg (38.4 lb)
MAX PAYLOAD (INCL FUEL): 25 kg (55.1 lb)
MAX T/O WEIGHT: 68 kg (150 lb)
MAX CRUISING SPEED: 49 kts (90 km/h; 56 mph)
MAX RATE OF CLIMB AT S/L: 180 m (590 ft)/min
SERVICE CEILING: 3000 m (9840 ft)
HOVER CEILING OGE: 1700 m (5575 ft)
MISSION RADIUS: standard datalink: 5.4 n miles (10 km; 6.2 miles); enhanced datalink: 54 n miles (100 km; 62 miles)
ENDURANCE: 6 hours

OIP Helimun Helicopter Pilot's Night-Vision System

BELGIUM

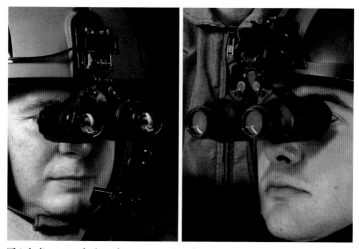

This helicopter pilot's night-vision system, known as Helimun, is available with 40° and 60° fields of view. Designed to fit easily onto a pilot's helmet, it has three principal enhancements: XD-4 image intensifiers; individual interpupillary adjustment; and greater eye relief. A power module is built into the back of the helmet. The system can be mounted on many kinds of pilot's helmets. The XD-4 image intensifiers provide a high-resolution image and have greater photocathode sensitivity, a higher signal-to-noise ratio, a more stringent blemish specification and a higher burn-in resis-tance compared to standard intensifiers, according to the manufacturer. Helimun provides a high image quality over a much greater range of eye positions than standard 15 mm eye-relief eyepieces, ensuring that all users have the full 40° or 60° field of view (FOV) and simplifying the task of centring the eyepiece directly in front of each eye. Furthermore, the new mechanism reduces monocular wobble.

SPECIFICATION:

USED BY:
Armed forces worldwide

CONTRACTOR:
OIP Sensor Systems, Oudenaarde, Belgium

FEATURES:
- 40° or 60° field of view
- Individual interpupillary distance adjustment
- Power module on the back of the helmet with back-up batteries
- Minus blue filters for cockpit lighting compatibility
- Low distortion optics

Bombardier CL-89 CANADA

CL-89 drone launch

SPECIFICATION:

USED BY:
Armies of France, Germany, Italy and UK for day/night surveillance and artillery target acquisition. First used operationally by British Army during Operations Desert Shield and Desert Storm

CONTRACTOR:
Bombardier Defence Services, Mirabel, Quebec, Canada

FEATURES:
One 0.56 kn (125 lb st) Williams WR2-6 turbojet
WINGSPAN: 0.94 m (3 ft 1.0 in)
FOREPLANE SPAN: 0.48 m (1 ft 7.0 in)
LENGTH (EXCL. ADMU PROBE): incl. booster: 3.73 m (12 ft 3.0 in); excl. booster: 2.60 m (8 ft 6.5 in)
BODY DIAMETER (MAX): 0.33 m (1 ft 1.0 in)
WEIGHT EMPTY: 78.2 kg (172.4 lb)
PAYLOAD: 17-20 kg (37.5-44.1 lb)
MAX LAUNCHING WEIGHT: incl. booster: 156 kg (344 lb); excl. booster: 108 kg (238 lb)
MAX LEVEL SPEED: 400 kts (741 km/h; 460 mph)
OPERATIONAL CEILING: 3050 m (10,000 ft)
MAX OPERATING RADIUS: standard: 32 n miles (60 km; 37 miles); with extended-range fuel tank: 38 n miles (70 km; 43 miles)

The CL-89 was developed to provide forward area field commanders with non-realtime visual information on territory within a 38 n mile (70 km; 43 mile) radius, using either a camera or an infrared linescanning systems. Major requirements were simplicity of operation and maintenance, high survivability in a sophisticated enemy air defence environment, ability to detect and record tactically significant enemy formations and weapons in all weathers, by day or night, and provision of accurate intelligence. The system had to be totally integrated, mobile and independent of such external services as electrical power supplies. The sensor pack is mounted in the lower central part of the drone body, just forward of the fuel and oil tanks. The daytime photographic reconnaissance sensor is a Zeiss KRb 8/24c camera. For nocturnal surveillance, this is replaced by a Vinten Type 201 IRLS. Recovery is by parachute.

Xian ASN-1 CHINA

Hand-launched Xian ASN-15

This is a lightweight, low-cost reconnaissance and surveillance UAV. It has a parasol-wing monoplane with dihedral on the outer panels, a slender pod-and-boom fuselage and is fitted with a T-tail. It is launched by hand or rail and is recovered by a belly skid landing or parachute. Its payload includes a CCD camera with realtime video downlink, or film camera. It is controlled by LOS radio control.

SPECIFICATION:

USED BY:
Chinese armed forces

CONTRACTOR:
Xian ASN Technology Group, Xian, Shaanxi, China

FEATURES:
One small single-cylinder piston engine, mounted above wing centre-section; two-blade propeller
WINGSPAN: 3 m (9 ft 10.1 in)
LENGTH OVERALL: 1.80 m (5 ft 10.9 in)
MAX LAUNCHING WEIGHT: 6.5 kg (14.3 lb)
MAX LEVEL SPEED AT S/L: 48 kts (90 km/h; 56 mph)
OPERATING ALTITUDE: Lower: 50 m (165 ft); upper: 500 m (1640 ft)
CONTROL RADIUS: 5.4 n miles (10 km; 6.2 miles)
ENDURANCE: 1 hour

VTÚL **Sojka** III CZECH REPUBLIC

Sojka III reconnaissance UAV

The Sojka (Jay) system was developed for tactical reconnaissance at ranges of up to 54 n miles (100 km; 62 miles) from the GCS, at altitudes from 200 – 2000 m (660 – 6560 ft), with real-time transmission of optical and telemetric data. High-wing monoplane with pusher engine and twin-boom tail unit; constructed of GFRP for rigidity, low weight and low radar signature. Standard reconnaissance payload is a colour TV camera installed in nose of air vehicle. Additional sensors are an A39 photographic camera and an Intertechnique Camelia IRLS for high-resolution electro-optical day/night reconnaissance. Also developed are a digital photographic system, and a gamma probe for radioactivity monitoring. Launch by reusable solid-fuel rocket booster from 14 m (50 ft), truck-mounted foldable ramp with 20° elevation. Underfuselage skids for belly landing on flat areas of grass, clay, sand or concrete. For more difficult terrain or emergency use, a recovery parachute and airbag are employed.

SPECIFICATION:

USED BY:
Czech army and air force

CONTRACTOR:
Czech Air Force Research Institute (VTÚL a PVO), Prague, Czech Republic

FEATURES:
One 22.0 kW (29.5 hp) UVMV M 115 two-cylinder two-stroke engine; two-blade fixed-pitch wooden pusher propeller. Fuel capacity 19 litres (5.0 US gallons; 4.2 Imp gallons)
WINGSPAN: 4.12 m (13 ft 6.2 in)
LENGTH OVERALL: 3.78 m (13 ft 4.2 in)
FUSELAGE LENGTH: 2.10 m (6 ft 10.7 in)
HEIGHT OVERALL: 1.08 m (3 ft 6.5 in)
PAYLOAD BAY VOLUME: 75.0 dm³ (2.12 cu ft)
FUEL WEIGHT: 12 kg (26.5 lb)
MAX PAYLOAD: 25 kg (55.1 lb)
MAX LAUNCHING WEIGHT: approx 180 kg (397 lb)
MAX LEVEL SPEED: 108 kts (200 km/h; 124 mph)
NORMAL OPERATING SPEED: 97 kts (180 km/h; 112 mph)
LOITER SPEED: 65 kts (120 km/h; 75 mph)
MAX RATE OF CLIMB AT S/L: 540 m (1771 ft)/min
OPERATING HEIGHT RANGE: lower: 50 m (165 ft); upper: 2000 m (6560 ft)
OPERATIONAL RADIUS: >54 n miles (100 km; 62 miles)
ENDURANCE: 2 hours

SAGEM Crecerelle FRANCE

SAGEM Crecerelle in flight

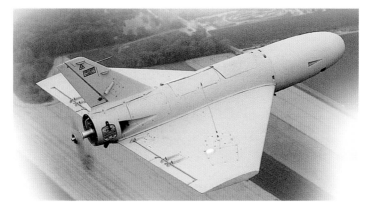

Crecerelle is derived directly from the interoperable ATAOS (autonomous tactical attack and observation systems) developed by SAGEM for observation, reconnaissance and neutralisation missions. The Meggitt Spectre is the air vehicle for the Crecerelle system and is a delta-wing monoplane, with elevons, mainly cylindrical fuselage, sweptback fin and rudder and a pusher engine. The fuselage and wings are of composites construction and it is launched by a pneumatic catapult from a trailer-mounted ramp. Recovery is by an autonomous parachute system with discard device for a safe landing in windy conditions.

SPECIFICATION:

USED BY:
French army

CONTRACTOR:
SAGEM, Division Defense et
Securité, Paris, France

FEATURES:
18.6 kw (25 hp) Meggitt WAE 342
two-cylinder two-stroke engine;
two-blade wooden pusher
propeller
WINGSPAN: 3.28 m (10 ft 9.0 in)
LENGTH OVERALL: 2.74 m
(9 ft 0.0 in)
HEIGHT OVERALL: 0.71 m
(2 ft 4.0 in)
PAYLOAD BAY VOLUME: 50.0 dm³
(1.76 cu ft)
MAX FUEL: 24 kg (52.9 lb)
MAX PAYLOAD: 35 kg (77.2 lb)
MAX LAUNCHING WEIGHT: 145 kg
(320 lb)
MAX LEVEL SPEED: 129 kts
(240 km/h; 149 mph)
CRUISING SPEED: 86 kts (160 km/h;
99 mph)
LOITER SPEED: 70 kts (130 km/h;
81 mph)
OPERATING HEIGHT: lower: 300 m
(985 ft); upper: 4000 m (13,120 ft)
MISSION RADIUS: 32-49 n miles
(60-90 km; 37-56 miles)
MAX RANGE: 108 n miles (200 km;
124 miles)
ENDURANCE: 5 hours

Dassault AVE FRANCE

Dessault Aéronef de Validation Expérimentale (AVE) UAV

Designed to carry payloads for surveillance, laser target designation and EW missions. The take-off and landing are under manual control; the rest of the mission can be autonomous, or under air- or ground-based operator control. It has GPS navigation and conventional runway take-off and landing or catapult (depending on type). It also features a parachute or parafoil for emergency recovery (depending on type).

SPECIFICATION:

USED BY:
Development as a stealth UCAV to meet French requirements

CONTRACTOR:
Dassault Aviation, St Cloud, France

FEATURES:
Two 0.2 kN (45 lb st) Aviation Microjet Technology (AMT) turbojets
WINGSPAN: 2.40 m (7 ft 10.5 in)
LENGTH OVERALL: 2.40 m (7 ft 10.5 in)
WEIGHT EMPTY: 35 kg (77.2 lb)
MAX T/O WEIGHT: 60 kg (132.3 lb)
DESIGN MAX LEVEL SPEED: M0.5
RANGE: approx 81 n miles (150 km; 93 miles)

EADS SDE **Eagle 2** FRANCE

Eagle UAV

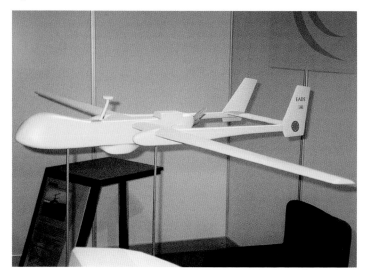

Medium-altitude, long-endurance strategic intelligence-gathering UAV.

SPECIFICATION:

USED BY:
French air force

CONTRACTOR:
EADS Defence and Communication Systems, ISR Operating Unit, Saint Quentin en Yvelines, France

FEATURES:
One 895 kw (1,200 shp) Pratt & Whitney Canada PT6A turboprop
WINGSPAN: 26.00 m (85 ft 3.6 in)
LENGTH OVERALL: 13.00 m (42 ft 7.8 in)
MAX PAYLOAD: 450 kg (992 lb)
MAX T/O WEIGHT: 3600 kg (7936 lb)
MAX LEVEL SPEED: 230 kts (426 km/h; 264 mph)
OPERATIONAL CEILING: 13,720 m (45,000 ft)
T/O AND LANDING RUN: <1000 m (3280 ft)
MAX RANGE: 1,565 n miles (2900 km; 1802 miles)
TIME ON STATION: (at 540 n miles (1000 km; 621 miles) from base) 24 hours

EADS Fox AT FRANCE

Fox AT with underwing weather sensors

High-wing monoplane with pod-and-boom fuselage, pusher engine and T-tail. It is constructed of duralumin, glass/carbon fibres and styrofoam and the wing and tail surfaces are attached by single bolts. Designed in co-operation with 10 other French aerospace companies to meet the requirements of the French Army and potential export customers, it has both civil and military applications. More than 1000 of all versions have been produced. Sensors can include fixed or gyrostabilised CCD and IR cameras, FLIR (3 – 5 or 8 – 12 microns), thermal analysers, Linescan 4000, VHF or radar jammers and NBC detectors. Another option includes meteorological sondes, up to four of which can be carried underwing and dropped by parachute to gauge temperature, air pressure and windspeed to aid fire correction for long-range artillery. There is a launch by bungee catapult or hydraulic launcher and normal recovery (no landing gear).

SPECIFICATION:

USED BY:
Austria, French army, Indonesia, the United Nations and an unidentified Persian Gulf country plus others

CONTRACTOR:
EADS Defence and Communication Systems, CAC Systemes, La Chapelle Vendomoise, France

FEATURES:
One 16.4 kw (22 hp) Limbach L 275 E flat-twin engine; two-blade pusher propeller
WINGSPAN: 3.60 m (11 ft 9.7 in)
LENGTH OVERALL: 2.75 m (9 ft 0.3 in)
HEIGHT OVERALL: 0.70 m (2 ft 3.6 in)
WEIGHT EMPTY: 65 kg (143.3 lb)
MAX PAYLOAD: 15 kg (33.1 lb)
MAX LAUNCHING WEIGHT: 90 kg (198.4 lb)
MAX LEVEL SPEED: 97 kts (180 km/h; 112 mph)
LOITER SPEED: 39 kts (72 km/h; 45 mph)
OPERATING HEIGHT RANGE: lower: 30 m (100 ft); upper: 3000 m (11,480 ft)
MAX DATALINK RANGE EXTENDABLE: 27 n miles (50 km; 31 miles)
MISSION RADIUS (AUTOMATIC): 54 n miles (100 km; 62 miles)
ENDURANCE: 3 hours

SAGEM **Sperwer and Ugglan** FRANCE

Sperwer in flight

Surveillance and target acquisition UAV. Sperwer (Sparrowhawk) is derived from the SAGEM Crecerelle but has a redesigned airframe: low/mid-mounted cropped-delta wings, with elevons; box-section fuselage; and twin outward-canted fins and rudders. The wings are de-iced by hot air from the engine exhaust. Mission payloads: the Sperwer and Ugglan are equipped with SAGEM IRIS dual E-O/IR sensor payload in a retractable turret, plus a piloting camera in nose. It can also be equipped with SAR, ESM/elint package, communications jammer or atmospheric data-gathering payload. It features an automatic launch by pneumatic catapult and recovery by parachute and a triple airbag recovery system.

SPECIFICATION:

USED BY:
Armies of Denmark, France, Greece, the Netherlands and Sweden

CONTRACTOR:
SAGEM, Division Defense et Securité, Paris, France

FEATURES:
One 52.2 kw (70 hp) Rotax 586 two-cylinder two-stroke engine; four-blade pusher propeller
WINGSPAN: 4.20 m (13 ft 9.4 in)
LENGTH OVERALL: 3.00 m (9 ft 10.1 in)
HEIGHT OVERALL: 1.10 m (3 ft 7.3 in)
WEIGHT EMPTY: 212 kg (467 lb)
MAX PAYLOAD: 45 kg (99.2 lb)
MAX LAUNCHING WEIGHT: 330 kg (728 lb)
MAX LEVEL SPEED: 127 kts (235 km/h; 146 mph)
LOITER SPEED: <90 kts (167 km/h; 103 mph)
CEILING: 5000 m (16,400 ft)
MISSION RADIUS: Sperwer: 108 n miles (200 km; 124 miles); Ugglan: 38 n miles (70 km; 43.5 miles)
ENDURANCE: 6 hours

STN Atlas KZO GERMANY

KZO prototype

The German army's KZO (Kleinfluggerat Zielortung: small air vehicle for target location) is a derivative of the former MBB Tucan (Toucan) series of experimental UAVs. It is designed for realtime and day and night observation of enemy forces. It is a small, low-wing monoplane with no horizontal tail surfaces, and has a pusher engine and wings which fold for container storage and transportation and incorporate hot-air de-icing. It has no landing gear and the nose is configured for the installation of various modular payloads. Known examples include a Zeiss OPHELIOS 12 micron stabilised day/night (FLIR) sensor or synthetic aperture radar, and optional playback recorder for deferred in-flight transmission, allowing data storage when realtime transmission is not possible. The sensory and real time data transmission links are highly resistant to jamming, and are capable of transmitting up to 54 n miles (100 km; 62 miles) through dense jamming, and up to 81 n miles (150 km; 93 miles) in more favourable conditions. There is also provision for a laser range-finder/designator. It is launched by a jettisonable booster rocket from a container mounted on a flatbed military truck.

SPECIFICATION:

USED BY:
German army

CONTRACTOR:
STN Atlas Elektronik GmbH, Bremen, Germany

FEATURES:
One 23.9 kw (32 hp) Fichtel & Sachs two-cylinder two-stroke engine; two-blade pusher propeller
WINGSPAN: 3.42 m (11 ft 2.6 in)
LENGTH OVERALL: 2.28 m (7 ft 5.8 in)
HEIGHT OVERALL: 0.96 m (3 ft 1.8 in)
MAX PAYLOAD: 35 kg (77.2 lb)
MAX LAUNCHING WEIGHT: 161 kg (355 lb)
MAX LEVEL SPEED: 135 kts (250 km/h; 155 mph)
NORMAL OPERATING SPEED: 81 kts (150 km/h; 93 mph)
LOITER SPEED: 65 kts (120 km/h; 75 mph)
OPERATING HEIGHT RANGE: lower: 300 m (985 ft); upper: 3500 m (11,480 ft)
CEILING: 4000 m (13,120 ft)
OPERATING RADIUS (DATALINK RANGE): 81 n miles (150 km; 93 miles)
ENDURANCE: >3 hours 30 minutes

EMT LUNA GERMANY

Prototype LUNA being prepared for launch

The LUNA takes its name from the German Army's Luftgestutzte Unbemannte Nahaufklarungs Ausstattung (airborne unmanned close reconnaissance system) programme and is a high-aspect ratio shoulder-wing monoplane with a cruciform tail unit, dependent auxiliary fins and rudders and a dorsally mounted pusher engine. It is of glass fibre epoxy composites construction. The LUNA is fitted with a daylight CCD colour TV camera, with zoom, or Zeiss P286D Attica non-stabilised, 1.7 kg (3.75 lb) thermal imager in ventral bay; a nose-mounted colour camera for piloting and a real-time imagery downlink. It is launched from 4 m (13.1 ft) rail by an EMT bungee catapult which is foldable for transport. Recovery is by parachute recovery with a optional guided parafoil and downward-looking descent video camera.

SPECIFICATION:

USED BY:
German Army; possible interest from other NATO countries

CONTRACTOR:
EMT GmbH, Penzberg, Germany

FEATURES:
One 5.0 kw (6.7 hp) two-cylinder two-stroke engine with restart capability; three-blade pusher propeller with folding blades
FUEL CAPACITY: 3 litres (0.8 US gallon; 0.7 Imp gallon)
WINGSPAN: 4.17 m (13 ft 8.2 in)
LENGTH OVERALL: 2.28 m (7 ft 5.8 in)
HEIGHT OVERALL: 0.78 m (2 ft 6.7 in)
PROPELLER DIAMETER: 0.56 m (1 ft 10.0 in)
PAYLOAD BAY VOLUME: 10.0 dm^3 (0.35 cu ft)
WEIGHT EMPTY: 20 kg (44.1 lb)
MAX PAYLOAD: 3 kg (6.6 lb)
MAX LAUNCHING WEIGHT: 30 kg (66.1 lb)
MAX LEVEL SPEED: 86 kts (160 km/h; 99 mph) IAS
TYPICAL CRUISING SPEED: 38 kts (70 km/h; 43.5 mph) IAS
LOITER SPEED: 26 kts (48 km/h; 30 mph) IAS
MAX RATE OF CLIMB AT S/L: 300 m (984 ft)/min
OPERATING HEIGHT RANGE: lower: S/L; upper: 500 m (1640 ft)
CEILING: 3000 m (9840 ft)
OPERATIONAL RADIUS: real-time (datalink limit): 43 n miles (80 km; 50 miles); off-line: >54 n miles (100 km; 62 miles)
ENDURANCE: 2-4 hours
BEST GLIDE RATIO: 18

ADE **Nishant** INDIA

India's ADE Nishant (Dawn) UAV made its public debut in December

This is a reconnaissance, surveillance and target acquisition UAV with a typical pod-and-twin tailboom layout, high-mounted wing, pusher engine and no landing gear. It is built largely of composites and has conventional ailerons, elevator and rudders. The platform is gyrostabilised with combined daylight TV and FLIR, or daylight TV only, as standard. Optional alternatives include 35 mm miniature panoramic camera or sigint payloads. It is launched by a mobile hydraulic/pneumatic catapult with a velocity 81 to 86 kts (150 – 160 km/h; 93 – 99 mph) and is recovered by parachute and twin airbag for a belly landing.

SPECIFICATION:

USED BY:
Indian army and navy

CONTRACTOR:
Aeronautical Development Establishment (ADE) of Indian Ministry of Defence, Bangalore, India

FEATUES:
One 37.3 kw (50 hp) UEL AR 801R rotary engine; two-blade pusher propeller
WINGSPAN: 6.64 m (21 ft 9.4 in)
LENGTH OVERALL: 4.63 m (15 ft 2.3 in)
HEIGHT OVERALL: 1.183 m (3 ft 10.6 in)
WEIGHT EMPTY: 252 kg (556 lb)
MAX PAYLOAD: 60 kg (132 lb)
MAX LAUNCHING WEIGHT: 375 kg (827 lb)
MAX LEVEL SPEED: 100 kts (185 km/h; 115 mph)
CRUISING SPEED: 67-81 kts (125-150 km/h; 93 mph)
LOITER SPEED: 51 kts (95 km/h; 59 miles)
CEILING: 3600 m (11,810 ft)
MISSION RADIUS: datalink range: 54 n miles (100 km; 62 miles); command range: 86 n miles (160 km; 99 miles)
ENDURANCE: 4 hours 30 minutes

HESA Ababil-s IRAN

Ababil-s surveillance UAV

This is a medium-range reconnaissance and surveillance UAV with a mainly cylindrical fuselage with ogival nosecone; large sweptback vertical fin; pusher engine; and rear swept wings mounted to the underside of the fuselage. The Abadil is of swept metal construction with foreplanes on top of the fuselage near the nose. Payload includes a camera with realtime imagery downlink. It is launched from a truck-mounted pneumatic launcher designed and manufactured by HESA but can also be launched with booster rocket assistance and from a ship's deck. Recovery is by belly skid landing or a HESA cruciform parachute.

SPECIFICATION:

USED BY:
Iranian armed forces. Also available for export

CONTRACTOR:
Iran Aircraft Manufacturing Industries (HESA), Esfahan, Iran

FEATURES:
One P 73 rotary piston engine (rating not known), driving two-blade pusher propeller
WINGSPAN: 3.33 m (10 ft 11.1 in)
LENGTH OVERALL: 2.80 m (9 ft 2.2 in)
HEIGHT OVERALL: 0.935 m (3 ft 0.8 in)
MAX LAUNCHING WEIGHT: 83 kg (183 lb)
MAX LEVEL SPEED: 162 kts (300 km/h; 186 mph)
CEILING: 4270 m (14,000 ft)
MISSION RADIUS: 81 n miles (150 km; 93 miles)

Qods Mohadjer 4 IRAN

Model of the Mohadjer 4

Mohadjer is Arabic for 'migrant' but it is also known as Hodhod (a hooded bird) and has mid-mounted, untapered wings; bullet-shaped fuselage; twin tailbooms; twin fins; and rudders bridged by horizontal tail surface. Construction is substantially of composites. It has retractable belly skid or wheeled landing gear, according to version. Mohadjer, the most recent and most capable version, is said to have 'impressive' ECM capability. It is equipped with GPS and designed for reconnaissance, surveillance, artillery fire support, ECM and communications relay. An IR camera is also fitted as is an onboard digital processor. The Mohadjer can downlink sensor imagery. It is launched by conventional wheeled take-off but can be rail truck-mounted or wheeled for independent mobility. Recovery is by parachute, skid or wheeled landing.

SPECIFICATION:

USED BY:
Iranian armed forces. Reported in use by Iranian Border Guards to detect drug trafficking

CONTRACTOR:
Qods Aviation Industries, Tehran, Iran

FEATURES:
Single 18.6 kw (25 hp) flat-twin piston engine (type not known); two-blade pusher propeller.
Basic dimensions for the earlier M 2 model unless stated otherwise:
WINGSPAN: 3.80 m (12 ft 5.6 in)
LENGTH OVERALL: 2.875 m (9 ft 5.2 in)
HEIGHT OVERALL: 1.03 m (3 ft 4.6 in)
TAIL UNIT SPAN: 0.915 m (3 ft 0.0 in)
MAX LAUNCHING WEIGHT (M 4): 175 kg (386 lb)
MAX LEVEL SPEED (M 4): 108 kts (200 km/h; 124 mph)
CEILING (M 4): 485 m (18,000 ft)
MISSION RADIUS (M 4): 81 n miles (150 km; 93 miles)
ENDURANCE (M 4): 7 hours

Aeronautics Aerolight, Aerosky and Aerostar ISRAEL

The close-range Aerosky

Variants:

Aerolight (A): Very close-range (OTH) reconnaissance and surveillance version; also suitable as operator training system.

Aerosky (B): Close-range version for reconnaissance, surveillance, target acquisition and designation; also suitable for operator training.

Aerostar (C): Short-range version; otherwise generally as for Aerosky.

These are high-wing monoplanes with pod fuselage, pusher engine and single (Aerolight) or twin (Aerosky, Aerostar) tailbooms and T-tail unit. Features include fixed tricycle landing gear and composites construction. Mission payloads: all off-the-shelf, to customer's requirements. There is a pan-tilt-zoom optical camera in the Aerolight and stabilised, gimbal-mounted day/night E-O/IR sensors in the Aerosky and Aerostar. They are all launched and recovered by conventional wheeled take-off and landing.

SPECIFICATION:

USED BY:
Israel Defence Forces, US navy and others

CONTRACTOR:
Aeronautics Defense Systems Ltd, Yavne, Israel

FEATURES:
A: One 4.5-8.2 kw (6-11 hp) piston engine; two-blade pusher propeller
B: One 11.2-14.9 kw (15-20 hp) piston engine; two- or three-blade pusher propeller
C: One 19.4-23.9 kw (26-32 hp) piston engine; two-blade pusher propeller
WINGSPAN: A: 4.00 m (13 ft 1.5 in); B: 4.50 m (14 ft 9.2 in); C: 6.20 m (20 ft 4.1 in)
MAX PAYLOAD: A: 8 kg (17.6 lb); B: 18 kg (39.7 lb); C: 50 kg (110.2 lb)
MAX T/O WEIGHT: A: 40 kg (88.2 lb); B: 70 kg (154.3 lb); C: 200 kg (441 lb)
OPERATIONAL CEILING: A: 3050 m (10,000 ft); B: 4575 m (15,000 ft); C: 5485 m (18,000 ft)
MISSION RADIUS: A: 27 n miles (50 km; 31 miles); B: 54 n miles (100 km; 62 miles); c: up to 108 n miles (200 km; 124 miles)
ENDURANCE: A: 5 hours; B: >5 hours; C: >10 hours

IAI **Heron** ISRAEL

Heron displaying its full-span slotted flaps

The Heron is an all-composites constructed, high-wing monoplane with very high-aspect ratio wings with full-span slotted flaps. It has a twin-boom tail unit with inward-canted fins and rudders. A pusher engine provides propulsion. The tricycle landing gear is retractable. The large fuselage volume is available for a wide variety of single or multiple payloads for day and night operation but is primarily a realtime UAV system for intelligence collection, surveillance, target acquisition/tracking and communications/data relay.

SPECIFICATION:

USED BY:
French Air Force, Israeli Air Force

MANUFACTURER/CONTRACTOR:
Israel Aircraft Industires, Malat UAV Division, Tel-Aviv, Israel

FEATURES:
WINGSPAN: 16.60 m (54 ft 5.5 in)
LENGTH OVERALL: 8.50 m (27 ft 10.6in)
FUSELAGE LENGTH: 5.20 m (17 ft 0.7 in)
HEIGHT OVERALL: 2.30 m (7 ft 6.6 in)
MAX FUEL WEIGHT: 430 kg (948 lb)
MAX PAYLOAD: 250 kg (551 lb)
LOITER SPEED: 70-80kt (130-148 km/h; 81-92 mph)
LOITER ALTITUDE: 6100 m (20,000 ft)
SERVICE CEILING: 8075 m (26,500 ft)
MAX OPERATING ALTITUDE: >540 n miles (1000 km; 621 miles)
MAX ENDURANCE: 50 hours

Meteor Mirach 100 Recce ITALY
Mirach 100 reconnaissance version on launch trailer

Reconnaissance UAV. Roles can include aerial reconnaissance, target acquisition and damage assessment. Reconnaissance payloads can include a low-light TV camera plus a photogrammetric zoom camera, or alternatively an infra-red imager. Electro-optical sensors are connected to an onboard wideband transmitter and/or a video recorder. TV or IR signals are transmitted in real or near-realtime to the GCS and recorded. Launch is by a pair of booster rockets from a zero-length ramp on land or the ship's deck or air launch, without boosters, from a helicopter (AgustaWestland A 109 or Eurocopter Dauphin/ Panther) or fixed-wing aircraft. For air launch, Mirach is connected to the airborne pylon by means of four supports directly connected to hardpoints in the central portion of the UAV's fuselage. Two air vehicles are carried by each helicopter. Mobile zero-length launchers are available for rapid deployment ground launch.

SPECIFICATION:

USED BY:
Italian army

CONTRACTOR:
Meteor Costruzioni Aeronautiche ed Elettroniche SpA, Ronchi dei Legionari, Italy

FEATURES:
WINGSPAN: 1.804 m (5 ft 11.0 in)
WING AREA: 0.82 m² (8.83 sq ft)
LENGTH OVERALL: 4.126 m (13 ft 6.4 in)
BODY DIAMETER (MAX): 0.383 m (1 ft 3.1 in)
HEIGHT OVERALL: 0.807 m (2 ft 7.8 in)
TAIL UNIT SPAN: 1.04 m (3 ft 4.9 in)
PAYLOAD VOLUME: 80.0 dm³ (2.82 cu ft)
MAX PAYLOAD: 40 kg (88.2 lb)
MAX LAUNCHING WEIGHT: from ramp: 280 kg (617 lb); from aircraft: 295 kg (650 lb)
MAX LEVEL SPEED: 459 kts (850 km/h; 528 mph)
OPERATING HEIGHT: min: 10 m (33 ft); max: 9000 m (29,525 ft)
RANGE: one-way: 270 n miles (500 km; 310 miles); two-way: 135 n miles (250 km; 155 miles) max
ENDURANCE: 1 hour
G LIMIT: +6

Meteor Mirach 150 ITALY

Mirach 150 on its truck-mounted launching ramp

Medium-range tactical UAV whose applications include aerial reconnaissance over land and sea areas with realtime or delayed near-realtime transmission of sensor imagery information; military support missions requiring deep radius of penetration, especially over well-protected enemy targets; damage assessment; enemy radar detection; and enemy radar and communications jamming. The Mirach 150 is a low-wing monoplane with a circular cross-section fuselage, v-tail, and short-span light alloy wings with glass fibre leading-edges. Payload sensors can include an IRLS, panoramic camera, high-altitude photographic camera, or a high-resolution TV camera and video recorder. The Mirach 150 can be launched from a mobile zero-length ramp on land or from the deck of a ship, using an automatic navigation launch system (ANLS). The UAV can land unattended at a pre-programmed recovery site. Descent is by parachute, and ground impact is absorbed by an automatically inflated airbag.

SPECIFICATION:

USED BY:
Italian army

CONTRACTOR:
Meteor Costruzioni Aeronautiche ed Elettroniche SpA, Ronchi dei Legionari, Italy

FEATURES:
One 1.47 kN (331 lb st) Microturbo TRS 18-1 turbojet
WINGSPAN: 2.60 m (8 ft 6.4 in)
WING AREA: 1.40 m² (15.07 sq ft)
LENGTH OVERALL: 4.70 m (15 ft 5.0 in)
HEIGHT OVERALL: 0.91 m (2 ft 11.8 in)
BODY DIAMETER (MAX): 0.383 m (1 ft 3.1 in)
PAYLOAD BAY VOLUME: 110.0 dm³ (3.88 cu ft)
WEIGHT EMPTY: 254 kg (560 lb)
MAX FUEL WEIGHT: 86 kg (190 lb)
MAX PAYLOAD: 50 kg (110 lb)
MAX LAUNCHING WEIGHT: incl. booster: 380 kg (838 lb); excl. booster: 340 kg (750 lb)
MAX LEVEL SPEED: 378 kts (700 km/h; 435 mph)
NORMAL CRUISING SPEED: 291 kts (540 km/h; 335 mph)
MAX RATE OF CLIMB AT S/L: 1500 m (4921 ft)/min
OPERATING HEIGHT RANGE: min: 200 m (660 ft); max: 9000 m (29,525 ft)
OPERATIONAL RADIUS: 135 n miles (250 km; 155 miles)
ENDURANCE: 1 hour

KAI **Night Intruder** KOREA, SOUTH

Night Intruder rail launch

The Night Intruder is a short-range tactical UAV with typical pod-and-twin boom configuration, high-mounted wings, pusher engine and mainly composites construction. It has a fixed tricycle landing gear, with self-sprung mainwheels and oleo nose leg. The wings, booms and tail surfaces are detachable for transport. It has a stabilised, gimbal-mounted, non-retractable dual-sensor ventral turret containing daylight TV and a FLIR, third-generation, 3 – 5 micron band thermal imager with 2° – 50° field of view with continuous zoom capability. The TV camera has a 2° – 28° field of view. It takes off conventionally but can also be launched from truck-mounted hydraulic or pneumatic catapult. Recovery is by wheeled landing although there is parafoil for emergency recovery.

SPECIFICATION:

USED BY:
Republic of Korea Army and Navy

CONTRACTOR:
Korea Aerospace Industries,
Changwon, South Korea

FEATURES:
One 38.8 kw (52 hp) AEL AR 801R
rotary engine, driving a four-
blade fixed-pitch wooden pusher
propeller
WINGSPAN: 6.40 m (21 ft 0.0 in)
LENGTH OVERALL: 4.80 m
(15 ft 9.0 in)
HEIGHT OVERALL: 1.47 m
(4 ft 9.9 in)
WEIGHT EMPTY: 215 kg (474 lb)
MAX PAYLOAD: 45 kg (99.2 lb)
MAX T/O WEIGHT: 300 kg (661 lb)
MAX LEVEL SPEED: 100 kts
(185 km/h; 115 mph)
CRUISING SPEED: 65-81 kts
(120-150 km/h; 75-93 mph)
CEILING: 4570 m (15,000 ft)
OPERATIONAL RADIUS: max
datalink range: >65 n miles
(120 km; 75 miles); with relay
system: >108 n miles (200 km;
124 miles)
ENDURANCE: 6 hours

This is a low-cost surveillance and target acquisition UAV with strut-braced high-wing monoplane of pod, twin tailboom configuration and twin engines. It is of composites construction with non-retractable tricycle landing gear. Standard payload is an 8 mm CCD colour TV camera with a 120 mm motorised zoom; optional alternative is a FLIR sensor. Take-off is conventional or with rocket booster assistance and recovery is either conventional or by parachute.

SPECIFICATION:

USED BY:
Pakistan army

CONTRACTOR:
Air Weapons Complex E-5, Wah Cantt, Pakistan

FEATURES:
Single 100 cc piston engine and a second 100 cc engine installed in rear of fuselage nacelle and driving a pusher propeller.
FUEL CAPACITY: 20 litres (5.3 US gallons; 4.4 Imp gallons)
WINGSPAN: 3.66 m (12 ft 0.0 in)
WING CHORD, CONSTANT: 0.61 m (2 ft 0.0 in)
LENGTH OVERALL: 2.74 m (9 ft)
WEIGHT EMPTY: 26 kg (57.3 lb)
MAX PAYLOAD: 34 kg (75.0 lb)
MAX T/O WEIGHT: 60 kg (132.3 lb)
MAX LEVEL SPEED: 94 kts (175 km/h; 109 mph)
CRUISING SPEED: 70 kts (130 km/h; 81 mph)
LOITER SPEED: 49 kts (90 km/h; 56 mph)
CEILING: 4000 m (13,120 ft)
RANGE: >27 n miles (50 km; 31 miles)
ENDURANCE: 3 hours

Yakovlev Pchela-т RUSSIA

Pchela-т tactical UAV

Short-range surveillance and tactical UAV. Features include: high-mounted wings with turned-down tips; cylindrical fuselage, with rear-mounted ducted propeller; and four non-retractable leaf spring landing legs. It is mainly composites construction. Onboard sensors are a TV camera with zoom lens (viewing angle 3° – 30°) on Pchela-1т or IRLS on Pchela-1IK. Data transmission in real time. The UAV is operated from a BTR-D tracked vehicle chassis, on top of which it is transported, with wings folded, in a drum-shaped container. Alongside this container is a launch rail, also folded during transportation. For deployment, the rail and UAV wings are unfolded, and the Pchela-1т is launched from the rail assisted by a pair of solid-propellant rocket boosters. Recovery is by parachute descent to a landing on the four spring-loaded landing legs.

SPECIFICATION:

USED BY:
Russian army, navy and naval infantry (used operationally against rebel forces in Chechnya in April 1995 and from October 1999) and North Korea

CONTRACTOR:
A S Yakovlev OKB, Moscow, Russia

FEATURES:
One 23.9 kw (32 hp) Samara P-032 two-cylinder two-stroke engine; three-blade ducted pusher propeller
WINGSPAN: 3.25 m (10 ft 7.9 in)
WING AREA: 1.83 m³ (19.7 sq ft)
LENGTH OVERALL: 2.78 m (9 ft 1.4 in)
HEIGHT OVERALL: 1.11 m (3 ft 7.7 in)
MAX LAUNCHING WEIGHT: 138 kg (304 lb)
MAX LEVEL SPEED: 97 kts (180 km/h; 112 mph)
CRUISING SPEED: 65 kts (120 km/h; 75 mph)
OPERATING HEIGHT RANGE: min: 100 m (330 ft); max: 2500 m (8200 ft)
OPERATIONAL RADIUS: 27 n miles (50 km; 31 miles)
ENDURANCE: 2 hours

INTA ALO SPAIN

Camouflaged ALO with tricycle landing gear

Surveillance UAV. High-wing monoplane with V-tail (included angle 110°); taper on wing and tail leading-edges. Optional fixed tricycle landing gear. Mission payloads include CCD colour TV camera or FLIR with real-time video imagery downlink. Launch by bungee catapult and recovery by parachute to belly landing.

SPECIFICATION:

USED BY:
Spanish army

CONTRACTOR:
Instituto Nacional de Tecnica
Aeroespacial, Madrid, Spain

FEATURES:
One 4.78 kw (6.4 hp) piston engine; two-blade propeller
WINGSPAN: 3.03 m (9 ft 11.3 in)
LENGTH OVERALL: 1.75 m (5 ft 8.9 in)
MAX PAYLOAD: 6 kg (13.2 lb)
MAX LAUNCHING WEIGHT: 20 kg (44.1 lb)
MAX LEVEL SPEED: 108 kts (200 km/h; 124 mph)
LOITER SPEED: 27 kts (50 km/h; 31 mph)
CEILING: 1000 – 1500 m (3280 – 4920 ft)
NORMAL RANGE: 27 n miles (50 km; 31 miles)
ENDURANCE: 2 hours

Watchkeeper UK

Close range, short-range intelligence, surveillance, target acquisition and reconnaissance (ISTAR) UAV.

SPECIFICATION:

USED BY:
Intended for the UK army

CONTRACTOR:
Defence Procurement Agency, UK

BAE Systems Phoenix UK

Phoenix UAV

Battlefield surveillance and target acquisition UAV system. The British Army's first all-weather, day/night unmanned aircraft for real-time surveillance and target acquisition. Among current UAV systems, Phoenix is unique in that the airborne component is totally sensor-orientated, to the extent that the air vehicle is an aerial 'taxi' for a detachable underfuselage pod containing the imaging sensor and the airborne portion of the datalink. The airframe, built almost entirely of composites (glass fibre, carbon fibre, Kevlar and Nomex honeycomb), is of modular construction for ease of maintenance, transportation on the battlefield and mounting of different payloads in the mission pod. Features include push-in wing and tailboom attachment, replaceable wing and fin tips and dorsal shock-absorber and single-pin attachment (with electrical umbilical) of the ventral mission pod. Thermal, visual, acoustic and radar signatures are low, to give the system a high

SPECIFICATION:

USED BY:
UK army

CONTRACTOR:
BAE Systems Avionics, Rochester, Kent, UK

FEATURES:
One 18.6 kw (25 hp) Meggitt MDS 342 two-cylinder two-stroke engine; two-blade fixed-pitch wooden propeller
WINGSPAN: 5.50 m (18 ft 0.5 in)
LENGTH OVERALL: 3.80 m (12 ft 5.6 in)
PROPELLER DIAMETER: 0.78 m (2 ft 6.7 in)
MAX PAYLOAD: 50 kg (110.2 lb)
MAX FUEL WEIGHT: 20 kg (44.1 lb)
MAX LAUNCHING WEIGHT: 180 kg (397 lb)
MAX LEVEL SPEED: 85 kts (157 km/h; 97 mph)
CRUISING SPEED: approx 70 kts (130 km/h; 81 mph)
CEILING: 2440 m (8000 ft)
OPERATIONAL RADIUS: 38 n miles (70 km; 43.5 miles)
ENDURANCE: 4 hours 30 minutes
RECOVERY ACCURACY: 100 m (330 ft) CEP

probability of survival. Subsystems onboard the 'taxi' include those for flight control, navigation, parachute/airbag recovery and pod stabilisation. An anti-icing system is under consideration. In the target acquisition and surveillance role, the payload comprises an infra-red sensor based on the UK Thermal Imaging Common Modules (TICM II), mounted in a two-axis stabilised turret. The third axis roll is steadied by stabilising the complete mission pod. This enables the imagery to be presented 'horizon up' for maximum ease of interpretation and correlation with the surrounding terrain. Also in the payload pod are the processing electronics and the airborne end of the datalink, which utilises two fully steerable antennas, one at each end of the pod to provide full directional coverage. The IR payload has a 360° scan in azimuth, a line of sight that can be steered through more than 70° in elevation and a zoom lens providing continuous magnifications from x2.5 – x10. It can be locked fore and aft, at a preset elevation, during the cruise phase of a mission. Sector scanning can be selected for area search, and the imager's sight-line can be steered automatically to remain aligned with a target being orbited by the UAV. A wider range of sensors such as SAR, a mine detection system or EW jammers is under consideration for possible future use. The air vehicle is launched from a hydraulic/pneumatic catapult, installed on a six-wheel, 14-tonne truck. At the end of a mission, the air vehicle descends inverted by parachute, to protect the mission pod, landing impact being absorbed by an inflatable airbag on top of the fuselage and by the frangible fin tips.

NRL Dragon Eye and Sea ALL USA

Dragon Eye concept demonstrator (1) and the essentially similar Sea ALL (2)

The Dragon Eye is a multirole, man-portable mini-UAV with a constant-chord, high-mounted wing; square-section fuselage; and a large triangular fin and rudder. There is no landing gear. The Dragon Eye dismantles into six components, storable in package 38 x 38 x18 cm (15 x 15 x 7 in).

Interchangeable noses contain two colour or monochrome daylight or LLTV cameras with options including IR imager and communications relay. It can be hand- or bungee-launched. Recovery is by autopilot-commanded, deep stall terminal descent to a belly landing, or automatic parachute recovery. The Sea ALL is steered into a net for shipboard recovery.

SPECIFICATION:

USED BY:
US Navy and Marine Corps

CONTRACTOR:
US Naval Research Laboratory, Washington DC, USA

FEATURES:
Twin 214 w electric motors (lithium disulphide batteries), each driving a two-blade tractor propeller with folding blades
WINGSPAN: 1.14 m (3 ft 9.0 in)
LENGTH OVERALL: 0.91 m (2 ft 11.75 in)
MAX PAYLOAD: 0.225 kg (0.5 lb)
MAX LAUNCHING WEIGHT: Dragon Eye: 2.49 kg (5.5 lb); Sea ALL: 2.04 kg (4.5 lb)
MAX LEVEL SPEED: 35 kts (65 km/h; 40 mph)
OPERATING HEIGHT RANGE: upper: 152 m (500 ft); lower: 92 m (300 ft)
MISSION RADIUS (DATALINK RANGE): 2.7 n miles (5 km; 3.1 miles)
ENDURANCE: approx 45 minutes

BAI BQM-147A Exdrone USA

Low-cost multirole mini-UAV. The Exdrone is a simple, symmetrical delta-winged mini-UAV (NACA 63A-012 aerofoil section) with single fin and rudder. The wings (including movable control surfaces) and vertical fin are of state-of-the-art monocoque composites construction with cured glass fibre/epoxy components. Features include: forward/downward-looking colour TV camera with pan/tilt/zoom capability; laser range-finder; IR camera; jammer; communications relay; or customer-specified equipment.

The standard launch method is by a compressed air rail system which consists of a 7.92 m (26 ft) rail to accelerate the UAV to a flying speed of 45 kts (84 km/h; 52 mph); near-vertical launches can be made using a zero-length launcher and UPC rocket-assisted take-off. Exdrone has also been deployed from naval ships using a pneumatic launcher and net recovery system. Landing is made on skids or by net recovery.

SPECIFICATION:

USED BY:
US navy, Marine Corps, army and Coast Guard. Deployed during the 1991 Gulf War, providing daytime surveillance of barriers and minefields in Kuwait prior to ground force advances

CONTRACTOR:
BAI Aerosystems Inc, Easton, Maryland, USA

FEATURES:
WINGSPAN: standard: 2.50 m (8 ft 2.4 in); wide-body: 2.71 m (8 ft 10.8 in)
WING AREA: standard: 1.86 m² (20.0 sq ft)
LENGTH OVERALL: 1.62 m (5 ft 3.6 in)
HEIGHT OVERALL: 0.49 m (1 ft 7.2 in)
PROPELLER DIAMETER: 0.51 m (1 ft 8.0 in)
WEIGHT EMPTY: standard: 32.2 kg (71 lb); Dragon Drone: 24.9 kg (55 lb)
MAX PAYLOAD (INCL. FUEL): standard: 9.1 kg (20 lb); wide-body: 17.2 kg (38 lb)
MAX LAUNCHING WEIGHT: standard: 41.3 kg (91 lb); Dragon Drone: 43.1 kg (95.1 lb)
NEVER-EXCEED SPEED: A: 165 kts (305 km/h; 190 mph); B: 195 kts (362 km/h; 225 mph)
MAX LEVEL SPEED: A: 100 kts (185 km/h; 115 mph); B: 152 kts (281 km/h; 175 mph)
LOITER SPEED: A: 39-65 kts (72-121 km/h; 45-75 mph)
STALLING SPEED: A: 26-35 kts (49-65 km/h; 30-40 mph); B: 31-40 kts (57-73 km/h; 35-45 mph)
OPERATING HEIGHT RANGE: 915-1,525 m (3000-5000 ft)
SERVICE CEILING: 3050 m (10,000 ft)
RANGE: A: standard fuel: 65 n miles (120 km; 75 miles); A: auxiliary fuel: 195 n miles (362 km; 225 miles); A: max demonstrated: 486 n miles (901 km; 560 miles); B: auxiliary fuel: 130 n miles (241 km; 150 miles)
DATALINK RANGE: approx 48 n miles (90 km; 56 miles)
ENDURANCE: 2 hours 30 minutes

General Atomics Gnat USA

All-altitude multimission long-endurance UAV. Low-wing monoplane with a slender fuselage, inverted v-tail, rear-mounted engine, and retractable tricycle undercarriage with steerable nosewheel, differential mainwheel braking and anti-skid capability. The airframe is made of carbon/epoxy composites, and is stressed for 6 G manoeuvres. Payloads are accommodated in the nose, the contours of which vary according to the particular sensor carried. Mission payloads can be carried for surveillance (radar, stabilised FLIR, TV and LLTV), reconnaissance (IR linescanner), ESM, direction-finding, radio and datalink relay, NBC detection, air-delivered payloads or custom designs. It features wheeled take-off from suitable terrain with canister launch optional or wheeled landing where terrain is suitable with parachute recovery optional. There is an automatic landing system.

SPECIFICATION:

USED BY:
Turkish and US armies

CONTRACTOR:
General Atomics Aeronautical Systems Inc, San Diego, California, USA

FEATURES:
A: Gnat 750, B: I-Gnat/Rotax 912, C: I-Gnat/Rotax 914
One 48.5 kw (65 hp) Rotax 582 two-cylinder two-stroke engine in Gnat 750; I-Gnat has a 59.7 kw (80 hp) Rotax 912 or 78.3 kw (105 hp) Rotax 914 turbocharged flat-four; two-blade fixed-pitch (optionally variable-pitch) pusher propeller in both cases
WINGSPAN: A: 10.76 m (35 ft 3.6 in); B, C: 12.80 m (42 ft 0.0 in)
WING AREA: A: 6.10 m² (65.66 sq ft)
LENGTH OVERALL: A: 5.33 m (17 ft 6.0 in); B, C: 5.76 m (18 ft 10.8 in)
PROPELLER DIAMETER: A: 1.52 m (5 ft)
WEIGHT EMPTY: A: 254 kg (560 lb); B, C: 385 kg (850 lb)
FUEL WEIGHT: A: 193 kg (426 lb); B, C: 227 kg (500 lb)
PAYLOAD (IN NOSE): A: 63.5 kg (140 lb); B, C: 91 kg (200 lb)
MAX T/O WEIGHT: A: 511 kg (1126 lb); B, C: 703 kg (1550 lb)
MAX LEVEL SPEED: A: 140 kts (259 km/h; 161 mph) IAS; B: 125 kts (231 km/h; 143 mph) IAS; C: 160 kts (296 km/h; 184 mph) IAS
LONG-RANGE CRUISING SPEED: A: 46 kts (85 km/h; 53 mph)
STALLING SPEED: A: 36 kts (67 km/h; 42 mph) IAS
MAX RATE OF CLIMB AT S/L: A: 335 m (1100 ft)/min; B: 244 m (800 ft)/min; C: 396 m (1300 ft)/min
CEILING: A: 7620 m (25,000 ft); B: >7620 m (25,000 ft); C: 9140 m (30,000 ft)
T/O DISTANCE: B: 366 m (1200 ft); C: 320 m (1,050 ft)
LANDING DISTANCE: B: 305 m (1000 ft); C: 320 m (1050 ft)
REAL-TIME LOS RANGE: 97 n miles (180 km; 112 miles)
MAX OPERATIONAL RADIUS: A, B, C: 1500 n miles (2778 km; 1726 miles)
LOITER: 1080 n miles (2000 km; 1243 miles)
RADIUS: A, B, C: 12 hours
ENDURANCE: 1525 m (5,000 ft): A, B, C: >40 hours

Hawkeye Aerial Surveillance System USA

The Hawkeye surveillance system is a totally self-contained unit and all of the equipment needed to operate the system comes in a single box. Hawkeye is portable in that, right out of the box, it fits in the trunk of a medium-sized car and can be set up to fly in ten minutes. There is a stealth operation and an electric motor is employed for quietness and low profile. Constructed from advanced composite materials, the airframe is as rugged as it needs to be for law enforcement operations. Night-vision cameras are available and the cost of Hawkeye is probably about 30 per cent of similar military systems.

SPECIFICATION:

USED BY:
In service

CONTRACTOR:
Autauga Arms Ltd, USA

FEATURES:
WEIGHT: 2.71 kg (6 lb)
PAYLOAD CAPACITY: 905 g (2 lb)
AIR SPEED: 30 kts
STALL SPEED: 5 kts
WINGSPAN: 2.43 m (8 ft)
LENGTH: 1.21 m (4 ft)
HEIGHT: 30.4 cm (1 ft)
FLIGHT DURATION: 30 minutes (expandable)
FLIGHT RANGE: 800 m (1/2 mile expandable)

Northrop Grumman/IAI RQ-5A Hunter USA

RQ-5A Hunter with underwing BUETSS (Bat UAV ejection tubes)

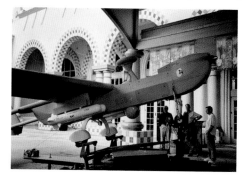

This is a short-range reconnaissance, surveillance and target acquisition UAV with a robust pod-and-twin tailboom high-wing monoplane, built of low-observable composites. The single pusher engine improves single-engine survivability as does the fixed tricycle landing gear. Basic payloads are the IAI Tamam MOSP combined TV/FLIR sensor and an IAI Elta G/H-band airborne data relay system. Take-off is conventional and it can operate from unprepared strips with rocket-assisted take-off an option. Landing is conventional using a retractable hook-and-arrester cable. Emergency recovery is by parachute.

SPECIFICATION:

USED BY:
Armies of Belgium, France, Israel and the US (deployed to Macedonia in late 1999 to monitor the Serbia/Kosovo conflict; one was shot down on 7 April 1999; a further five had been lost by the end of the NATO air campaign two months later)

CONTRACTOR:
Northrop Grumman Integrated Systems, Ryan Aeronautical Centre, San Diego, California, USA

FEATURES:
Two 50.7 kw (68 hp) Moto Guzzi two-cylinder four-stroke engines, one at front and one at rear of fuselage nacelle; two-blade wooden propellers (one tractor, one pusher). Fuel capacity 189 litres (50 US gallons; 41.6 Imp gallons)
WINGSPAN: 8.84 m (29 ft 0.0 in)
LENGTH OVERALL: 7.01 m (23 ft 0.0 in)
HEIGHT OVERALL: 1.65 m (5 ft 5.0 in)
PAYLOAD BAY VOLUME: 282.5 dm³ (8.0 cu ft)
WEIGHT EMPTY: 540 kg (1190 lb)
FUEL WEIGHT (MAX): 136 kg (300 lb)
PAYLOAD (MAX): 113 kg (250 lb)
MAX FUEL PLUS PAYLOAD WEIGHT: 178 kg (393 lb)
MAX T/O WEIGHT: 726 kg (1600 lb)
MAX LEVEL SPEED: 110 kts (204 km/h; 126 mph)
MAX CRUISING SPEED: 80 kts (148 km/h; 92 mph)
LOITER SPEED: 60 kts (111 km/h; 69 mph)
MAX RATE OF CLIMB AT S/L: 232 m (761 ft)/min
CEILING: 4575 m (15,000 ft)
T/O RUN AT S/L: 200 m (656 ft)
MISSION RADIUS: standard (LOS): up to 108 n miles (200 km; 124 miles) with airborne relay; (OLOS): 162 n miles (300 km; 186 miles)
ENDURANCE: 4575 m (15,000 ft) at 100 n miles (185 km; 115 miles) from base: 8 hours
ENDURANCE: 12 hours

AAI/IAI RQ-2 Pioneer USA

Rocket-boosted shipboard launch of a Pioneer UAV

A short/medium-range surveillance and intelligence-gathering UAV with houlder-wing, pod-and-twin-tailboom monoplane, pusher engine and a fixed tricycle landing gear plus arrester hook. The radar cross-section is approximately 0.5 m² (5.38 sq ft). The Pioneer can be assembled in the field, allowing the prompt despatch of several vehicles at one time. Payloads include IAI Tamam gyrostabilised high-resolution TV (Moked 200) or FLIR (Moked 400) and (from May 1997) dual-sensor (E-O/IR) Wescam 12DS200 for day and night or reduced visibility operations; ECM, decoy, communications (VHF and UHF) relay, and laser designator/range-finder packages. The aircraft is also equipped with a transponder and Mode III IFF. It can be launched from a wheeled take-off, be catapulted from a pneumatically operated twin-rail launcher, or be rocket-assisted. At sea, it is launched by rocket. Recovery is by wheeled landing using a tail hook to catch one of two arresting cables, or by flying into a net attached to an energy absorbing system.

SPECIFICATION:

USED BY:
US navy, US Marine Corps

CONTRACTOR:
Pioneer UAV Inc, California, Maryland, USA

FEATURES:
Originally one 19.4 kw (26 hp) Sachs SF 350 two-cylinder two-stroke engine; two-blade pusher propeller. Replaced by 28.3 kw (38 hp) UEL AR 741 rotary (first flight with this engine March 1997). Fuel capacity 41.6 litres (11.0 US gallons; 9.2 Imp gallons) in Option 2, 45.4 litres (12.0 US gallons; 10.0 Imp gallons) in Option2+
WINGSPAN: 5.11 m (16 ft 9.2 in)
LENGTH OVERALL: 4.26 m (13 ft 11.7 in)
FUSELAGE (POD) LENGTH: 2.90 m (9 ft 6.2 in)
PAYLOAD BAY VOLUME: 100.0 dm³ (3.53 cu ft)
WEIGHT EMPTY: A:125 kg (276 lb); B:138 kg (304 lb)
FUEL WEIGHT: A:29.9 kg (66 lb); B:32.7 kg (72 lb)
MAX PAYLOAD: A, B:45.4 kg (100 lb)
MAX T/O/LAUNCHING WEIGHT: A:190 kg (419 lb); B:205 kg (452 lb)
MAX LEVEL SPEED (BOTH): 100 kts (185 km/h; 115 mph)
CRUISING/LOITER SPEED: (both) 80 kts (148 km/h; 92 mph)
MAX RATE OF CLIMB AT S/L: A: 246 m (807 ft)/min
OPERATING HEIGHT RANGE: lower (both): 305 m (1000 ft); upper: A: 3660 m (12,000 ft); B: 4575 m (15,000 ft)
DATALINK RANGE: (both) 100 n miles (185 km; 115 miles)
ENDURANCE: (both) 5 – 6 hours 30 minutes

AeroVironment FQM-151A Pointer USA

Hand-launching a Pointer

SPECIFICATION:

USED BY:
French army and the US Marine
Corps, army, air force and
National Guard plus US civilian
law enforcement and other
agencies

CONTRACTOR:
AeroVironment Inc, Simi Valley,
California, USA

FEATURES:
One 300 W electric (samarium
cobalt) motor, powered by two
Li/SO₂ primary or Ni/cd
rechargeable batteries; pusher
propeller with two folding blades
WINGSPAN: 2.74 m (9 ft 0.0 in)
LENGTH: 1.83 m (6 ft 0.0 in)
WEIGHT EMPTY: 2.27 kg (5.0 lb)
MAX PAYLOAD: 0.91 kg (2.0 lb)
MAX LAUNCHING WEIGHT: colour
camera: 4.17 kg (9.2 lb); night
vision camera: 4.35 kg (9.6 lb)
MAX LEVEL SPEED: 43 kts (80 km/h;
50 mph)
CRUISING SPEED: 16 kts (30 km/h;
19 mph)
MAX RATE OF CLIMB AT S/L: 91 m
(300 ft)/min
OPERATING HEIGHT RANGE: lower:
30 m (100 ft); upper: 300 m
(985 ft)
OPERATIONAL RADIUS: 4.3 n miles
(8 km; 5 miles)
ENDURANCE: primary batteries:
1 hour 30 minutes; rechargeable
batteries: 20 minutes

Hand-launched UAV. The Pointer air vehicle is a
small and very lightweight hand-launched,
powered sailplane, intended initially as a semi-
expendable vehicle for aerial surveillance of a
battlefield. However, the majority of air vehicles
delivered to date remain in operational condition,
many having logged more than 200 – 300 flights. It
is a parasol monoplane with pylon-mounted wing,
pod-and-boom fuselage and T-tail. The aircraft,
which has a Kevlar and composites primary
structure, consists of six components; these push-
fit together and can be assembled on site in less
than five minutes. A wide variety of possible
sensors includes: a colour CCD video camera with
in-flight switchable pointing; an IR micro-
bolometer thermal imager; a Surface Acoustic
Wave Chemical Agent Detector; particulate filters
and volumetric air samplers; pressure, temperature
and humidity sensors; and monochrome, colour or
IR film 35 mm cameras. It is hand-launched with
autoland on the belly after being placed in a deep
stall following engine shutdown.

DRS Sentry USA

The redesigned Sentry HP

The Sentry is a short-range relay UAV with high-mounted, broad-delta wing and deep centre-section fuselage. Construction is mainly of carbon fibre, Kevlar and glass fibre and it has wheeled or skid landing gear. A realtime video camera is fitted as standard while E-O/IR sensors and other payloads are optional. It also has a E-band or G-band uplink and downlink. The Sentry is launched by pneumatic launcher with a wheeled take-off or wheeled dolly option and a wheeled or skid landing. A parafoil precision approach and landing system is optional, enabling recovery in small or unimproved landing areas.

SPECIFICATION:

USED BY:
US army; others – not identified – may include US intelligence agencies

CONTRACTOR:
DRS Unmanned Technologies, Mineral Wells, Texas, USA

FEATURES:
A: One 19.0 kw (25.5 hp) Herbrandson Dyad 290 cc (17.7 cu in) two-cylinder two-stroke engine; two-blade propeller
FUEL CAPACITY: 37.9 litres (10 US gallons; 8.3 Imp gallons) in A; 45.4 litres (12 US gallons; 10.0 Imp gallons) in B
WINGSPAN: A: 3.35 m (11 ft 0.0 in); B: 3.90 m (12 ft 9.5 in)
WING AREA: A: 2.84 m² (30.62 sq ft); B: 2.91 m² (31.37 sq ft)
LENGTH OVERALL: A: 2.43 m (7 ft 11.5 in); B: 2.68 m (8 ft 9.6 in)
FUSELAGE: Length: A: 1.65 m (5 ft 5.0 in); Max width: A: 0.76 m (2 ft 5.9 in)
PROPELLER DIAMETER: A: 0.74 m (2 ft 5.0 in)
PAYLOAD VOLUME (A): Internal: 48.5 dm³ (1.71 cu ft); external pods: 37.1 or 53.3 dm³ (1.31 or 1.88 cu ft)
WEIGHT EMPTY: A: 59.0 kg (130 lb); B: 81.6 kg (180 lb)
FUEL WEIGHT: A: 27.2 kg (60 lb); B: 32.7 kg (72 lb)
MAX PAYLOAD WITH FULL FUEL: A: 27.2 kg (60 lb); B: 34.0 kg (75 lb)
MAX LAUNCHING WEIGHT: A: 113.4 kg (250 lb); B: 147.4 kg (325 lb)
MAX LEVEL SPEED: A: 95 ks (176 km/h; 109 mph); B: 110 kts (203 km/h; 126 mph)
CRUISING SPEED: A: 70 kts (130 km/h; 81 mph); B: 75 kts (139 km/h; 86 mph)
LOITER SPEED: A, B: 65 kts (120 km/h; 75 mph)
STALLING SPEED: power on: A: 28 kts (52 km/h; 33 mph) IAS; power off: A: 32 kts (60 km/h; 37 mph) IAS
CEILING: A, B: 3050 m (10,000 ft)
MISSION RADIUS: A: 200 n miles (370 km; 230 miles)
ENDURANCE: standard fuel, with reserves, A and B 6 hours

AAI RQ-7A Shadow 200 USA

Surveillance and target acquisition UAV. Small, stealthy shoulder-wing monoplane, with pusher engine, twin tailbooms and inverted v-tail unit. Construction is mainly (90 per cent) of composites (graphite and Kevlar epoxy).

There is an optionally detachable tricycle landing and automatic ground launch by hydraulic catapult or by conventional wheeled take-off. Recovery is by automatic wheeled landing.

SPECIFICATION:

USED BY:
US army

CONTRACTOR:
AAI Corporation, Hunt Valley, Maryland, USA

FEATURES:
One 28.3 kw (38 hp) UEL AR 741 rotary engine; two-blade fixed-pitch wooden pusher propeller. Fuel (39.7 litres; 10.5 US gallons; 8.7 Imp gallons) in fire-retardant, explosion-proof wing cells. Growth option for eventual heavy fuel power plant
WINGSPAN: 3.89 m (12 ft 9.0 in)
WING AREA: 2.14 m² (23.0 ft²)
LENGTH OVERALL: 3.40 m (11 ft 2.0 in)
HEIGHT OVERALL: 0.91 m (3 ft 0.0 in)
PROPELLER DIAMETER: 0.66 m (2 ft 2.0 in)
WEIGHT EMPTY: 91.0 kg (200.6 lb)
MAX FUEL WEIGHT: 28.6 kg (63 lb)
MAX PAYLOAD: 25.3 kg (55.7 lb)
MAX LAUNCHING WEIGHT: 149 kg (328 lb)
MAX LEVEL SPEED AT S/L: 123 kts (228 km/h; 141 mph)

MAX CRUISING SPEED: 84 kts (156 km/h; 97 mph)
LOITER SPEED: at S/L: 53 kts (99 km/h; 61 mph) at 4,575 m (15,000 ft); 57 kts (106 km/h; 66 mph)
OPTIMUM CLIMBING SPEED: 80-85 kts (148-157 km/h; 92-98 mph)
STALLING SPEED AT S/L: 55 kts (102 km/h; 64 mph)
MAX RATE OF CLIMB AT S/L: 457 m (1,500 ft)/min
OPERATIONAL RADIUS: 43 n miles (80 km; 69 miles)
MAX DATALINK RANGE: 67.5 n miles (125 km; 78 miles)
ENDURANCE: 5-6 hours
G LIMIT: +3.6

AAI Shadow 400 and 600 USA

Straight-winged Shadow 400 (1) and angle-winged Shadow 600 (2)

Surveillance and target acquisition UAV. Small, stealthy shoulder-wing monoplane, with pusher engine, twin tailbooms and inverted v-tail unit. Construction is mainly (90 per cent) of composites (graphite and Kevlar epoxy). There is an optionally detachable tricycle landing gear and automatic ground launch by hydraulic catapult or by conventional wheeled take-off. Recovery is by automatic wheeled landing.

SPECIFICATION:

USED BY:
US army

CONTRACTOR:
AAI Corporation, Hunt Valley, Maryland, USA

FEATURES:
One 28.3 kw (38 hp) UEL AR 741 rotary engine; two-blade fixed-pitch wooden pusher propeller. Fuel (39.7 litres; 10.5 US gallons; 8.7 Imp gallons) in fire-retardant, explosion-proof wing cells. Growth option for eventual heavy fuel power plant
WINGSPAN: 3.89 m (12 ft 9.0 in)
WING AREA: 2.14 m² (23.0 ft²)
LENGTH OVERALL: 3.40 m (11 ft 2.0 in)
HEIGHT OVERALL: 0.91 m (3 ft)
PROPELLER DIAMETER: 0.66 m (2 ft 2.0 in)
WEIGHT EMPTY: 91.0 kg (200.6 lb)
MAX FUEL WEIGHT: 28.6 kg (63 lb)
MAX PAYLOAD: 25.3 kg (55.7 lb)
MAX LAUNCHING WEIGHT: 149 kg (328 lb)
MAX LEVEL SPEED AT S/L: 123 kts (228 km/h; 141 mph)
MAX CRUISING SPEED: 84 kts (156 km/h; 97 mph)
LOITER SPEED: at S/L: 53 kts (99 km/h; 61 mph) at 4575 m (15,000 ft); 57 kts (106 km/h; 66 mph)
OPTIMUM CLIMBING SPEED: 80-85 kts (148-157 km/h; 92-98 mph)
STALLING SPEED AT S/L: 55 kts (102 km/h; 64 mph)
MAX RATE OF CLIMB AT S/L: 457 m (1500 ft)/min
CEILING: 4575 m (15,000 ft)
T/O RUN: 250 m (820 ft)
OPERATIONAL RADIUS: 43 n miles (80 km; 69 miles)
MAX DATALINK RANGE: 67.5 n miles (125 km; 78 miles)
ENDURANCE: 5-6 hours
G LIMIT: +3.6

Sikorsky Dragon Warrior USA

Simulated photograph of Sikorsky's Dragon Warrior in flight

Close-range VTOL tactical UAV. Circular, composites (graphite/epoxy) ring, within which rotates a pair of four-blade, co-axial, bearingless shrouded rotors with composites blades. The shroud contributes a proportion of overall lift. The engine, fuel tank, sensor payload and recovery parachute are also contained within the shroud 'fuselage'. It has detachable wings and shrouded pusher propeller and can fly with or without wings attached. It also features a daylight TV camera, FLIR and laser designator and is transportable in a single HMMWV. It has vertical take-off and landing and a parachute emergency recovery system.

SPECIFICATION:

USED BY:
Evaluated by USMC

CONTRACTOR:
Sikorsky Aircraft, Stratford, Connecticut, USA

FEATURES:
Two 18.6 kw (25 hp) Herbrandson Dyad 290 two-cylinder two-stroke engines, converted to utilise heavy fuel
WINGSPAN: 3.05 m (10 ft)
ROTOR DIAMETER (EACH): 0.99 m (3 ft 3.0 in)
SENSOR PAYLOAD: 11.3-15.9 kg (25-35 lb)
MAX T/O WEIGHT: 113 kg (250 lb)
MAX LEVEL SPEED: 117 kts (217 km/h; 135 mph)
MISSION RADIUS: 100 n miles (185 km; 115 miles)
TIME ON STATION: (at 1830 m (6000 ft) altitude, 50 n miles (93 km; 58 miles) from base) 2 hours

BAE Systems R4E SkyEye USA

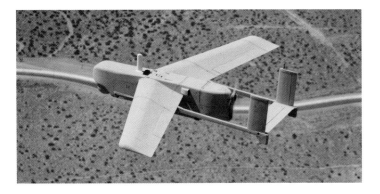

Multimission UAV. The SkyEye's pod-and-twin-tailboom airframe is built primarily of carbon fibre and Kevlar-reinforced epoxy, fully sealed for long life in hot and humid climates. It can be equipped with two underwing rails or pods for the carriage of external stores and multiple sensor packages such as a comint or elint sensor, combined with a FLIR, IRLS or daylight video imager for target identification. A stabilised gimbal provides 360° field of regard in azimuth and +20/-110° in elevation. Egyptian R4E-50s can carry a daylight TV, 127 mm (5 in) and 70 mm (2.75 in) panoramic cameras, a 35.4 kg (78 lb) Honeywell Mk III mini-FLIR, an IRLS (Honeywell D-500 derivative) and an onboard recorder for OLOS missions. The type of datalink used depends upon customer specification, and both analogue and digital links can be utilised. It is catapult-launched from a self-contained and optionally truck-mounted ESCO hydraulic/pneumatic launcher. Recovery is on a retractable ventral skid in suitable terrain, or by an onboard parafoil or parachute system. An autoland capability is optional.

SPECIFICATION:

USED BY:
Egyptian army, Moroccan army, Thai air force and the US army plus other unidentified customers

CONTRACTOR:
BAE Systems Aircraft Controls, (formerly Marconi Astronics), Santa Monica, California, USA

FEATURES:
One 73.1 kw (98 hp) twin-rotor rotary engine; four-blade pusher propeller
WINGSPAN: 7.315 m (24 ft)
LENGTH OVERALL: 4.12 m (13 ft 6.2 in)
WEIGHT EMPTY: 334 kg (737 lb)
MAX FUEL WEIGHT: 109 kg (240 lb)
PAYLOAD WITH MAX FUEL: 125 kg (275 lb)
MAX LAUNCHING WEIGHT: 567 kg (1250 lb)
MAX LEVEL SPEED: 110 kts (204 km/h; 127 mph)
ECON CRUISING SPEED: 70 kts (130 km/h; 80 mph)
MAX RATE OF CLIMB AT S/L: 229 m (750 ft)/min
CEILING: 4880 m (16,000 ft)
TYPICAL COMMAND AND CONTROL RANGE: (extendable by airborne or ground-based data relays) 100 n miles (185 km; 115 miles)
ENDURANCE: >12 hours

NRL **Dragon Warrior** USA

Mid-2002 display model of the NRL Dragon Warrior

The Warrior is a close-range VTOL tactical UAV with a three-blade main rotor, streamlined fuselage with T-tailplane and shrouded tail rotor. It has twin, non-retractable main landing legs and an undertail bumper. It can be transported by a HMMWV. Take-off and landing is conventional for a helicopter.

SPECIFICATION:

USED BY:
US Marine Corps

CONTRACTOR:
US Naval Research Laboratory, Washington DC, USA

FEATURES:
MAIN ROTOR DIAMETER: 2.44 m (8 ft 0 in)
FUSELAGE LENGTH: 2.13 m (7 ft 0 in)
PAYLOAD CAPACITY: 11.3-15.9 kg (25-35 lb)
MAX T/O WEIGHT: 113 kg (250 lb)
MAX LEVEL SPEED: 100 kts (185 km/h; 115 mph)
ENDURANCE: 3-5 hours

Surveillance:
Land

oip Holographic Night-Vision Goggles BELGIUM

oip holographic night-vision dual-view goggles

The use of Holographic Optical Elements (HOES) provides these lightweight HNV-1 holographic night-vision goggles (NVGs) with the ability to allow the wearer to see through the night-vision image and view the real-life surroundings. The user will always maintain an image of the world, irrespective of possible flares or flashes, while still accessing a large area of peripheral vision during the night. The use of holographic technology permits the operator to perform night tasks under better conditions than could ever be achieved with classic goggles. HNV-1 goggles are suitable for Special Task Force missions.

SPECIFICATION:

USED BY:
Issued to Belgian Army and to Special Task Forces in other NATO armies

CONTRACTOR:
OIP Sensor Systems, Oudenaarde, Belgium

FEATURES:
MAGNIFICATION: X1
DISTORTION: <7%
FIELD OF VIEW: night-vision image: vertical 30°, horizontal 40°, overlapping L + R 20°; see-through image: unobstructed peripheral vision
FOCUSING: Continuously adjustable from <25 cm to infinity
INTERPUPILLARY DISTANCE: >57-69 mm without adjustment
RESOLUTION (TYPICAL): 2 lp/mrad
BATTERY: Standard AA size, two x 1.5 V
WEIGHT: Approx 1 kg
CENTRE OF GRAVITY: <50 mm from forehead

oip Head-Mounted Optical Projection System (HOPROS) BELGIUM

HOPROS projects visual information before the user's eye

This Head-mounted Optical Projection System (HOPROS) projects visual information before the observer's eye while at the same time ensuring an undisturbed image of the environment, thereby keeping the hands free. Specialists such as technicians, engineers and doctors often need, for example, to refer to step-by-step instructions while working, and HOPROS projects these instructions in front of their eyes without obstructing their view of their surroundings. The applications for HOPROS include c4I integration of individual soldiers at war, real-time transfer of operations information in the field (GPS location, reports, instructions and so on), online updates of enemy movements, assignments of trajectories, maintenance and logistics and even telesurgery.

SPECIFICATION:

USED BY:
Armed forces worldwide

CONTRACTOR:
oip Sensor Systems, Oudenaarde, Belgium

FEATURES:
• Hands-free operation
• Free movement for user
• Data or image projection
• Unique see-through capability
• Lightweight and comfortable

OIP Infra-Red Laser Target Pointer BELGIUM

OIP's infra-red (IR) laser target pointers are for close-range combat with small arms at night. They are designed to enable the user to aim at an enemy with great accuracy under low light conditions as well as in complete darkness and without visual recognition by the enemy. The laser pointers are used primarily on basic infantry weapons such as rifles, sub-machine guns and other single-person portable weapons. They are aligned to the axis of these weapons. When the user activates the pointer for some seconds by means of a remote switch on the weapon, the emitted laser beam projects a bright IR spot exactly where the weapon is aimed and where the bullet will hit the target. This enables a precise shot without aiming through scopes or customary mechanical sights. Eye strain during long shooting sessions is thus said to be reduced. Shooting can be done from the hip, and the laser circular spot is visible only by means of night-vision goggles.

SPECIFICATION:

USED BY:
Armed forces worldwide

CONTRACTOR:
OIP Sensor Systems, Oudenaarde, Belgium

FEATURES:
• Small and lightweight
• Designed for close combat
• Enables shooting from the hip
• MIL-STD 1913 interface

OIP Lightweight Universal Night-Observation System

BELGIUM

OIP's Lightweight Universal Night-Observation System (LUNOS) is a passive night-vision family consisting of a binocular body, several objective lenses with different magnification factors (x1, x4 and x6) and a number of options, such as face mask, grip, monopod carry bag and transport case, plus reticle for the x6 version. The LUNOS system allows exchange of objectives on the spot in the field. Switching from one objective lens to another is comparable with changing the lens of a photo camera. The system allows the user to change in the field within one minute from lightweight, mask-mounted, hands-free, night-driving goggles to medium-range or long-range tripod-mounted observation binoculars. The modular nature of the system allows for a wide variety of applications, and later extensions to the family of equipment can be easily integrated.

SPECIFICATION:

USED BY:
Armed forces worldwide

CONTRACTOR:
OIP Sensor Systems, Oudenaarde, Belgium

FEATURES:
- Lightweight
- Modular design (interchangeable objectives)
- In-field exchange of accessories
- No image blooming
- Little or no image smear
- Fast-speed lens for x1 system
- Fast-speed mirror objective for x4 and x6 systems
- Built-in IR illuminator
- Operational under severe conditions

OIP MLR30 and MLR40 Handheld Laser Range-finders

BELGIUM

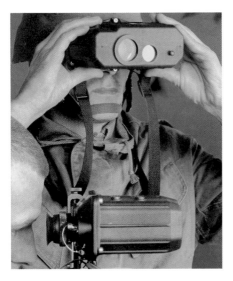

OIP's MLR30 and MLR40 minilasers are suited for hand-held or tripod-mounted applications. The MLR30 is of the neodymium-doped yttrium aluminium garnet (Nd YAG) type, and the MLR40 is the eye-safe version. With ranging performance of 20 km for both, they are extremely small and lightweight. The MLR40 is also available in a 7 km range version. Target ranging is performed within seconds, and the ranges are displayed in the eyepiece. In combination with the goniometer, complete triangulation of the target is possible, and the data can be externally processed if required. The applications of the range-finders include orientation of forward observers, range information for direct-fire weapons, target information for artillery and mortar positions, and target ranging for armoured vehicles and helicopters. The ranging data can be fed to a computer.

SPECIFICATION:

USED BY:
Armed forces worldwide

CONTRACTOR:
OIP Sensor Systems, Oudenaarde, Belgium

FEATURES:
• Eye-safe option
• Standard AA batteries
• Lightweight
• Digital readout

ANGENIEUX Lucie Night-vision Goggles FRANCE

Lucie multipurpose night-vision goggles have been developed by Angenieux, a subsidiary of Thales, for the French Army and security forces. It is designed for night-time patrolling, driving or observation tasks. Lucie takes advantage of the latest improvements of technology regarding night vision. A new patented optical design gives a very compact head-mounted goggle. Lucie can be fitted with a second-, super- or third-generation image intensifier with automatic brightness control and has a 50° field of view. The system also has x4 or x6 magnification quick-mounting magnifier lenses which are fully compliant with military specifications. There is a built-in infra-red illuminator with IR-on indicator in the left eyepiece. Lucie can be helmet mounted with flip-up face mask or hand-held.

SPECIFICATION:

USED BY:
French Special Forces

CONTRACTOR:
Thales Angenieux SA, France

FEATURES:
MAGNIFICATION: x1, x4, x6
FIELD OF VIEW: x1: 50° x4: 10°
IMAGE INTENSIFIER: GEN II
SuperGEN or GEN III
RESOLUTION: (x1)
DIOPTRE ADJUSTMENT: -5 to +3
dioptres
INTERPUPILLARY DISTANCE:
56 – 74 mm
EYE RELIEF: >20 mm
FOCUS RANGE: 20 cm to infinity
WEIGHT (WITH BATTERY): <0.45 kg
POWER SUPPLY: 1.5 V or 3.6 V
(lithium) AA battery

SAGEM MATIS MP Hand-held Third-generation Thermal Imager FRANCE

MATIS MP is a member of the SAGEM MATIS family of third-generation thermal imagers, based on the latest generation of cooled equipment operating in the 3-5 µm waveband. Lightweight and compact, the MATIS MP is intended for day and night short- and long-range observation. It is particularly well adapted to highly mobile operators like police and customs officers, in operations such as urban safety, border surveillance and search and rescue. Based on a dual field-of-view telescope, it also includes an ergonomic binocular display with integrated controls, which as a whole can be easily separated from the thermal imager. It is powered directly from its own battery or from an external source.

SPECIFICATION:

USED BY:
In service worldwide

CONTRACTOR:
SAGEM SA, France

FEATURES:
SPECTRAL BAND: 3-5 µm
DETECTOR: focal plane array
FIELD OF VIEW: (wide) 12 x 8°;
(narrow) 2.5 x 1.7°
ELECTRONIC ZOOM: 1.5 x 1°
EEIGHT: <6.5 kg
POWER CONSUMPTION: 8 w
OPERATING TIME: >7 hours in
ambient temperature
RETICLE: aiming mark
VIDEO OUTPUT: CCIR

UGO Day and Night Goggles FRANCE

This device is designed for day/night observation and can be used for vehicle driving and performing different tasks by night. The day/night binoculars (UGO) provide three functions integrated into a single unit.

Day observation with magnification x8 is ensured through a conventional binocular lens assembly. The field of view is >6°, the input lens diameter is 24 mm and the reticle graduated in millimetres.

The night-vision capability with magnification x1 is designed to enable driving a vehicle and performing tasks under very low-light conditions. The binoculars are secured to the driver's head by a facial mask. The mask is quickly fitted and removed. The field of view is 40°, the definition is <1.5 mrad/lp and it has an auxiliary IR source.

Night observation with magnification x4 is possible by adding an afocal lens to the binocular body. The field of view is 10° and night vision is ensured through a second-generation image intensifier tube (interchangeable with the third-generation system. Its weight is 750 g without mask or afocal lens.

SPECIFICATION:

USED BY:
In service worldwide

CONTRACTOR:
Thales Optronique, France

VIGY 10 Naval Surveillance System FRANCE

SPECIFICATION:

USED BY:
In service in France and an unknown Southeast Asian country

CONTRACTOR:
SAGEM SA, France

The VIGY 10 electro-optical system is a lightweight day-and-night surveillance system for use onboard a wide range of surface vessels, coastal surveillance patrol boats, and harbour installations. The VIGY 10 covers a large variety of missions: day-and-night surveillance; law enforcement operations; surveillance of sensitive areas; assistance in search and rescue operations; navigation assistance in shallow waters; and port entry and so on.

Underwater Night Sights and Homing Beacons ISRAEL

Sentry M18 underwater night sight

SPECIFICATION:

USED BY:
Israeli Maritime Special Forces

MANUFACTURER/CONTRACTOR:
Technical Equipment International, Israel

The Night Sentry M18UW monocular sight incorporates an 18 mm Super Gen II image intensification tube and 25 mm f/0.85 objective lens which provides divers with a night-vision capability that can operate down to depths of 50 m. The system, which weighs 460 g without the head harness, allows the diver to identify a human-sized target at a range of 150 m in starlight. For close inspection of objects, the equipment incorporates a small infra-red (IR) source.

The Night Fighter M81 is a fully submersible individual weapons sight, which is capable of operating down to depths of 50 m. The system is based on a Gen II intensifier which permits identification of human-sized objects at ranges of 285 m in starlight. The Night Fly is an IR beacon used to mark beachheads for amphibious operations.

OGVN6 Night-vision Binoculars ITALY

This optical system is equipped with a second-generation microchannel light amplifier tube which has Automatic Brightness Control and a system for automatic switch off when the brightness of the viewing field rises above a certain level. The instrument may be used for night surveillance, naval manoeuvres, battlefield observation or police surveillance and patrolling.

SPECIFICATION:

USED BY:
In service worldwide

CONTRACTOR:
Galileo Avionica SpA, Italy

FEATURES:
DIMENSIONS: 360 x 130 x 110 mm
WEIGHT: 1.95 kg
MAGNIFICATION: x4
FIELD OF VIEW: 11°
DIOPTRE ADJUSTMENT:
+-5 dioptres
INTERPUPILLARY ADJUSTMENT:
58 – 72 mm
FOCUS RANGE: adjustable 12 m to infinity
RESOLUTION: 0.8 mrad at 10^3 lx
POWER SUPPLY: 2 manganese alkali batteries, 1.5 v LR14
BATTERY LIFE: 100 hours at 25°C

Thales Mono Night-vision Goggle UK

The idea behind this mono goggle was to provide enhanced night vision for one eye and normal vision for the other. This is a unique miniature system that provides a high-resolution image. It can be either hand-held or mounted on a facemask or helmet. It is compatible with a nuclear, biological and chemical protective mask. A rotating mechanism allows the device to be adjusted to either eye or to be stored when not in use. There are an infra-red illuminator for close-order tasks and a high-light sensor which automatically shuts off the image intensifier in high-light environments. The goggle can be used for weapon aiming in conjunction with a laser target marker.

SPECIFICATION:

USED BY:
UK armed forces

CONTRACTOR:
Thales Optics, St Asaph, UK

FEATURES:
MAGNIFICATION: day x1; night x3
FIELD OF VIEW: day 40°;
night 13.3°
DIMENSIONS: 115 x 65 x 40 mm

Thales Jay Night-vision Goggles UK

This is a head-mounted night-vision system that can also be used in a weapon-aiming role in conjunction with a laser target marker. The goggles can be supplied with either a second- or third-generation image intensifier tube. An infra-red light source is incorporated. These goggles can be adapted to medium-range or long-range surveillance (x 4.5 magnification). Even longer ranges can be achieved by adding the Thales Maxi-Kite adapter.

SPECIFICATION:

USED BY:
UK Special Forces

CONTRACTOR:
Thales Optics, St Asaph, UK

FEATURES:
MAGNIFICATION: day x 1 (unity)
FIELD OF VIEW: 40°
WEIGHT: 680 g
DIMENSIONS: (l x h x w) 160 x 90 x
160 mm
POWER SOURCE: 2 x 1.5 v batteries
(commercially available)

Portaguard – Hand-held Microwave Radar Ground Surveillance System UK

Movement is indicated by readily identifiable audible tones. For example, a man moving produces a series of zipping sounds, a vehicle produces a rushing sound and so on. The varying signal tones make it possible to identify easily whether the target is human, vehicular (wheeled or tracked) or animal. The Portaguard system has a 'see-through capability' to identify movement type behind doors, windows or walls. The effective range of the unit is 200 – 300 m for a human moving and 500 – 600 m for vehicles. The arc of the unit is approximately 90°. A small antenna extension increases the range by approximately 30 per cent. The unit is also capable of remote operation via a simple receiver and transmitter over 5000 – 8000 m and can be interfaced with most other sensor technologies. The receivers are also fitted with a RS-232 output which links to a PC. Border control, local perimeter and security base protection are some of the more conventional applications.

SPECIFICATION:

USED BY:
In service

CONTRACTOR:
Wylam Defence Systems, UK

AN/PVS-7D Gen III Night-vision Goggles UK

ITT Industries Night Vision offers the AV/PVS-7D night-vision goggles with various image-intensifier tube options designed to meet the individual customer performance requirements. It enables personnel to conduct critical operations during the darkest nights of the year. Lightweight, the device has been human-engineered for long-wearing comfort. It can be hand-held, helmet-mounted or head-harness-mounted. The AN/PVS-7D features Gen III tube performance offering optimum resolution, high gain and photo response to near infra-red. A quick-release lever permits one-handed attachment/detachment, an automatic highlight cutoff to protect the image intensifier, an 'IR-on' indicator and momentary IR switch. Optional accessories include: x3 and x5 magnifier lenses; a slip-on compass; and an IR spot or flood lens. The device uses universally available AA batteries and has a low-voltage indicator. It is supplied in a flexible carrying case with shoulder strap and belt-mount clip. A rugged environmentally protective shipping and storage case is also available.

SPECIFICATION:

USED BY:
In service

CONTRACTOR:
ITT Industries Night Vision, USA

FEATURES:
SCENE ILLUMINATION: $10^6 - 1$ fc
SPECTRAL RESPONSE: visible to 0.90 μm (IR)
FIELD OF VIEW: 40°
MAGNIFICATION: unity
DIOPTRIC ADJUSTMENT: +2 − -6 dioptres
INTERPUPILLARY ADJUSTMENT: 55 – 71 mm
OBJECT LENS: EFL 26 mm, f/1.2, T/1.3
FOCUS RANGE: 20 cm to infinity
BATTERY: two AA 1.5 v alkaline or 1 x 3 v lithium (BA-5567)
WEIGHT: 680 g

KillFlash USA

KillFlash

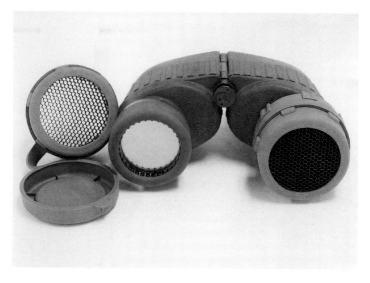

Reflections from the objective lens of observation, surveillance or weapon sight optics can give away an operator's location or compromise a mission. Tenebraex Corporation's KillFlash Anti-Reflection Devices (ARDS) are a lightweight, field-practical solution to glint. They hide reflections without resolution loss, significant light loss or reduction in the optic's field of view; they also contain a specially configured honeycomb of small tubes that act like a much larger traditional cylindrical lens hood. They both hide reflections and shield the optic from internal glare caused by light sources outside its field of view. In a 25.4 mm (1 in) thick package, the Model M22-G2 KillFlash for the US Army's M22 binocular gives the same protection as a traditional tube over 533 mm (21 in) long. KillFlash ARDS are available for a wide range of optics, including binoculars, night-vision surveillance optics and goggles, weapon sights and thermal viewers.

SPECIFICATION:

USED BY:
In service

CONTRACTOR:
Tenebraex Corporation, USA

FEATURES:
INTERIOR: 66.5 mm (2.62 in)
EXTERIOR: 90 mm (3.5 in)
LENGTH: 57 mm (2.25 in)
WEIGHT: 113 g (4 oz)
HOUSING MATERIAL: rubber over thermoplastic core
FILTER MATERIAL: resin-reinforced composite honeycomb with special matt-black coating

Transport:
Air, Fixed
Wing

IA 58 Pucara ARGENTINA

Highly manoeuvrable, single-seat aircraft for close ground support in counter-insurgency and conventional operations.

SPECIFICATION:

USED BY:
Argentinian air force

CONTRACTOR:
Argentina's Military Aircraft Factory (FMA) and Lockheed Martin Aircraft Argentina (LMAA), Argentina

ACCOMMODATION:
All versions = pilot and navigator/WSO in a jettisonable escape capsule

PERFORMANCE:
MAX SPEED: M = 2.2
RANGE: 2750+ nm (5093 km)

ARMAMENT:
INTERNAL GUN: one 20mm M61 cannon (optional)
HARDPOINTS: eight
MAX WEAPON LOAD: about 14,228 kg (31,500 lb)
REPRESENTATIVE WEAPONS: AIM-9 AAM; Mk.80-series bombs; Paveway II LGB; AGM-84 Harpoon; EW/ECM or desigator pods; external fuel tanks

DIMENSIONS:
LENGTH: 22.4 m (73 ft 6 in)
WINGSPAN: spread 21.3 m (70 ft 0 in); fully-swept 10.3 m (33 ft 11 in)
HEIGHT: 5.2 m (17 ft 1 in)

FEATURES:
Shoulder-mounted variable geometry wings; twin P&W TF30-P-3 turbofans; side-by-side cockpit; wide sleek nose

DHC-5 Buffalo CANADA

All-weather, STOL tactical transport.

SPECIFICATION:

USED BY:
Variants operated by the air forces of Brazil, Canada, Cameroon, Democratic Republic of Congo, Ecuador, Egypt, Indonesia, Kenya, Mexico, Sudan, Tanzania, Togo and Zambia

CONTRACTOR:
de Havilland Canada (Bombardier), Canada

ACCOMMODATION:
Two flight crew and crew chief, plus 41 troops, 35 paratroops or 8164 kg (18,000 lb) of freight

PERFORMANCE:
MAX SPEED: 252 kts (467 km/h)
RANGE: 225 nm (415 km)

DIMENSIONS:
LENGTH: 24.1 m (79 ft 0 in)
WINGSPAN: 29.3 m (96 ft 0 in)
HEIGHT: 8.7 m (28 ft 8 in)

FEATURES:
High-wing; T-tail; two GE CT-82-4 turboprops

DHC-4A Caribou CANADA

STOL tactical transport aircraft.

SPECIFICATION:

USED BY:
Now operated by air forces of
Australia, Costa Rica and Malaysia

CONTRACTOR:
de Havilland Canada
(Bombardier), Canada

ACCOMMODATION:
Two flight crew plus 32 troops,
26 paratroops or 3965 kg (8740 lb)
of freight

PERFORMANCE:
MAX SPEED: 188 kts (347 km/h)
RANGE: 210 nm (390 km)

DIMENSIONS:
LENGTH: 22.1 m (72 ft 7 in)
WINGSPAN: 29.1 m (95 ft 7 in)
WEIGHT: 9.7 m (31 ft 9 in)

FEATURES:
High straight wing; high beavertail; two P&W R-2000-7M2 piston
engines

J-7 (F-7) CHINA

Single-seat (twin-seat variant) ground attack/ fighter aircraft.

SPECIFICATION:

USED BY:
Air force of the Chinese People's Liberation Army

CONTRACTOR:
Chengdu Aircraft Industrial Group, China

ACCOMMODATION:
J-7/F-7 variants = pilot; JJ-7 (FT-7) = student and instructor

PERFORMANCE:
MAX SPEED: M = 2.05 (1175 kts, 2,275 km/h)
RADIUS OF ACTION: 259 nm (480 km)

ARMAMENT (F-7MG):

INTERNAL GUN: one 30mm Type 30-1 cannon
HARDPOINTS: five
MAX WEAPON LOAD: about 1500 kg (3300 lb)
REPRESENTATIVE WEAPONS: PL-7, AIM-9, Magic AAMs; bombs; FFAR pods; external fuel tanks

DIMENSIONS:

LENGTH: 12.2 m (39 ft 11 in)
WINGSPAN: 8.3 m (27 ft 3 in)
HEIGHT: 4.1 m (13 ft 5 in)

FEATURES:

Low, double-delta wing; swept tailplanes; single LMC (Liyang) WP13F turbojet; nose intake with central radome

Q-5 'Fantan' CHINA

Single-seat, close air support fighter.

SPECIFICATION:

USED BY:
Air force of the Chinese People's Liberation Army

CONTRACTOR:
Nanchang Aircraft Manufacturing Company, China

ACCOMMODATION:
Pilot

PERFORMANCE:
MAX SPEED: M = 1.12 (643 kts, 1190 km/h)
RADIUS OF ACTION: 324 nm (600 km)

ARMAMENT:
INTERNAL GUN: one 23 mm cannon
HARDPOINTS: ten
MAX WEAPON LOAD: 2000 kg (4410 lb)
REPRESENTATIVE WEAPONS: PL-2, PL-7, AIM-9, Magic AAMS; bombs, FFAR pods; external fuel tanks

DIMENSIONS:
LENGTH: 16.2 m (53 ft 4 in)
WINGSPAN: 9.7 m (31 ft 10 in)
HEIGHT: 4.5 m (14 ft 9 in)

FEATURES:
Swept wing; two Shenyang WP6 turbojets; intakes by cockpit; pointed nose

Alpha Jet FRANCE

Twin-seat training aircraft that can be operated in the close air support/ground attack role.

SPECIFICATION:

USED BY:
Variants operated by air forces of Belgium, Cameroon, Egypt, France, Ivory Coast, Morocco, Nigeria, Portugal, Qatar, Thailand, Togo, UAE and the UK

CONTRACTOR:
Dassault, France

ACCOMMODATION:
Student and instructor

PERFORMANCE:
MAX SPEED: 560 kts (1038 km/h)
RANGE: 315 nm (583 km)

ARMAMENT:
INTERNAL GUN: one 30 mm DEFA or 27 mm Mauser cannon in underfuselage pod
HARDPOINTS: five
MAX WEAPON LOAD: 2500 kg (5510 lb)
REPRESENTATIVE WEAPONS: Magic, AIM-9 AAMs; AGM-65 Maverick; Mk.81/82 bombs; FFAR pods; recce and gun pods; external fuel tanks

DIMENSIONS:
LENGTH: 11.8 m (38 ft 6 in)
WINGSPAN: 9.1 m (29 ft 10 in)
HEIGHT: 4.2 m (13 ft 9 in)

FEATURES:
Shoulder-swept wing; lateral intakes; tandem cockpit; 2 SNECMA/Turbomeca Larzac 04-c6/20 turbofans

G222 (C-27) ITALY

Tactical transport aircraft.

SPECIFICATION:

USED BY:
Variants operated by air forces of
Argentina, Nigeria, Thailand,
Tunisia and Venezuela

CONTRACTOR:
Alenia, Italy

ACCOMMODATION:
Three flight crew and one
loadmaster plus 53 troops,
40 paratroopers or 9000 kg
(19,840 lb) cargo

PERFORMANCE:
MAX SPEED: 291 kts (540 km/h)
RANGE: 740 nm (1,371 km)

DIMENSIONS:
LENGTH: 22.7 m (74 ft 5 in)
WINGSPAN: 28.7 m (94 ft 2 in)
HEIGHT: 9.8 m (32 ft 2 in)

FEATURES:
High-tail; shoulder-tapered wing;
two GE T64-GE-P4D turboprops;
fuselage undercarriage fairings

C-27J Spartan ITALY

Tactical transport aircraft.

SPECIFICATION:

USED BY:
Air forces of Greece and Italy

CONTRACTOR:
Alenia, Italy, in conjunction with
Lockheed Martin, USA

ACCOMMODATION:
Two flight crew and one
loadmaster plus 53 troops,
40 paratroopers or 10,000 kg
(22,046 lb) cargo

PERFORMANCE:
MAX SPEED: 325 kts (602 km/h)
RANGE: 1350 nm (2500 km)

DIMENSIONS:
LENGTH: 22.7 m (74 ft 5 in)
WINGSPAN: 28.7 m (94 ft 2 in)
HEIGHT: 9.8 m (32 ft 2 in)

FEATURES:
High-tail; shoulder-tapered wing;
two R-R AE 2100D2 turboprops;
fuselage undercarriage fairings

Single-seat, close air support fighter.

SPECIFICATION:

USED BY:
Japanese Air Self Defence Force

CONTRACTOR:
Mitsubishi, Japan

ACCOMMODATION:
Pilot

PERFORMANCE:
MAX SPEED: M = 1.6
RADIUS OF ACTION: n/a

ARMAMENT:
INTERNAL GUN: one 20 mm JM61 cannon
HARDPOINTS: five
MAX WEAPON LOAD: 2721 kg (5997 lb)
REPRESENTATIVE WEAPONS: ASM-1 ASM; bombs, FFAR pods; external fuel tanks

DIMENSIONS:
LENGTH: 17.8 m (58 ft 6 in)
WINGSPAN: 7.9 m (25 ft 10 in)
HEIGHT: 4.5 m (14 ft 8 in)

FEATURES:
Shoulder-swept wing; two Rolls-Royce/Turbomeca Adour 108 turbofans; rear ventral fins

F-2 JAPAN

Single-seat, close air support fighter.

SPECIFICATION:

USED BY:
Japanese Air Self Defence Force

CONTRACTOR:
Mitsubishi, Japan

ACCOMMODATION:
F-2A = pilot, F-2B = student and
instructor

PERFORMANCE:
MAX SPEED: M = 2.0
RADIUS OF ACTION: n/a

ARMAMENT:
INTERNAL GUN: one 20 mm M61
cannon
HARDPOINTS: 13
MAX WEAPON LOAD: 6498 kg
(14,320 lb)
REPRESENTATIVE WEAPONS: AAM-3,
AIM-7, AIM-9 AAMS; ASM-1/-2 ASMS;
bombs; FFAR pods; external
fuel tanks

DIMENSIONS:
LENGTH: 15.5 m (58 ft 6 in)
WINGSPAN: 11.1 m (36 ft 6 in)
HEIGHT: 4.9 m (16 ft 3 in)

FEATURES:
Mid-swept wing; 2 GE F110
turbofans; chin intake

IAR-93/SOKO J-22 Orao (Eagle) ROMANIA

J-22 Orao

Single-seat (twin-seat for training) ground attack/
reconnaissance aircraft.

SPECIFICATION:

USED BY:
Romanian and Yugoslavian
(Bosnia-Herzegovenia) air forces

CONTRACTOR:
Avione, Romania

PERFORMANCE:
MAX SPEED: 586 kts (1086 km/h)
RADIUS OF ACTION: 248 nm
(460 km)

ARMAMENT:
(IAR-93A/B)
INTERNAL GUN: two 23 mm
twin-barrel cannon
HARDPOINTS: five
MAX WEAPON LOAD: 1500 kg
(3307 lb)
REPRESENTATIVE WEAPONS: AAMS;
250 kg or 500 kg bombs; FFAR
pods; external fuel tanks

DIMENSIONS:
LENGTH: 14.9 m (48 ft 11 in)
Length (trainer): 15.4 m (50 ft 6 in)
WINGSPAN: 9.3 m (30 ft 6 in)
HEIGHT: 4.5 m (14 ft 0 in)

FEATURES:
Shoulder-swept wing; twin
Rolls-Royce Viper turbojets;
short pointed nose

An-12 (Y-8) 'Cub' RUSSIA

Tactical transport aircraft.

SPECIFICATION:

USED BY:
Variants operated by air forces of
Afghanistan, Algeria, Angola,
Azerbaijan, Belarus, Kazakhstan,
Russia, Ukraine, Uzbekistan and
Yemen

CONTRACTOR:
Antonov, Russia

PAYLOAD/ACCOMMODATION:
Five flight crew and one rear
gunner plus 90 troops, 60
paratroopers or 20,000 kg
(44,090 lb) cargo

PERFORMANCE:
MAX SPEED: 419 kts (777 km/h)
RANGE: 1942 nm (3600 km)

DIMENSIONS:
LENGTH: 33.1 m (108 ft 7 in)
WINGSPAN: 38.0 m (124 ft 8 in)
HEIGHT: 12.2 m (40 ft)

ARMAMENT:
Two 23 mm NK-23 cannon in
tail turret

FEATURES:
High-tail; shoulder-tapered wing;
anhedral on outer wing panels;
four Ivchenko AI-20 turboprops;
fuselage undercarriage fairings

su-17/-20/-22 'Fitter-D/K' RUSSIA

su-17

Single-seat (twin-seat for training) ground attack and reconnaissance aircraft.

SPECIFICATION:

USED BY:
Variants operated by air forces of Afghanistan, Angola, Azerbaijan, Bulgaria, Czech Republic, Ethiopia, Iran, Libya, Peru, Poland, Slovak Republic, Syria, Turkmenistan, Ukraine, Uzbekistan, Vietnam and Yemen

CONTRACTOR:
Sukhoi, Russia

ACCOMMODATION:
All but su-22U/UM3 = pilot, su-22U/UM3 = student and instructor

PERFORMANCE:
MAX SPEED: M = 2.09
RADIUS OF ACTION: approx 550 nm (1017 km)

ARMAMENT:
INTERNAL GUNS: two 30 mm NR-30 cannon
HARDPOINTS: nine
MAX WEAPON LOAD: 4250 kg (9370 lb)
REPRESENTATIVE WEAPONS: Kh-23 'Kerry', Kh-25 'Karen', Kh-28 'Kyle'; AGMs; bombs; rockets; external fuel tanks

DIMENSIONS:
LENGTH: 18.8 m (61 ft 6 in)
WINGSPAN: spread – 10.0 m (32 ft 10 in); swept – 8.8 m (28 ft 9 in)
HEIGHT: 5.0 m (16 ft 5 in)

FEATURES:
V-G wing; one Lyulka AL-21F-3 turbojet; nose intake

su-27 'Flanker' RUSSIA

Single-seat (twin-seat for training) ground attack and fighter aircraft.

SPECIFICATION:

USED BY:
Variants operated by air forces of Belarus, China, Ethiopia, Kazakhstan, Russia, Ukraine, Uzbekistan and Vietnam

CONTRACTOR:
Sukhoi, Russia

ACCOMMODATION:
su-27 = pilot, su-27UB = student and instructor

PERFORMANCE:
MAX SPEED: M = 2.35 (1350 kts, 2500 km/h)
RADIUS OF ACTION: 810 nm (1500 km)

ARMAMENT:
INTERNAL GUN: one 30 mm GSh-30-1 cannon
HARDPOINTS: eight (plus wingtips)
MAX WEAPON LOAD: 4000 kg (8818 lb)
REPRESENTATIVE WEAPONS: R-27 'Alamo', R-33 'Amos', R-60 'Aphid', R-73 'Archer' AAMS; bombs; rockets; 23 mm gun pod; external fuel tanks

DIMENSIONS:
LENGTH: 21.9 m (71 ft 11 in)
WINGSPAN: 14.7 m (48 ft 3 in)
HEIGHT: 5.9 m (19 ft 5 in)

FEATURES:
Twin fins; shoulder-swept wing; two Saturn/Lyulka AL-31F turbofans; intakes under fuselage/wing; ventral fins; tailcone between jetpipes

su-30/-33 'Flanker' RUSSIA

su-30

Twin-seat, ground attack and fighter aircraft capable of operating from aircraft carriers in support of amphibious operations.

SPECIFICATION:

USED BY:
Variants operated by air forces of India and Russia

CONTRACTOR:
Sukhoi, Russia

ACCOMMODATION:
Pilot and WSO

PERFORMANCE:
MAX SPEED: M = 2.35 (1350 kts, 2500 km/h)
RADIUS OF ACTION: 810 nm (1500 km)

ARMAMENT:
INTERNAL GUN: one 30 mm GSh-30-1 cannon
HARDPOINTS: ten (plus wingtips)
MAX WEAPON LOAD: 8000 kg (17,635 lb)
REPRESENTATIVE WEAPONS: R-27 'Alamo', R-73 'Archer', R-77 'Adder' AAMs; Kh-29 'Kedge', Kh-31 'Krypton', Kh-59 'Kazoo' AGMs; Raduga 3 M80E ASM; bombs; rockets; external fuel tanks

DIMENSIONS:
LENGTH: 21.9 m (71 ft 11 in)
WINGSPAN: 14.7 m (48 ft 3 in)
HEIGHT: 5.9 m (19 ft 5 in)

FEATURES:
Twin fins; shoulder-swept wing; two Saturn/Lyulka AL-31F turbofans; intakes under fuselage/wing; ventral fins; tailcone between jetpipes

su-25 'Frogfoot' RUSSIA

Single-seat (twin-seat for training) close air support aircraft.

SPECIFICATION:

USED BY:
Variants operated by air forces of Angola, Armenia, Azerbaijan, Belarus, Bulgaria, Democratic Republic of Congo, Czech Republic, Georgia, Iran, Macedonia, North Korea, Peru, Russia, Slovak Republic, Turkmenistan, Ukraine and Uzbekistan

CONTRACTOR:
Sukhoi, Russia

ACCOMMODATION:
su-25/T/TM/su-39 = pilot,
su-25UB/UBK/UTG = student and instructor

PERFORMANCE:
MAX SPEED: 526 kts (975 km/h)
RANGE: 675 nm (1250 km)

ARMAMENT:
INTERNAL GUN: one 30 mm
AO-17A two-barrel cannon
HARDPOINTS: ten
MAX WEAPON LOAD: 4400 kg (9700 lb)
REPRESENTATIVE WEAPONS: R-3S 'Atoll', R-60 'Aphid' AAMS; kh-23 'Kerry', кh-25 'Karen', kh-29 'Kedge' AGMS; LGBS; bombs; rockets; 23 mm gun pod; external fuel tanks

DIMENSIONS:
LENGTH: 15.5 m (50 ft 11 in)
WINGSPAN: 14.4 m (47 ft 1 in)
HEIGHT: 4.8 m (15 ft 9 in)

FEATURES:
Shoulder-slightly-swept wing; ECM pod wingtips; two Soyuz/Gavrilov R-195 turbojets; lateral intakes and jetpipes

Be-12 Chaika 'Mail' RUSSIA

Amphibian.

SPECIFICATION:

USED BY:
Russian and Ukrainian air forces

CONTRACTOR:
Beriev, Russia

ACCOMMODATION:
Five flight crew plus mission
specialists. Cabin accomodates
specialised mission equipment

PERFORMANCE:
MAX SPEED: 297 kts (550 km/h)
RANGE: 4050 nm (7500 km)

DIMENSIONS:
LENGTH: 30.2 m (99 ft 0 in)
WINGSPAN: 29.8 m (97 ft 9 in)
HEIGHT: 7.0 m (22 ft 11 in)

ARMAMENT:
No internal gun
HARDPOINTS: four plus internal
weapons bay
MAX WEAPON LOAD: n/a
REPRESENTATIVE WEAPONS:
torpedoes; depth charges; mines

FEATURES:
Twin-tail; shoulder-swept wing
with cranked inner wings; wing
floats; two Ivchenko AI-20D
turboprops' tail MAD boom

C-295 M SPAIN

Multi-role tactical transport.

SPECIFICATION:

USED BY:
Spanish air force

CONTRACTOR:
CASA (EADS), Spain

PAYLOAD/ACCOMMODATION:
Two flight crew plus up to 78
passengers, 48 paratroopers or
7500 kg (16,535 lb) of freight

PERFORMANCE:
MAX SPEED: 260 kts (481 km/h)
RANGE: 728 nm (1348 km)

DIMENSIONS:
LENGTH: 24.4 m (80 ft 2 in)
WINGSPAN: 25.8 m (84 ft 8 in)
HEIGHT: 8.6 m (28 ft 2 in)

FEATURES:
Shoulder-tapered wing; fuselage
undercarriage fairings; two
P&WC PW127G turboprops

105 (SK 60) SWEDEN

Twin-seat, training aircraft also used in the ground attack and the reconnaissance roles.

SPECIFICATION:

USED BY:
Variants operated by air forces of Austria and Sweden

CONTRACTOR:
Saab, Sweden

ACCOMMODATION:
Student and instructor

PERFORMANCE:
MAX SPEED: 432 kts (1800 km/h)
RANGE (INTERNAL FUEL): 1350 nm (2500 km)

ARMAMENT:
No internal gun
HARDPOINTS: six
MAX WEAPON LOAD: 700 kg (1543 lb)
REPRESENTATIVE WEAPONS: bombs; FFAR pods; gun pods

DIMENSIONS:
LENGTH: 10.8 m (35 ft 4 in)
WINGSPAN: 9.5 m (31 ft 2 in)
HEIGHT: 2.7 m (8 ft 9 in)

FEATURES:
Shoulder-swept wing; side-by-side cockpit; two Williams-Rolls FJ44 turbofans

Canberra UK

Bomber, intruder and reconnaissance aircraft still in use (for instance, in Afghanistan).

SPECIFICATION:

USED BY:
Australia, UK and US airforces

CONTRACTOR:
English Electric/British Aerospace, UK and under licence in US

ACCOMMODATION:
B.2 = pilot and two navigators
T.4/T.54 = student and instructor (plus one)
B(I) versions = pilot and navigator
PR.9 = pilot and navigator

PERFORMANCE:
MAX SPEED: 470 kts (871 km/h)
RADIUS OF ACTION: 700 nm (1296 km)

ARMAMENT:
B(I).12/58/68
INTERNAL GUNS: 4 20 mm Hispano cannon (optional)
HARDPOINTS: four in bomb bay, two underwing
MAX WEAPON LOAD: 3630 kg (8000 lb)
REPRESENTATIVE WEAPONS: 500 lb, 1000 lb and 4000 lb bombs; AS.30 AGM; wingtip fuel tanks and underwing target-towing stores

DIMENSIONS:
LENGTH: B(I).12/58/68: 19.9 m (65 ft 6 in); PR.9: 20.3 m (66 ft 8 in)
WINGSPAN: B(I).12/58/68: 19.5 m (64 ft); PR.9: 20.7 m (67 ft 10 in)
HEIGHT: 4.8 m (15 ft 8 in)

FEATURES:
Mid-straight wing; offset canopy on B(I).12/58/68 and PR.9; two mid-wing-mounted Rolls-Royce Avon 206 turbojets

Sea Harrier UK

Single-seat VTOL aircraft for air defence and close support of land forces. Operates from aircraft carriers and (unusually) from single-spot ships.

SPECIFICATION:

USED BY:
Variants operated by India (navy), Spain (navy), Thailand (navy), UK (navy) and US (USMC)

CONTRACTOR:
BAE Systems, UK and under licence in the US

ACCOMMODATION:
Sea Harrier FA.2 = pilot

PERFORMANCE:
MAX SPEED: 618 kts (1144 km/h)
RADIUS OF ACTION: 200 nm (370 km)

ARMAMENT:
No internal guns, but two 30 mm Aden cannon fuselage pods
HARDPOINTS: five
MAX WEAPON LOAD: 3630 kg (8000 lb)
REPRESENTATIVE WEAPONS:
ASRAAM, AIM-9, AIM-120 AAMS; 1000 lb bombs; PGMS; AGM; external fuel tanks

DIMENSIONS:
LENGTH: 14.2 m (46 ft 6 in)
WINGSPAN: 7.7 m (25 ft 3 in)
HEIGHT: 3.7 m (12 ft 2 in)

FEATURES:
Shoulder-swept wing with LERX; single Rolls-Royce Pegasus Mk.106 vectored-thrust turbofan; four nozzles; blown canopy

AV-8B Harrier GR.7/9 UK

Harrier GR7

Single-seat, STOVL, ground-attack aircraft capable of operating from aircraft carriers and forward edges of the battlefield. The USMC also operate a night-attack version.

SPECIFICATION:

USED BY:
Variants operated by the air forces of Italy, Spain, UK and US (also the US Marines Corps)

CONTRACTOR:
BAE Systems, UK/McDonnell Douglas (Boeing), USA

ACCOMMODATION:
AV-8B/Harrier GR.5/7/9 = pilot
TAV-8B/Harrier T.10 = student and instructor

PERFORMANCE:
MAX SPEED: 575 kts (065 km/h)
RADIUS OF ACTION: 594 nm (1101 km)

ARMAMENT:
INTERNAL GUN: one 25 mm GAU-12/U cannon (USMC), two 25 mm Aden cannon (now abandoned by RAF)
HARDPOINTS: seven (nine on AF and Harrier II Plus)
REPRESENTATIVE WEAPONS: AIM-9; Mk.80-series bombs; AGM-65 Maverick; Paveway LGBs; FFAR pods; Brimstone AAAW; external fuel tanks

DIMENSIONS:
LENGTH: AV-8B, 14.1 m (46 ft 4 in); Harrier GR.5/7/9: 14.4 m (47 ft 1 in)
WINGSPAN: 9.2 m (30 ft 4 in)
HEIGHT: 3.5 m (11 ft 7 in)

Hunter UK

Single-seat (twin-seat variant) fighter/ground attack aircraft.

SPECIFICATION:

USED BY:
Worldwide in ground support role; still in service with at least two countries

CONTRACTOR:
Hawker (HAS/BAE), UK

ACCOMMODATION:
Hunter FGA.9/70/70A = pilot
Hunter T.7/66C/81 = student and instructor

PERFORMANCE:
MAX SPEED: 620 kts (1149 km/h)
RADIUS OF ACTION: about 600 nm (1111 km)

ARMAMENT:
FGA.9/70/70A
INTERNAL GUNS: four 30 mm Aden cannon
HARDPOINTS: four
MAX WEAPON LOAD: 3357 kg (7400 lb)
REPRESENTATIVE WEAPONS: 500 lb and 1000 lb bombs; 2 in/2.75 in FFAR pods; 3 in rocket projectiles: CBLS and external fuel tanks

DIMENSIONS:
LENGTH: 13.9 m (45 ft 10 in)
WINGSPAN: 10.3 m (33 ft 8 in)
HEIGHT: 4.0 m (13 ft 2 in)

FEATURES:
Swept-fin; mid-mounted; swept-wings; single Rolls-Royce Avon 207 turbojet; wing-root intakes

A-10A USA

Single-seat, ground-support aircraft for operations, particularly against hard targets and tanks.

SPECIFICATION:

USED BY:
US air force

CONTRACTOR:
Fairchild Republic/Lockheed Martin, USA

ACCOMMODATION:
Pilot

PERFORMANCE:
MAX SPEED: 390 kts (722 km/h)
RADIUS OF ACTION: 540 nm (1000 km)

ARMAMENT:
INTERNAL GUN: one 30 mm GAU-8/A cannon
HARDPOINTS: 11
MAX WEAPON LOAD: 9450 kg (21,000 lb)
REPRESENTATIVE WEAPONS: AIM-9 AAMs; Mk.80-series bombs; BLU-27/B Rockeye cluster bombs; Paveway II LGBs; AGM-65 Maverick AGMs; designator and EW/ECM pods; external fuel tanks

DIMENSIONS:
LENGTH: 16.3 m (53 ft 4 in)
WINGSPAN: 17.5 m (57 ft 6 in)
HEIGHT: 4.5 m (14 ft 8 in)

FEATURES:
Twin fins; low 'plank' wings; twin GE TF34 turbofans on rear-fuselage pods

B-2A **Spirit** USA

Two-pilot (plus third seat) stealth, long-range bomber.

SPECIFICATION:

USED BY:
us air force

CONTRACTOR:
Northrop, USA

ACCOMMODATION:
Two pilots (plus third seat)

PERFORMANCE:
MAX SPEED: n/a
RANGE: (internal fuel) 4500 nm
(8334 km)

ARMAMENT:
No internal gun. Two weapons
bays, each with 8-store rotary
launcher, no external hardpoints
MAX WEAPON LOAD: 18,144 kg
(40,000 lb)
REPRESENTATIVE WEAPONS:
AGM-129 ACM; JDAM, JSOW and
JASSM weapons; nuclear and
conventional bombs

DIMENSIONS:
LENGTH: 21.0 m (69 ft)
WINGSPAN: 52.4 m (172 ft)
HEIGHT: 5.2 m (17 ft)

FEATURES:
No fin; flying wing with blended
fuselage (tadpole-like); serrated
trailing edge; four GE F118
turbofans

OV-10 **Bronco** USA

Twin-seat, highly manoeuvrable, multi-purpose, counter-insurgency aircraft.

SPECIFICATION:

USED BY:
Originally by US air force and marines now in variants by air forces from Colombia, Indonesia, Morocco, Philippines, Thailand and Venezuela

CONTRACTOR:
Rockwell (Boeing), USA

ACCOMMODATION:
Two pilots

PERFORMANCE:
MAX SPEED: 244 kts (452 km/h)
RADIUS OF ACTION: 198 nm (367 km)

ARMAMENT:
INTERNAL GUNS: four 7.62 mm M60C machine guns
HARDPOINTS: seven
MAX WEAPON LOAD: 1633 kg (3600 lb)
REPRESENTATIVE WEAPONS:
AIM-9 AAM; Mk.80-series bombs; FFAR pods; gun pods; external fuel tank

DIMENSIONS:
LENGTH: 12.7 m (41 ft 7 in)
WINGSPAN: 12.2 m (40 ft)
HEIGHT: 4.6 m (15 ft 2 in)

FEATURES:
Twin boom tail; podded fuselage; two Garrett T76 turboprops; fuselage stores sponsons

C-17 Globemaster III USA

Strategic transport aircraft.

SPECIFICATION:

USED BY:
UK and US air forces

CONTRACTOR:
Boeing (McDonnell Douglas), USA

ACCOMMODATION:
Two flight crew and one
loadmaster, plus 154 passengers,
102 paratroops or a max of
76,655 kg (169,000 lb) of cargo

PERFORMANCE:
MAX SPEED: M = 0.77
RANGE: 2400 nm (8704 km)

DIMENSIONS:
LENGTH: 53.0 m (174 ft)
WINGSPAN: 51.7 m (169 ft 9 in)
HEIGHT: 16.8 m (55 ft 1 in)

FEATURES:
T-tail; shoulder-swept wing with
winglet tips; four wing-mounted
P&W F117-PW-100 (PW2040)
turbofans; fuselage undercarriage
sponsons

Hercules AC-130H/U: C-130A/B/E/H/C-130J USA

Hercules special operations gunship

A ubiquitous aircraft used in many roles including those of Special Operations Gunship and delivery of paratroopers. It is capable of high and very low level delivery and even the recovery of personnel from the ground while in flight. Details given here are for the gunship used solely by the USAF. The stretched version (130-J) is 34.4 m (112 ft 9 in) long and can carry 92 paratroopers.

SPECIFICATION:

USED BY:
US air force (gunship) otherwise all other variants are in use world-wide by at least sixty air forces

CONTRACTOR:
Lockheed Martin, USA

ACCOMMODATION:
Three flight crew plus mission crew of ten (AC-130U) or 11 (AC-130H)

PERFORMANCE:
MAX SPEED: 325 kts (602 km/h)
RANGE: 2046 nm (3791 km)

ARMAMENT:
(AC-130U)
INTERNAL GUNS: one 25 mm GAU-12/U cannon; one 40 mm M2A1 Bofors gun; one 105 mm M137A1 howitzer; on port side of fuselage
HARDPOINTS: four
REPRESENTATIVE WEAPONS: use of AGM-114 Hellfire AGM studied; external fuel tanks under wing

DIMENSIONS:
LENGTH: 29.8 m (97 ft 9 in)
WINGSPAN: 40.4 m (132 ft 7 in)
HEIGHT: 11.7 m (38 ft 3 in)

FEATURES:
High-straight wings; four Allison (Rolls-Royce) T56 turboprops

C-141B Starlifter USA

Tactical transport aircraft.

SPECIFICATION:

USED BY:
US air force

CONTRACTOR:
Lockheed Martin, USA

PAYLOAD/ACCOMMODATION:
Four flight crew plus 205 troops,
168 paratroops or 41,222 kg
(90,800 lb) freight

PERFORMANCE:
MAX SPEED: 492 kts (910 km/h)
RANGE: 2550 nm (4725 km)

DIMENSIONS:
LENGTH: 51.3 m (168 ft 3 in)
WINGSPAN: 48.7 m (159 ft 11 in)
HEIGHT: 12.0 m (39 ft 3 in)

FEATURES:
T-tail; shoulder-swept wing; with
four underwing-mounted P&W
TF33-P-7 turbofans; lower
fuselage undercarriage fairings;
56 turboprops

F-117A Nighthawk USA

Single-seat, stealth attack fighter.

SPECIFICATION:

USED BY:
US air force

CONTRACTOR:
Lockheed Martin, USA

ACCOMMODATION:
Pilot

PERFORMANCE:
MAX SPEED: M = 1.0+
RADIUS OF ACTION: n/a

ARMAMENT:
No internal gun. Weapons bays
but no external hardpoints
REPRESENTATIVE WEAPONS:
Mk.84 bomb; BLU-109B; GBU-10;
GBU-27 LGBS; AGM-65 Maverick;
AGM-88 HARM

DIMENSIONS:
LENGTH: 20.1 m (65 ft 11 in)
WINGSPAN: 13.2 m (43 ft 4 in)
HEIGHT: 3.8 m (12 ft 5 in)

FEATURES:
Swept butterfly fins; low-swept
wings blended to angular
fuselage; two GE F404 turbofans

Transport: Air, Rotary Wing

AS 532 Cougar (Super Puma) FRANCE

Medium-lift transport helicopter used, additionally, by Special Forces.

SPECIFICATION:

USED BY:
Variants operated by Argentina, Brazil, Cameroon, Chile, China, Democratic Republic of Congo, Ecuador, France, Germany, Greece, Iceland, Indonesia, Japan, Jordan, Kuwait, Malawi, Mexico, Netherlands, Nepal, Nigeria, Oman, Saudi Arabia, Singapore, South Africa, South Korea, Spain, Sweden, Switzerland, Thailand, Turkey, UAE, Venezuela and Zimbabwe

CONTRACTOR:
Eurocopter, France. Built under licence in Indonesia (Dirgantara) and Turkey (TAI)

ACCOMMODATION:
Two (plus one) flight crew plus 21 passengers or 4500 kg (9920 lb) external slung cargo

PERFORMANCE:
MAX SPEED: 170 kts (315 km/h)
RANGE: 656 nm (1215 km)

ARMAMENT (OPTIONAL):
HARDPOINTS: two pylons
REPRESENTATIVE WEAPONS: Exocet ASMs, FFAR pods, 20 mm cannon or 12.7 mm machine gun pods, homing torpedoes

DIMENSIONS:
MAIN ROTOR DIAMETER: (Cougar Mk II) 16.2 m (53 ft 1 in)
LENGTH: 19.5 m (63 ft 11 in)
HEIGHT: 5.0 m (16 ft 5 in)

FEATURES:
Air intakes over cabin; rear-fuselage sponsons; two Turbomeca Makila 1A2 turboshafts; retractable wheeled undercarriage; starboard tailplane; port tail rotor

AS 565 Panther (Dauphin 2) FRANCE

General purpose light helicopter used, additionally, for support of amphibious and Special Forces.

SPECIFICATION:

USED BY:
Variants operated by naval, army and air forces of Angola, Argentina, Brazil, Burkina Faso, Cambodia, Cameroon, Democratic Republic of Congo, Côte d'Ivoire, China, France, Iceland, Ireland, Israel, Mexico, Morocco, Romania, Saudi Arabia, UAE, Uruguay and US

CONTRACTOR:
Eurocopter, France

ACCOMMODATION:
One pilot and second front seat plus up to 12 passengers or 1600 kg (3525 lb) cargo sling

PERFORMANCE:
MAX SPEED: 155 kts (287 km/h)
RANGE: 464 nm (859 km)

ARMAMENT:
(AS 365N)
HARDPOINTS: four on two pylons
REPRESENTATIVE WEAPONS:
AS-15TT ASMS, torpedoes, 7.62 mm or 12.7 mm machine gun or 20 mm cannon pods

DIMENSIONS:
MAIN ROTOR DIAMETER: 11.9 m (39 ft 2 in)
LENGTH: 13.7 m (45 ft)
HEIGHT: 4.1 m (13 ft 4 in)

FEATURES:
Fenestron tail rotor; two Turbomeca Arriel 1C2 or 2C turboshafts; retractable wheeled undercarriage

SA 316/319 Alouette III FRANCE

SA 316

General purpose, light helicopter used, additionally, by Special Forces and for ground attack.

SPECIFICATION:

USED BY:
Variants operated by air and land forces of Albania, Angola, Argentina, Austria, Belgium, Burundi, Cameroon, Chad, Democratic Republic of Congo, Côte d'Ivoire, Ecuador, Ethiopia, France, Gabon, Ghana, Greece, Guinea-Bissau, Guinea Republic, India, Indonesia, Ireland, Jordan, Lebanon, Malaysia, Malta, Mauritius, Mexico, Namibia, Nepal, Netherlands, Pakistan, Portugal, Romania, South Africa, South Korea, Suriname, Swaziland, Switzerland, Tunisia, Venezuela and Zimbabwe

CONTRACTOR:
Aerospatiale (Eurocopter), France

ACCOMMODATION:
One pilot plus six passengers plus 750 kg (1650 lb) external sling load

PERFORMANCE:
MAX SPEED: 113 kts (210 km/h)
RANGE: 290 nm (540 km)

ARMAMENT: (WHEN FITTED)
INTERNAL GUN: (if fitted) cabin-mounted 7.62 mm machine gun or 20 mm MG 151/20 cannon
HARDPOINTS: up to four on cabin-mounted pylons
REPRESENTATIVE WEAPONS: four AS 11 or two AS 12 missiles

DIMENSIONS:
MAIN ROTOR DIAMETER: 11.0 m (36 ft 2 in)
LENGTH: 12.8 m (42 ft 1 in)
HEIGHT: 3.0 m (9 ft 10 in)

FEATURES:
Rounded, glazed nose; single Turbomeca Artouste III B (SA 316) or Astazou XIV (SA 319) turboshaft; skid undercarriage (ground forces) or wheel undercarriage (at sea)

AS 550/555 Ecureuil   FRANCE

AS 550

Light utility helicopter also used in support of amphibious and Special Forces.

SPECIFICATION:

USED BY:
Variants operated by army and air forces of Albania, Argentina, Australia, Botswana, Brazil, Burkina Faso, Burundi, Cambodia, Comoros, Denmark, Djibouti, Ecuador, France, Gabon, Guinea Republic, Ireland, Jamaica, Malawi, Mali, Mauritius, Mexico, Nepal, Paraguay, Peru, Rwanda, Sierra Leone, Singapore, Thailand, Tunisia, UAE, UK and Venzuela

CONTRACTOR:
Eurocopter, France. Built under licence in Brazil

ACCOMMODATION:
One pilot and second front seat plus four passengers or 907 kg (2000 lb) cargo sling

PERFORMANCE:
MAX SPEED: 155 kts (287 km/h)
RANGE: 362 nm (670 km)

ARMAMENT:
(AS 550C3)
HARDPOINTS: two
REPRESENTATIVE WEAPONS: two AGMS; one torpedo; FFAR pods; 7.62 mm or 12.7 mm machine gun or 20 mm cannon pods

DIMENSIONS:
MAIN ROTOR DIAMETER: 10.7 m (35 ft 1 in)
LENGTH: 12.9 m (42 ft 5 in)
HEIGHT: 3.4 m (10 ft 11 in)

FEATURES:
Starboard tail rotor; one Turbomeca Arriel 1D1 or 2B (AS 350/550) or two Turbomeca Arrius 1A turboshafts (AS 355/555); skid undercarriage

SA 341/342 Gazelle FRANCE

Light utility helicopter used, additionally, for support of Special Forces and in the ground attack role. Adapted for ship-borne operations.

SPECIFICATION:

USED BY:
Angola, Yugoslavia, Burundi, Cameroon, China, Cyprus, Ecuador, Egypt, France, Gabon, Guinea Republic, Ireland, Kuwait, Libya, Morocco, Qatar, Syria, UAE and the UK

CONTRACTOR:
Aerospatiale (Eurocopter), France

ACCOMMODATION:
One or two flight crew plus three passengers

PERFORMANCE:
MAX SPEED: 167 kts (310 km/h)
RANGE: 194 nm (360 km)

ARMAMENT:
(SA 342L/M)
HARDPOINTS: up to four on cabin pylons
REPRESENTATIVE WEAPONS: Mistral AAM; AS 11; AS 12 or HOT ATGWS; 2.75 in or 67 mm rocket pods

DIMENSIONS:
MAIN ROTOR DIAMETER: 10.5 m (34 ft 5 in)
LENGTH: 12.0 m (39 ft 4 in)
HEIGHT: 3.1 m (10 ft 3 in)

FEATURES:
Glazed cabin; one Turbomeca Astazou IIIA (SA 341) or Astazou XIVM (SA 342L) turboshaft with upturned exhaust; skid undercarriage; fenestron in tailboom

SA 330 **Puma** FRANCE

Medium-lift tactical helicopter used, additionally, by Special Forces.

SPECIFICATION:

USED BY:
Variants operated by the air forces and armies of Argentina, Cameroon, Chile, Democratic Republic of Congo, Côte d'Ivoire, Ecuador, Ethiopia, France, Gabon, Guinea Republic, Indonesia, Kenya, Kuwait, Lebanon, Malawi, Mexico, Morocco, Nepal, Oman, Pakistan, Philippines, Portugal, Romania, Spain, Sudan, UAE and the UK

CONTRACTOR:
Aerospatiale (Eurocopter), France

ACCOMMODATION:
Two (plus one) flight crew plus 16-20 passengers or 3200 kg (7055 lb) external slung cargo

PERFORMANCE:
MAX SPEED: 158 kts (294 km/h)
RANGE: 309 nm (572 km)

ARMAMENT:
(Puma SOCAT)
INTERNAL GUN: Giat 20 mm cannon in undernose turret
HARDPOINTS: up to four on cabin pylons
REPRESENTATIVE WEAPONS: AAMS; ATGWS; 57 mm or 70 mm rocket pods

DIMENSIONS:
MAIN ROTOR DIAMETER: 15.0 m (49 ft 2 in)
LENGTH: 18.5 m (59 ft 6 in)
HEIGHT: 5.1 m (16 ft 10 in)

FEATURES:
Air intakes over cabin; rear-fuselage sponsons; two Turbomeca Turmo IVC turbo-shafts; wheeled undercarriage; tailplane to port of boom; tail rotor to right

AS 665 Tiger FRANCE

Multi-role combat helicopter used, additionally, for the support of Special Forces.

SPECIFICATION:

USED BY:
Variants are operated by the armies and air forces of Australia, France and Germany

CONTRACTOR:
Eurocopter, France and Germany

ACCOMMODATION:
Two pilots

PERFORMANCE:
MAX SPEED: 175 kts (322 km/h)
RANGE: 432 nm (800 km)

ARMAMENT:
INTERNAL GUN: (HAP/HCP) Giat 30 mm cannon in undernose turret
HARDPOINTS: four on two pylons
MAX WEAPON LOAD: n/a
REPRESENTATIVE WEAPONS:
Mistral or Stinger AAMs; Hellfire (RAAF); HOT or Trigat ATGWS; FFAR pods; 12.7 mm machine gun or 20 mm cannon pods; external fuel tanks

DIMENSIONS:
MAIN ROTOR DIAMETER: 13.0 m (42 ft 8 in)
LENGTH: 15.8 m (51 ft 10 in)
HEIGHT: 4.3 m (14 ft 2 in)

FEATURES:
Tandem cockpit; twin-finned tailplanes; starboard tail rotor; two MTU/R-R/Turbomeca MTR 390 turboshafts; fixed wheeled undercarriage

Dhruvs ALH INDIA

Multi-role, utility helicopter additionally used in support of naval and coast guard operations.

SPECIFICATION:

USED BY:
Indian navy and army

CONTRACTOR:
Hindustan Aeronautics Ltd, India

ACCOMMODATION:
Two pilots plus 12-14 passengers or 1500 kg (3307 lb) external cargo sling

PERFORMANCE:
MAX SPEED: 178 kts (330 km/h)
RANGE: 432 nm (800 km)

ARMAMENT:
INTERNAL GUN: provision for 20 mm cannon under nose
HARDPOINTS: four on two pylons
MAX WEAPON LOAD: n/a
REPRESENTATIVE WEAPONS: AAMS; ASMS; ARGWS; torpedoes; depth charges; 68 mm or 71 mm FFAR pods; 12.7 mm machine gun or 20 mm cannon pods

DIMENSIONS:

MAIN ROTOR DIAMETER: 13.2 m (43 ft 4 in)
LENGTH: 15.9 m (52 ft 1 in)
HEIGHT: 4.9 m (16 ft 1 in)

FEATURES:
Side-by-side cockpit; twin-finned tailplanes; starboard tail rotor; two Turbomeca TM 333-2B turboshafts; skid undercarriage (utility); retractable wheeled undercarriage (naval)

Medium-lift transport and naval helicopter suitable for amphibious operations.

SPECIFICATION:

USED BY:
Variants operated by forces from France, Germany, Italy, Netherlands, Norway and Sweden

CONTRACTOR:
NATO Helicopters

ACCOMMODATION:
Two flight crew plus mission specialists (NFH) or 14-20 troops (TTH)

PERFORMANCE:
MAX SPEED: 157 kts (291 km/h)
RANGE: 650 nm (1203 km)

ARMAMENT:
INTERNAL GUN: 7.62 mm machine gun(s) in door mountings
HARDPOINTS: two pylons
MAX WEAPON LOAD: 4600 kg (10,143 lb)
REPRESENTATIVE WEAPONS:
ASV: Marte Mk 2/s ASMS
ASW: torpedoes; depth charges

DIMENSIONS:

MAIN ROTOR DIAMETER: 16.3 m (53 ft 5 in)
LENGTH: 19.6 m (64 ft 2 in)
HEIGHT: 4.1 m (13 ft 5 in)

FEATURES:
Side-by-side cockpit; port tail rotor; starboard tailplane; two RTM 322 or GE T700-T6E turbo-shafts; fuselage sponsons for retractable wheeled undercarriage

A 129 Mangusta ITALY

Light attack helicopter used, additionally, in support of Italian Special Forces.

SPECIFICATION:

USED BY:
Italian air force

CONTRACTOR:
Agusta, Italy

ACCOMMODATION:
Two flight crew

PERFORMANCE:
MAX SPEED: 159 kts (294 km/h)
RANGE: 303 nm (561 km)

ARMAMENT:
INTERNAL GUNS: 20 mm cannon in nose turret on International version
HARDPOINTS: four pylons
MAX WEAPON LOAD: 1000 kg (2204 lb)
REPRESENTATIVE WEAPONS: Stinger or Mistral AAMs; two ATGWS; 2.75 in, 70 mm or 81 mm rocket pods; 12.7 mm machine gun or 20 mm cannon pods

DIMENSIONS:
MAIN ROTOR DIAMETER: 11.9 m (39 ft)
LENGTH: 14.3 m (46 ft 10 in)
HEIGHT: 2.3 m (9 ft)

FEATURES:
Tandem cockpit; port tail rotor; 2 R-R Gem 1004 (A 129) or LHTEC T800-LHT-800 (A 129 International) turboshafts; fixed wheel undercarriage

EH 101 Merlin ITALY & UK

Multi-role, medium-lift helicopter used, additionally, to insert and extract Special Forces. Operates from ships and aircraft carriers in support of amphibious operations.

SPECIFICATION:

USED BY:
Variants operated by navies and air forces of Canada, Denmark, Italy, Japan and the UK

CONTRACTOR:
Augusta, Italy and Westland, UK

ACCOMMODATION:
Two pilots plus specialised mission crew or 30 passengers (Series 300) or 30-45 troops

PERFORMANCE:
MAX SPEED: 167 kts (309 km/h)
Radius of action (SAR): 350 nm (648 km)

ARMAMENT:
INTERNAL GUN: provision for a nose-mounted 0.5 in (12.7 mm) machine gun chin turret
HARDPOINTS: four (plus optional two)
MAX WEAPON LOAD: four torpedoes = 960 kg (2116 lb)
REPRESENTATIVE WEAPONS:
Marte Mk 2 ASMs; Sting Ray; Mk 46 or MU90 torpedoes; depth charges; FFAR pods

DIMENSIONS:
MAIN ROTOR DIAMETER: 18.6 m (61 ft)
LENGTH: 22.8 m (74 ft 10 in)
HEIGHT: 6.6 m (21 ft 9 in)

FEATURES:
Starboard tailplane; port tail rotor; 3 R-R/Turbomeca RTM 322-01/8 (UK versions) or GE T700-GE-T6A/A1 (Canadian/Italian versions) turboshafts; retractable undercarriage

Mi-8/-17 'Hip' RUSSIA

Mi-8

Heavy, assault helicopter widely used, additionally, for the insertion and extraction of Special Forces.

SPECIFICATION:

USED BY:
Variants operated by the ground and air forces of Afghanistan, Albania, Algeria, Angola, Armenia, Azerbaijan, Bangladesh, Belarus, Bhutan, Bosnia-Herzegovina, Burkina Faso, Cambodia, China, Costa Rica, Croatia, Cuba, Czech Republic, Djibouti, Ecuador, Egypt, Eritrea, Estonia, Ethiopia, Finland, Georgia, Guinea-Bisseau, Guyana, Hungary, India, Iran, Kazakhstan, Kenya, Kyrgyz, Laos, Libya, Lithuania, Malaysia, Maldives, Mali, Moldova, Mongolia, Mozambique, Myanmar, North Korea, Pakistan, Peru, Poland, Romania, Russia, Rwanda, Slovak Republic, Sudan, Syria, Tajikistan, Turkmenistan, Turkey, Uganda, Ukraine, US, Uzbekistan, Vietnam, Yemen and Yugoslavia

CONTRACTOR:
MIL, Russia

ACCOMMODATION:
Two pilots and (Mi-8T 'Hip-c') up to 24 troops and (Mi-17-1V) up to 30 troops, or 3000 kg (6614 lb) external cargo sling

PERFORMANCE:
MAX SPEED: 135 kts (250 km/h)
RANGE: 545 nm (1010 km)

ARMAMENT:
(Mi-8TB 'Hip-E')
INTERNAL GUN: one 12.7 mm machine gun in nose
HARDPOINTS: six on outrigger pylons
MAX WEAPON LOAD: n/a
REPRESENTATIVE WEAPONS:
AT-2 'Swatter' ATGWS; 57 mm rocket pods

DIMENSIONS:
MAIN ROTOR DIAMETER: 21.3 m (69 ft 10 in)
LENGTH: 25.3 m (83 ft 1 in)
HEIGHT: 5.5 m (18 ft 2 in)

FEATURES:
Round windows on military cabin; square windows on civil variants; port tail rotor; two Klimov TV2-117AG (Mi-8) and TV3-117 MT (Mi-17) turboshafts; fixed wheeled undercarriage

Mi-28 'Havoc' RUSSIA

Attack helicopter.

SPECIFICATION:

USED BY:
Russian forces

CONTRACTOR:
MIL, Russia

ACCOMMODATION:
Two pilots

PERFORMANCE:
MAX SPEED: 162 kts (300 km/h)
RANGE: 234 nm (435 km)

ARMAMENT:
INTERNAL GUN: one 30 mm
cannon in under-nose turret
HARDPOINTS: two pylons under
each stub-wing
MAX WEAPON LOAD: 11,500 kg
(24,961 lb)
REPRESENTATIVE WEAPONS:
Vikhr, Igla-v or AT-6 'Spiral'
ATGWS; 80 mm or 122 mm rocket
pod; 23 mm cannon pods;
mine dispensers

DIMENSIONS:
MAIN ROTOR DIAMETER: 17.2 m
(56 ft 5 in)
LENGTH: 17.0 m (55 ft 10 in)
HEIGHT: 4.7 m (15 ft 5 in)

FEATURES:
Angular fuselage; starboard tail
rotor; port tailplane; two laterally-
mounted Klimov TV3-117VMA
turboshafts; fixed wheeled
undercarriage

Mi-24/-25/-35 'Hind' RUSSIA

Mi-24

Attack, assault helicopter used, additionally, in support of Special Forces operations.

SPECIFICATION:

USED BY:
Variants operated by the armies or air forces of Afghanistan, Algeria, Angola, Armenia, Azerbaijan, Belarus, Bosnia-Herzegovina, Bulgaria, Croatia, Cuba, Czech Republic, Eritrea, Ethiopia, Georgia, Guinea Republic, Hungary, India, Kazakhstan, Krgizia, Libya, Mexico, Mozambique, Nigeria, North Korea, Peru, Poland, Russia, Rwanda, Sierra Leone, Slovak Republic, Sri Lanka, Sudan, Syria, Tajikistan, Tanzania, Turkmenistan, Ukraine, US, Uzbekistan, Vietnam, Yemen and Zimbabwe

CONTRACTOR:
MIL, Russia

ACCOMMODATION:
Pilot and WSO

PERFORMANCE:
MAX SPEED: 172 kts (320 km/h)
COMBAT RADIUS: (internal fuel) 86 nm (160 km)

ARMAMENT:
INTERNAL GUN: one 12.7 mm four-barrel Gatling-type machine gun in undernose turret
HARDPOINTS: four pylons on stub wings, and twin rails under endplate
MAX WEAPON LOAD: 2860 kg (6305 lb)
REPRESENTATIVE WEAPONS:
AA-8 'Aphid', AA-11 'Archer' or Igla AAMS; AT-2 ATGWS; 57 mm rocket pods; 80 mm, 130 mm or 240 mm rockets; twin-barrel 23 mm gun pod; external fuel tanks

DIMENSIONS:
MAIN ROTOR DIAMETER: 17.3 m (56 ft 9 in)
LENGTH: 21.3 m (70 ft)
HEIGHT: 5.1 m (16 ft 8 in)

FEATURES:
Tandem cockpit; undernose sensor fairings on some versions; port tail rotor; two Klimov TV3-117 MT turboshafts; fixed wheeled undercarriage

ка 50/-52 Hokum-A/-B RUSSIA

Close support helicopter operated, additionally, in support of Special Forces.

SPECIFICATION:

USED BY:
Russian forces

CONTRACTOR:
Kamov, Russia

ACCOMMODATION:
ка-50: one pilot on Zvelda K-37-800 ejection seat; ка-52: two pilots on same ejection seats

PERFORMANCE:
MAX SPEED: 210 kts (390 km/h)
RANGE: 595 nm (1100 km)

ARMAMENT:
INTERNAL GUN: 30 mm cannon on starboard fuselage
HARDPOINTS: four pylons on stub wings
MAX WEAPON LOAD: 3000 kg (6610 lb)
REPRESENTATIVE WEAPONS: AA-11 'Archer' AAMS; AS-12 'Kegler' ARMS; AT-6 ATGWS; 80 mm or 122 mm rocket pods; FAB-500 bombs; external fuel tanks

DIMENSIONS:
ROTOR DIAMETER: (each) 14.5 m (47 ft 7 in)
LENGTH: 16.0 m (52 ft 6 in)
HEIGHT: 4.9 m (16 ft 2 in)

FEATURES:
E-O fairings under nose; small twin fin tailplane; single main fin; two Klimov TV3-117VMA turboshafts; retractable wheeled undercarriage

AH-2A **Rooivalk** SOUTH AFRICA

Attack helicopter operated in support of ground operations.

SPECIFICATION:

USED BY:
South African air force

CONTRACTOR:
Denel Aviation (Atlas), SA

ACCOMMODATION:
Two pilots

PERFORMANCE:
MAX SPEED: (PAH-1), 167 kts
(309 km/h)
RANGE: 720 nm (1,335 km)

ARMAMENT:
INTERNAL GUN: F2 20 mm cannon
in undernose turret
HARDPOINTS: six pylons (three on
each stub wing)
MAX WEAPON LOAD: 2032 kg
(4480 lb)
REPRESENTATIVE WEAPONS: Mistral
AAMS; Mokapa ATGWS; 68 mm
FFAR pods

DIMENSIONS:
MAIN ROTOR DIAMETER: 15.6 m
(51 ft 1 in)
LENGTH: 18.7 m (61 ft 5 in)
HEIGHT: 5.2 m (17 ft)

FEATURES:
Tandem cockpit; starboard tail
rotor; port tailplane; two
Turbomeca Makila 1K2
turboshafts; fixed wheeled
undercarriage

WG.13 Lynx UK

Naval and battlefield helicopter used, additionally, for the insertion and extraction of maritime Special Forces.

SPECIFICATION:

USED BY:
Variants operated by navies, marines and armies of Brazil, Denmark, France, Norway, Germany, Malaysia, Netherlands, Nigeria, Oman, Portugal, South Africa, South Korea and the UK

CONTRACTOR:
Westland, UK

ACCOMMODATION:
One pilot and one WSO (naval) or two pilots plus ten troops (battlefield) Army/Navy Super Lynx

PERFORMANCE:
MAX SPEED: 145 kts (269 km/h) 138 kts (256 km/h)
RADIUS OF ACTION: 292 nm (540 km); 320 nm (593 km)

ARMAMENT:
INTERNAL GUN: provision for door-mounted 7.62 mm GPMG or 0.5 in (12.7 mm) M3 machine gun
HARDPOINTS: two pylons (battlefield), or four (naval)
MAX WEAPON LOAD: 3949 kg (8707 lb) battlefield or 4618 kg (10,181 lb) naval

REPRESENTATIVE WEAPONS:
BATTLEFIELD: HOT, Hellfire or TOW ATGWs; FFAR pods; 7.62 mm machine gun or 20 mm cannon pods
NAVAL-ASW: Mk 44/46, A244S or Sting Ray torpedoes; depth charges
NAVAL-ASV: Sea Skua, Penguin or Marte ASMs; 7.62 mm machine guns or 20 mm cannon pods

DIMENSIONS:
Main rotor Army/Navy Super Lynx
DIAMETER: 12.8 m (42 ft); 12.8 m (42 ft)
LENGTH: 15.1 m (49 ft 9 in); 15.2 m (50 ft)
HEIGHT: 3.5 m (11 ft 6 in); 3.7 m (12 ft)

FEATURES:
Side-by-side cockpit; square windows in fuselage; port tail rotor; starboard tailplane; two R-R Gem 42-1 turboshafts; skid (army) or fixed wheeled undercarriage (naval and AH.9)

HC Mk 4 Sea King UK

Sea King HC Mk 4 (Commando)

Medium-lift naval and battlefield helicopter used, especially, by the UK's amphibious and maritime Special Forces.

SPECIFICATION:

USED BY:
Variants operated by navies, marines and air forces of Australia, Belgium, Egypt, Germany, India, Norway, Pakistan, Qatar and the UK

CONTRACTOR:
Westland, UK

ACCOMMODATION:
Two pilots plus two WSOs (ASW/ASVW) or two pilots plus 28 troops (Sea King C.4/Commando) or 3628 kg (8000 lb) external slung cargo

PERFORMANCE:
MAX SPEED: 122 kts (226 km/h)
RANGE: (Commando) 300 nm (556 km)

ARMAMENT:
INTERNAL GUN: one 7.62 mm GPMG, starboard door mounted
HARDPOINTS: four
MAX WEAPON LOAD: n/a
REPRESENTATIVE WEAPONS: Sea Eagle or Exocet ASMs; Mk 46; A224S; Sting Ray torpedoes; depth charges

DIMENSIONS:
MAIN ROTOR DIAMETER: 18.9 m (62 ft)
LENGTH: 22.1 m (72 ft 8 in)
HEIGHT: 5.1 m (16 ft 10 in)

FEATURES:
'Boat-hulled' fuselage; port tail rotor; two R-R Gnome H.1400-1T turboshafts; outrigger sponsons for retractable wheeled undercarriage

AH-64 Apache USA

Attack and reconnaissance helicopter used, additionally, in support of Special Forces.

SPECIFICATION:

USED BY:
Variants operated by marines, armies and air forces of Egypt, Greece, Israel, Netherlands, Saudi Arabia, Singapore, UAE, UK and the US

CONTRACTOR:
Boeing, US. Under licence in the UK by Augusta/Westland

ACCOMMODATION:
Two pilots

PERFORMANCE:
MAX SPEED: 197 kts (365 km/h)
RANGE: (AH-64D) 220 nm (407 km)

ARMAMENT:
INTERNAL GUN: M230 30 mm Chain Gun in undernose mounting

HARDPOINTS: four (plus two planned) pylons
MAX WEAPON LOAD: n/a
REPRESENTATIVE WEAPONS: Mistral, Sidewinder, Starstreak or Stinger AAMS; Hellfire ATGWS; 2.75 in FFAR pods

DIMENSIONS:
MAIN ROTOR DIAMETER: 14.6 m (48 ft)
LENGTH: 17.8 m (58 ft 3 in)
HEIGHT: (AH-64D) 4.9 m (16 ft 3 in)

FEATURES:
Tandem cockpit; two GE T700-GE-701C turboshaft; port tail rotor; fixed wheeled undercarriage

UH-1 Iroquois/Bell 204/205/212 USA

UH-1

Utility helicopter (known as the Huey) used, additionally, to insert, extract and support Special Forces. Dimensions here are for the 204/205; the 212 is slightly larger and can carry up to fourteen passengers.

SPECIFICATION:

USED BY:
Variants operated by marines, air forces and armies of Argentina, Austria, Bolivia, Bosnia-Herzegovina, Brazil, Chile, Colombia, Dominican Republic, El Salvador, Germany, Greece, Indonesia, Iran, Italy, Libya, Mexico, Morocco, Myanmar, Oman, Pakistan, Panama, Paraguay, Philippines, Singapore, Thailand, Tunisia, Turkey, UAE, Venezuela, US and Zambia

CONTRACTOR:
Bell Helicopter Textron Inc, US. Under licence in Germany, Italy, Japan and Thailand

ACCOMMODATION:
2 flight crew plus 8 passengers (204) and 11-14 passengers (205)

PERFORMANCE:
MAX SPEED:(UH-1C) 128 kts (238 km/h)
RANGE: (UH-1C) 332 nm (615 km)

ARMAMENT: (OPTIONAL)
INTERNAL GUN: 7.62 mm, 12.7 mm machine guns or 20 mm cannon in cabin
HARDPOINTS: four pylons
MAX WEAPON LOAD: n/a
REPRESENTATIVE WEAPONS: 2.75 in, 68 mm, 71 mm, 81 mm rocket pods; 12.7 mm machine gun or 20 mm cannon pods

DIMENSIONS:
(UH-1D)
MAIN ROTOR DIAMETER: 14.6 m (48 ft)
LENGTH: 16.4 m (53 ft 11 in)
HEIGHT: 4.1 m (13 ft 5 in)

FEATURES:
Squat fuselage; tail rotor – port on 204, starboard on 205; one Lycoming T53-L turboshaft; skid undercarriage

S-70A/UH-60 Black Hawk USA

Battlefield helicopter also operated in support of Special Forces.

SPECIFICATION:

USED BY:
Variants operated by armies and air forces of Argentina, Australia, Austria, Bahrain, Brazil, Brunei, Chile, China, Colombia, Egypt, Israel, Japan, Jordan, Malaysia, Mexico, Morocco, Philippines, Saudi Arabia, South Korea, Taiwan, Turkey and the US

CONTRACTOR:
Sikorsky, USA

ACCOMMODATION:
Three flight crew plus 11 troops or 4082 kg (9000 lb) external cargo sling

PERFORMANCE:
MAX SPEED: (UH-60L/Q) 194 kts (359 km/h)
RANGE: (with external tanks) 1200 nm (2222 km)

ARMAMENT: (OPTIONAL)
INTERNAL GUNS: provision for two 7.62 mm Miniguns or 0.5 in (12.7 mm) GECAL 50 machine guns in fuselage doors
HARDPOINTS: four mounted on the outrigger ESSS
MAX WEAPON LOAD: (ESSS) 2268 kg (5000 lb)
REPRESENTATIVE WEAPONS: (ESSS) Stinger AAMs; Hellfire ATGWs; 2.75 in FFAR pod; mine dispensers; ECM pods; external fuel tanks

DIMENSIONS:
MAIN ROTOR DIAMETER: 16.7 m (53 ft 8 in)
LENGTH: 19.8 m (64 ft 10 in)
HEIGHT: 5.1 m (16 ft 10 in)

FEATURES:
Side-by-side cockpit; square windows in fuselage; starboard tail rotor; full tailplane at base of fin; two GE T700-GE-700/-701 turboshafts; fixed wheeled undercarriage

CH-47 Chinook USA

CH-47 lifting Special Operations Craft (Reverine) during Operation Telic, Iraq

Transport helicopter used, additionally, (as CH-47D) to insert, extract and support Special Forces especially in the US and UK. Operates from aircraft carriers in support of amphibious operations.

SPECIFICATION:

USED BY:
Variants operated by marines, air forces and armies of Argentina, Australia, Egypt, Greece, Iran, Italy, Japan, Libya, Morocco, Netherlands, Singapore, South Korea, Spain, Taiwan, Thailand, the UK and US

CONTRACTOR:
Boeing, US. Built under licence in Japan and Italy

ACCOMMODATION:
Two pilots plus crew chief plus 33-55 troops

PERFORMANCE:
MAX SPEED: 154 kts (285 km/h)
RADIUS OF ACTION: (MH-47E) 505 nm (935 km)

ARMAMENT:
INTERNAL GUNS: two or three pintle-mounted 7.62 mm M134 Miniguns or 0.5 in (12.7 mm) machine guns in cabin

DIMENSIONS:
ROTOR DIAMETER: 18.3 m (60 ft)
LENGTH: 30.1 m (98 ft 11 in)
HEIGHT: 5.7 m (18 ft 11 in)

FEATURES:
Twi-rotor configuration; two Honeywell (Lycoming) T55-L-712 turboshafts; fuselage sponsons; fixed wheeled undercarriage

RAH-66 Comanche USA

Stealth, attack, reconnaissance helicopter destined, additionally, to support Special Forces.

As this publication was going to press the US Army terminated its order for 1205 RAH-66 Comanche armed reconnaissance helicopters, saying that the system was too vulnerable to anti-aircraft threats and did not now fit in with future army plans.

SPECIFICATION:

USED BY:
US army (not yet in service)

CONTRACTOR:
Boeing/Sikorsky, USA

ACCOMMODATION:
Two pilots

PERFORMANCE:
MAX SPEED: 175 kts (324 km/h)
RADIUS OF ACTION: 150 nm
(278 km)

ARMAMENT:
INTERNAL GUN: XM301 20 mm
cannon in nose turret
HARDPOINTS: three in each
weapons bay (one each side) plus
two optional external pylons
MAX WEAPON LOAD: n/a
REPRESENTATIVE WEAPONS:
Stinger AAMS; Hellfire ATGWS;
2.75 in rocket pods

DIMENSIONS:
MAIN ROTOR DIAMETER: 12.2 m
(40 ft)
LENGTH: 14.3 m (46 ft 10 in)
HEIGHT: 3.4 m (11 ft 1 in)

FEATURES:
Smooth, stealthy exterior; two
LHTEC T800-LHT-801 turboshafts;
T-tail; 'fan-in-fin' tail rotor;
retractable undercarriage

AH-1 HueyCobra/Super Cobra USA

Attack helicopter used, additionally, to support Special Forces.

SPECIFICATION:

USED BY:
Variants operated in Bahrain, Iran, Israel, Japan, Jordan, Pakistan, South Korea, Thailand, Turkey and the US

CONTRACTOR:
Bell Helicopter Textron Inc, USA

ACCOMMODATION:
Two flight crew

PERFORMANCE:
MAX SPEED: 222 kts (411 km/h)
RADIUS OF ACTION: 125 nm (232 km)

ARMAMENT:
(AH-1Z)
INTERNAL GUN: M197 20 mm cannon in nose turret
HARDPOINTS: six pylons
MAX WEAPON LOAD: 1556 kg (3430 lb)
REPRESENTATIVE WEAPONS:
Sidewinder AAMS; TOW or Hellfire ATGWS; Maverick AGMS; 2.75 in rocket pods; 12.7 mm machine gun or 20 mm cannon pods

DIMENSIONS:
MAIN ROTOR DIAMETER: 14.6 m (48 ft)
LENGTH: 17.7 m (58 ft)
HEIGHT: 4.4 m (14 ft 7 in)

FEATURES:
Lateral intakes behind tandem cockpit; port tail rotor; two GE T700-GE-401 turboshafts; skid undercarriage

V-22 Osprey USA

Utility, tilt-wing aircraft
due in service with the
USMC, to support
amphibious operations.

SPECIFICATION:

USED BY:
US Navy, Marine Corps and Army

CONTRACTOR:
Bell/Boeing, USA

ACCOMMODATION:
Two pilots plus crew chief and up
to 24 combat-equipped troops

PERFORMANCE:
MAX SPEED: 305 kts (565 km/h)
RANGE: (VTO) 515 nm (953 km)

ARMAMENT:
INTERNAL GUN: possibly a
7.62 mm or 0.5 in (12.7 mm)
machine gun in nose turret

DIMENSIONS:
ROTOR DIAMETER: 11.6 m
(38 ft 1 in)
LENGTH: (wings folded) 19.2 m
(63 ft)
HEIGHT: (nacelles vertical) 6.7 m
(22 ft 1 in)

FEATURES:
Twin fins; two R-R (Allison)
T406-AD-400 turboshafts in
rotating nacelles at wingtips;
retractable wheeled
undercarriage

Transport:
Land,
Amphibians

ARIS ARK Tracked Amphibious Support Vehicle FRANCE

The ARK is based on the lower hull and running gear of the United Defense M548 tracked cargo carrier. To improve the relatively poor amphibious capability of the M548, the ARK features an extended light alloy bow on the front of the vehicle and the engine compartment is now completely watertight. The extended bow was designed to offer the minimum of hydrodynamic drag. The cab has also been redesigned and a new snorkel-type device has been fitted to the cab rear to provide air for the engine. Hydraulic power for water propulsion is generated by two variable displacement hydraulic pumps. If required, the ARK can be carried inside a transport aircraft or slung under a heavy lift helicopter.

SPECIFICATION:

OPERATED BY:
Italian amphibious forces

CONTRACTOR:
Applicazioni Rielaborazioni Impianti Speciali (ARIS) SpA, Lomabardore, Italy

FEATURES:
CAB SEATING: one plus one
WEIGHT: (kerb) 7600 kg; (GVW) 12, 800 kg
MAX LOAD: 5200 kg
POWER TO WEIGHT RATIO: 16.16 hp/tonne
LENGTH: 6.96 m
WIDTH: 2.45 m
HEIGHT: (unloaded) 2.767 m
GROUND CLEARANCE: 0.41-0.45 m
MAX SPEED: (road) 60 km/h; (water) 6 kts
RANGE: (road) >500 km
MAX GRADIENT: 60%
MAX SIDE SLOPE: 30%
FORDING: amphibious
ENGINE: Detroit Diesel 6v-52 6-cylinder water-cooled two-stroke diesel developing 202 hp
TRANSMISSION: Allison automatic with four forward and one reverse gears

EXTRA FEATURES:
Water jet intakes and exhaust nozzles under bow; forward cockpit; large, open body (can be covered with a canvas hood; rear tailgate for loading

IVECO Model 6640G Amphibious Cargo Carrier ITALY

IVECO Model 6640 G 2000 kg amphibious cargo carrier with tarpaulin cover

This vehicle, announced in 1980, is very similar to the earlier IVECO Model 6640A (4 x 4) amphibious cargo carrier. The 6640G has a much greater weight due to stronger construction and a slightly longer wheelbase; it also has a more powerful diesel engine coupled to automatic transmission and is propelled in the water by a water-jet.

SPECIFICATION:

OPERATED BY:
Italian amphibious forces

CONTRACTOR:
IVECO SpA, Bolzano, Italy

FEATURES:
CAB SEATING: one plus two
CONFIGURATION: 4 x 4
WEIGHT: (kerb) 6700 kg; (loaded) 8700 kg; (on front axle, loaded) 3400 kg; (on rear axle, loaded) 5300 kg
MAX LOAD: 2000 kg
LOAD AREA: 3.21 x 1.95 m
LENGTH: 8.2 m
WIDTH: 2.5 m
HEIGHT: (cab) approx 2.7 m; (tarpaulin) 3.16 m
GROUND CLEARANCE: 0.35 m
TRACK: 1.96 m
WHEELBASE: 3.1 m
ANGLE OF APPROACH/DEPARTURE: 30°/25°
MAX SPEED: (road) 100 km/h; (water, propelled by water-jet) 11 km/h
RANGE: (road) >600 km; (water, propelled by water-jet) >5 hours
MAX GRADIENT: 60%
MAX SIDE SLOPE: 30%

FORDING: amphibious
ENGINE: Model 8062.24 6-cylinder inline turbocharged water-cooled four-stroke diesel developing 195 hp at 3200 rpm (6640 H, 220 hp at 3000 rpm)
TRANSMISSION: automatic, three forward and one reverse gears with power take-off for waterjet
STEERING: power assisted
TURNING RADIUS: (land) 7.5 m
TYRES: 14.5 x 20 PS 12 (13.00 x 20 optional)

EXTRA FEATURES:
Four wheels; horizontal fenders around hull; forward control with large, open cargo area aft

DAC 2.65 FAEG Amphibious Vehicle ROMANIA

The DAC 2.65 FAEG amphibious vehicle is, in effect, a light, two-seater 4 x 4 vehicle that is kept afloat when crossing waterways or swamps by four floats on side struts. When afloat it is driven by a propeller with an adjustable immersion depth to deal with shallow water. The propeller height can be adjusted from the dashboard and it is driven from the main engine by two reduction gears manually engaged once afloat. Steering is carried out using the normal steering wheel.

SPECIFICATION:

OPERATED BY:
Romanian army

CONTRACTOR:
ROMAN SA, Brasov, Romania

FEATURES:
CAB SEATING: one plus one
CONFIGURATION: 4 x 4
WEIGHT: (laden) 2100 kg;
(unladen) 1700 kg; (permissible front axle load) 1140 kg;
(permissible rear axle load) 960 kg
PAYLOAD: 400 kg
LENGTH: 3.45 m
WIDTH: 2.075 m
HEIGHT: (cab, laden) 2.04 m; (cab, unladen) 2.05 m; (over floats) 2.5 m; (loading platform) 0.93 m
GROUND CLEARANCE: 0.26 m
WHEELBASE: 1.634 m
MAX SPEED: (road) 50 km/h
FUEL CAPACITY: 40 litres
MAX GRADIENT: 73%
SIDESLOPE: 66%
FORDING: amphibious
VERTICAL STEP: 0.26 m
DITCH CROSSING: 0.54 m
ENGINE: 102.13.MAS 1.397 litre 4-cylinder in-line water-cooled four-stroke diesel developing 62 hp at 5000 rpm
TRANSMISSION: manual, lockable centre differential
TRANSFER BOX: two-speed
STEERING: mechanical on all wheels via steering cables
TYRES: 31 x 15, 5/15 tubeless

EXTRA FEATURES:
4 x 4 appearance with propeller; large floats either side when at sea

PTS, PTS-M and PTS-2 Tracked Amphibious Vehicles

RUSSIA

Ukrainian Army PTS-2 with trim vane erected ready for amphibious operation

These three vehicles are essentially similar and are based on the elongated chassis of the ATS-59 tracked artillery tractor. The vehicles were designed to carry 5000 kg on land or 10,000 kg on water, or up to 70 personnel. In the ambulance role, up to 12 stretchers can be carried in the open cargo area. The PTS-M has also been used to lay portable trackway across beach areas.

SPECIFICATION:

OPERATED BY:
Armies of Algeria, Angola, Bulgaria, Congo, Cuba, Egypt, India, Iran, Latvia, Libya, Poland, Serbia and Montenegro, Tanzania, Vietnam and Yemen

CONTRACTOR:
Coral Small State Enterprise, St Petersburg, Russia

FEATURES:
CAB SEATING: one plus one (up to 70 troops in rear)
WEIGHT: (empty) 17,700 kg; (loaded, land) 22,700 kg; (loaded, water) 27,700 kg
MAX LOAD: (land) 5000 kg; (water) 10,000 kg
LOAD AREA: 7.9 x 2.6 m
LENGTH: 11.426 m
WIDTH: 3.3 m
HEIGHT: 2.65 m
GROUND CLEARANCE: (loaded) 0.4 m
TRACK: 2.8 m
TRACK WIDTH: 480 mm
LENGTH OF TRACK ON GROUND: 5.63 m

GROUND PRESSURE: (empty) 0.382 kg/cm; (with 5000 kg load) 0.483 kg/cm; (with 10,000 kg load) 0.582 kg/cm
MAX SPEED: (dirt road, with 5000 kg load) 25-27 km/h; (road, with 5000 kg load) 42 km/h; (water, with 10,000 kg load) 10.6 km/h; (water, towing 5000 kg trailer) 8.5 km/h
RANGE: (land, 5000 kg load) up to 380 km (water, 10,000 kg load) 12 km
FUEL CAPACITY: 705 litres
MAX GRADIENT: (empty) 60%; (loaded) 20%
VERTICAL OBSTACLE: 0.65 m
TRENCH: 2.5 m
ENGINE: V-54P V-12 diesel developing 350 hp at 1800 rpm

EXTRA FEATURES:
Flush, flat-topped hull; cockpit starboard side forward

VAP 3550/1 3000 kg Amphibious Vehicle SPAIN

The VAP 3550/1 (4 x 4) 3000 kg amphibious vehicle was developed to meet Spanish Navy requirements for a vehicle to be launched from LSTs and other amphibious craft offshore, reach the coast under its own power and then travel inland over rough country. VAP is the export name of this vehicle, within Spain it is known as the Pegaso 3550. The VAP is fully amphibious, propelled in the water by two waterjets at the rear of the hull immediately behind the second axle. The two single water-jets are driven by a hydraulic system composed of a pump directly connected to the vehicle's engine and two hydraulic motors acting directly on the hydrojets. It features a pressurising system for the mechanical units in contact with the water which operates as soon as the VAP enters the water. When afloat, pivot turns can be accomplished.

SPECIFICATION:

OPERATED BY:
Armies of Egypt, Mexico and the Spanish Marines

CONTRACTOR:
IVECO Pegaso SA, Madrid, Spain

FEATURES:
CAB SEATING: one plus two (rear, up to 18)
CONFIGURATION: 4 x 4
WEIGHT: (laden) 12,500 kg; (unladen) 9500 kg
MAX LOAD: 3000 kg
LOAD AREA: 3.2 x 2.05 m
LENGTH: 8.85 m
WIDTH: 2.5 m
HEIGHT: (cab) 2.5 m; (crane) 2.83 m
GROUND CLEARANCE: 0.32 m
TRACK: 1.927 m
WHEELBASE: 3.45 m
ANGLE OF APPROACH/DEPARTURE: 33°/27°
MAX SPEED: (road) 87 km/h; (water) 5.5 kts
RANGE: (road) 800 km; (water) 80 km
FUEL CAPACITY: 250 litres
MAX GRADIENT: 60%
MAX SIDE SLOPE: 30%
FORDING: amphibious
ENGINE: Pegaso 9135/5 6.55 litre 6-cylinder inline turbocharged diesel developing 170 hp at 2600 rpm
TRANSMISSION: Pegaso manual, six forward and one reverse gears
TURNING RADIUS: 9 m
TYRES: 13.00 x 20

EXTRA FEATURES:
Sharply angled bow; four wheels; high sided with cockpit forwards; two sets of recessed steps each side of hull

Aquatrack Tracked 8000 kg Amphibious Vehicle UK

The Aquatrack tracked 8000 kg amphibious vehicle was developed by GKN Defence (now Alvis Vickers Limited) to provide a vehicle capable of carrying up to 8000 kg of payload or forty seated personnel in a fully amphibious environment and over a wide variety of terrains. Power is provided by a single diesel engine driving twin variable-pitch propellers in Kort nozzles. Twin rudders assist in allowing the vehicle to manoeuvre and operate fully laden in Sea State 5 at water speeds up to 13 km/h. The vehicle can operate in up to 3.05 m of plunging surf. It can also negotiate harsh terrain, mud, soft sand or frozen ground.

SPECIFICATION:

OPERATED BY:
Philippines Marine Corps

CONTRACTOR:
Alvis Vickers Limited, Shropshire, UK

FEATURES:
CAB SEATING: one plus one plus two
WEIGHT: (laden) approx 21,750 kg; (unladen) approx 13,750 kg
MAX LOAD: 8000 kg
LENGTH: 9.6 m
WIDTH: (min) 3.2 m
HEIGHT: approx 3.7 m
DECK HEIGHT: 1.43 m
LOAD AREA: 4.45 x 2.6 m
GROUND CLEARANCE: (at centre) 0.41 m
ANGLE OF APPROACH/DEPARTURE: 40°/40°
MAX SPEED: (land) 75 km/h; (water) 13 km/h
RANGE: (road) 500 km; (water, cruising) 70 km
FUEL CAPACITY: 400 litres
MAX GRADIENT: 50%
VERTICAL OBSTACLE: 0.5 m
TRENCH: 2 m
FORDING: amphibious
ENGINE: Deutz BF6 M1015 11.9 litre v-6 water-cooled diesel developing 322 bhp at 2300 rpm
TRANSMISSION: (land) x200-6 automatic, four forward and one reverse gears, with torque converter
TURNING CIRCLE: pivot turn

EXTRA FEATURES:
High-sided hull with enclosed cockpit over bow; one set of recessed, staggered steps each side of the hull

Advanced Amphibious Assault Vehicle – AAAV USA

AAAV at speed

Tracked, amphibious APC due into service in 2006 to replace the AAV7A1 (LVTP7). To be renamed the Littoral Fighting Vehicle.

SPECIFICATION:

OPERATED BY:
US Marine Corps

CONTRACTOR:
General Dynamics, Michigan, USA

FEATURES:
CREW: three plus 18
WEIGHT LOADED: 34,476 kg
WEIGHT EMPTY: 28,576 kg
GROUND PRESSURE: 0.625 kg/cm
LENGTH: (overall, land) 9.271 m; (overall, water) 10.566 m
WIDTH ACROSS SKIRTS: 3.632 m
HEIGHT TO TURRET ROOF: 3.20 m
GROUND CLEARANCE: 0.406 m
TRACK WIDTH: 533 mm
MAX ROAD SPEED: 72.41 km/h
MAX WATER SPEED: 37-46.61 km/h
TRANSITION MODE SPEED: 16.6 km/h
RANGE: (land) 643 km; (water) 121 km
FUEL CAPACITY: 1506 litres
ENGINE: MTU MT 883 ka-523 diesel developing 2700 hp in water mode and 850 hp in land mode
TRANSMISSION: Allison Transmission x4560
SUSPENSION: hydropneumatic (retractable)

ARMAMENT: (main) one 30 mm MK 44 cannon; (coaxial) one 7.62 mm M240 MG
AMMUNITION: (main) 200 (ready) plus 400 (stowed); (coaxial) 800 (ready) plus 1600 (stowed)

Amphibious Assault Vehicle – AAV7A1 (LVTP7 AAV) USA

AAV7A1

The AAV7A1 is a tracked, amphibious APC that is due to be replaced in US service in 2006 by the AAAV. The AAV7A1 has a boat-shaped hull with a nose that slopes backwards, down to the tracks: its sides are vertical but ribbed. It has six road wheels and a rear, drive sprocket. The driver's cupola is at the front left-hand side with the commander's cupola behind and central. A machine gun cupola is on the front right side.

SPECIFICATION:

OPERATED BY:
US Marine Corps

CONTRACTOR:
FMC Corporation, USA

FEATURES:
CREW: Three plus 25
COMBAT WEIGHT: 22,838 kg
UNLOADED WEIGHT: 17,441 kg
POWER TO WEIGHT RATIO:
17.51 hp/t
GROUND PRESSURE: 0.57 kg/cm
LENGTH: 8.16 m
WIDTH: 3.27 m
HEIGHT: (overall) 3.31 m
GROUND CLEARANCE: 0.406 m
TRACK: 2.609 m
TRACK WIDTH: 533 mm
LENGTH OF TRACK ON GROUND:
3.94 m
MAX SPEED: (road, forwards)
64 km/h; (water, waterjets)
13.5 km/h; (water, tracks) 7.2 km/h
FUEL CAPACITY: 681 litres
MAX RANGE: (land at 40 km/h)
482 km
MAX ENDURANCE (WATER): 7 hours
FORDING: amphibious
GRADIENT: 60%
SIDE SLOPE: 40%
VERTICAL OBSTACLE: 0.914 m
TRENCH: 2.438 m
TURNING RADIUS: pivot
ENGINE: Detroit Diesel model
8V-53T, 8-cylinder, water-cooled,
turbocharged diesel developing
400 hp at 2800 rpm
TRANSMISSION: HS-400 with
hydraulic torque converter, four
forward and two reverse ratios
ARMAMENT: (main) one 12.7 mm
M85 MG (one 40 mm MK 19
grenade launcher and one 12.7
mm machine gun)
AMMUNITION: (12.7 mm) 1000

LARC-5 4545 kg Amphibious Cargo Carrier USA

SPECIFICATION:

OPERATED BY:
Amphibious forces of Argentina,
Australia, Philippines, Portugal,
Singapore, Thailand and the us

CONTRACTOR:
ConDiesel Mobile Equipment,
Connecticut, usa (no longer
trading)

FEATURES:
CAB SEATING: one plus two
CONFIGURATION: 4 x 4
WEIGHT: (laden) 14,053 kg;
(unladen) 9508 kg
MAX LOAD: 4545 kg
LOAD AREA: 4.876 x 2.971 m
LENGTH: 10.07 m
WIDTH: 3.05 m
HEIGHT: (overall) 3.1 m; (reduced)
2.41 m
GROUND CLEARANCE: 0.406 m
TRACK: 2.565 m
WHEELBASE: 4.876 m
ANGLE OF APPROACH/DEPARTURE:
$27°/20.7°$
MAX SPEED: (road) 48.2 km/h;
(water) 13.92 km/h
RANGE: (land, laden) 322 km;
(land, unladen) 400 km; (water,
laden) 56 km; (water, unladen)
65 km
FUEL CAPACITY: 547.2 litres
MAX GRADIENT: 60%
MAX SIDE SLOPE: 25%
FORDING: amphibious
ENGINE: (early vehicles) 8-cylinder
petrol developing 300 hp at
3000 rpm; (late production
vehicles) Cummins v-8 water-
cooled four-stroke diesel
developing 300 hp
TURNING RADIUS: 13.26 m
SUSPENSION: rigid
TYRES: 18.00 x 25

EXTRA FEATURES:
Substantial rubber fending
around hull at deck level; stepped
deck

The LARC-5 (Lighter, Amphibious, Resupply, Cargo,
5 ton) (4 x 4) was developed by the Borg Warner
Corporation from 1958 under the direction of the
us Transportation Engineering Command at Fort
Eustis, Virginia. The vehicle was designed to carry
4545 kg of cargo, or 15 – 20 fully equipped troops
from ships offshore to the beach or, if required,
farther inland. It was issued on the scale of
thirty-four per Army light amphibious company.
The vehicle is propelled in the water by a
three-bladed propeller under the rear of the hull.

Transport:
Land, Light
Vehicles

LOHR Fardier FL 500 and FL 501 Light Vehicle FRANCE

SOFRAME Fardier FL 501

These light air-portable vehicles were developed by SOFRAMAG (later LOHR and now SOFRAME) for use by airborne troops. A C-130 or C-160 Transall transport aircraft can carry six FL 500s ready for air-dropping or 12 FL 500s for delivery as cargo. The SA 330 Puma helicopter can carry one FL 500 and one 120 mm mortar. The vehicle can tow a trailer or weapon such as a 120 mm TDA mortar, weighing a maximum of 500 kg.

SPECIFICATION:

USED BY:
French and Spanish airborne brigades

CONTRACTOR:
SOFRAME, Hangenbieten, France

FEATURES:
CAB SEATING: one
CONFIGURATION: 4 × 4
WEIGHT: (laden) 1,180 kg; (unladen) 680 kg
MAX LOAD: 500 kg
LOAD AREA: 1.93 m²
LENGTH: (laden) 2.41 m; (unladen) 2.375 m
WIDTH: 1.5 m
HEIGHT: (steering wheel) 1.18 m; (load area) 0.92 m
GROUND CLEARANCE: (laden) 0.2 m; (unladen) 0.26 m
TRACK: 1.26 m
WHEELBASE: 1.735 m
ANGLE OF APPROACH/DEPARTURE: 90°/90°
MAX SPEED: (road) 80 km/h
RANGE: (road) 200 km
FUEL CAPACITY: 25 litres
MAX GRADIENT: 60%
MAX SIDE SLOPE: 30%
VERTICAL OBSTACLE: 0.2 m
FORDING: 0.4 m
ENGINE: (FL 500) Citroen AK 2 flat twin petrol developing 29 hp (DIN) at 6750 rpm; (FL 501) Citroen VO6/630 flat twin, air-cooled petrol developing 36 hp at 5500 rpm
TURNING RADIUS: 4.8 m

EXTRA FEATURES:
'Bug-eye' headlights

SOFRAME VLA (Véhicule Léger Aermobile) FRANCE

Netherlands Army VLA

In service with the Royal Netherlands Army, the VLA is known as the Luchtmobiel Speciaal Voertuig, or LSV.

SPECIFICATION:

USED BY:
Netherlands airborne troops

CONTRACTOR:
SOFRAME, Hangenbieten, France

FEATURES:
SEATING: two plus four
CONFIGURATION: 4 x 4
WEIGHT EMPTY: 1350 kg
COMBAT WEIGHT: 2250 kg
MAX LOAD: 900 kg
TOWED LOAD: 1200 kg
LENGTH: (overall) 3.36 m
WIDTH: 1.72 m
HEIGHT: (body) 1.08 m;
(windscreen and roll bars folded)
1.32 m; (roll bar, laden) 1.72 m
(roll bar, laden) 1.79 m
GROUND CLEARANCE: (laden)
0.27 m; (unladen) 0.34 m
WHEELBASE: 1.965 m
TRACK: (front) 1.446 m
ANGLE OF APPROACH/DEPARTURE:
40°/50°

MAX SPEED: 80 km/h
RANGE: 700 km
FUEL CAPACITY: 80 litres
MAX GRADIENT: 60%
MAX SIDE SLOPE: 50%
FORDING: 0.55 m
VERTICAL OBSTACLE: 0.35 m
ENGINE: Peugeot XUD 9A
4-cylinder in-line diesel
developing 70 hp
TRANSMISSION: automatic with
four forward and one reverse
gears
TURNING RADIUS: 5.5 m

EXTRA FEATURES:
Unusual shape

M-240 Storm MultiMission Vehicle (MMV) ISRAEL

The M-240 Storm MultiMission Vehicle (MMV) was designed to fulfil several military functions including general utility, patrol and reconnaissance, command and anti-tank weapons vehicle.

SPECIFICATION:

USED BY:
Israeli Defence Forces

CONTRACTOR:
AIL, Nazareth Illit, Israel

FEATURES:
CAB SEATING: one plus three – five
CONFIGURATION: 4 x 4
GROSS VEHICLE WEIGHT: 2350 kg
MAX LOAD: (off road) 850 kg
LENGTH: (long frame) 4.5 m;
(short frame) 4.15 m
WIDTH: 1.676 m
HEIGHT: (overall) 2.02 m
GROUND CLEARANCE: 0.24 m
WHEELBASE: 2.63 m
ANGLE OF APPROACH/DEPARTURE:
(SWB) 40°/37°; (LWB) 40°/26.5°
MAX SPEED: 160 km/h
FUEL CAPACITY: 76 litres
RANGE: (petrol) 450 km;
(diesel) 600 km
FORDING: 0.45 m
MAX GRADIENT: 75%
VERTICAL OBSTACLE: 0.35 m

ENGINE: Chrysler 3.983 litre 6-cylinder in-line petrol with fuel injection developing 180 hp at 4700 rpm, fitted with Vortox two-stage air cleaner or VW 2.498 litre 4-cylinder in-line turbo-charged diesel developing 118 hp at 4200 rpm
TRANSMISSION: Aisin AX15 with five forward and one reverse gears

EXTRA FEATURES:
High anti-roll bar on patrol version

LuAZ-96 Amphibious Battlefield Support Vehicle RUSSIA

LuAZ-967 M

The driver sits immediately behind the windscreen which folds forward to reduce the overall height. His seat is on the centreline of the vehicle and can be folded down so that he can drive lying flat. The steering column and steering wheel can also be lowered. As a battlefield medical evacuation vehicle, the LuAZ-967 M has two folding seats for walking wounded as well as two stretchers, but its normal load is two patients plus the driver. It is fully amphibious, being propelled in the water by its wheels. A treadway is carried on each side of the vehicle for crossing trenches and other obstacles. There is a winch with a capacity of 200 kg and 100 m of cable mounted at the front of the vehicle; this winch may be used to winch in wounded personnel on a canvas mat. The LuAZ-967 M is also used by airborne forces as a light support vehicle and as a weapon carrier; in the latter role it has been observed carrying an AGS-17 grenade launcher, the 9K111 Fagot anti-tank guided missile and an 82 mm B-10 recoilless rifle.

SPECIFICATION:

USED BY:
Russian armed forces

CONTRACTOR:
Lutsk Motor Vehicle Plant,
Ukraine

FEATURES:
SEATING: one plus two, or three
CONFIGURATION: 4 x 4
WEIGHT: (empty) 930 kg;
(loaded) 1350 kg
MAX LOAD: 420 kg
MAX TOWED LOAD: 300 kg
LENGTH: 3.682 m
WIDTH: 1.74 m
HEIGHT: (incl windscreen) 1.625 m
GROUND CLEARANCE: 0.285 m
WHEELBASE: 1.8 m
ANGLE OF APPROACH/DEPARTURE:
34°/36°
MAX ROAD SPEED: 75 km/h
MAX WATER SPEED: 5-6 km/h
RANGE: 285 km
FUEL CAPACITY: 34 litres
GRADIENT: 58%
FORDING: amphibious
ENGINE: MeMZ-967A 4-cylinder
air-cooled petrol developing
37 hp at 4300 rpm
TRANSMISSION: manual, four
forward and one reverse gears,
plus cross-country gear
TURNING RADIUS: 5.8 m

EXTRA FEATURES:
Central driving position; folding
windscreen

Jakkals Lightweight Airborne Vehicle SOUTH AFRICA

Jakkals (4 x 4) LAV carrying four FT5 light anti-tank weapon tubes

The Jakkals (Jackal) lightweight airborne vehicle is a 4 x 4 utility vehicle designed for use by airborne forces. It resembles a small jeep and is conventional in layout, with the engine at the front and the driver and single passenger in the centre; space behind the seats is very limited. It is assembled using standard, commonly available vehicle components, including the engine.

SPECIFICATION:

USED BY:
South African National Defence Forces

CONTRACTOR:
Armscor, Pretoria, South Africa

FEATURES:
SEATING: two
CONFIGURATION: 4 x 4
WEIGHT: (tractor) 940 kg; (trailer) 180 kg
MAX LOAD: (tractor) 350 kg
TOWED LOAD: 350 kg
LENGTH: 2.408 m
WIDTH: (tractor) 1.211 m; (trailer) 1.191 m
HEIGHT: (packed, tractor) 0.963 m; (packed, trailer) 0.91 m (operational) 1.23 m
GROUND CLEARANCE: 0.19 m
TRACK: 1.027 m
WHEELBASE: 1.539 m
ANGLE OF APPROACH/DEPARTURE: 45/44°
RANGE: 200 km
FUEL CAPACITY: 60 litres
ENGINE: 1.6 litre 4-cylinder petrol developing 63 hp at 5200 rpm
TRANSMISSION: manual, synchromesh, with four forward and one reverse gears
TURNING CIRCLE: 9.74 m

EINSA Model MM-1 MATV SPAIN

EINSA Multipurpose All-Terrain Vehicle

The EINSA Model MM-1 Multipurpose All-Terrain Vehicle (MATC) is a lightweight 4 x 4 vehicle capable of being used as a personnel carrier, supplies carrier or light tractor. Up to twelve vehicles can be carried stacked in the hold of a C-130 transport aircraft and up to six vehicles can be paradropped together, each with a load of 400 kg. Vehicles can also be underslung from helicopters.

SPECIFICATION:

USED BY:
Spanish armed forces

CONTRACTOR:
Equipos Industriales de Manutencion SA (EINSA), Madrid, Spain

FEATURES:
SEATING: one (up to six in rear)
CONFIGURATION: 4 x 4
WEIGHT: (on road) 1650 kg
LOAD: 1000 kg
TOWED LOAD: 1850 kg
LENGTH: (air drop) 2.64 m
WIDTH: 1.78 m
HEIGHT: (load platform, loaded) 0.89 m
TRACK: 1.48 m
WHEELBASE: 1.88 m
ANGLE OF APPROACH/DEPARTURE: 90°/60-90°
MAX SPEED: 65-92 km/h according to engine
GRADIENT: (max load) 60%
MAX SIDE SLOPE: 40%
FORDING: 0.45 m
ENGINE: water-cooled diesel developing 68, 74 or 90 hp
TRANSMISSION: automatic with torque converter with four forward and one reverse gears

Santana Model 88 Militar Light Vehicle SPAIN

Santana Model 88 Militar prepared for deep wading

Metalurgica de Santa Ana (to become known as
Santana, and later Santana-Motor S.A.) began
manufacturing licence-produced Land Rover (4 x 4)
light vehicles in 1958, the company's association
with Land Rover ending in 1985, although Santana-
manufactured components were used in Land
Rover models until the end of the 1980s. Apart
from the basic personnel and load (up to 500 kg)
carried, the Model 88 Militar can be readily
converted to a number of special purpose
configurations and weapon carriers. The Model 88
Militar may also be paradropped on a platform
which, together with the parachute and fittings,
weighs 2200 kg.

SPECIFICATION:

USED BY:
Egyptian, Moroccan and Spanish
armed forces and others

CONTRACTOR:
Santana-Motor SA, Madrid, Spain

FEATURES:
CAB SEATING: one plus one (up to
four in rear)
CONFIGURATION: 4 x 4
WEIGHT: (max) 2160 kg; (empty)
1660 kg
LOAD: 500 kg
LENGTH: 3.725 m
WIDTH: 1.574 m
HEIGHT: (with hood) 1.905 m
TRACK: 1.309 m
WHEELBASE: 2.235 m
FUEL CAPACITY: 97 litres
ANGLE OF APPROACH/DEPARTURE:
48°/32°
ENGINE: 2.286 litre 4-cylinder
in-line water-cooled petrol
developing 61 hp at 4000 rpm or
2.286 litre 4-cylinder in-line
water-cooled diesel developing
59 hp at 4000 rpm
TRANSMISSION: manual with four
forward and one reverse gears
TURNING RADIUS: 6.25 m

EXTRA FEATURES:
Similar to a Land Rover

Santana Model 109 Militar Light Vehicle SPAIN

Santana Model 109 prepared for parachuting

A deep wading version of the Model 109 Militar was produced and is in service with the Spanish Marines. The Model 109 Militar can also be prepared for parachute drops by lashing it to a special platform in a stripped-down state. The complete load of prepared vehicle, fixtures and platform weighs 2800 kg.

SPECIFICATION:

USED BY:
Egyptian, Moroccan and Spanish armed forces (including marines) and others

CONTRACTOR:
Santana-Motor SA, Madrid, Spain

FEATURES:
CAB SEATING: one plus one (plus six in rear)
CONFIGURATION: 4 x 4
WEIGHT: (max) 3150 kg; (empty) 1890 kg
MAX LOAD: 1000 kg
LENGTH: 4.546 m
WIDTH: 1.574 m
HEIGHT: (with hood) 2.008 m
TRACK: 1.309 m
WHEELBASE: 2.768 m
FUEL CAPACITY: 114 litres
ANGLE OF APPROACH/DEPARTURE: 52°/31°
ENGINE: (basic model) 2.286 litre 4-cylinder in-line water-cooled petrol developing 61 hp at 4000 rpm or variations
TRANSMISSION: manual with four forward and one reverse gears
TURNING RADIUS: 6.25 m

EXTRA FEATURES:
Similar to a Land Rover

Land Rover Defender UK

Land Rover Defender XD 110

A Weapons Mount Installation Kit was developed for the UK MOD and, following minimal preparation, can be fitted to any Defender XD 110 by four soldiers in under four hours. 16 Air Assault Brigade currently operate approaching 200 so-converted vehicles. This gives the vehicles a defensive/offensive capability by allowing the mounting and stable firing of heavy machine guns, grenade launchers or anti-armour missiles from a ring or pulpit mount attached to a full-length roll protection cage. A second, forward firing light machine is also fitted to the vehicle. The Defender XD TUL/TUM contract required for the first time that vehicles be delivered with enhanced cold weather and wading abilities built in. Originally two programmes, these merged for practical and cost reasons and a total of 686 Winter Water Defender XD vehicles were delivered. The bulk of these are operated by the Royal Marines. These vehicles are modified to operate in temperatures as low as -49°C, and following a maximum of two hours preparation can wade in 1.5 m of seawater for up to six minutes.

SPECIFICATION:

USED BY:
British armed forces (especially the Royal Marines and Parachute Regiment) and many others worldwide

CONTRACTOR:
Land Rover, Warwick, UK

FEATURES:
(XD 110)
SEATING: one plus one (eight in rear)
CONFIGURATION: 4 x 4
WEIGHT: (GVW) 3344 kg
MAX LOAD: 1200 kg
TOWED LOAD: up to 4000 kg
LENGTH: 4.55 m
WIDTH: 1.79 m
HEIGHT: 2.08 m
GROUND CLEARANCE: 0.23 m
TRACK: (front) 1.52 m; (rear) 1.51 m
WHEELBASE: 2.79 m
FUEL CAPACITY: 82 litres
FORDING: 0.6 m (Winter Water, 1.5 m of sea water for six minutes)
ENGINE: 2.5 litre 4-cylinder in-line direct injection turbocharged water-cooled diesel developing 111 hp at 4000 rpm
TRANSMISSION: manual, five forward and one reverse gears

EXTRA FEATURES:
Air intake on offside windscreen; side-mounted spare tyre

Supacat Mk III All Terrain Mobile Platform (ATMP) UK

Supacat ATMP Mk III towing an SLLPT trailer and 105 mm light gun

The Supacat Mk III is a 6 x 6 low ground pressure vehicle running on 31 x 15.5 x 15 wide section low-pressure tyres. The Supacat has a limited amphibious capability and can be fitted with tracks for extremely soft conditions and for deep snow. It is primarily an open vehicle but can be fitted with a variety of hard, soft or lightweight removable canopies. The Supacat is fully air-portable. Schemes are approved for single, dual and quadruple vehicle underslung loads under suitable helicopters such as the Sea King (1), Black Hawk (2) and Chinook (4). Two Supacats can be driven into the Chinook and the vehicle is compatible with the EH 101. Supacat can be air-dropped and a number of schemes have been proved. These include two vehicles on one platform or one vehicle plus trailer or mixed stores. Supacats have been airlifted in a variety of aircraft such as the C-130 Hercules and trials have been carried out for the CASA 235. Vehicles can be stacked one on the other for air transport, using the vehicle's own equipment. Supacats can be used for troop transport and as weapon platforms and carriers.

SPECIFICATION:

USED BY:
Canadian, Mexican, UK (including the Royal Marines) and US armed forces and one undisclosed Asian nation

CONTRACTOR:
Supacat Limited, Honiton, UK

FEATURES:
SEATING: one plus five
CONFIGURATION: 6 x 6
WEIGHT: (maximum) 2650 kg (3050 kg limited application); (empty) 1800 kg
PAYLOAD: 1600 kg
LOAD AREA: 1.445 x 1.87 m
TOWED LOAD: (ideal conditions) up to approx 2400 kg
LENGTH: 3.44 m
WIDTH: 2 m
HEIGHT: (roll bar) 1.87 m; (cab) 2.01 m; (folded down) 1.21 m; (load platform) 0.94 m
GROUND CLEARANCE: 0.215 m
TRACK: 1.601 m
WHEELBASE: 0.923 m + 0.923 m
ANGLE OF APPROACH/DEPARTURE: 57°/58°
MAX SPEED: (road) 64 km/h
FUEL CAPACITY: 63.6 litres
MAX GRADIENT: 100%
MAX SIDE SLOPE: 40°
VERTICAL OBSTACLE: 0.5 m
FORDING: amphibious

M151 Light Vehicle and Variants USA

M151A2

The body and chassis of the M151 are integral and are of all-welded construction. The layout of the vehicle is conventional, with the engine at the front and the crew area at the rear with a removable canvas top and side curtains and a windscreen that can be folded forward flat on the bonnet. Nearly all US armed forces' M151 models were replaced by the HMMWV series, apart from some which are retained by the US Marine Corps.

SPECIFICATION:

Variants in use by armies and Special Forces in over 100 countries including the Democratic Republic of Congo, Egypt, Gambia, Greece, Indonesia, Israel, South Korea, Netherlands, Pakistan, Peru, Philippines, Portugal, Saudi Arabia, Senegal, Singapore, Somalia, Spain (marines only), Thailand, Turkey, US (Marine Corps) and Venezuela

CONTRACTOR:
AM General Corporation, Indiana, USA

FEATURES:
(M151)
CAB SEATING: one plus three
CONFIGURATION: 4 x 4
WEIGHT: (empty) 1012 kg; (loaded) 1575 kg
WEIGHT ON FRONT AXLE: (empty) 574 kg
WEIGHT ON REAR AXLE: (loaded) 448 kg
MAX LOAD: (road) 554 kg; (cross-country) 362 kg
TOWED LOAD: (road) 970 kg; (cross-country) 680 kg

LENGTH: 3.352 m
WIDTH: 1.58 m
HEIGHT: (overall) 1.803 m; (reduced) 1.332 m
GROUND CLEARANCE: 0.26 m
TRACK: 1.346 m
WHEELBASE: 2.159 m
ANGLE OF APPROACH/DEPARTURE: 66°/37°
MAX SPEED: 106 km/h
RANGE: 482 km
FUEL CAPACITY: 56 litres
MAX GRADIENT: 60%
MAX SIDE SLOPE: 40%
FORDING: (without preparation) 0.533 m; (with preparation) 1.524 m
ENGINE: L-142 4-cylinder water-cooled OHV petrol developing 72 hp at 4000 rpm
TRANSMISSION: manual with four forward and one reverse gears
TURNING RADIUS: 5.486 m

EXTRA FEATURES:
Substantial anti-roll bar; Jeep-like construction

Transport: Land, Oversnow and ATV

Singapore Technologies Kinetics All Terrain Tracked Carrier (ATTC) SINGAPORE

Singapore Technologies Kinetics ATTC (in basic troop carrier configuration)

This All Terrain Tracked Carrier (ATTC) known as Bronco is a multipurpose articulated tracked carrier that can be configured to meet a wide range of payload requirements, from personnel or cargo carrier to command post and weapon platform. It was designed to traverse any type of terrain, including mud, snow and swamps. The vehicle can ford water obstacles up to 1.2 m deep and can float and swim following a minimum of preparation. The ATTC travels on heavy-duty seamless rubber tracks for low noise level running.

SPECIFICATION:

USED BY:
Singaporean armed forces

CONTRACTOR:
Singapore Technologies Kinetics, Singapore

FEATURES:
CAB SEATING: (front module) one plus five; (rear module) ten
WEIGHT: (enclosed version, kerb, total) 11,200 kg; (flatbed version, kerb, total) 10,700 kg; (GVW, both versions) 16,000 kg
PAYLOAD: (enclosed version) 4200 kg; (flatbed version) 4700 kg
LENGTH: 8.6 m
WIDTH: (over track) 2.3 m
HEIGHT: (overall) 2.2 m
TRACK WIDTH: 600 mm
MAX SPEED: (road) 60 km/h; (cross country) 25 km/h; (swimming) 5 km/h
GRADIENT: 60%
MAX SIDE SLOPE: 30%
VERTICAL OBSTACLE: 0.6 m
TRENCH: 1.5 m
FORDING: 1.2 m; amphibious with preparation
ENGINE: Caterpillar 3126B turbocharged diesel developing 350 hp at 2400 rpm
TRANSMISSION: Allison MD3560P fully automatic
STEERING: hydraulic, articulated

EXTRA FEATURES:
Close resemblance to the Alvis Hägglunds Vehicle Bandvagn BV 206

Alvis Hagglunds Vehicle Bandvagn BV 206 SWEDEN

Alvis Hagglunds Vehicle Bandvagn BV 206 all-terrain carrier

The BV 206 consists of two tracked units linked together with a steering unit, each unit consisting of a chassis with the body mounted on four rubber elements. The BV 206 is fully amphibious, being propelled in the water by its tracks.

SPECIFICATION:

USED BY:
More than 11,000 ordered or in military service with Brazil, Canada, Chile, China, Finland, France, Germany, Italy, South Korea, Malaysia, Netherlands, Norway, Pakistan, Singapore, Spain, Sweden, UK and US Army

CONTRACTOR:
Alvis Hagglunds AB, Ornskoldsvik, Sweden

FEATURES:
(cargo carrier)
CAB SEATING: (front unit) five to six; (rear unit) 11
WEIGHT: (empty) 4490 kg; (loaded) 6740 kg
WEIGHT OF FRONT UNIT: (empty) 2740 kg
WEIGHT OF REAR UNIT: (empty) 1730 kg
MAX LOAD: 2250 kg; (front unit) 610 kg; (rear unit) 1640 kg
TOWED LOAD: 2500 kg
LOAD AREA: (front unit) 0.81 x 1.4 m; (rear unit) 2.5 x 1.4 m
LENGTH: 6.9 m
WIDTH: 1.87 or 2 m
HEIGHT: 2.4 m

GROUND CLEARANCE: 0.35 m
TRACK WIDTH: 620 mm
MAX SPEED: (road) 52 km/h; (water) 3 km/h
MAX GRADIENT: (hard surface) 100%; (snow) 30%
MAX SIDE SLOPE: 90%
FORDING: amphibious
RANGE: (roads) 300 km
ENGINE: Mercedes-Benz OM 603.950 2.996 litre 6-cylinder diesel developing 136 hp at 4600 rpm; (early production) Ford Model 2658 E V-6 water-cooled petrol developing 136 bhp at 5200 rpm (could also be fitted with Mercedes-Benz 5-cylinder in-line turbocharged diesel engine developing 125 bhp at 4500 rpm)
TRANSMISSION: Daimler-Benz W4A-040 fully automatic with torque converter, with four forward and one reverse gears
STEERING: articulated hydrostatic
TURNING RADIUS: 8 m (6 m with pitch control)

EXTRA FEATURES:
Twin-hulled, blunt front, slab-sided; rubber tracks equal approx one third of the vehicle's width

241

Alvis Hagglunds BVS 10 Armoured Personnel Carrier

SWEDEN

BVS 10 Viking ATV(P) armed with 12.7 mm MG in service with the Royal Marines

The Royal Marines deploy three basic versions of the ATV(P): Troop Carrying Vehicle; Command Vehicle; and Repair and Recovery Vehicle. Like all other BV 206/BV 206S all-terrain vehicles, the BVS 10 is fully amphibious, being propelled in the water by its rubber band tracks at a maximum speed of 5 km/h. It can be carried inside a CH-53 helicopter.

SPECIFICATION:

USED BY:
UK Royal Marines (known as the Viking)

CONTRACTOR:
Alvis Hagglunds AB, Ornskoldsvik, Sweden

FEATURES:
CREW: four plus ten
MAX COMBAT WEIGHT: 10,500 kg – 11,500 kg
UNLOADED WEIGHT: 760 kg; (front unit) 4670 kg; (rear unit) 3090 kg
PAYLOAD: 2840 kg; (front unit) 730 kg; (rear unit) 2110 kg
POWER TO WEIGHT RATIO: 23.80 hp/t
LENGTH: 7.55 m
WIDTH: 2.10 m
HEIGHT: (front) 2.19 m; (rear) 2.08 m
GROUND CLEARANCE: 0.35 m
TRACK: 1.48 m
TRACK WIDTH: 620 mm
MAX ROAD SPEED: 65 km/h
MAX WATER SPEED: 5 km/h
GRADIENT: 100% (limited by friction)
RANGE: (road) 300 km

ENGINE: Cummins 5.9 litre 6-cylinder in-line heavy-duty diesel developing 250 hp at 2500 rpm with 300 hp engine available in future
TRANSMISSION: Allison MD 3560 automatic with six forward gears and one reverse
STEERING: hydrostatic, articulated, damped
TURNING RADIUS: 6 m

ARMAMENT:
UK vehicles are fitted with a roof-mounted 7.62 mm or 12.7 mm machine gun and standard equipment includes banks of two electrically-operated smoke grenade launchers

EXTRA FEATURES:
Similar in silhouette appearance to earlier BVs; rear unit as vertical sides with no windows and one rear-opening door; front unit has almost vertical hull front that slopes up to windscreen and two doors each side but with windows only in the front

Over-snow Strike/Support Vehicle (OSV) UK

Seafire Over-snow Strike/Support Vehicle (1) and sledges for Seafire Over-snow Strike/Support Vehicle (2)

The Over-Snow Strike/Support Vehicle was developed as a military up-grade package for the Bombardier-Nordtrac Skandic Super Wide Track over-snow vehicle – part of the Skidoo range. The package includes a modified vehicle console with additional electrics, displays and infra-red lighting, a front vehicle frame for weapons or other equipment and a high-performance sledge. The sledge is based on modern materials designed for arctic conditions and is able to carry loads in excess of 250 kg, including heavy machine guns and mortars. It is also used for casualty transport. The sledge floats: several may be joined together to form a pontoon.

SPECIFICATION:

USED BY:
UK Royal Marines

CONTRACTOR:
Seafire Limited, Cullompton, UK

FEATURES:
Handle bar controls; pointed 'bows'; two forward, steering skids; a central, rubber track for propulsion

GT-T Tracked Amphibious Over-snow Vehicle UKRAINE

Troops boarding GT-T amphibious over-snow vehicles

The GT-T can tow a trailer weighing up to 4000 kg. The KLP-2 wheeled/ski trailer was designed for use with the GT-T. The GT-T is fully amphibious. Most sources state that it is propelled in the water by its tracks at a speed between 5 and 6 km/h.

SPECIFICATION:

USED BY:
Russian amphibious forces

CONTRACTOR:
Ordzhonikidze Kharkov Tractor Plant JSC, Ukraine

FEATURES:
CAB SEATING: one plus two (up to ten in rear)
WEIGHT: (empty) 8200 kg; (loaded) 10,200 kg
MAX LOAD: 2000 kg
TOWED LOAD: 4000 kg
LENGTH: 6.34 m
WIDTH: 3.14 m
HEIGHT: 2.16 m
GROUND CLEARANCE: 0.45 m
TRACK WIDTH: 540 mm
LENGTH OF TRACK ON GROUND: 3.914 m
GROUND PRESSURE: (loaded) 0.24 kg/cm^2
MAX SPEED: (road) 45.5 km/h; (water) 6 km/h
RANGE: 500 km
MAX GRADIENT: 60%
ENGINE: 1Z-6 6-cylinder water-cooled diesel developing 192 hp

EXTRA FEATURES:
Very wide chassis, sloping sides to body; an unusual feature of the GT-T is that the fuel tanks are positioned externally above the tracks on each side at the rear

MT-L Tracked Amphibious Over-snow/All Terrain Vehicle UKRAINE

MT-L tracked amphibious over-snow vehicle

The MT-L is fully amphibious without preparation, being propelled in the water by its tracks at a maximum speed of 6 km/h. A bilge pump is fitted as standard.

SPECIFICATION:

USED BY:
Russian amphibious forces

CONTRACTOR:
Ordzhonikidze Kharkov Tractor Plant JSC, Ukraine

FEATURES:
CAB SEATING: one plus seven (up to ten in rear)
WEIGHT: (laden, without trailer) 13,000 kg; (laden, with trailer) 11,000 kg; (unladen) 8500 kg
MAX LOAD: (without trailer) 4500 kg; (laden, with trailer) 2500 kg
TOWED LOAD: 7000 kg
LENGTH: 6.364 m
WIDTH: 2.85 m
HEIGHT: 2.013 m
GROUND CLEARANCE: 0.4 m
TRACK WIDTH: 350 mm
LENGTH OF TRACK ON GROUND: 3.7 m
TRACK: 2.5 m
GROUND PRESSURE: 0.428 kg/cm^2
MAX SPEED: (road, without trailer) 61.5 km/h; (road, with trailer) 46.8 km/h; (water) 5-6 km/h
RANGE: 500 km
MAX GRADIENT: (without trailer) 60%; (with trailer) 40%
MAX SIDE SLOPE: 40%
ENGINE: YaMZ-238V v-8 diesel developing 230 hp at 2100 rpm
TRANSMISSION: manual with six forward and one reverse gears
STEERING: clutch and brake

EXTRA FEATURES:
Similar to the GT-T

LMC 1200 Over-snow Vehicle USA

LMC 1200 over-snow vehicle with 10-man fully enclosed body

Although designed primarily for over-snow operation, the LMC 1200 can be used over other types of marginal terrain such as swamps. The basic vehicle has a two-seat, fully enclosed cab at the front of the vehicle and optional rollbars can be fitted to enable it to withstand twice its weight.

SPECIFICATION:

USED BY:
US Marine Corps (among other us forces)

CONTRACTOR:
Logan Manufacturing Company, Utah, USA (no longer trading)

FEATURES:
CAB SEATING: two plus up to ten
WEIGHT: (empty) 2803 kg
MAX LOAD: 1361 kg
NORMAL LOAD: 453-907 kg
LENGTH: 4.114 m
WIDTH: 2.526 m
HEIGHT: 2.108 m
GROUND CLEARANCE: 0.254 m
TRACK WIDTH: 914 mm
GROUND PRESSURE: 0.07 kg/cm^2
MAX SPEED: (with outboard reduction gearing) 27 km/h
FUEL CAPACITY: 159 litres
GRADIENT: (dirt) 80%; (snow) 60%
ENGINE: Ford 6-cylinder petrol developing 124 hp
TRANSMISSION: Ford c-6 automatic, three forward and one reverse gears
DIFFERENTIAL STEERING: planetary controlled
TURNING RADIUS: 4.572 m

FEATURES:
Box shaped hull with three large windows either side; large driver's door with window

LMC 1500 Over-snow Vehicle USA

LMC 1500 over-snow vehicle with roll-bars

The LMC 1500 over-snow vehicle was initially available in three versions. One was a two-seat cab version with an uncovered cargo area measuring 1.7 x 1.778 m and another a five-seat cab with a reduced cargo area measuring 1.122 x 1.7 m. A fully enclosed full cab version with a covered cargo area, or seating for the driver and up to seven passengers was also available.

SPECIFICATION:

USED BY:
US Marine Corps (among other US forces)

CONTRACTOR:
Logan Manufacturing Company, Utah, USA (no longer trading)

FEATURES:
CREW: two plus up to six
WEIGHT: (base vehicle); (empty, summer tracks) 1950 kg; (empty, wide tracks) 2086 kg
MAX LOAD: 1088 kg
LENGTH: (four axles) 2.972 m; (three axles) 2.667 m
WIDTH: (cab) 1.71 m; (overall, summer tracks) 2.13 m; (overall, wide tracks) 2.489 m
HEIGHT: 2.11 m
GROUND CLEARANCE: (with differential guard) 0.23 m
TREAD WIDTH: 1.422 m
TRACK WIDTH: 711 or 914 mm
MAX SPEED: (hard surface) 32 km/h
FUEL CAPACITY: 110 litres
FORDING: 0.355 m
GRADIENT: (hard snow) 80%
VERTICAL OBSTACLE: 0.254 m
ENGINE: Ford 6-cylinder petrol developing 124 hp
TRANSMISSION: Ford C-6 automatic with three forward and one reverse gears
TURNING RADIUS: 3.048 m

LMC 1800 Over-snow Vehicle USA

LMC 1800 over-snow vehicle with five-man cab

The LMC 1800 over-snow vehicle was available in three versions. One is the standard two-seat cab with a 3.01 m² cargo platform and another a five-seat cab with a reduced cargo area. Also available was a fully enclosed full cab version with a covered cargo area or seating for the driver and up to ten passengers. The final production models were marketed as the LMC 1800 Bearcat.

SPECIFICATION:

USED BY:
US Marine Corps (among other US forces)

CONTRACTOR:
Logan Manufacturing Company, Utah, USA (no longer trading)

FEATURES:
CAB SEATING: two plus up to ten
MAX LOAD: 1360 kg
LENGTH: 3.607 m
WIDTH: (cab) 1.829 m; (overall, standard tracks) 2.438 m (overall, wide tracks) 2.54 or 2.794 m
HEIGHT: 2.337 m
GROUND CLEARANCE: 0.305 m
TRACK WIDTH: 711 mm, 813 mm, 914 mm or 1.041 m
MAX SPEED: 17 km/h
FUEL CAPACITY: 114 litres (228 or 356 litres optional)
GRADIENT: (hard snow) 80%
MAX SIDE SLOPE: 60%
ENGINE: Caterpillar 6.6 litre 3116T diesel developing 173 hp
TRANSMISSION: Sundstrand Series 90 hydrostatic, variable speed pumps, fixed speed motors and external adjustable relief valves
STEERING: hydrostatic

EXTRA FEATURES:
Tracks proud of the body either side; full-width windscreen

Transport: Land, Special Attack Vehicles

NORINCO **Fast Attack Vehicle** CHINA

NORINCO fitted with a roof-mounted 23 mm cannon and a pintle-mounted 7.62 machine gun

The vehicle has been fielded by airborne units of the People's Liberation Army and, despite disclosing the type being available for export sales, very little specific information has become available.

The NORINCO fast attack vehicle appears to be of rear-wheel drive 4 x 2 configuration with a rear-mounted engine and, in a central roll-over protected cage, seating for either four people, including the driver, or two people plus additional stores. The forward part of the vehicle carries a replacement wheel and on/off-road tyre, and a front-mounted electric winch is provided for self-recovery operations.

The vehicle is 4 m long, 2.095 m wide and 2.21 m high, and combat weight is given as 1,950 kg. No further dimensional or driveline details have been released.

SPECIFICATION:

USED BY:
People's Liberation Army

CONTRACTOR:
China North Industries Corporation, Beijing, People's Republic of China

ARMAMENT:
A wide range of weapon stations can be fitted and the example shown in released photographs is armed with a 7.62 mm machine gun on a swivel mount to the right of the driver's position and a new Chinese 23 mm cannon installed in a circular mount on top of the roll-over protection system. The 23 mm cannon is fitted with a muzzle brake to reduce recoil forces so allowing it to be installed on light vehicles. The weapon can be traversed through a full 360° with elevation from -10° to +52° and the operator can fire single shots or automatic fire at the rate of 200 rpm or 400 rpm. The weapon is driven from a 24 v power source. Maximum effective range is 2000 m. A total of 200 rounds of ready-to-use 23 mm ammunition is carried and, for increased accuracy, a day/night sighting system is installed above the weapon.

FEATURES:
Skeletal anti-roll cage

Auverland Type A3F Fast Attack Vehicle FRANCE

Auverland Type A3F airmobile vehicle in VAC command form

The dimensions of the A3F allow it to be carried inside the NH 90 helicopters ordered for the French Army and scheduled for delivery commencement in 2011. The A3F can also be dropped by parachute. The French Army has tested a longer wheelbase version, the A3F SL.

SPECIFICATION:

USED BY:
French airborne forces, possibly Swedish army

CONTRACTOR:
SNAA (Societe Nouvelle des Automobiles Auverland), Saint-Germain-Laval, France

FEATURES:
SEATING: one plus two
CONFIGURATION: 4 x 4
WEIGHT: (GVW) 2510 kg; (kerb) 1350 kg
PAYLOAD: 1160 kg
LENGTH: 3.4 m
WIDTH: 1.58 m
HEIGHT: (overall) 1.9 m; (roll bars folded) 1.4 m
GROUND CLEARANCE: 0.255 m
WHEELBASE: 2.25 m
ANGLE OF APPROACH/DEPARTURE: 50°/50°
MAX SPEED: 130 km/h
RANGE: 700 km
FUEL CAPACITY: 80 litres
MAX GRADIENT: 100%
FORDING: (unprepared) 0.6 m

ENGINE: Peugeot XUD 9TF 1.905 litre 4-cylinder in-line turbocharged water-cooled four-stroke diesel developing 92 hp at 4000 rpm
TRANSMISSION: Peugeot with five forward and one reverse gears
CLUTCH: single dry plate
TURNING RADIUS: 5 m

ARMAMENT:
The VAC command version can carry a 5.56 or 7.62 mm machine gun on a front mounting. It also has a central mounting suitable for a 0.50 in/12.7 mm heavy machine gun, a Giat M 621 20 mm cannon, a 40 mm grenade launcher or a MILAN anti-tank missile launcher

EXTRA FEATURES:
Skeletal anti-roll cage

Szöcske Light Strike Vehicle HUNGARY

The Szöcske (Cricket)
Light Strike Vehicle
may be produced in
either a 4 x 2 or 4 x 4
drive configuration and
with a choice of air- or
water-cooled engines.
There is also the option
of a turbo-diesel
engine.

SPECIFICATION:

CONTRACTOR:
GEPFET Kft, Budapest, Hungary

FEATURES:
SEATING: two plus two
CONFIGURATION: 4 x 2 or 4 x 4
WEIGHT: 1100 or 1200 kg
PAYLOAD: 500 kg
LENGTH: 3.8 m
WIDTH: 1.8 m
HEIGHT: 1.5 m
GROUND CLEARANCE: 0.3 m
WHEELBASE: 2.48 m
ANGLE OF APPROACH/DEPARTURE:
80°/35°
MAX SPEED: 130 km/h
RANGE: (cruising) 600 km/h
MAX GRADIENT: 80%
FORDING: 0.4 m
ENGINE: 1.9 litre air-cooled
petrol developing 87 hp or
1.9 litre water-cooled diesel
developing 77 hp
TRANSMISSION: (4 x 4) manual
with four forward plus one
climbing and reverse gears

ARMAMENT:
The Szöcske roll-over frame can
be used to mount several types of
weapon, including missile
launchers or recoilless guns of
various calibres. The vehicle can
also be used to tow a trailer or
light weapons such as automatic
mortars

EXTRA FEATURES:
Skeletal anti-roll cage; electric
winch forwards as standard

AIL Desert Raider Special Operations Vehicle (SOV)

ISRAEL

AIL Desert Raider 6 x 6 reconnaissance and fast attack vehicle

Air-portable, highly mobile surveillance and strike vehicle capable of operating behind the front lines of a modern battlefield. The Desert Raider can be carried internally by a CH-53 helicopter.

SPECIFICATION:

USED BY:
Israel Special Forces and an unknown customer

CONTRACTOR:
Automotive Industries Limited, Israel

FEATURES:
SEATING: one plus two (plus two optional)
CONFIGURATION: 6 x 6
WEIGHT: (kerb) 1450 kg, (GVW) 2650 kg
PAYLOAD: 1200 kg
LENGTH: (with spare wheel) 4.1 m; (overall) 3.86 m
WIDTH: (body) 1.95 m; (wheels) 2 m
HEIGHT: (overall) 1.85 m; (roll bars folded) 1.32 m
GROUND CLEARANCE: 0.39 m
ANGLE OF APPROACH/DEPARTURE: 75°/89°
MAX SPEED: 110 km/h
RANGE: (operational) 500 km
MAX GRADIENT: 70%
MAX SIDE SLOPE: 70%

FORDING: (without preparation) 0.7 m
VERTICAL STEP: 0.6 m

ARMAMENT:
Special Forces personal and light support weapons

EXTRA FEATURES:
Six wheels with a gap between the front pair and the rear four; skeletal anti-roll frame; central driving position

AB3 Black Iris and Desert Iris Light Special Forces Vehicle JORDAN

AB3 Black Iris light special forces vehicle armed with Browning 12.7 mm M2 heavy machine gun

SPECIFICATION:

USED BY:
Jordanian armed forces including the Special Operations Command (SOCOM)

CONTRACTOR:
King Abdullah II Design and Development Bureau (KADDB), Amman, Jordan

FEATURES:
SEATING: one plus one or up to six
CONFIGURATION: 4 x 2 or 4 x 4
PAYLOAD: 500 kg (options 750 or 1000 kg)
LENGTH: 4.1 m
WIDTH: 1.9 m
HEIGHT: 1.5 m
GROUND CLEARANCE: 0.35 m
WHEELBASE: 2.75 m
MAX SPEED: (on-road) 140 km/h
MAX RANGE: 600 km on road (400 km off-road)
GRADIENT: 60%
MAX SIDE SLOPE: 40%
ENGINE: 2.8-litre Toyota 4-cylinder in-line SOHC diesel developing 102 hp at 4200 rpm and maximum torque of 192 Nm at 2400 rpm (options available)
TRANSMISSION: manual, five forward and one reverse gears

ARMAMENT:
Various weapons options are available including 12.7 mm or 7.62 mm machine gun mounts, or platforms for a TOW launcher or 106 mm recoilless rifle

EXTRA FEATURES:
Very low chassis; partially-solid anti-roll cage

The AB3 Black Iris/Desert Iris Special Forces utility vehicle was developed by the King Abdullah II Design and Development Bureau working in association with SHP Motorsports of the United Kingdom. Extensive prototype field trials were conducted in Jordan and South Africa from mid-1999 to mid-2001 and included deployment of some 4 x 2 Black Iris vehicles with Jordanian forces on UN operations in Sierra Leone. Since then SOCOM has placed orders for initial quantities of the vehicle in both anti-tank and reconnaissance configurations. Further quantities of the vehicle in both 4 x 2 and later 4 x 4 versions have been ordered by GHQ Jordan Armed Forces and these are intended as replacements for M151 Jeeps and light trucks. The 4 x 4 version is known as the Desert Iris.

AB5 Special Forces Vehicle JORDAN

AB5 special forces vehicles in convoy

The AB5 special forces vehicle has been built onto the chassis of a Land Rover Defender 110 and is intended for numerous tactical roles including fast attack, reconnaissance, border patrol and peacekeeping missions. The AB5 was designed around Jordanian Special Forces requirements and has been produced in several versions. The type has been deployed with Jordanian Special Forces on operations with the United Nations in Sierra Leone. This version has retained the Land Rover body but features roll-over protection and weapons mounts derived from the AB3 Black Iris/ Desert Iris programme.

SPECIFICATION:

USED BY:
Jordanian Special Operations Command (SOCOM)

CONTRACTOR:
King Abdullah II Design and Development Bureau (KADDB), Amman, Jordan

FEATURES:
SEATING: one plus one or two (plus six)
CONFIGURATION: 4 X 4
PAYLOAD: 1000 kg (max)
UNLADEN WEIGHT: 3050 kg
LENGTH: 4.5 m
WIDTH: 2 m
HEIGHT: 1.94 m
GROUND CLEARANCE: 0.2 m
WHEELBASE: 2.8 m
ANGLE OF APPROACH/DEPARTURE: 60/38°
MAX SPEED: (on-road) 180 km/h
MAX RANGE: 600 km on road (400 km off-road)
ENGINE: Rover 3.5 litre V8 petrol developing 134 hp
TRANSMISSION: LT 85, manual, five forward and one reverse

ARMAMENT:
Roof weapon ring installation for a 12.7 mm machine gun. There is also provision for a 7.62 mm M60 machine gun to be mounted on the front right-hand side for the front-seat passenger

EXTRA FEATURES:
Land Rover body and chassis

Turbomecanica Hamster 3 Special Purpose Off-road Vehicle ROMANIA

The Turbomecanica Hamster 3 special purpose off-road vehicle is intended to fulfil a wide range of military and other roles where high mobility is required; 4 x 2 and 4 x 4 configurations are available. A special 'Jumper' version with seating for the driver and up to five passengers is available for airborne and paradrop roles.

SPECIFICATION:

CONTRACTOR:
Societatea Comerciala Turbomecanica SA, Bucharest, Romania

USED BY:
Unspecified countries

FEATURES:
SEATING: one plus up to five
CONFIGURATION: 4 x 2 or 4 x 4
WEIGHT: (kerb) 750 kg; (kerb, lightweight model) 650 kg; (loaded) 1500 kg
PAYLOAD: 750 kg
TOWED LOAD: 1000 kg
LENGTH: 3.8 m
WIDTH: 1.7 m
HEIGHT: 1.18 m
GROUND CLEARANCE: 0.2 m
TRACK: (front and rear) 1.4 m
WHEELBASE: 2.5 m
MAX SPEED: (road) 130 km/h
RANGE: 400 km
MAX GRADIENT: 40°
MAX SIDE SLOPE: 30°
ENGINE: Renault 1.397 litre 4-cylinder water-cooled petrol developing 62 hp at 5250 rpm
TRANSMISSION: manual, five forward and one reverse gears

EXTRA FEATURES:
Body work is entirely tubular; no anti-roll bar

ST Kinetics Flyer Light Strike Vehicle SINGAPORE

SPECIFICATION:

USED BY:
Singapore armed forces

CONTRACTOR:
Singapore Technologies Kinetics
Limited, Singapore

FEATURES:
SEATING: one plus two or three
CONFIGURATION: 4 x 4
WEIGHT: (kerb) 1400 kg
PAYLOAD: 1000 kg
LENGTH: 4.5 m
WIDTH: 2.03 m
HEIGHT: 1.9 m
GROUND CLEARANCE: 0.4 m
WHEELBASE: 2.85 m
ANGLE OF APPROACH/DEPARTURE:
70°/40°
MAX SPEED: 110 km/h
RANGE: 525 km
GRADIENT: 60%
MAX SIDE SLOPE: 50%
FORDING: 0.6 m
VERTICAL OBSTACLE: 0.4 m
ENGINE: 2-litre turbocharged
intercooled diesel developing
110 hp at 4500 rpm

TRANSMISSION: semi-automatic
transaxle, three forward and one
reverse gears
TURNING RADIUS: 6.5 m

ARMAMENT:
The roll cage can be configured in
a number of ways to
accommodate various weapon
installations. A typical weapon
installation could be a 7.62 mm
machine gun forward plus a
pedestal mount for a missile
launcher or a 40 mm grenade
launcher such as the 40AGL.
Vehicles in service with the
Singapore defence forces carry a
rear-mounted pedestal for two
Spike anti-tank guided weapons,
with stowage for five missiles

EXTRA FEATURES:
Skeletal body; raised 'boot' with
spare tyre above

Mechem BAT Special Forces Utility Vehicle SOUTH AFRICA

Mechem BAT special forces utility vehicle with 68 mm rocket launcher

The Mechem BAT lightweight, airdrop-capable Special Forces utility vehicle is based on a civilian lightweight overland vehicle design and embodies numerous standard commercial components.

SPECIFICATION:

USED BY:
South African Defence Force (SANDF)

CONTRACTOR:
Mechem, Silverton, South Africa

FEATURES:
SEATING: one plus up to five
CONFIGURATION: 4 x 4
LENGTH: 3.1 m
WIDTH: 1.8 m
HEIGHT: 1.8 m
GROUND CLEARANCE: (min) 0.26 m
MAX SPEED: 120 km/h
RANGE: 500 km
ENGINE: 3-litre v-6 petrol
developing 138 hp at 5000 rpm or
2-litre 4-cylinder turbocharged
diesel
TRANSMISSION: manual, five
forward and one reverse gears
TURNING RADIUS: 5.25 m

ARMAMENT:
A mounting point for single or
twin machine guns is standard
between the bullet protected twin
windscreens. Some examples
carry a single 20 mm cannon

EXTRA FEATURES:
Sharply sloping bonnet; spare
wheel on left-hand side

CSIR Defencetek G BAT Mk 2 Rapid Reaction Utility Vehicle SOUTH AFRICA

Fully armed CSIR Defencetek BAT Mk 2 showing the interchangeable weapons mounting pad

The CSIR G BAT Mk 2 lightweight, airdrop-capable rapid reaction utility vehicle is a development of the earlier Mechem BAT vehicle: an optional innovation is an add-on frontal armour kit to provide protection against 7.62 mm x 51 NATO ball ammunition for the power pack from the side and 7.62 x 54 Draganov API protection from the front. Hand-grenade protection can also be offered as an add-on. No protection is offered for the crew. The BAT Mk 2 is qualified for both high- and low-level airdrop from transport aircraft such as the C-130 Hercules. It can also be carried slung under helicopters such as the Denel Aviation Oryx.

SPECIFICATION:

USED BY:
French and South African armed forces

CONTRACTOR:
CSIR Defencetek, Pretoria, South Africa

FEATURES:
SEATING: two plus up to five
CONFIGURATION: 4 x 4
WEIGHT: (kerb) 2300 kg with add-on armour, (GVW) 3800 kg
PAYLOAD: 1500 kg
LENGTH: 3.8 m
WIDTH: 1.8 m
HEIGHT: 1.8 m
GROUND CLEARANCE: (min) 0.246 m
WHEELBASE: 2.4 m
ANGLE OF APPROACH/DEPARTURE: 39°/39°
MAX SPEED: 137 km/h
RANGE: (road) 1,054 km
FUEL CAPACITY: 96 litres
GRADIENT: 80%
FORDING: 0.6 m
ENGINE: Mercedes-Benz 5-cylinder in-line water-cooled diesel developing 120 hp at 3800 rpm
TRANSMISSION: Mercedes-Benz automatic with four forward and one reverse gear
TURNING RADIUS: 5.25 m

ARMAMENT:
Mountings for machine guns and light weapons up to 20 mm can also be provided. Storage space is provided underneath the mounting pallet for ammunition. A mounting point for a single 5.56 or 7.62 mm machine gun is standard between the bullet-protected twin windscreens

EXTRA FEATURES:
Heavily armed; spare wheel on left-hand door

Alvis OMC Wasp Rapid Deployment Reconnaissance Vehicle (RDRV) SOUTH AFRICA

Alvis OMC Wasp rapid deployment reconnaissance vehicle configured to seat eight soldiers

The Wasp rapid deployment reconnaissance vehicle (RDRV) was developed for use by Special and Airborne Forces and was designed to be self-deployable by road or airlifted/dropped by helicopter or transport aircraft. A C-130 Hercules aircraft is capable of transporting four vehicles. In its basic configuration the Alvis OMC Wasp provides three side-by-side seats in the front, the centre of these having dual (high/low) positions that enable the gunner to fire from a mounting on the windscreen frame.

SPECIFICATION:

USED BY:
South African National Defence Force

CONTRACTOR:
Alvis OMC, Benoni, South Africa

FEATURES:
CAB SEATING: one plus seven (standard configuration); (one plus five in 60 mm mortar or 107 mm multiple rocket launcher configuration)
CONFIGURATION: 4 x 4
WEIGHT: (unladen) 2150 kg; (laden) 3600 kg
PAYLOAD: 1450 kg
TOWED LOAD: 1500 kg (in RDLV configuration)
LENGTH: 3.15 m
WIDTH: 2.3 m
HEIGHT: 1.875 m (to top of rollbar)
GROUND CLEARANCE: 243 mm
TRACK: (front) 1.62 m; (rear) 1.62 m
WHEELBASE: 2.2 m
ANGLE OF APPROACH/DEPARTURE: 63°/90°
MAX ROAD SPEED: 120 km/h
MAX RANGE: 420 km at 80 km/h (on road)
FUEL CAPACITY: 60 litres (plus optional 60 litres)
MAX GRADIENT: 60%
ENGINE: VM Motori Detroit Diesel 2.5-litre 4-cylinder in-line turbocharged and intercooled water-cooled diesel developing 113 hp at 3800 rpm
TRANSMISSION: DaimlerChrysler three-speed automatic
TURNING RADIUS: 5.5 m

ARMAMENT:
Typically a 7.62 mm machine gun, but the mounting will also accept a 12.7 mm machine gun, a light-recoil 20 mm MG-151 type cannon, or a 40 mm automatic grenade launcher. The rear of the vehicle features a reconfigurable seat and the weapons pallet which can be fitted with light support weapons including a 60 mm mortar, a 107 mm multiple rocket launcher, or a pedestal mounted 20 mm cannon or 12.7 mm machine gun

EXTRA FEATURES:
Tubular anti-roll cage

ADCOM H2A Fast Attack Vehicle UNITED ARAB EMIRATES

ADCOM H2A fast attack vehicle configured for the anti-armour harassment role

The ADCOM H2A fast attack vehicle is offered in kit form or for local production if ordered in sufficient numbers. Available in a variety of configurations, the vehicle has been displayed prominently in an anti-armour harassment configuration; it is claimed to be able to strike at armour from ranges in excess of 5000 m, its relative small size, stealthiness, speed and agility ensuring it remains difficult to locate and target.

In the armour harassment role, weapons fit consists of two 5.56 minimi guns for self-protection, eight 66 mm smoke grenade launchers and a 12.7 mm heavy machine gun (HMG) capable of air defence. Anti-tank missile armament is not specified and is presumably of customer choice. Laser guided maximum ranges of 5500 m (day) and 3500 m (night) are quoted and eight missile reloads can be carried. The weapons mounting system allows the HMG and missile launcher to be mounted together and used as required.

SPECIFICATION:

CONTRACTOR:
ADCOM Trading Limited, Abu Dhabi, UAE

FEATURES:
CAB SEATING: one plus one
CONFIGURATION: 4 x 2/4 (selectable)
WEIGHT: (laden) 3245 kg; (unladen) 2042 kg;
PAYLOAD: 1203 kg
LENGTH: (with rear-mounted spare wheel) 4.724 m
WIDTH: 2.108 m
HEIGHT: weapons fit dependent
GROUND CLEARANCE: 0.410 m
WHEELBASE: 3.124 m
MAX SPEED: 140 km/h
MAX RANGE: (standard tank) 800 km
FUEL CAPACITY: 190 litres
MAX GRADIENT: >60%
MAX SIDE SLOPE: >30%
ENGINE: Cummins 5.9 litre 6-cylinder in-line turbocharged and intercooled diesel developing 300 hp at 3200 rpm
TRANSMISSION: GM 4L80E 3-speed automatic with overdrive

ARMAMENT:
(see main entry)

EXTRA FEATURES:
Long bonnet; long running boards; spare wheel mounted on back; anti-roll cage

Cobra Light Strike Vehicle (LSV) UK

The Cobra is a highly mobile vehicle for military use in hostile environments. It was designed as a weapon platform and for military missions such as reconnaissance and airborne operations. Commercially available major components and assemblies are used in its construction where possible. The Cobra can be transported inside a standard ISO container and may be slung under CH-47D, Puma and Sea King helicopters. It has been paradropped from a C-130 transport aircraft.

Weapons that can be mounted on the LSV's UMI (Universal Mount Interface) include 7.62 mm and 12.7 mm machine guns (including the 12.7 mm GECAL Gatling gun), a 40 mm grenade launcher, a 30 mm ASP-30 cannon, or six MILAN anti-tank missiles and their launcher. A 51 mm or 60 mm mortar may be carried for dismounted use.

SPECIFICATION:

USED BY:
Some may still be in service with the British army

CONTRACTOR:
Cobra Defence Systems Ltd, Brighton, UK

FEATURES:
SEATING: one plus one
CONFIGURATION: 4 x 4
WEIGHT: (unladen) 1220 kg; (fully laden) 1810 kg
LOAD CAPACITY: 590 kg
LENGTH: 4.166 m
WIDTH: 1.728 m
HEIGHT: (top of roll cage) 1.6 m
GROUND CLEARANCE: 0.3 m
WHEELBASE: 2.54 m
MAX SPEED: 130 km/h
RANGE: over 610 km
FUEL CAPACITY: 75 litres
GRADIENT: 50%
MAX SIDE SLOPE: (with weapons fitted) 50°
FORDING: (unprepared) 0.5 m
TRENCH: 1 m
ENGINE: VAG 1.9-litre turbo diesel developing 95 bhp
TRANSMISSION: manual with four forward (plus crawler) and one reverse gear
TURNING RADIUS: approx 6 m

ARMAMENT:
(see main entry)

EXTRA FEATURES:
Long, low silhouette

Special Operations Vehicle UK

US Army SOV

Based on the Land Rover Defender chassis. Can be para-dropped or carried inside a C-130, CH-47 or CH-53.

SPECIFICATION:

USED BY:
US Rangers

CONTRACTOR:
Land Rover, UK

FEATURES:
ACCOMMODATION: up to seven
CONFIGURATION: 4 x 4
WEIGHT: 3515 kg
LENGTH: 5.445 m
WIDTH: 1.89 m
HEIGHT: (gun ring) 1.93 m
GROUND CLEARANCE: 0.216 m
TRACK: 1.486 m
WHEELBASE: 2.794 m

ARMAMENT:
Mk 19 40 mm grenade launcher
or 12.7 mm (0.5 in) machine gun
and front passenger 7.62 mm
machine gun

EXTRA FEATURES:
Pintle-mounted machine gun;
Land Rover configuration; solid
anti-roll cage

Chenowth Light Strike Vehicle (LSV) USA

Chenowth Light Strike Vehicle (LSV) armed with TOW anti-tank missile launcher

The original military model was the two-seat Fast Attack Vehicle (FAV) produced during the mid-1980s from which the three-seat LSV was further developed. The LSV can be carried internally by CH-47 and CH-53 helicopters. Two may be carried by a C-130 Hercules for paradropping, or three as cargo. During Operation Desert Shield/Storm the FAV and LSV were operated by US and UK Special Forces and by the US Marines and the USN's SEALS.

Weapons can include two 7.62 mm machine guns, mounted fore and aft, together with one 12.7 mm M2 machine gun or a 40 mm MK 19 automatic grenade launcher. The LSV can also carry a TOW 2 anti-tank missile launcher, a 30 mm ASP-30 cannon, an AT-4 anti-tank rocket launcher or the Stinger SAM. Light armour may be added as required, as can special stowage configurations.

SPECIFICATION:

USED BY:
Greece, Mexico, Oman, Portugal, Spain and the US Navy, Marine Corps and Army

CONTRACTOR:
Chenowth Corporation, Washington DC, USA

FEATURES:
SEATING: one plus two
CONFIGURATION: 4 x 2
WEIGHT: (kerb) 960 kg; (loaded) 1660 kg
PAYLOAD: 700 kg
LENGTH: 4.08 m
WIDTH: 2.11 m
HEIGHT: 2.01 m
GROUND CLEARANCE: 0.41 m
WHEELBASE: 2.84 m
ANGLE OF APPROACH/DEPARTURE: 81°/48°
MAX SPEED: (road) 130 km/h; (off road) 110 km/h
RANGE: 500 km
GRADIENT: 75%
MAX SIDE SLOPE: >45%
ENGINE: 2.2-litre air-cooled petrol delivering 125 hp
TRANSMISSION: manual, four forward and one reverse gears

ARMAMENT:
(see main entry)

FEATURES:
Very low bonnet; wide wheel base

Transport:
Sea,
Air-Cushion
Vessels

Jingsah II Class Medium-lift Hovercraft CHINA

The prototype was built at Dagu in 1979. This may now have been scrapped and been superseded by ten of this improved version which has a bow door for disembarkation. Numbers are uncertain.

SPECIFICATION:

USED BY:
Chinese amphibious forces

FEATURES:
DISPLACEMENT: 70 tons
DIMENSIONS: 22 x 8 m
 (72.2 x 26.2 ft)
MAIN MACHINERY: two propulsion
motors; two lift motors
SPEED: 55 kts
MILITARY LIFT: 15 tons

ARMAMENT:
GUNS: 4-14.5 mm (two twin) MGS

EXTRA FEATURES:
Twin, ducted propellers; angled
drive shafts; bridge forwards;
bow ramp

T 2000 Class Medium-lift Hovercraft FINLAND

Prototype ordered 9 July 1999 and delivered in 2002. Subject to results of trials, three further craft may be ordered. Constructed of welded aluminium sheets and lightweight composite materials to reduce magnetic and radar signatures.

SPECIFICATION:

USED BY:
Finnish navy

CONTRACTOR:
Aker Finnyards, Finland

SPECIFICATIONS:
DISPLACEMENT: 84 tons full load
DIMENSIONS: 27.4 x 15.4 m
(89.9 x 50.5 ft)
MAIN MACHINERY: two gas
turbines (drive and lift);
8046 hp(m)
(6 MW); six cp air props
SPEED: 50 kts
COMPLEMENT: ten
RADARS: Surface search

ARMAMENT:
A surface-to-surface missile fit
has not been confirmed. A new
mine (Seamine 2000) is also
under development

LCAC Type KOREA, SOUTH
Hovercraft

There are reported to be plans to build up to
twenty small hovercraft for special forces; the first
two were reported building in 1994, and one was
seen on sea trials in May 1995.

SPECIFICATION:

USED BY:
South Korean Special Forces

Solgae Class – Heavy Lift Hovercraft

Strong resemblance to the USN LCAC although developed without consultation with US. Unloaded speed is 65 kts.

SPECIFICATION:

USED BY:
South Korean amphibious forces

FEATURES:
DISPLACEMENT: 120 tons full load
DIMENSIONS: 25.2 x 12 x 7.8 m
(82.7 x 39.4 x 25.6 ft)
MAIN MACHINERY: two gas
turbines; 5000 hp(m) (3.68 MW)
propulsion; two gas turbines;
3000 hp(m) (2.2 MW) lift; two
airscrews
SPEED: 65 kts; 40 kts (loaded)
RANGE: 500 miles at 45 kts
COMPLEMENT: eight
MILITARY LIFT: 27 tons; one
vehicle; 65 troops
RADARS: Navigation: Raytheon SPS
64(v)2; I-band

ARMAMENT:
GUNS: 1 Vulcan 20 mm Gatling

EXTRA FEATURES:
Large, open-plan deck; twin,
ducted propellers; cockpit
forward on starboard side; twin
nozzles for vectored thrust abaft
the cockpit

Aist (Dzheyran – project 1232.1) Heavy-lift Hovercraft

RUSSIA

Aist 730

First produced at Leningrad in 1970, with subsequent production at a rate of about six every four years. It is the first large hovercraft for naval use and is similar to the UK SR. N4. The type name is *maly desantny korabl na vozdushnoy podushke* meaning 'small ACV'. Modifications have been made to the original engines and some units have been reported as carrying two SA-N-5 quadruple SAM systems and chaff launchers. Three (700 series) are based in the Baltic, the other three are in the Caspian.

SPECIFICATION:

USED BY:
Russian naval forces

FEATURES:
DISPLACEMENT: 298 tons full load
DIMENSIONS: 47.3 x 17.8 m
(155.2 x 58.4 ft)
MAIN MACHINERY: two Type
NK-12 M gas turbines driving four
axial lift fans and four propeller
units for propulsion; 19,200
hp(m)(14.1 MW) nominal
SPEED: 70 kts
RANGE: 120 miles at 50 kts
COMPLEMENT: 15 (three officers)
MILITARY LIFT: 80 tons or four
light tanks plus 50 troops or two
medium tanks plus 200 troops or
three APCs plus 100 troops
COUNTERMEASURES: Decoys: two
PK 16 chaff launchers
RADARS: Surface search: Kivach;
I-band
FIRE CONTROL: Drum Tilt; H/I-band
IFF: High Pole B. Square Head

ARMAMENT:
GUNS: four 30 mm/65 (two twin)
AK 630; six barrels per mounting;
3000 rds/min combined to 2 km

Czilim (Project 20910) Class Light Hovercraft RUSSIA

Ordered from *Jaroslawski Sudostroiteinyj Zawod* to an Almaz design for Special Forces of the Border Guard. The first one was laid down on 24 February 1998 and in service in early 2001. Three further vessels may be in service.

SPECIFICATION:

USED BY:
Russian Border Guard Special Forces

FEATURES:
DISPLACEMENT: six tons full load
DIMENSIONS: 12 x 5.8 m
(9.4 x 19 ft)
MAIN MACHINERY: Deutz B F 6 M
1013 diesels; 435 hp(m) (320 kw)
sustained; for lift and propulsion
SPEED: 33 kts
RANGE: 300 miles at 30 kts
COMPLEMENT: two plus six Border Guard
RADARS: Navigation: I-band

ARMAMENT:
GUNS: 1-7.62 mm MG. 1-40 mm
RPG.

EXTRA FEATURES:
Twin, ducted propellers; box-section superstructure with wheelhouse forward

Lebed (Kalmar – Project 1206) Heavy-lift Hovercraft

RUSSIA

Lebed class

First entered service 1975 and can be carried in
'Ivan Rogov' class. It has a bow ramp with a gun on
the starboard side and the bridge to port.

SPECIFICATION:

USED BY:
Russian naval forces

FEATURES:
DISPLACEMENT: 87 tons full load
DIMENSIONS: 24.4 x 11.2 m
(80.1 x 36.7 ft)
MAIN MACHINERY: two Ivchenko
AI-20K gas turbines for lift and
propulsion; 8000 hp (m)
(5.88 MW)
SPEED: 50 kts
RANGE: 100 miles at 50 kts
COMPLEMENT: six (two officers)
MILITARY LIFT: two light tanks or
40 tons cargo or 120 troops
RADARS: Navigation: Kivach;
I-band

ARMAMENT:
GUNS: 2-30 mm (twin) MGS.

EXTRA FEATURES:
Two-ducted propellers; twin
rudders; twin gas turbine
exhausts; square-sided
superstructure

Pomornik (Zubr, Type 1232) Heavy Hovercraft RUSSIA

Pomornik 782

SPECIFICATION:

USED BY:
Navies of Greece, Russia and the
Ukraine

FEATURES:
DISPLACEMENT: 550 tons full load
DIMENSIONS: 57.6 x 25.6 m
(189 x 84 ft)
MAIN MACHINERY: five Type
NK-12 MV gas-turbines; two for
lift, 23,672 hp (m) (17.4 MW)
nominal; three for drive, 35,508
hp(m) (26.1 MW) nominal
SPEED: 63 kts
RANGE: 300 miles at 55 kts
COMPLEMENT: 31 (four officers)
MILITARY LIFT: three MBT or ten
APC plus 230 troops (total
130 tons)
COUNTERMEASURES: decoys:
MS227 chaff launcher
ESM: Tool Box; intercept
WEAPONS CONTROL: Quad Look
(DWU-3) (modified Squeeze Box)
Optronic director
RADARS: Surface search: Curl
Stone; I-band
FIRE CONTROL: Bass Tilt; H/I-band
IFF: Salt Pot A/B. Square Head

ARMAMENT:
MISSILES: SAM: 2 SA-N-5 Grail
quad launchers; manual aiming;
IR homing to 6 km (3.2 n miles) at
1.5 Mach; altitude to 2500 m
(8000 ft); warhead 1.5 kg
GUNS: two 30 mm/65 AK 630; six
barrels per mounting; 3000
rds/min combined to 2 km. Two
retractable 122 mm rocket
launchers (not in first of class)
MINES: two rails can be carried
for 80

EXTRA FEATURES:
Large, three-ducted propellers;
warship-style bridge; sloping bow
configuration with internal ramp

Slingsby SAH 2200 Light Hovercraft UK

Slingsby 2200

SPECIFICATION:

USED BY:
Finnish Frontier Guard, Libyan
and Saudi Arabian maritime
Special Forces

CONTRACTOR:
Slingsby, UK

FEATURES:
DISPLACEMENT: 5.5 tons full load
DIMENSIONS: 10.6 x 4.2 m
(34.8 x 13.8 ft)
MAIN MACHINERY: one Cummins
6CTA-8-3 M-1 diesel; 300 hp
(224 kW)
SPEED: 40 kts
RANGE: 400 miles at 30 kts
COMPLEMENT: two
MILITARY LIFT: 2.2 tons or 12
troops
RADARS: Navigation: Raytheon
R41; I-band

ARMAMENT:
GUNS: 1-12.7 mm MG

EXTRA FEATURES:
Composite hull and
superstructure; box-sectioned
superstructure; single, ducted
propeller; radar above forward
wheelhouse

ABS M-10 Medium-lift Hovercraft UK

ABS M-10 assault version on operations in Sri Lanka

All have Kevlar-reinforced composite hulls and superstructure. Speeds of 60 kts fully laden have been achieved. The vessel performs well in rough weather conditions, operating on cushion, in gale force winds and swells of more than 4 m (13 ft). The 2.5 m (8.2 ft) wide bow ramp allows rapid deployment of troops and vehicles well inland of the waterline.

SPECIFICATION:

USED BY:
Sri Lankan and Swedish maritime Special Forces

CONTRACTOR:
ABS Hovercraft, UK (built under licence in Sweden)

FEATURES:
DIMENSIONS: 20.6 x 8.8 m (67.8 x 28.9 ft)
PAYLOAD: 10 tons
CREW: two
FUEL CAPACITY: 4000 litres
PROPULSIVE POWER: two Deutz diesels; 1050 hp(m), 1000 kw
SPEED: 50 kts
RANGE: 600 n miles
MILITARY LIFT: 77 lightly equipped troops or 20 troops plus two vehicles
OBSTACLE CLEARANCE: 1 m

ARMAMENT:
Infantry weapons and hand-held anti-tank and surface-to-air missile systems. A heavy machine gun can be operated from the port bow

EXTRA FEATURES:
Third-generation craft; twin, ducted, controllable-pitch propellers; SSF version has low profile and a rounded superstructure; SF version usually painted in disruptive pattern colour scheme

Griffon 1000 TD Light Hovercraft UK

Three acquired in mid-1990. Although having an obvious amphibious capability they are also used for rescue and flood control.

SPECIFICATION:

USED BY:
Thailand amphibious forces

CONTRACTOR:
Griffon, UK

FEATURES:
DIMENSIONS: 8.4 x 3.8 m
(27.6 x 12.5 ft)
MAIN MACHINERY: one Deutz
BF6L913C diesel; 190 hp(m)
(140 kw)
SPEED: 33 kts
RANGE: 200 miles at 27 kts
COMPLEMENT: two
CARGO CAPACITY: 1000 kg plus
nine troops
RADARS: Navigation: Raytheon;
I-band

EXTRA FEATURES:
Single, ducted propeller with
three incorporated rudders; four
side windows; mast above control
position; radar antenna
immediately abaft the mast

Griffon 2000 TDX(M) Light Hovercraft   UK

Can be embarked in an LCU or carried on a wheeled, low-loader. Speed indicated is at Sea State 3 with a full load.

SPECIFICATION:

USED BY:
Estonia Border Guard, Finnish Frontier Guard, Lithuanian State Border Service, Swedish Coast Guard and the UK Royal Marines

CONTRACTOR:
Griffon, UK

FEATURES:
DISPLACEMENT: 6.8 tons full load
DIMENSIONS: 11 x 4.6 m (36.1 x 15.1 ft)
MAIN MACHINERY: one Deutz BF8L513 diesel; 320 hp (239 kw) sustained
SPEED: 33 kts
RANGE: 300 miles at 25 kts
COMPLEMENT: two
MILITARY LIFT: 16 troops or 2 tons
RADARS: Navigation: I-band

ARMAMENT:
GUNS: 1-7.62 mm MG

EXTRA FEATURES:
Aluminium hull and superstructure; box-sectioned superstructure; single, ducted propeller; radar above passenger compartment; UK craft are painted in a disruptive camouflage pattern

Griffon 8000 TD(M) Hovercraft UK

Indian Coast Guard Griffon 8000

Six hovercraft were ordered from GRSE Calcutta in May 1999 for construction in technical collaboration with Griffon UK. It is a second generation craft with aluminium hulls.

SPECIFICATION:

USED BY:
Indian Coast Guard in anti-smuggling/drug-running role

FEATURES:
DISPLACEMENT: 18.2 tons; 24.6 tons full load
DIMENSIONS: 21.15 x 11 x 0.32 m (69.5 x 36.1 x 1 ft)
MAIN MACHINERY: two MTU 12V 183 TB 32 V12 diesels; 800 hp (596 kw)
SPEED: 50 kts
RANGE: 400 miles at 45 kts
COMPLEMENT: 13 (two officers)
RADAR: Raytheon R-80; I-band

ARMAMENT:
GUNS: 1-12.7 mm MG

EXTRA FEATURES:
Twin, ducted propellers aft; forward cockpit; low superstructure

Wellington (BH.7) Class Medium-lift Hovercraft UK

Can embark troops and vehicles or normal support cargoes. The Iranian Aircraft Manufacturing Industries (HESA) is reported to be able to maintain these craft in service.

SPECIFICATION:

USED BY:
Iranian amphibious forces

CONTRACTOR:
British Hovercraft Corporation, UK

FEATURES:
DISPLACEMENT: 53.8 tons full load
DIMENSIONS: 23.9 x 13.9 x 1.7 m (78.3 x 45.6 x 5.6 ft) (skirt)
MAIN MACHINERY: one RR Proteus 15 M/541 gas turbine; 1250 hp (3.17 MW) sustained
SPEED: 70 kts; 30 kts in Sea State 5 or more
RANGE: 620 miles at 66 kts
RADARS: Surface search: Decca 1226; I-band

ARMAMENT:
GUNS: 2 Browning 12.7 mm MGS. Mk 5 craft fitted for, but not with Standard missiles

EXTRA FEATURES:
One un-ducted propeller on vertical pod; one angle tail fin; painted in disruptive-pattern camouflage

Textron Marine (LCAC/MCAC) Heavy Lift Hovercraft USA

LCAC 19

SPECIFICATION:

USED BY:
Japanese amphibious forces, US navy

CONTRACTOR:
Textron Marine, USA

FEATURES:
DISPLACEMENT: 87.2 tons light; 170-182 full load
DIMENSIONS: 26.8 m oa (on-cushion) (24.7 ft between hard structures) x 14.3 m beam (on-cushion) (13.1 ft beam hard structure) x 0.9 m draught (off-cushion) (on cushion: 87.9 x 46.9 ft x 2.9 ft off cushion)
MAIN MACHINERY: four Avco-Lycoming TF-40B gas turbines; two for propulsion and two for lift; 16,000 hp (12 MW) sustained; two shrouded reversible-pitch airscrews (propulsion); four double entry fans, centrifugal or mixed flow (lift)

SPEED: 40 kts (loaded)
RANGE: 300 miles at 35 kts; 200 at 40 kts
COMPLEMENT: five
MILITARY LIFT: 24 troops; one MBT or 60-75 tons
RADARS: Navigation: Marconi LN66; I-band

ARMAMENT:
30 mm Gatling guns can be fitted

FEATURES:
Large, open-plan deck; twin, ducted propellers; cockpit forward on starboard side; twin nozzles for vectored thrust abaft the cockpit

Transport:
Sea,
Sub-surface

s-10 Oxygen Rebreather Diving Apparatus CANADA

s-10 diving apparatus

The s-10 is a chest-mounted rebreather diving set designed for specific military and law enforcement agency work in shallow waters. It is a closed-circuit pure oxygen rebreather for use to depths of 8 m. Specific user rules and regulations on oxygen swimming operations may permit the use of the s-10, for brief intervals, to greater depths.

SPECIFICATION:

USED BY:
Some NATO navies

CONTRACTOR:
Carleton Life Support
Technologies Ltd, Canada

FEATURES:
LENGTH: 36 cm
WIDTH: 30 cm
DEPTH: 17 cm
WEIGHT: 12.5 kg
OXYGEN FLASK VOLUME: 1.3 or
1.9 litres
BREATHING BAG CAPACITY: 5.5 litres
ENDURANCE: 4 hours
CHARGING PRESSURE: 206 bar

EXTRA FEATURES:
Large chest bag

R-1 Swimmer Delivery Vehicle (SDV) CROATIA

R-1 submersible

The R-1 is a single-seat underwater SDV designed for covert tasks such as reconnaissance, harbour protection, minefield surveillance and so on. The monohull vehicle is built of aluminium alloy and comprises light bow and stern sections that can be flooded. The vehicle can be transported in a submarine torpedo tube and used in both freshwater and open seas. Navigation instruments are housed in a watertight container and comprise a gyro-magnetic compass, sonar, echo-sounder, electric clock and other measuring systems.

SPECIFICATION:

USED BY:
Croatian, Libyan, Russian, Serbian and Montenegran, Swedish and Syrian maritime Special Forces

CONTRACTOR:
Brodosplit, Split, Croatia

FEATURES:
LENGTH: 3.72 m (12.2 ft)
WIDTH: 1.05 m (3.4 ft)
HEIGHT: 0.76 m (2.5 ft)
DIAMETER: 0.52 m (1.7 ft)
DISPLACEMENT: 320 lbs (145 kg) (less payload)
PAYLOAD: 40 kg (88 lbs)
PROPULSION: DC electric motor, 1 kw; 24 v silver-zinc battery
SPEED: 3 (max); 2.5 kts (cruising)
RANGE: 6 n miles (at max speed); 8 n miles (at cruising speed)
OPERATING DEPTH: 60 m (197 ft)

ARMAMENT:
MINES: 12 limpets

EXTRA FEATURES:
Torpedo-shaped bow section; single crew lying horizontally; handlebar controls

R-2 Mala Class Swimmer Delivery Vehicle (SDV) CROATIA

R-2 dry delivery mode

Croatia operates three R-2 Mala class SDVs. It is a free-flood craft with the main motor, battery, navigation pod and electronic equipment housed in separate watertight cylinders. Instrumentation includes aircraft-type gyrocompass, magnetic compass, depth gauge (with 0 – 100 m scale), echo-sounder, sonar and two searchlights. Constructed of light aluminium and Plexiglas, it is fitted with fore and after-hydroplanes, the tail being a conventional cruciform with a single rudder abaft the screw. Large Perspex windows give a good all-round view.

SPECIFICATION:

USED BY:
Maritime special forces of Croatia, Libya, Russia, Sweden and Syria

CONTRACTOR:
Brodosplit, Split, Croatia

FEATURES:
DISPLACEMENT: 1.4 tons
DIMENSIONS: 4.9 x 1.4 x 1.3 m
(16.1 x 4.6 x 4.3 ft)
MAIN MACHINERY: one motor;
4.5 hp(m) (3.3 kw); one shaft
SPEED: 4.4 kts
RANGE: 18 miles at 4.4 kts;
23 at 3.7 kts
COMPLEMENT: two

ARMAMENT:
MINES: 250 kg of limpet mines

EXTRA FEATURES:
Bulbous shape; large Perspex windows; can operate 'dry' on the surface for delivery

Una Class Midget Submarine CROATIA

The Una Class has exit/re-entry capability with mining capacity. It can carry six combat swimmers, plus four Swimmer Delivery Vehicles and limpet mines. The diving depth is 120 m (394 ft). Batteries can only be charged from shore or from a depot ship. Variations exist between the two operated by Croatia and the six operated by Yugoslavia.

SPECIFICATION:

USED BY:
Croatian maritime Special Forces, Yugoslavian Naval Combat Divers Unit

CONTRACTOR:
Brodosplit, Split, Croatia

FEATURES:
DISPLACEMENT: 76 tons surfaced; 88 dived
DIMENSIONS: 18.8 x 2.7 x 2.5 m (61.7 x 9 x 8.2 ft)
MAIN MACHINERY: two motors; 49 hp(m) (36 kw); one shaft
SPEED: 6 kts surfaced; 7 kts dived
RANGE: 200 miles at 4 kts
COMPLEMENT: six plus four swimmers
SONARS: Atlas Elektronik; passive/active search; high frequency

ARMAMENT:
Either four mines or two torpedoes

EXTRA FEATURES:
Very small; no fin on the Yugoslavian version; snorkel induction mast and exhaust at aft end of fin (Croatia); low profile on the surface; steep, narrow casing running the length of the hull

Orca Swimmer Delivery Vehicle (SDV) GERMANY

The Orca is designed to carry out a broad range of covert missions and is able to operate autonomously in the littoral environment carrying out visual and sensor reconnaissance operations, intelligence gathering and anti-mine warfare tasks. The 'dry' vehicle allows divers to exit and enter through the top or bottom of the hull using a lock-in/lock-out chamber. Stealth is assured as no air bubbles are emitted and the water is not disturbed in any way. The Orca can be fitted with a five-step telescopic mast carrying above-water sensors such as colour video camera with pan and tilt functions, together with HF/VHF radio antenna and GPS antennas. A second video camera fitted in the bow is used for classification and observation. An obstacle avoidance sonar with a range of 200 m is also mounted in the bow. Up to five divers (including the pilot) can be carried to a range in excess of 150 n miles (depending on mission profile and equipment carried).

SPECIFICATION:

USED BY:
German navy combat divers

FEATURES:
DISPLACEMENT: 28 tons
LENGTH: 13.27 m (45 ft o in)
DIAMETER: 2.1 m (6.8 ft)
SPEED: >5 kts
RANGE: 150 n miles
OPERATING DEPTH: 100 m
PAYLOAD: 250 kg

EXTRA FEATURES:
Torpedo-shaped hull with cruciform tail fins

Cakra (209) Class Submarine (SSK) GERMANY

Indonesian Navy Cakra class SSK

SPECIFICATION:

USED BY:
Indonesian navy for the launching and recovering of maritime Special Forces using inflatable craft

CONTRACTOR:
Howaldtswerke, Germany

FEATURES:
DISPLACEMENT: 1 ton, 285 surfaced; 1390 dived
DIMENSIONS: 59.5 x 6.2 x 5.4 m (95.2 x 20.3 x 17.9 ft)
MAIN MACHINERY: Diesel-electric; four MTU 12V 493 AZ80 GA31L diesels; 2400 hp(m) (1.76 MW) sustained; four Siemens alternators; 1.7 MW; one Siemens motor; 4600 hp(m) (3.38 MW) sustained; one shaft
SPEED: 11 kts surfaced; 21.5 kts dived
RANGE: 8200 miles at 8 kts
COMPLEMENT: 34 (six officers)

COUNTERMEASURES: ESM: Thomson-CSF DR 2000U; radar warning
WEAPONS CONTROL: Signaal Sinbad system
RADARS: Surface search: Thomson-CSF Calypso; I-band
SONARS: Atlas Elektronik CSU 3-2; active/passive search and attack; medium frequency. PRS-3/4; (integral with CSU) passive ranging
OPERATIONAL ENDURANCE: 50 days

ARMAMENT:
TORPEDOES: 8-21 in (533 mm) bow tubes; 14 AEG SUT Mod 0; dual purpose; wire-guided; active/passive homing to 12 km (6.5 n miles) at 35 kts; 28 km (15 n miles) at 23 kts; warhead 250 kg

EXTRA FEATURES:
High bow section; low stern; rudder breaks surface

MG 110 Midget Submarine ITALY

Three MG 110 types built in Pakistan under supervision by Cosmos. These are enlarged SX 756 of Italian Cosmos design. They have a diving depth of 150 m and can carry eight swimmers with 2 tons of explosives as well as two CF2 FX 60 SDVS (swimmer delivery vehicles). It features Pilkington Optronics CK 39 periscopes and is reported as having a range of 1000 n miles and an endurance of twenty days. All have been upgraded since 1995 with improved sensors and weapons. All are active.

SPECIFICATION:

USED BY:
Pakistan navy and maritime
Special Forces

CONTRACTOR:
Cosmos SpA, Livorno, Italy (built under licence in Pakistan)

FEATURES:
DISPLACEMENT: 118 tons dived
DIMENSIONS: 27.8 x 5.6 m
(91.2 x 18.4 ft)
SPEED: 7 kts dived
RANGE: 2200 miles surfaced;
60 dived
COMPLEMENT: eight + eight
swimmers
SONARS: hull mounted; active/
passive; high frequency

ARMAMENT:
TORPEDOES: two 21 in (533 mm)
tubes; two AEG SUT; wire-guided;
active homing to 12 km
(6.5 n miles) at 35 kts; passive
homing to 28 km (15 n miles) at
23 kts; warhead 250 kg plus either
two short range active/passive
homing torpedoes or two SDVS.
MINES: 12 Mk 414 Limpet type

EXTRA FEATURES:
Sharp bow; low fin; distinctive
'dorsal' strut at forward end of
casing; similar to the MG 120/ER

MG 120/ER Shallow Water Attack Submarine (SWAT) ITALY

SWAT MG 120/ER on the surface

The MG 120/ER SWATS is designed to carry out both offensive and defensive operations in shallow waters where larger submarines are unable to fully exploit their potential capabilities. The submarine is also able to crawl along the seabed further enhancing its stealth capability. One of the outstanding characteristics of the MG 120/ER SWATS is its range, which exceeds 2000 n miles surfaced. The submarine is also fitted with an AIP system called the Underwater Auxiliary Propulsion Engine comprising a closed circuit diesel fuelled by liquid oxygen. This gives a submerged radius of 400 n miles. The boat is manned by a crew of six and can carry up to fifteen combat divers.

SPECIFICATION:

USED BY:
Maritime Special Forces of Italy; variants also with the navies of Colombia, South Korea, Pakistan and others

CONTRACTOR:
Cosmos SpA, Livorno, Italy

ARMAMENT:
Armament configurations can be varied according to the mission in hand and may comprise up to four wire-guided torpedoes, two chariots, 16 mini-torpedoes, four remote-controlled Chariots, up to 12 ground influence (magnetic/ acoustic) mines, 20 limpet mines, or commando gear containers

EXTRA FEATURES:
Sharp bow; low fin; distinctive 'dorsal' strut forward end of casing; similar to the MG 110

Midget Submarine ITALY

Colombian Navy midget submarine

Two listed by the Colombian Navy as 'Tactical Submarines'. They can carry eight swimmers with two tons of explosive as well as two swimmer delivery vehicles (SDVs). It was commissioned at 40 tons, but subsequently enlarged in the early 1980s.

SPECIFICATION:

USED BY:
Colombian navy

CONTRACTOR:
Cosmos SpA, Livorno, Italy

FEATURES:
DISPLACEMENT: 58 tons surfaced; 70 dived
DIMENSIONS: 23 x 4 m (75.5 x 13.1 ft)
MAIN MACHINERY: Diesel-electric; one diesel; one motor; 300 hp(m) (221 kw); one shaft
SPEED: 11 kts surfaced; 6 kts dived
RANGE: 1200 miles surfaced; 60 dived
COMPLEMENT: four

ARMAMENT:
MINES: six Mk 21 with 300 kg warhead; eight Mk 11 with 50 kg warhead

EXTRA FEATURES:
Snort mast abaft the fin; sharp bow

Chariot CE2F/X100T Swimmer Delivery Vehicle ITALY

Chariot CE2F/X100T with relative armamants

The Chariot or SDV (Swimmer Delivery Vehicle) is the result of a continuing upgrade project of the famous Italian Maiali of the Second World War. Because of their endurance, chariots are normally transported to within their operating range by a parent ship such as a SWAT, patrol submarine, helicopter or even an innocent-looking fishing vessel. The Chariot is designed to navigate undetected in hostile waters and carry two combat divers to their target (harbour, oil rig, coastal installation and so on) and then back to the parent ship after completion of the mission.

SPECIFICATION:

USED BY:
Argentinian, Egyptian, Indian and Italian maritime Special Forces

CONTRACTOR:
Cosmos SpA, Livorno, Italy

FEATURES:
LENGTH: 7.0 m (23 ft)
DIAMETER: 0.8 m (2.6 ft)
HEIGHT: 1.50 m (4.9 ft)
DISPLACEMENT: 2.1 tons
OPERATING DEPTH: 100 m (328 ft)
SPEED: 5 kts (max); 4 kts (cruise)
RANGE: 50 n miles (at cruise speed)
CREW: two

ARMAMENT:
One Mk 31 (230 kg explosive) or two Mk 41s (105 kg explosive) or one Mk 41 and five mini-torpedoes, 12 Mk 414 limpet mines (7 kg explosive each) or ten Mk 430 limpet mines (15 kg explosive each)

EXTRA FEATURES:
Two crew sitting astride the SDV; torpedo-shaped hull

Sang-o Class Mini Submarine

PEOPLE'S DEMOCRATIC REPUBLIC OF KOREA (NORTH)

Used extensively for infiltration operations. The submarine can bottom, and swimmer disembarkation is reported as being normally exercised from periscope depth. One of the class grounded and was captured by South Korea on 18 September 1996. Some crew members may be replaced by Special Forces for short operations.

SPECIFICATION:

USED BY:
North Korean maritime Special Forces

CONTRACTOR:
Sinpo, North Korea

FEATURES:
DISPLACEMENT: 256 tons surfaced; 277 dived
DIMENSIONS: 35.5 x 3.8 x 3.7 m (116.5 x 12.5 x 12.1 ft)
MAIN MACHINERY: one Russian diesel generator; one North Korean motor; one shaft; shrouded prop
SPEED: 7.6 kts surfaced; 7.2 kts snorting; 8.8 kts dived
RANGE: 2700 miles at 7 kts
COMPLEMENT: 19 (two officers) plus six swimmers
RADARS: Surface search: Furuno; I-band
SONARS: Russian hull-mounted; passive/active search and attack

ARMAMENT:
TORPEDOES: two or four 21 in (533 mm) tubes (in some); probably Russian Type 53-56
MINES: 16 can be carried (in some)

Yugo and P-4 Class Midget Submarines

PEOPLE'S DEMOCRATIC REPUBLIC OF KOREA (NORTH)

More than one design. Details given are for the latest type, at least one of which has been exported to Iran, who have been building since 1987 to a Yugoslavian design. Some have two short external torpedo tubes and some have a snort mast. The conning tower acts as a wet and dry compartment for divers. There is a second and smaller propeller for slow speed manoeuvring while dived. Two of the class are designated P-4s. This type has two internal torpedo tubes and operate from merchant mother ships. Some North Korean craft have been lost in operations against South Korea, the latest in June 1998. Two were exported to Vietnam in June 1997.

SPECIFICATION:

USED BY:
Iran and North Korean maritime Special Forces and the Vietnamese Peoples Navy

CONTRACTOR:
Yukdaesu-ri shipyard, North Korea

FEATURES:
DISPLACEMENT: 90 tons surfaced; 110 dived
DIMENSIONS: 20 x 3.1 x 4.6 m (65.6 x 10.2 x 15.1 ft)
MAIN MACHINERY: two diesels; 320 hp(m)(236 kw); one shaft
SPEED: 12 kts surfaced; 8 kts dived
RANGE: 550 miles at 10 kts; surfaced; 50 at 4 kts dived
COMPLEMENT: four plus six to seven divers
RADARS: Navigation: I-band

ARMAMENT:
TORPEDOES: two 406 mm tubes

EXTRA FEATURES:
Very small; disruptive pattern camouflage scheme

Swimmer Delivery Vehicle (SDV) IRAN

Al Sabehat 15

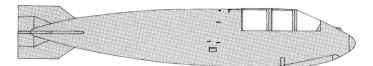

On 29 August 2000, the first Iranian-built
Swimmer Delivery Vehicle (SDV) Al Sabehat 15 was
launched at Bandar Abbas. The 8 m (26.2 feet) craft
can accommodate a two-man crew and has the
capability to carry three additional divers. It is well
suited for coastal reconnaissance, Special Forces
insertion/extraction and mining (it can carry
fourteen limpet mines) of ports and anchorages
but not for open water operations.

SPECIFICATION:

USED BY:
Iranian maritime Special Forces

CONTRACTOR:
Not known. Bandar Abbas, Iran

FEATURES:
Torpedo-shaped hull with
aircraft-style windows; enclosed
propeller within combined
rudder and diving planes

Midget Submarine SWEDEN

Spiggen II

SPECIFICATION:

USED BY:
Swedish navy

CONTRACTOR:
Forsvarets Materielverk, Sweden

FEATURES:
DISPLACEMENT: 17 tons dived
DIMENSIONS: 10.6 x 1.7 x 1.4 m
(34.8 x 5.6 x 4.6 ft)
MAIN MACHINERY: one Volvo
Penta diesel; one shaft
SPEED: 5 kts dived; 6 kts surfaced
COMPLEMENT: four
ENDURANCE: 14 days
DIVING DEPTH: 100 m (300 ft)

FEATURES:
Bulbous fin; mast abaft fin

Class 4 and Class 5 Long Range Submersible Carriers (LRSC) UNITED ARAB EMIRATES

Class 5 diver controls

Both Class 4 and Class 5 are fitted with on board computers, sonars with a range of 150 m (492 ft), echo sounders, GPS and navigational aids. Both carry a crew of two divers.

SPECIFICATION:

USED BY:
UAE Special Forces

MANUFACTURER:
Emirates Marine Technologies, UAE

FEATURES:
LENGTH: Class 4: 7.35 m (24 ft); Class 5: 9.1 m (30 ft)
CRUISING SPEED: 6 kts (maximum speed of 7 kts)
RANGE: 60 n miles
DEPTH: 50 m (164 ft)
ENDURANCE: 6 hours with a built-in breathing system; rebreathers giving longer time underwater

DISPLACEMENT: (surface) Class 4: 1.5 tonnes; Class 5: 3.5 tonnes
PAYLOAD: Class 4: 200 kg; Class 5: 450 kg

ARMAMENT:
Both classes can deliver explosives and place limpet mines while their divers/crew can carry out sabotage or surveillance

EXTRA FEATURES:
Two crew; glass and carbon fibre construction

Stealth Divex Rebreather Diving Equipment UK

Divex closed-circuit mixed-gas rebreather

This system was designed to meet the requirements of Explosive Ordnance Disposal and Special Forces and incorporates modern materials, microprocessing power and the latest technology in underwater breathing apparatus design.

The Divex rebreather is an electronically controlled closed-circuit mixed-gas system available as two options for military diving. It features a buoyancy compensator and can be fitted with a bailout system. Closed-circuit breathing systems function by maintaining a breathable gas mixture for the diver at depth through removing the CO_2 from exhaled gas via the scrubber unit, and injecting pure oxygen to replace the oxygen metabolised by the diver. The aim is to replace the oxygen in the quantity at which it is consumed, whatever the breathing rate and metabolic rate. With the rebreather a diver can stay at a depth of 100 m (328 feet) for up to 20 minutes. Operating endurance is between four and six hours.

SPECIFICATION:

USED BY:
UK SBS

MANUFACTURER:
Divex Ltd, Aberdeen, UK

FEATURES:
Large 'back-pack'

Oxymax Closed-circuit Oxygen Diving Set UK

Oxymax 3 is a compact oxygen rebreather set providing up to three hours' endurance at depths of up to 10 m (33 ft), depending on conditions. It is inherently non-magnetic in construction (but can be ratified as fully 'non-magnetic' to special order) and is characteristically low in operating noise.

SPECIFICATION:

USED BY:
In service with an unspecified number of maritime Special Forces

CONTRACTOR:
Divex Ltd, Aberdeen, UK

FEATURES:
Large chest bag; horizontal oxygen cylinder beneath

ssk 96 Subskimmer Rigid Inflatable Boat UK

ssk 96 in awash mode

The ssk 96 Subskimmer is designed especially for combat swimmers. The hull is that of a rigid-hulled inflatable fitted with a two-stroke, three-cylinder 90 hp Yamaha outboard engine which is also capable of operating submerged. Conversion to submersible mode is quick and simple, taking approximately 90 seconds. Underwater the craft is manoeuvrable and easy to control. Electric propulsion units, flexibly mounted near the bows, provide forward motion that is achieved by simply pointing the unit in the desired direction. As all the dry systems are in water-tight and pressure-tight housings, the vehicle may be left parked on the seabed for days as operational needs dictate. Underwater its endurance is over two hours on standard batteries. It can be operated single-handed.

SPECIFICATION:

USED BY:
Thailand maritime Special Forces and others

CONTRACTOR:
KSA (Underwater) Ltd, Alston, UK

FEATURES:
LENGTH: (inflated) 5.80 m (19 ft); (deflated) 5.40 m (17.7 ft)
WIDTH: (inflated) 1.90 m (6.2 ft); (deflated) 1.60 m (5.2 ft)
HEIGHT: 1.20 m (3.9 ft)
DRAFT: (max/min): 0.70/0.30 m (2.3/0.9 ft)
DISPLACEMENT: 1520 kg
PAYLOAD (CREW, FUEL, AND STORES): 600 kg
SPEED: 25 kts
SURFACE RANGE: 70 n miles

EXTRA FEATURES:
RIB configuration on the surface but with snorkel tubes

Advanced SEAL Delivery System (ASDS) USA

These are dry submersibles capable of deploying from a mother submarine to a hostile shore. Optical and comms periscopes are fitted plus a small sonar. It can be carried by a C-5 or C-17 transport aircraft or on the deck of a submarine.

SPECIFICATION:

USED BY:
US SEAL teams

CONTRACTOR:
Northrop Grumman, USA

SPECIFICATIONS:
LENGTH: 20 m (65 ft)
BREADTH: 3 m (10 ft)
DISPLACEMENT: 55 tons
CREW: two
EMBARKED FORCE: eight SEALS
RANGE: 125 n miles at 8 kts
PROPULSION: 55hp motor and
four thrusters

Dry Deck Shelter USA

USS Philadelphia with DDS

The DDS (Dry Deck Shelter) was developed to fit on submarines for the carriage of Swimmer Delivery Vehicles (SDVs). These shelters are used to transport and launch the SDV or to lock out combat swimmers. Submarines are equipped with special fittings and with modifications to their air systems as well as additional systems to enable them to carry the DDS abaft the sail. These adaptations permit free passage between the submarine and the DDS while submerged. The watertight connection allows the divers to enter the DDS while the boat is still submerged and to exit the DDS together with their SDV, equipment and/or rubber inflatables and carry out their mission. The air transportable DDS can be installed on modified submarines in about twelve hours.

The DDS is subdivided into three watertight compartments housed within a GRP fairing. The forward spherical compartment is used to treat injured divers. The middle spherical compartment is a transfer chamber which allows divers to enter and exit from the submarine and to enter either or both of the other compartments in the DDS. The aft compartment is a hangar with elliptical ends, used to carry an SDV or special equipment for the divers.

SPECIFICATION:

USED BY:
UK (in due course) and US maritime Special Forces

CONTRACTOR:
General Dynamics Electric Boat Division, Northrop Grumman, USA

FEATURES:
LENGTH: 11.6 m (38 ft)
DIAMETER: 2.75 m (9 ft)
DISPLACEMENT: 30 tons
PAYLOAD: one SDV

EXTRA FEATURES:
Large tubular structure abaft the fin of a submarine; hinged after end opens for the full circumference

Mk VIII Mod 1 SEAL Delivery Vehicle USA

The USN operates ten; the UK's SBS took delivery of three in 1999. In both countries these have replaced the ageing Mk 8 Mod 0 SDVs. These new SDVs have twice the range (67 km or 36 n miles at a maximum speed of 9 kts) of their predecessors. This all-electric Mod 1 can transport six fully equipped combat swimmers in its fully flooded compartments.

SPECIFICATION:

USED BY:
UK SBS and US SEAL teams

MANUFACTURER:
Not known; possibly Northrop Grumman, USA

FEATURES:
LENGTH: 6.7 m (22 ft)

ARMAMENT:
Six combat divers

EXTRA FEATURES:
Full flooding crew compartment; uniform hull shape with enclosed propeller

Transport:
Sea, Surface

High Speed Interceptor Craft (HSIC) AUSTRALIA

Eight have been built by Queensland Ships and delivered in September 1997. These craft replaced earlier high speed craft.

SPECIFICATION:

USED BY:
Hong Kong Police Anti-Smuggling Task Force

CONTRACTOR:
Queensland Ships, Australia

FEATURES:
DISPLACEMENT: 2.7 tons full load
DIMENSIONS: 8.5 x 2.6 x 0.7 m
(28.3 x 8.7 x 2.4 ft)
MAIN MACHINERY: two Mercury
outboards; 500 hp (373 kw)
SPEED: 51 kts
COMPLEMENT: three

ARMAMENT:
Personal weapons: as required

EXTRA FEATURES:
Twin outboards; sectional
inflatable collar; midships control
station; high-backed seats aft

High Speed Logistics Craft AUSTRALIA

HSV-X1

Chartered by US from Incat, Tasmania.
Modifications to the commercial design include
deck strengthening, a 472 m² helicopter deck,
suitable for SH-60 and CH-46 and a two-part
hydraulically operated vehicle ramp to facilitate
rapid loading/unloading from stern or alongside.
Military communications have also been fitted.
Manned by a joint Army/Navy crew, the ship is
being used by both services in a series of exercises
and trials. Typical roles being examined include
Naval Special Warfare, Ship-to-Objective
Manoeuvre and intra-theatre lift of a Brigade
Combat Team.

SPECIFICATION:

USED BY:
On trial by, amongst others, US
Special Operations Command

CONTRACTOR:
Incat, Tasmania, Australia

FEATURES:
DISPLACEMENT: 1872 tons
DIMENSIONS: 96.0 x 27.0 x 3.7 m
(315.0 x 88.5 x 12.1 ft)
MAIN MACHINERY: four CAT 3618
diesels; 38,620 hp (28.8 MW);
four LIPS 150D waterjets
SPEED: 48 kts (light); 38 kts
(full load)
RANGE: 2400 miles at 35 kts
MILITARY LIFT: 815 tonnes cargo
and 350 personnel

EXTRA FEATURES:
Distinctive large catamaran hull;
US Navy colour scheme;
aluminium construction

Inshore Patrol Craft CHINA

Border Security Force speedboat

Details given are for the standard small patrol craft. In addition there are a number of speedboats confiscated from smugglers and used for interception duties.

SPECIFICATION:

USED BY:
Chinese Maritime Security Force

FEATURES:
DISPLACEMENT: 32 tons full load
DIMENSIONS: 62 x 13.1 x 3.6 m
(18.9 x 4 x 1.1 ft)
MAIN MACHINERY: two diesels;
900 hp(m)(662 kw); two shafts
SPEED: 15 kts
COMPLEMENT: five

ARMAMENT:
GUNS: one 12.7 mm MG

EXTRA FEATURES:
Small; not fast; lightly armed

Stealth High Speed Insertion Craft (HSIC) CHINA

Stealth assault craft

Since 1996 large numbers of low profile stealth craft have been active in the South Sea areas, and have been reported as far away as the Philippines. Sizes vary from 30 to 60 m (98 – 197 ft) in length and many are capable of speeds in excess of 30 kts. Most are paramilitary vessels but some may be privately owned.

SPECIFICATION:

USED BY:
Chinese maritime Special Forces

FEATURES:
Long, flushed deck hulls; single superstructure resembling a submarine's fin

Assault and River Craft COLOMBIA

Eduardoño class (1 & 2) and high speed interceptor class (3)

Fifty-one Colombian-built 'Eduardoño' class assault craft of about 10 m (33 ft) length and powered by two Yamaha outboards; 400 hp (298 kw). In addition there are five high-speed interceptor craft whose country of origin is not known.

SPECIFICATION:

USED BY:
Nicaraguan maritime Special Forces

CONTRACTOR:
Not known, Colombia

Fast Raiding Craft FINLAND

Based on Swedish 'Gruppbat'.

SPECIFICATION:

USED BY:
Finnish Naval Special Operations Units

CONTRACTOR:
Alutech Ltd, Finland

FEATURES:
DISPLACEMENT: 3 tons full load
DIMENSIONS: 8 x 2.1 x 0.3 m
(26.2 x 6.9 x 1 ft)

MAIN MACHINERY: one Yanmar 4;
LHA-STE diesel; 240 hp (179 kw);
one RR FF-jet 240 waterjet
SPEED: 30 kts
COMPLEMENT: one
MILITARY LIFT: nine troops with
equipment

EXTRA FEATURES:
Control consul aft with
windscreen; solid guard-rails aft;
grey painted; waterjet

Jurmo Class Fast Raiding Craft FINLAND

Developed for a troop carrying role. The prototype was delivered in 1999. It features a cargo hatch of composite material to provide ballistic protection.

SPECIFICATION:

USED BY:
Finnish Naval Special Operations Unit

CONTRACTOR:
Alutech Ltd, Finland

FEATURES:
DISPLACEMENT: 10 tons full load
DIMENSIONS: 13.3 x 3.5 x 0.6 m (43.6 x 11.5 x 2.0 ft)
MAIN MACHINERY: two Caterpillar diesels; two FF-jet 375 waterjets
SPEED: 30+ kts
COMPLEMENT: two
MILITARY LIFT: 21 troops with equipment or 2.5 tons cargo
RADARS: Navigation: I-band

ARMAMENT:
GUNS: one 12.7 mm MG

EXTRA FEATURES:
Downward sloping fore-deck; double, ribbed, rubbing strake; solid mast; disruptive pattern camouflage; two waterjets

Baklan Class High Speed Interceptor Class FRANCE

Top speed up to Sea State 3 and a composite hull construction.

SPECIFICATION:

USED BY
Yemeni combined navy/army Special Forces unit

CONTRACTOR:
CMN, France

FEATURES:
DISPLACEMENT: 12 tons full load
DIMENSIONS: 15.5 x 3 x 0.8 m (50.9 x 9.8 x 2.6 ft)
MAIN MACHINERY: two diesels; two surface drives
SPEED: 55 kts
RANGE: 400 miles at 30 kts
COMPLEMENT: four
RADARS: Surface search: Furuno; I-band

ARMAMENT:
GUNS: two 12.7 mm MG

EXTRA FEATURES:
Long, slim hull; central, enclosed cockpit; semi-solid goal post aft for antennae

Manta Class High Speed Patrol/Interceptor Craft FRANCE

Aluminium construction. This version has two inboard engines. Pennant numbers are in odd number sequence.

SPECIFICATION:

USED BY:
Kuwaiti navy

CONTRACTOR:
Simmonneau, France

FEATURES:
DISPLACEMENT: 10 tons full load
DIMENSIONS: 14 x 3.8 x 0.7 m
(45.9 x 12.5 x 2.3 ft)
MAIN MACHINERY: two Caterpillar
3208 diesels; 810 hp(m) (595 kw)
sustained; two shafts
SPEED: 40 kts
RANGE: 180 miles at 35 kts
COMPLEMENT: four
RADARS: Surface search: Furuno;
I-band

ARMAMENT:
GUNS: three Herstal M2HB
12.7 mm MG

EXTRA FEATURES:
Fully enclosed wheelhouse; raked
goalpost for antennae; single gun
position forward; twin gun
position aft

Inshore Patrol Craft FRANCE

Simonneau type

About five hundred, mostly Task Force Boats, of which the illustration is an example. Many are based at Jiddah with the rest spread around the other bases. Most are armed with MGs and the larger craft have I-band radars.

SPECIFICATION:

USED BY:
Saudi Arabian Coast Guard Task
Force

CONTRACTOR:
Simonneau, France

FEATURES: (TYPE/DATE/SPEED)
RAPIER: 15.2 m/1976/28 kts
ENFORCER: USA 9.4 m/1980s/
30 kts
SIMONNEAU: SM 331 9.3 m/1992/
40 kts
BOSTON WHALERS: 8.3 m/1980s/
30 kts
CATAMARANS: 6.4 m/1977/30 kts
TASK FORCE BOATS: 5.25 m/1976/
20 kts
VIPER: 5.1 m/1980s/25 kts
COBRA: 3.9 m/1984/40 kts

Klepper Kayak GERMANY

17.5 ft long, folding, two-man canoe.

SPECIFICATION:

USED BY:
UK Royal Marines SBS

CONTRACTOR:
Klepper Kayaks, Rosenheim,
Germany

Lürssen Very Slim High Speed Interceptor Craft GERMANY

SPECIFICATION:

USED BY:
Indonesian Customs in
interceptor role

CONTRACTOR:
Lürssen, Germany

FEATURES:
DISPLACEMENT: 11 tons full load
DIMENSIONS: 16 x 2.8 x 1 m
(52.5 x 9.2 x 3.3 ft)
MAIN MACHINERY: two MTU
diesels; 600 hp(m) (441 kw);
two shafts
SPEED: 50 kts
RANGE: 750 miles at 30 kts
COMPLEMENT: five (one officer)

ARMAMENT:
GUNS: one 7.62 mm MG

EXTRA FEATURES:
Very slim; extreme, sloping
windshield and enclosed control
position; forward-raked bow

Ashoora Class Inshore Patrol Craft IRAN

Eight acquired from Iran in 1992-94. Based at Flamingo Bay.

SPECIFICATION:

USED BY:
Sudanese naval forces

CONTRACTOR:
IRI Marine Industries, Iran

FEATURES:
DISPLACEMENT: 3 tons full load
DIMENSIONS: 8.1 x 2.4 x 0.5 m
(26.6 x 8 x 1.6 ft)
MAIN MACHINERY: two Yamaha
outboards; 400 hp(m) (294 kw)
SPEED: 42 kts
COMPLEMENT: two

ARMAMENT:
GUNS: one 7.62 mm MG

EXTRA FEATURES:
Twin outboard engines; control
consul aft

Ashoora Assault Craft IRAN

SPECIFICATION:

USED BY:
Iranian Revolutionary Guard
maritime Special Forces,
Sudanese maritime forces

CONTRACTOR:
Not known, Iran

FEATURES:
DIMENSIONS: 8.1 x 2.4 m
(26.6 x 7.9 ft)
PROPULSION: two outboards
SPEED: 42 kts

ARMAMENT:
GUNS: one 7.62 mm MG

EXTRA FEATURES:
Covered bow, open stern; twin
outboards

Jet Ski Assault Craft IRAN

SPECIFICATION:

USED BY:
Revolutionary Guard maritime
Special Forces

CONTRACTOR:
Not known, Iran

ARMAMENT:
One RPG (as an example)

FEATURES:
Jet ski with a two-man, armed
crew

MIG-G-0800 IRAN

SPECIFICATION:

USED BY:
Pasdaran Marine Special Forces

CONTRACTOR:
Not known but local build based
on the Boston Whaler (US) and
Watercraft (UK)

FEATURES:
DISPLACEMENT: 3.5 tons full load
DIMENSIONS: 9.2 x 2.8 x 0.45 m
(30.2 x 9.2 x 1.5 ft)
MAIN MACHINERY: two Volvo
Penta diesels; 1260 hp (940 kw)
SPEED: 30 kts
COMPLEMENT: three
Radar: Surface search: I-band

ARMAMENT:
ROCKETS: one RPG-7 rocket
launcher or 106 mm recoilless
rifle; one 12-barrelled 107 mm
rocket launcher (MRL)
GUNS: three 12.7 mm MGS

EXTRA FEATURES:
Boston Whaler type; aft control
consul

Type 4 Fast Patrol Craft IRAN

SPECIFICATION:

USED BY:
Iranian Revolutionary Guard
maritime Special Forces

CONTRACTOR:
Not known, Iran

FEATURES:
DIMENSIONS: 3.9 x 1.6 m
(13.1 x 5.2 ft)
PROPULSION: two outboard
engines

ARMAMENT:
Small arms

EXTRA FEATURES:
Twin outboards; heavy rubbing
strake

Army Craft ITALY

SPECIFICATION:

USED BY:
Italy's Serenissima Amphibious
Regiment on the Venice Lagoon

CONTRACTOR:
Not known, Italy

High Speed Intercept Craft (HSIC) ITALY

Donated by the Angelopoulos family to the Hellenic Navy for use by Special Forces. It is a Rigid Hull Inflatable Boat with removable synthetic armour panels.

SPECIFICATION:

USED BY:
Hellenic Navy Special Forces

CONTRACTOR:
Fabio Buzzi, Italy

FEATURES:
DISPLACEMENT: 6.3 tons full load
DIMENSIONS: 12.8 x ? x ? m
(42 x ? x ? ft)
SPEED: 60+ kts
COMPLEMENT: four

ARMAMENT:
GRENADE LAUNCHER: one 40 mm
Mk 19
GUNS: one 12.7 mm MG; two 7.62
mm MGS

EXTRA FEATURES:
Very low and flat, rigid inflatable
hull; light coloured, disruptive
camouflage; goal post
arrangement for radar above
conning position

V 5000/6000 High Speed Interceptors (HSIC) ITALY

V 6001 (1) and V 5006 (2)

Details are for V 6003-6012. V 6001-6002 are smaller prototype craft with three engines and a top speed of 64 kts. The V 5000 class are smaller craft with a top speed of 55 kts.

SPECIFICATION:

USED BY:
Italy's *Servizio Navale Guardia de Finanza* in pursuit of maritime criminals

CONTRACTOR:
Not known, Italy

FEATURES:
DISPLACEMENT: 16 tons full load
DIMENSIONS: 16.4 x 2.8 x 0.8 m
(53.8 x 9.2 x 2.6 ft)
MAIN MACHINERY: four Seatek
6-4V-10D diesels; 2856 hp(m)
(2.13 MW) sustained; four surface-piercing propellers
SPEED: 72 kts
COMPLEMENT: four
RADARS: Surface search: I-band

EXTRA FEATURES:
Long, slim, sleek and very fast;
fully enclosed wheelhouse

High Speed Infiltration Craft (HSIC) and Semi-submersible NORTH KOREA

SPECIFICATION:

USED BY:
North Korean maritime Special Forces

CONTRACTOR:
Not known, North Korea

FEATURES:
DISPLACEMENT: 5 tons full load
DIMENSIONS: 9.3 x 2.5 x 1 m
(30.5 x 8.2 x 3.1 ft)
MAIN MACHINERY: one diesel;
260 hp(m) (191 kw); one shaft
SPEED: 35 kts
COMPLEMENT: two
RADARS: Navigation: Furuno 701;
I-band

ARMAMENT:
GUNS: one 7.62 mm MG

Large numbers built for agent infiltration and covert operations. These craft have a very low radar cross-section and 'squat' at high speeds. A newer version was reported in 1998. This is 12.8 m (14 ft) in length and has a top speed of about 45 kts. It is reported to travel on the surface until submerging to a depth of 3 m (10 ft) using a snort mast. It has a dived speed of 4 kts.

High Speed Patrol/Interceptor Craft (HSIC) MALAYSIA

SPECIFICATION:

USED BY:
Malaysian Customs

Fast Patrol Boats MEXICO

G 19 (1), C 101-01 (2) and C 2001-01 (3)

Details are for the 36 G 01-36 'Pirana' class. C 101-01 is the 50-knot 'Interceptor' class launch. There are also ten 8.8 m (29 feet) Mako Marine craft, with twin Mercury outboards and five Sea Force 730 RIBS with Hamilton waterjets.

SPECIFICATION:

USED BY:
Mexican navy

FEATURES:
DIMENSIONS: 6.8 x 2.3 x 0.3 m (22.3 x 7.5 x 1 ft)
MAIN MACHINERY: two Johnson outboards; 280 hp (209 kw)
SPEED: 40 kts
RANGE: 190 miles at 40 kts
COMPLEMENT: two

ARMAMENT:
GUNS: one or two 7.62 mm MGS

Sea Stalker 1500 Class High Speed Insertion Craft (HSIC) NETHERLANDS

SPECIFICATION:

USED BY:
Hong Kong Police Anti-
Smuggling Task Force

CONTRACTOR:
Damen, Gorinchem, Netherlands

FEATURES:
DISPLACEMENT: 7.5 tons full load
DIMENSIONS: 14.8 x 2.9 x 0.8 m
(48.6 x 9.5 x 2.6 ft)
MAIN MACHINERY: three
Mercruiser Bulldog v8;
1500 hp(m)(1.1 MW); three shafts
SPEED: 55 kts; 45 kts in Sea State 3
COMPLEMENT: eight
RADARS: Surface search:
Raytheon; I-band

ARMAMENT:
GUNS: two 2 12.7 mm MGS

EXTRA FEATURES:
Smooth, downward sloping
foredeck; three shafts

Fast Patrol Boat PANAMA

SPECIFICATION:

USED BY:
Panamanian maritime forces

FEATURES:
DIMENSIONS: 10.2 x 2.3 x 0.6 m
(33.5 x 7.5 x 2 ft)
MAIN MACHINERY: two Yamaha
outboards; 400 hp(m)(294 kw)

SPEED: 35 kts
COMPLEMENT: four

ARMAMENT:
GUNS: one 7.62 mm MG

EXTRA FEATURES:
Long, hard-chine, open hulls;
control consol aft

Lake and River Patrol Craft PERU

PF 264 Lake and river patrol craft

Based at Puno on Lake Titicaca. GRP hulls built in 1982. Various types.

SPECIFICATION:

USED BY:
Peruvian Coast Guard

SPECIFICATIONS:
DISPLACEMENT: 5 tons full load
DIMENSIONS: 10 x 3.4 x 0.8 m
(32.8 x 11.2 x 2.6 ft)
MAIN MACHINERY: two Perkins
diesels; 480 hp (358 kw);
two shafts
SPEED: 15 kts
RANGE: 450 miles at 28 kts
COMPLEMENT: three
RADARS: Surface search: Raytheon
2800; I-band

ARMAMENT:
GUNS: one 12.7 mm MG

FEATURES:
Machine gun mounted well
forward; open control consul aft;
some have twin outboards;
deep hull

Rigid Inflatable POLAND

SG 005 (1) and SG 004 (2)

SPECIFICATION:

USED BY:
Sea Department of the Border
Guard (MOSG) maritime Special
Forces

FEATURES:
Rigid inflatable hulls; inboard
engines

Assault Craft SINGAPORE

Man-portable craft which can carry a section of troops in the rivers and creeks surrounding Singapore island.

SPECIFICATION:

USED BY:
Singapore Army Special Forces Battalion

CONTRACTOR:
SBEC, Singapore

FEATURES:
DIMENSIONS: 5.4 x 1.8 x 0.7 m (17.7 x 5.9 x 2.3 ft)
MAIN MACHINERY: one outboard; 50 hp(m) (37 kw)
SPEED: 12 kts
MILITARY LIFT: 12 troops

ARMAMENT:
GUNS: one 7.62 mm MG or 40 mm grenade launcher

EXTRA FEATURES:
Slab topsides; metal, exterior hand-grabs; single outboard

Harbour Craft SINGAPORE

RHIB

There are large numbers of harbour craft, many of them armed. These include four RHIBs with Yamaha 200 hp outboards capable of 43 kts.

High Speed Interceptor Class (HSIC) SINGAPORE

SPECIFICATION:

USED BY:
Singapore Navy Diving Unit

CONTRACTOR:
Boston Whaler, USA

FEATURES:
DISPLACEMENT: 12.5 tons full load
DIMENSIONS: 14.5 x 2.85 x 1.35 m
(47.6 x 9.4 x 4.4 ft)
MAIN MACHINERY: Triple Seatek
diesels coupled to Trimax drives
SPEED: 55+ kts
RADARS: Raytheon SL 72

ARMAMENT:
GUNS: two CIS 40 mm AGL;
two CIS 50 12.7 mm MGs;
one 7.62 mm GPMG

EXTRA FEATURES:
Long, slim, low hull; very fast;
streamlined, enclosed cockpit

High Speed Interceptor Craft SINGAPORE

FEATURES:
DIMENSIONS: 12.8 x 3.2 x 0.5 m
(42 x 10.5 x 1.6 ft)
MAIN MACHINERY: three
Mercruiser 502 Magnum diesels;
three shafts
SPEED: 50 kts
COMPLEMENT: five

ARMAMENT:
GUNS: one 7.62 mm MG

EXTRA FEATURES:
Dark blue hulls; fully enclosed
cockpit; goalpost on transom for
antennae

Dark blue hulls and grey superstructures, to make
the craft less visible at sea.

Delta 80 LCU SOUTH AFRICA

Two each can be carried in the fleet replenishment ships.

SPECIFICATION:

USED BY:
South African navy

FEATURES:
DISPLACEMENT: 5.5 tons full load
DIMENSIONS: 8.3 x 3.1 x 0.9 m
(27.2 x 10.2 x 3 ft)
MAIN MACHINERY: two outboards;
350 hp (261 kw)
SPEED: 37 kts
RANGE: 150 miles at 35 kts
COMPLEMENT: five

EXTRA FEATURES:
Full length rubbing strakes along
flared bow; control position aft

Stingray Interceptor Class Patrol Boat SOUTH AFRICA

SPECIFICATION:

USED BY:
Israeli maritime Special Forces

CONTRACTOR:
Stingray Marine, South Africa

FEATURES:
DISPLACEMENT: 10.5 tons full load
DIMENSIONS: 12 x 4.4 x 0.9 m
(39.4 x 14.5 x 2.9 ft)
MAIN MACHINERY: two Caterpillar
marine diesels; two shafts
SPEED: 35 kts
RANGE: 300 miles at cruising
speed
COMPLEMENT: five
RADAR: Surface search: I-band

EXTRA FEATURES:
Catamaran hull; high goal-post
for the radar and radio antenna

High Speed Intercept Craft (HSIC) SPAIN

SPECIFICATION:

USED BY:
Spanish maritime forces

FEATURES:
Twin outboard engines; tubular goalpost aft for navigation lights and antennae

Details not known but likely to be capable of speeds in excess of 45 kts.

Combatboat 90 E (Stridsbåt) SWEDEN

SPECIFICATION:

USED BY:
Chinese Customs Service, Malaysian Customs Service and the Swedish Amphibious Corps

CONTRACTOR:
Storebro Royal Cruiser, Sweden

FEATURES:
DISPLACEMENT: 9 tons full load
DIMENSIONS: 11.9 x 2.9 x 0.7 m (39 x 9.5 x 2.3 ft)
MAIN MACHINERY: one Scania AB DSI 14 diesel; 398 hp(m) (293 kW) sustained; FFJet 410 waterjet
SPEED: 40 kts; 37 kts (laden)
COMPLEMENT: two
MILITARY LIFT: 2 tons or six to ten troops
RADARS: Furuno 8050; I-band

EXTRA FEATURES:
Short, stubby bow ramp; three oblong ports in superstructure; fully enclosed cockpit forward

Malaysian craft have more powerful engines than the boats in Swedish service.

Combatboat 90 H (Stridsbåt) SWEDEN

Combatboat with twin 120 mm mortar (1) and Combatboat (2)

This craft has a large hatch forward to aid disembarkation. All have a 20° deadrise and all carry four six-man inflatable rafts.

SPECIFICATION:

USED BY:
Chinese paramilitary forces, Greek Coast Guard, Malaysian paramilitary forces, Mexican maritime Special Forces, Norwegian maritime Special Forces and the Swedish maritime police

CONTRACTOR:
Dockstavarvet and Gotlands Varv, Sweden

FEATURES:
DISPLACEMENT: 19 tons full load
DIMENSIONS: 15.9 x 3.8 x 0.8 m (52.2 x 12.5 x 2.6 ft)
MAIN MACHINERY: two Saab Scania DSI 14 diesels; 1104 hp(m) (812 kw); two Kamewa waterjets
SPEED: 35-50 kts; 20 kts (Sea State 3)
RANGE: 240 miles at 30 kts
COMPLEMENT: three
MILITARY LIFT: 20 troops plus equipment or 2.8 tons
RADARS: Racal Decca; RD 360 or Furuno 8050; I-band

ARMAMENT:
MISSILES: SSM: Rockwell RBS 17 Hellfire; semi-active laser guidance to 5 km (3 n miles) at 1.0 Mach; warhead 8 kg
GUNS: 3-12.7 mm MGS
MINES: four (or six depth charges)

EXTRA FEATURES:
Short, stubby bow ramp; two or three oblong ports in topsides; fully enclosed cockpit

Raiding Craft (Gruppbåt) LCVP SWEDEN

Small raiding craft used throughout the Swedish Archipelago.

SPECIFICATION:

USED BY:
Swedish Amphibious Corps

FEATURES:
DISPLACEMENT: 3 tons full load
DIMENSIONS: 8 x 2.1 x 0.3 m
(26.2 x 6.9 x 1 ft)
MAIN MACHINERY: one Volvo
Penta TAMD 42WJ diesel;
230 hp(m) (169 kw); one
Kamewa 240 waterjet
SPEED: 30 kts
COMPLEMENT: two
MILITARY LIFT: 1 ton

EXTRA FEATURES:
Aft, open control position; solid
guard-rails around transom;
blunt bow

Aquarius Class Fast Patrol Boat – Patrouillenboot 80

SWITZERLAND

SPECIFICATION:

USED BY:
Swiss army maritime forces

CONTRACTOR:
Müller AG, Spiez, Switzerland

FEATURES:
DISPLACEMENT: 7 tons full load
DIMENSIONS: 10.7 x 3.3 x 0.9 m
(35.1 x 10.8 x 3 ft)
MAIN MACHINERY: two Volvo KAD
42 diesels; 460 hp(m) (338 kw);
two shafts
SPEED: 35 kts
COMPLEMENT: eight
RADARS: Surface search: JFS
Electronic 364; I-band

ARMAMENT:
GUNS: two 12.7 mm MGS between
1978 and 1984

Moulded, three-quarter-length superstructure.
Weapons right forward in hatch and on open
stern deck.

High Speed Interceptor Craft (HSIC) TRINIDAD & TOBAGO

Kenneth Mohammed

SPECIFICATION:

USED BY:
Trinidad and Tobago Customs

FEATURES:
Long and slim; both fore-deck
and aft decks are covered;
tubular goalpost over control
position for antennae

Amongst other slower craft, the Customs service
operate this single, high speed interception vessel
named *Kenneth Mohammed*.

High Speed Intervention/Interceptor Craft TURKEY

Capable of carrying a RIB and used by Special Forces. Details are speculative.

SPECIFICATION:

USED BY:
Turkish maritime Special Forces

FEATURES:
DISPLACEMENT: 18 tons full load
DIMENSIONS: 16.8 x 4.04 x 1.0 m
(55.1 x 13.2 x 3.2 ft)
MAIN MACHINERY: two MTU 12V
183 TE94 diesels; 2588 hp(m)
(1.93 MW); two Arneson ASD 12 B1L
surface drives
SPEED: 50+ kts
COMPLEMENT: two plus ten
mission crew

EXTRA FEATURES:
Angled tumblehome; low superstructure silhouette; hard chine
hull; open cockpit; open transom

Kaan 15 Class High Speed Intervention/Interceptor Craft (HSIC) TURKEY

SPECIFICATION:

USED BY:
Turkish Coast Guard

FEATURES:
DISPLACEMENT: 19 tons full load
DIMENSIONS: 15.4 x 4.04 x 0.96 m
(54.2 x 13.2 x 3.15 ft)
MAIN MACHINERY: two MTU 12V
183 TE93 diesels; 2300 hp(m)
(1.69 MW); two Arneson ASD 12 B1L
surface drives
SPEED: 54 kts
RANGE: 350 miles at 35 kts
COMPLEMENT: four plus eight
mission crew
RADARS: Surface search: Raytheon;
I-band

ARMAMENT:
GUNS: two 12.7 mm MGS

EXTRA FEATURES:
Fibreglass hulls; fully enclosed
wheelhouse; Coast Guard
markings

Colvic Craft UK

Hellenic Coast Guard Colvic craft

The craft features GRP hulls with a stern platform for recovery of divers.

SPECIFICATION:

USED BY:
Hellenic Coast Guard Underwater Mission Squad

CONTRACTOR:
Colvic Craft, UK

FEATURES:
DISPLACEMENT: 24 tons full load
DIMENSIONS: 16.5 x 4.7 x 1.4 m
(54.1 x 15.4 x 4.6 ft)
MAIN MACHINERY: two MAN D2840
LE 401 diesels; 1644 hp(m)
(1.21 MW) sustained; two shafts
SPEED: 34 kts
RANGE: 500 miles at 25 kts
COMPLEMENT: five (one officer)
RADARS: Surface search: Raytheon;
I-band

ARMAMENT:
GUNS: one 12.7 mm MG; one
7.62 mm MG

EXTRA FEATURES:
Coast Guard diagonal stripes;
stern davits for dinghy

Cougar Enforcer Class High Speed Interceptor Craft (HSIC) UK

The craft has a v-monohull design.

SPECIFICATION:

USED BY:
Kuwaiti Coast Guard

CONTRACTOR:
Cougar Marine, UK

FEATURES:
DISPLACEMENT: 5.7 tons full load
DIMENSIONS: 12.2 x 2.8 x 0.8 m
(40 x 9 x 2.1 ft)
MAIN MACHINERY: two Sabre 380 s
diesels; 760 hp(m) (559 kw);
two Arneson ASD 8 surface drives;
two shafts
SPEED: 45 kts
RANGE: 250 miles at 35 kts
COMPLEMENT: four
RADARS: Surface search: Koden;
I-band

ARMAMENT:
GUNS: 1-12.7 mm MG

EXTRA FEATURES:
Open cockpit; v-monohull design;
split pulpit guard-rails forward

High Speed Interceptor Craft (HSIC) UK

HSIC, FIC 145 (1) and HSIC, VSV (2)

Two main types in service. Both are around 15 m (49 ft) in length and powered by two 750 hp diesels to give speeds in excess of 55 kts. One has a VSV wave-piercing hull which can maintain fast speeds in high sea states. Both types can be transported by air.

SPECIFICATION:

USED BY:
UK Royal Marines Special Boat Service

FEATURES:
Usually painted in a disruptive pattern camouflage scheme; fully enclosed wheelhouse

Port Patrol Craft (HSIC) UK

Miscellaneous craft. Two are Cougar 40-knot fast patrol craft of two tons. Three are one ton and one is four tons. Four are 14-15 ton craft.

SPECIFICATION:

USED BY:
Peruvian Coast Guard

CONTRACTOR:
Cougar Marine, UK

FEATURES:
Long, slim hull; very raked goal post for navigation lights and antennae

Arctic 28 and Al-Shaali Type RIBS UK

Arctic RIB

SPECIFICATION:

USED BY:
UAE Maritime Special Forces

FEATURES:
DISPLACEMENT: 4 tons full load
DIMENSIONS: 8.5 x 3 x 0.6 m
(27.9 x 9.7 x 2 ft)
MAIN MACHINERY: two outboards;
450 hp (336 kw)
SPEED: 38 kts
COMPLEMENT: one plus 11 troops

EXTRA FEATURES:
Central control consul; sectioned rubbing strake

GRP hulls. Used by Special Forces. The twelve Al-Shaali type were ordered in 1994 and built in Dubai.

Hashim (Rotork) Patrol Boat UK

Procured for patrolling the Dead Sea but due to the annual decrease of water depth, the craft were moved to Aqaba.

SPECIFICATION:

USED BY:
Jordanian maritime forces

CONTRACTOR:
Rotork, UK

FEATURES:
DISPLACEMENT: 9 tons full load
DIMENSIONS: 12.7 x 3.2 x 0.9 m
(41.7 x 10.5 x 3 ft)
MAIN MACHINERY: two Deutz
diesels; 240 hp (179 kw);
two shafts
SPEED: 28 kts
COMPLEMENT: five
MILITARY LIFT: 30 troops
RADARS: Surface search: Furuno;
I-band

ARMAMENT:
GUNS: one 12.7 mm MG; one
7.62 mm MG

EXTRA FEATURES:
Bow ramp; large-windowed,
double-height superstructure

Rigid Raiding Craft and Rigid Inflatable Boat UK

Rigid Raiding Craft (1) and Rigid Inflatable Boat (2)

The Rigid Raiding Craft (RRC) Mk 3 is 2.6 tons, 7.4 m (24.2 ft) and powered by a single Yamaha 220 hp (162 kw) diesel engine. It can travel up to 36 kts fully laden (up to 40 kts light) and carries eight troops. Some are used by the army. There are four types of Rigid Inflatable Boats (RIBs): Halmatic Arctic 22; Pacific 22; Arctic 28; and Pacific 28. They are capable of carrying 10–15 fully laden troops at speeds of 26–35 kts.

SPECIFICATION:

USED BY:
UK Royal Marines Special Forces

FEATURES:

RRC:
- Diesel powered
- Inward facing seats forward
- Flat-bowed
- Open consul aft

RIB:
- Forward facing seats abaft the open consul
- Two outboard engines

Mk v Class HSIC USA

This was the winning design of a competition held in 1994 to find a high-speed craft to insert and withdraw Navy SEAL teams and other special operations forces personnel. The craft has an aluminium hull and is transportable by C-5 aircraft. The Mexican Navy's three engine version is known as the Isla Class.

SPECIFICATION:

USED BY:
Mexico (as Isla class) and the US

CONTRACTOR:
Halter Marine Equitable Shipyard in New Orleans, USA

FEATURES:
DISPLACEMENT: 54 tons full load
Dimensions: 24.7 x 5.3 x 1.3 m (81.2 x 17.5 x 4.3 ft)
MAIN MACHINERY: two MTU 12V 396 TE94 diesels; 4506 hp (3.36 MW) sustained; two Kamewa waterjets
SPEED: 45 kts
RANGE: 515 miles at 35 kts
COMPLEMENT: five plus four spare
MILITARY LIFT: 16 fully equipped troops
RADARS: Navigation: Furuno; I-band
IFF: APX-100(V)

ARMAMENT:
Five Mk 46 Mod 4 mountings for twin 12.7 mm or 7.6 mm MGs; one Mk 19 40 mm grenade launcher; three Bushmaster 25 mm Mk 38s; Stinger missiles may be carried and gun armaments can be varied

EXTRA FEATURES:
Deep v-hull; RIB on ramp aft; solid, slanted mast

Assault Craft USA

SPECIFICATION:

USED BY:
Royal Thai Navy Riverine
Squadron

ARMAMENT:
Most are armed with one or two
7.62 mm MGS

FEATURES:
Rigid raiding raft type; one
outboard; control position on
starboard side forward

Diving Support Craft USA

Boston Whaler

SPECIFICATION:

USED BY:
Singapore Navy Diving Unit

CONTRACTOR:
Boston Whaler, USA

ARMAMENT:
GUNS: 7.62 MG and 40 mm
grenade launcher

FEATURES:
Boston Whaler hull; twin
outboards

High Speed Interceptor Craft (HSIC) USA

Used in the anti-narcotics role.

SPECIFICATION:

USED BY:
The Jamaica Defence Force Coast
Guard in the anti-narcotics role

CONTRACTOR:
Offshore Performance Marine,
USA

FEATURES:
DISPLACEMENT: 3 tons full load
DIMENSIONS: 10.1 x 2.4 x 0.6 m
(33 x 8 x 1.8 ft)
MAIN MACHINERY: two Johnson
OMC outboards; 450 hp (336 kw)
SPEED: 48 kts
COMPLEMENT: three
RADARS: Surface search: Raytheon
40X; I-band

ARMAMENT:
GUNS: one 7.62 mm MG (can be
carried)

EXTRA FEATURES:
Twin outboards; goalpost for
radar antenna

Isla Class Fast Attack Craft USA

Isla Corondo (old number)

The design is based on the USN Mk V class special operations craft. It features deep v-hulls with FRP/Kevlar construction and may be fitted with MM 15 SSMS in due course and armed with 40 mm or 20 mm guns.

SPECIFICATION:

USED BY:
Mexican navy

CONTRACTOR:
Trinity Marine Group, USA

FEATURES:
DISPLACEMENT: 52 tons full load
DIMENSIONS: 25 x 5.5 x 1.2 m
(82 x 17.9 x 4 ft)
MAIN MACHINERY: three Detroit
diesels; 16,200 hp (12.9 MW);
three Arneson surface drives
SPEED: 50 kts
RANGE: 1200 miles at 30 kts
COMPLEMENT: nine (three officers)
RADARS: Surface search: Raytheon
SPS 69; I-band
FIRE CONTROL: Thomson-CSF
Agrion; J-band

ARMAMENT:
GUNS: one 12.7 mm MG; two
7.62 mm MGS

EXTRA FEATURES:
Central, enclosed cockpit; deep
v-hull; raiding craft on after deck;
lattice mast

River Assault Boats USA

Colombian Marine Corps river assault boat

SPECIFICATION:

USED BY:
Colombian Marine Corps

CONTRACTOR:
Boston Whaler, USA

FEATURES:
LENGTH: 6.8 m (22.3 ft)

SPEED: 25 to 30 kts depending
on load

ARMAMENT:

GUNS: one 12.7 mm and two
7.62 mm MGS

EXTRA FEATURES:
Outboard propulsion; central
control consul; well-armed

Seafox Class Swimmer Delivery Craft USA

SPECIFICATION:

USED BY:
Egyptian Navy combat swimmers

CONTRACTOR:
Uniflite, USA

FEATURES:
DISPLACEMENT: 11.3 tons full load
DIMENSIONS: 11 x 3 x 0.8 m
(36.1 x 9.8 x 2.6 ft)
MAIN MACHINERY: two GM 6V-92TA
diesels; 520 hp (388 kw)
sustained; two shafts
SPEED: 30 kts
RANGE: 200 miles at 20 kts
COMPLEMENT: three
RADARS: Surface search: LN66;
I-band

ARMAMENT:
GUNS: two 12.7 mm MGS; two
7.62 mm MGS

EXTRA FEATURES:
GRP construction; painted black

Swiftships Class River Patrol Craft USA

Can carry up to eight troops. Used as command craft for river flotillas.

SPECIFICATION:

USED BY:
Ecuadorian Marine Corps and
Coast Guard

FEATURES:
DISPLACEMENT: 17 tons full load
DIMENSIONS: 13.9 x 3.6 x 0.6 m
(45.5 x 11.8 x 1.8 ft)
SPEED: 22 kts
RANGE: 600 miles at 22 kts
COMPLEMENT: four

ARMAMENT:
GUNS: two M2HB 12.7 mm MGS;
two M60D 7.62 mm MGS

EXTRA FEATURES:
Hard chine; v-hull; flush deck;
enclosed cockpit forward with
forward facing hatch

Tenerife Class River Patrol Craft USA

Colombia Tenerife class river patrol craft

Used for anti-narcotics patrols by the Colombian Marine Corps. It features aluminium hulls and can be transported by aircraft.

SPECIFICATION:

USED BY:
Colombian Marine Corps

CONTRACTOR:
Bender Marine, USA

FEATURES:
DISPLACEMENT: 12 tons full load
DIMENSIONS: 12.4 x 2.9 x 0.6 m
(40.7 x 9.5 x 2 ft)
MAIN MACHINERY: two Caterpillar
3208 TA diesels; 850 hp (634 kw)
sustained; two shafts
SPEED: 29 kts
RANGE: 530 miles at 15 kts
COMPLEMENT: five plus 12 troops
RADARS: Surface search: Raytheon
1900; I-band

ARMAMENT:
GUNS: three 12.7 mm MGs (one
twin, one single); one Mk 19
grenade launcher; one
7.62 mm MG

EXTRA FEATURES:
Painted in disruptive pattern
camouflage scheme; central
box-shaped wheelhouse;
armament fore and aft

Guardian Class Rigid Raiding Craft (RRC) USA

Argentine Marine Corps Guardian

Argentine craft have twin 150 hp Johnson outboards and are capable of carrying eight troops. They can be transported by aircraft.

SPECIFICATION:

USED BY:
Argentine Marine Corps and US Coast Guard port security units

FEATURES:
DISPLACEMENT: 3 tons full load
DIMENSIONS: 7.5 x 2.5 x 0.4 m (24.6 x 8.2 x 0.4 ft)
MAIN MACHINERY: two Evinrude outboards; 350 hp (261 kw)
SPEED: 35 kts
COMPLEMENT: four
RADARS: Navigation: Raytheon; I-band

ARMAMENT:
GUNS: one 12.7 mm MG; two 7.62 mm MGs

EXTRA FEATURES:
Twin outboards; central open control console; tubular goalpost aft for antennae

Light Patrol Boats USA

Built for US Special Operations Command. Air transportable.

SPECIFICATION:

USED BY:
USA Special Operations
Command

CONTRACTOR:
Boston Whaler, USA

FEATURES:
DISPLACEMENT: 3.3 tons full load
DIMENSIONS: 7.6 x 2.6 x 0.5 m
(25 x 8.6 x 1.5 ft)
MAIN MACHINERY: two OMC
outboards; 300 hp (224 kw)
SPEED: 35 kts
COMPLEMENT: three
RADARS: Surface search: Furuno
1731; I-band

ARMAMENT:
GUNS: three 12.7 mm MGS; one
7.62 mm MG

EXTRA FEATURES:
Two outboard engines; glass fibre
hulls; tubular goalpost for
antennae abaft the control
console

Mini Armoured Troop Carriers USA

Ten small troop carriers for riverine and SEAL operations.

SPECIFICATION:

USED BY:
US maritime Special Forces

CONTRACTOR:
Sewart, USA

FEATURES:
DISPLACEMENT: 14.8 tons full load
DIMENSIONS: 11 x 3.9 x 1.1 m
(36 x 12.7 x 3.5 ft). Draft of 0.3 m
(1 ft) when at speed
MAIN MACHINERY: two Detroit
6V-92TA diesels; 445 hp (332 kw)
sustained; two Jacuzzi 20YJ
waterjets
SPEED: 33 kts
RANGE: 280 n miles at 28 kts
COMPLEMENT: three
MILITARY LIFT: 16 SEALS
RADARS: Navigation; Marconi
LN66; I-band

ARMAMENT:
GUNS: seven 12.7 mm MGS

EXTRA FEATURES:
Aluminium hull; ceramic armour;
two waterjets; horizontally-ribbed
hull (rubbing strakes); flat,
sloping bow ramp

Rigid Inflatable Boats USA

The craft are capable of carrying eight SEALS at 32 kts. Details given are for the latest type being built by USMI, New Orleans.

SPECIFICATION:

USED BY:
US navy SEAL teams

CONTRACTOR:
USMI, New Orleans, USA

FEATURES:
DISPLACEMENT: 9 tons full load
DIMENSIONS: 11 x 3.2 x 0.9 m
(36.1 x 10.5 x 3 ft)
MAIN MACHINERY: two Caterpillar
3126 diesels; 940 hp (700 kw);
two Kamewa FF 280 waterjets
SPEED: 32 kts
RANGE: 200 miles at 33 kts
COMPLEMENT: three plus
eight SEALS

ARMAMENT:
GUNS: one 12.7 mm MG; one
7.62 mm MG or Mk 19 Mod 3
grenade launcher

EXTRA FEATURES:
Large RIB; two waterjets;
prominent central consul with
radar dome above; seats/grab-
rails for standing passengers aft

River Patrol Craft USA

SPECIFICATION:

USED BY:
Bolivian Navy and Marine Corps

FEATURES:
DISPLACEMENT: 5 tons full load
DIMENSIONS: 12.9 x 3.9 x 1 m
(42.3 x 12.7 x 3.3 ft)
MAIN MACHINERY: two diesels;
two shafts
SPEED: 15 kts
COMPLEMENT: five
RADARS: Surface search:
Raytheon; I-band

ARMAMENT:
GUNS: one 12.7 mm MG

EXTRA FEATURES:
Forward, enclosed cockpit;
prominent anchor stowage
over bow

Pirana Mk II Class River Patrol Craft USA

SPECIFICATION:

USED BY:
Bolivian Navy and Marine Corps
and Panama maritime forces

FEATURES:
DIMENSIONS: 6.8 x 2.3 x 0.6 m
(22.3 x 7.5 x 2 ft)
MAIN MACHINERY: two Johnson
outboards; 280 hp (209 kw)
SPEED: 35 kts
COMPLEMENT: four

ARMAMENT:
GUNS: one 12.7 mm MG

EXTRA FEATURES:
Open-shelled craft; central
control console; twin outboards

Mark v Class Special Operations High Speed Interceptor Craft (soc/hsic) USA

Mk v soc

This was the winning design of a competition held in 1994 to find a high-speed craft to insert and withdraw Navy SEAL teams and other special operations forces personnel. The craft has an aluminium hull and is transportable by c-5 aircraft. Stinger missiles may be carried and gun armaments can be varied. A variant with three engines is in service with the Mexican Navy.

SPECIFICATION:

USED BY:
us SEAL teams

CONTRACTOR:
Halter Marine, USA

FEATURES:
DISPLACEMENT: 54 tons full load
DIMENSIONS: 24.7 x 5.3 x 1.3 m
(81.2 x 17.5 x 4.3 ft)
MAIN MACHINERY: two MTU 12V
396 TE94 diesels; 4506 hp
(3.36 MW) sustained; two Kamewa
waterjets
SPEED: 45 kts
RANGE: 515 miles at 35 kts
COMPLEMENT: five plus four spare
MILITARY LIFT: 16 fully equipped
troops
RADARS: Navigation: Furuno;
ı-band
IFF: APX-100(V)

ARMAMENT:
GUNS: five Mk 46 Mod four
mountings for twin 12.7 mm or
7.6 mm MGS; one Mk 19 40 mm
grenade launcher; three
Bushmaster 25 mm Mk 38

EXTRA FEATURES:
Aluminium hull; long, fully
enclosed wheelhouse amidships

Riverine Assault Craft USA

SPECIFICATION:

USED BY:
US Marine Corps

FEATURES:
DISPLACEMENT: 7.5 tons full load
DIMENSIONS: 10.7 x 2.8 x 0.7 m
(35.1 x 9.2 x 2.3 ft)
MAIN MACHINERY: two Cummins
diesels; 600 hp (447 kw); two
waterjets
SPEED: 43 kts
COMPLEMENT: four to five, plus
10-15 marines

ARMAMENT:
GUNS: one 12.7 mm M2HB MG;
one 40 mm Mk 19 grenade
launcher

EXTRA FEATURES:
Heavily armed; two waterjets;
horizontally-ribbed hull (rubbing
strakes); usually painted dark
green or disruptive pattern
camouflage

River Patrol Craft URUGUAY

Uruguay 1

Used by the Naval Infantry for river patrols.

SPECIFICATION:

USED BY:
Uruguay's Corps of Naval
Infantry

CONTRACTOR:
Nuevos Ayres, Uruguay

FEATURES:
DISPLACEMENT: 5 tons full load
DIMENSIONS: 11.8 x 3.6 x 1 m
(38.7 x 11.8 x 3.2 ft)
MAIN MACHINERY: three Volvo
AD41P 220 MOP diesels
SPEED: 32 kts
RANGE: 1500 miles at 24 kts
COMPLEMENT: four

ARMAMENT:
GUNS: two 12.7 mm MGS

EXTRA FEATURES:
Civilian-style hull and superstructure; central, open cockpit;
in-board engines; three oblong
hull port lights

Polaris Class High Speed Interceptor Craft (HSIC)

VENEZUELA

Used for drug interdiction.

SPECIFICATION:

USED BY:
Venezuelan Coast Guard

FEATURES:
DISPLACEMENT: 5 tons full load
DIMENSIONS: 7.9 x 2.6 x 0.8 m
(26 wl x 8.5 x 2.6 ft)
MAIN MACHINERY: one diesel
outdrive; 400 hp(m) (294 kw)
SPEED: 50 kts
COMPLEMENT: ten
RADARS: Surface search:
Raytheon; I-band

ARMAMENT:
GUNS: one 12.7 mm MG

EXTRA FEATURES:
Long slim hull; open cockpit;
covered engine space aft with
single out outdrive

Inshore Patrol Craft VENEZUELA

Guardian

Details given are for the first of two built at Guatire of GRP construction. Further craft (example in photograph) are Boston Whaler 'Guardian' class capable of 25 kts, mounting two 12.7 mm and two 6.72 mm MGs, and with Raytheon radars.

SPECIFICATION:

USED BY:
Venezuelan Marine Corps

FEATURES:
DISPLACEMENT: 11 tons full load
DIMENSIONS: 12 x 2.8 x 1.7 m
(39.4 x 9.2 x 5.6 ft)
MAIN MACHINERY: two diesels;
640 hp(m) (470 kw); two shafts
SPEED: 38 kts
COMPLEMENT: four

ARMAMENT:
GUNS: two 7.62 mm MGS

Weapons:
Hand Guns

FN 9 mm High Power Pistol ARGENTINA

The 9 mm High Power pistol is the standard pistol of the Argentine armed services, produced under licence from FN Herstal at the Argentine government factory at Rosario. The pistol is very similar to the original Belgian design, but there are dimensional differences. Argentine production covers three distinct variations. The 'Militar' model is the standard fixed sight, blued-finish pattern with plastic anatomical grip surfaces; it is generally the same as the original Belgian design. The Model M90 has a lengthened slide stop lever and a reshaped safety catch, making both easier to operate. The anatomical grip is fitted and there is a plastic addition to the base of the magazine to give a greater area for the hand. The 'Detective' model has the same changes as the M90 but is shorter and more convenient for concealed carrying.

SPECIFICATION:

USED BY:
Argentine armed forces

CONTRACTOR:
Fabrica Militar Fray Luis Beltran,
Fray Luis Beltran, Argentina

FEATURES:
CARTRIDGE: 9 x 19 mm Parabellum
OPERATION: recoil; semi-
automatic; single-action
LOCKING: projecting lugs
FEED: 14-rd box magazine
WEIGHT: Militar, 929 g; M90,
968 g; Detective, empty without
magazine, 916 g
LENGTH: Militar and M90,
197 mm; Detective, 172 mm
BARREL: Militar, M90, 118 mm;
Detective, 93 mm
RIFLING: six grooves; rh; one turn
in 250 mm
SIGHTS: fore, adjustable blade;
rear, laterally adjustable notch

Steyr Special Purpose Pistol (SPP) AUSTRIA

The Special Purpose Pistol (SPP) is a locked-breech weapon in 9 x 19 mm parabellum calibre. There are only 41 component parts and the frame and top cover are made from a plastic material. The locking system relies upon a rotating barrel, using a single lug which moves in a groove in the frame to rotate and thus lock and unlock from the bolt. The cocking handle is at the rear of the weapon, beneath the rearsight and is pulled back to cock.

SPECIFICATION:

USED BY:
Austrian police

CONTRACTOR:
Steyr Mannlicher AG & Co KG,
Vienna, Austria

FEATURES:
CARTRIDGE: 9 x 19 mm parabellum
OPERATION: recoil; semi-automatic
LOCKING: rotating barrel
FEED: 15-rd or 30-rd magazines
WEIGHT: 1.20 kg (without magazine)
LENGTH: 322 mm
BARREL: 130 mm
SIGHTS: blade (fore); notch (rear)
SIGHT BASE: 188 mm

9 mm FN BDA9 Pistol BELGIUM

9 mm FN Herstal BDA9 pistol

The BDA9 is derived from its predecessor, the
FN Herstal High-Power and functions in the same
way, using short recoil and a cam beneath the
breech to disengage the barrel from the slide. It
differs in having a double-action trigger and a
hammer decocking lever in place of the safety
catch; this decocking lever is duplicated on both
sides of the frame and can thus be used with either
hand. The magazine release is normally fitted for
right-handed users, but it can be removed easily
and reassembled for left-handed use. The trigger
guard is shaped to facilitate a two-handed grip.

SPECIFICATION:

USED BY:
In use worldwide

CONTRACTOR:
FN Herstal SA, Herstal, Belgium

FEATURES:
CARTRIDGE: 9 x 19 mm parabellum
OPERATION: short recoil; semi-
automatic
LOCKING: dropping barrel, cam
actuated
FEED: 15-rd box magazine
WEIGHT: 875 g (DA/SA)
LENGTH: 200 mm
BARREL: 118 mm
RIFLING: six grooves; one turn in
250 mm
SIGHTS: adjustable blade (fore);
fixed notch; adjustable laterally
by an armourer (rear)
MUZZLE VELOCITY: 350 m/s

FN Herstal 5.7 mm Five-seveN pistol BELGIUM

Developed primarily to meet the needs of Special Forces and law-enforcement agencies, the Five-seveN tactical is a single-action pistol with a short, light trigger pull. The hammer is shrouded to prevent it from snagging on equipment and is protected from impacts. A firing-pin safety avoids accidental firing, while a manual safety can be used to block the trigger. The pistol has a manual slide stop for rapid reloading.

SPECIFICATION:

USED BY:
Cyprus National Guard Special Forces

CONTRACTOR:
FN Herstal SA, Herstal, Belgium

FEATURES:
CARTRIDGE: 5.7 x 28 mm
OPERATION: self-loading; double-action only
LOCKING: delayed blowback
FEED: 20-rd box magazine
WEIGHT: empty, 618 g; loaded, approx 744 g
LENGTH: 208 mm
HEIGHT: 143.5 mm
WIDTH: 31 mm
BARREL: 122.5 mm
SIGHTS: fore, fixed blade; rear, fixed notch
MUZZLE VELOCITY: nominal, 650 m/s

GC-IMBEL MD1 0.45 Pistol BRAZIL

The Pistol 45 GC-IMBEL MD1 0.45 semi-automatic pistol was developed from the classic Colt 0.45 M1911A1 but with an increased magazine capacity of fourteen rounds.

SPECIFICATION:

USED BY:
Brazilian Special Forces

CONTRACTOR:
Industria de Material Belico do Brasil – IMBEL, Piquete-SP, Brazil

FEATURES:
CARTRIDGE: 0.45 ACP
OPERATION: recoil; semi-automatic; single-action
LOCKING: projecting lug
FEED: 14-rd box magazine
WEIGHT: empty, 940 g; loaded, 1.3 kg
LENGTH: 216 mm
BARREL: 128 mm
RIFLING: six grooves; rh; one turn in 406 mm
SIGHTS: fore, fixed blade; rear, fixed notch
MUZZLE VELOCITY: 240 m/s

Para-Ordnance P14-45, P13-45, P12-45 and P10-45 0.45 Pistols CANADA

Para-Ordnance P14-45 0.45 pistols: blue steel finish (1); duotone stainless/blue (2); stainless steel (3)

SPECIFICATION:

USED BY:
Canadian special operations units

CONTRACTOR:
Para-Ordnance Inc, Ontario, Canada

FEATURES:
CARTRIDGE: 0.45 ACP
OPERATION: short recoil; semi-automatic; single-action
LOCKING: projecting lugs
FEED: detachable box magazine:
P14-45, 14 rds; P13-45, 13 rds;
P12-45, 12 rds; P10-45, 10 rds
WEIGHT: P14-45 steel, 1.1 kg; alloy frame, 880 g; P13-45 steel, 1.02 kg; alloy frame, 790 g; P12-45 steel, 960 g; P12-45 alloy frame, 730 g; P10-45 steel, 680 g; alloy, 530 g
LENGTH: P14-45, 216 mm; P13-45, 197 mm; P12-45, 180 mm; P10-45, 165 mm
BARREL: P14-45, 127 mm; P13-45, 120.6 mm; P12-45, 89 mm, P10-45, 76 mm
HEIGHT: P14-45, 146 mm; P13-45, 133.3 mm; P12-45, 127 mm; P10-45, 114 mm
SIGHTS: fore, blade; rear, laterally adjustable notch

The P14-45 is a full-size semi-automatic pistol derived from the Colt M1911A1, but with greater magazine capacity. The P13-45 has a slightly shorter grip and barrel and one round less magazine capacity. The pocket-size P12-45 is designed for concealment and is even more compact than the P13, while giving up only one round magazine capacity. The P10-45 is more compact still for maximum concealment, while retaining a large magazine capacity. The Para-Ordnance P-Series pistols incorporate not only the traditional M1911A1 grip safety, manual safety and inertia firing pin, but also have a firing pin lock which physically blocks the firing pin unless the trigger is pressed.

9 mm HS 2000 Pistol CROATIA

Three types of sights can be provided. Apart from the usual fixed rear and fore sights, sights adjustable for windage are available, while the third version features a ramp rearsight. The trigger mechanism is double-action only. When a round is loaded in the chamber, a rounded pinhead protrudes from a slightly dished recess in the rear of the slide to provide a visual and tactile indication of a loaded pistol. A grip safety is provided.

SPECIFICATION:

USED BY:
Croatian Special Forces

CONTRACTOR:
IM-METAL, Kolodvorska, Croatia

FEATURES:
CARTRIDGE: 9 x 19 mm Parabellum
OPERATION: short recoil;
self-loading; single-action
LOCKING: projecting lug
FEED: 15-rd box magazine
WEIGHT: with empty magazine,
700 g
LENGTH: 180 mm
HEIGHT: 139 mm
WIDTH: 30 mm
BARREL: 102.5 mm
RIFLING: six grooves; rh; one turn
in 250 mm
SIGHT RADIUS: 143 mm
MUZZLE VELOCITY: 340 m/s

9 mm HS 95 Pistol CROATIA

Both single- and double-action operation is possible. There is an automatic firing pin safety, and the pistol can be handled and operated by right-handed and left-handed firers. No tools are required for field stripping. The 9 mm HS 95 pistol is intended for both military and police use and is provided with a 15-round box magazine.

SPECIFICATION:

USED BY:
Croatian Special Forces

CONTRACTOR:
IM-METAL, Kolodvorska, Croatia

FEATURES:
CARTRIDGE: 9 x 19 mm Parabellum
OPERATION: short recoil;
self-loading; single- or
double-action
LOCKING: projecting lug
FEED: 15-rd box magazine
WEIGHT: empty, 1.032 kg
LENGTH: 180 mm
HEIGHT: 140 mm
WIDTH: 35 mm
BARREL: 102.5 mm
RIFLING: six grooves; rh; one turn
in 250 mm
SIGHTS: fore, fixed blade; rear,
laterally adjustable notch
SIGHT RADIUS: 145 mm
MUZZLE VELOCITY: 340 m/s

CZ 100 CZECH REPUBLIC

cz 100 with laser aiming device

This pistol incorporates the modern concept of a frame with a high-impact plastic and steel slide and a consequent weight reduction that significantly enhances the comfort of day-to-day carriage. The trigger mechanism belongs in the double-action only category, incorporating a firing pin safety. The pistol is equipped with a single-side slide stop and magazine catch. The slide is locked open when the last cartridge from the magazine has been fired. The cz 100 pistol can be provided with a compact laser aiming device which is mounted into the grooves in a frame located in front of the trigger guard. The laser aiming device incorporates a sensor responding to a trigger movement.

SPECIFICATION:

USED BY:
Czech Special Forces

CONTRACTOR:
Ceska Zbrojovka, Uherskv Brod, Czech Republic

FEATURES:
CALIBRE: 9 mm Luger/.40 S&W
MAGAZINE CAPACITY: 13/10 rds
OVERALL LENGTH: 177 mm
BARREL LENGTH: 95 mm
HEIGHT: 130 mm
WIDTH: 32 mm
WEIGHT: 680 g (empty)
SAFETY ELEMENTS: firing-pin safety; DAO mode of fire

CZ 97 B CZECH REPUBLIC

The CZ 97 B calibre .45 Auto is a semi-automatic hand gun designed for aimed shooting up to a range of 50 m. The weapon incorporates a locked breech principle and the semi-automatic function is achieved through the short barrel recoil. The hand gun is equipped with a manual safety, firing pin safety (block) and loaded chamber indicator. The CZ 97 B features double-action mode of fire. The magazine is a double column type with a single cartridge outlet and has a 10-round capacity. The slide is locked open when the last cartridge from the magazine has been fired.

SPECIFICATION:

USED BY:
Czech Special Forces

CONTRACTOR:
Ceska Zbrojovka, Ukerskv Brod, Czech Republic

FEATURES:
CALIBRE: .45 Auto (ACP)
OVERALL LENGTH: 212 mm
BARREL LENGTH: 123 mm
HEIGHT: 150 mm
WIDTH: 35 mm
MAGAZINE CAPACITY: 10 cartridges
WEIGHT: with empty magazine, 1150 g

MAB PA15 9 mm Pistol FRANCE

The MAB PA15 has a delayed-blowback action, relying on a rotating barrel. The barrel carries two lugs, above and below the chamber. The lower lug engages in a slot cut in the return spring guide, which is pinned to the frame, so that the lug can rotate but cannot move backward or forward. The upper lug engages in a track cut in the inner surface of the slide; this track is shaped so that the initial opening movement of the slide will rotate the barrel through about 35°, after which the track is straight so that the slide can recoil while the barrel remains still. Rotation of the barrel is initially resisted by a combination of its inertia and the torque effect of the bullet passing through the rifling. When the chamber pressure has reached a safe level, the slide is blown back, compressing the return spring, rotating the hammer and depressing the trigger bar. The empty case is extracted and ejected to the right of the gun.

The return spring forces the slide forward. The top round in the magazine is pushed forward up the bullet guide and enters the chamber. The cam groove on the slide then causes the barrel to rotate, and the extractor grips the rim of the case. The trigger bar rises into its recess when the slide is fully forward.

SPECIFICATION:

USED BY:
French and Yugoslavian Special Forces

CONTRACTOR:
Manufacture d'Armes Automatiques de Bayonne (MAB), Bayonne, France

FEATURES:
CARTRIDGE: 9 x 19 mm Parabellum
OPERATION: delayed blowback; semi-automatic
LOCKING: barrel lug rotates in cam path in slide
FEED: 15-rd box magazine
WEIGHT: 1.09 kg
LENGTH: 203 mm
BARREL: 114 mm
RIFLING: six grooves; rh
SIGHTS: fore, blade; rear, notch
MUZZLE VELOCITY: 350 m/s

.45 Heckler & Koch SOCOM Pistol GERMANY

.45 Heckler & Koch SOCOM pistol with Knight

Designed to meet specifications drawn up by the US Government for a new 'Offensive Handgun Weapons System' for US Special Operations Command (USSOCOM). The SOCOM pistol is a .45 ACP calibre semi-automatic weapon of more or less conventional type, to which a flash and noise suppressor and a laser aiming module can be readily attached and removed. The laser aiming module has been specially developed for the pistol. A mechanical recoil reduction system is incorporated in the design, reducing the recoil force felt by the firer by some 30 per cent. The frame is of polymer plastic material, the slide is a one-piece machined component and the polymer magazine has a capacity of 13 .45 ACP rounds. The pistol is both single- and double- action, with an ambidextrous manual safety lever. The laser module, powered by two AA batteries, provides visible or IR aiming marks alone or in conjunction with a visible or IR illuminator. The laser aiming mark is adjustable for windage and elevation and the entire module may be removed and replaced on the pistol without affecting zero.

SPECIFICATION:

USED BY:
US Special Forces

CONTRACTOR:
Heckler & Koch GmbH,
Oberndorf, Germany

FEATURES:
CARTRIDGE: .45 ACP
OPERATION: recoil; semi-automatic
LOCKING: modified Browning
drop-barrel
FEED: 12-rd box magazine
WEIGHT: 1210 g (empty
magazine); 2250 g (full magazine)
suppressor and laser aiming
module
LENGTH: 245 mm without,
399 mm with suppressor
BARREL: 149 mm; six grooves; lh;
one turn in 406 mm
SIGHTS: iron 3-dot or laser
SIGHT RADIUS: 197 mm
MUZZLE VELOCITY: 270 m/s
M1911 ball

Walther 7.65 mm Models PP and PPK Pistols GERMANY

Walther 7.65 mm Model PP pistol

The Walther PP and PPK are straight blowback pistols with external hammers, double-action triggers and very adequate safety arrangements. The hammer is prevented from reaching the firing pin until the sear movement, when the trigger is pulled, moves the block clear. The disconnector works into a recess in the slide, and until the disconnector can rise, the sear cannot rotate. This occurs only when the slide is fully forward.

SPECIFICATION:

USED BY:
Widespread use by European Special Forces

CONTRACTOR:
Carl Walther Waffenfabrik, Ulm, Germany

FEATURES:
CARTRIDGE: 5 mm/0.32 ACP 9 mm short/0.38 ACP
OPERATION: blowback
FEED: 8-rd (PP) or 7-rd (PPK) box magazine
WEIGHT: PP, 682 g; PPK, 568 g
LENGTH OVERALL: PP, 173 mm; PPK, 155 mm
BARREL: PP, 99 mm; PPK, 86 mm
RIFLING: six grooves; rh
SIGHTS: fore: blade; rear: notch
MUZZLE VELOCITY: 7.65 mm PP, 290 m/s; PPK, 280 m/s

Walther 9 mm Model P5 Pistol GERMANY

Walther 9 mm Model P5 compact pistol

The Walther P5 is a locked-breech recoil-operated pistol of conventional appearance, but with several unusual features incorporated in the lockwork.

There are four built-in safety operations:

(1) The firing pin is held out of line with the hammer nose until the hammer is released by the trigger;

(2) Until the moment of firing, the firing pin is held opposite a recess in the face of the hammer;

(3) Should the hammer be released by any means other than the trigger, it will not move the firing pin – even if it strikes with full force the hammer has a safety notch;

(4) The trigger bar is disconnected unless the slide is fully closed and the barrel locked to it.

SPECIFICATION:

USED BY:
Taiwan police forces. Procured by the UK MOD as the L102A1. Also in service with Netherlands police and in Nigeria, Portugal and various South American countries

CONTRACTOR:
Carl Walther Waffenfabrik, Ulm, Germany

FEATURES:
CARTRIDGES: 9 x 19 mm Para-bellum; 7.65 x 21 mm Parabellum; 9 x 21 mm
OPERATION: recoil; locked-breech
LOCKING: pivoting locking piece
FEED: box magazine
MAGAZINE CAPACITY: 8 rds
WEIGHT: empty, 795 g; loaded, 885 g
LENGTH: overall, 180 mm; barrel, 90 mm
RIFLING: six grooves; rh
SIGHTS: (adjustable for elevation and line) fore, blade; rear, square notch with white contrast markings
SIGHT RADIUS: 134 mm
MUZZLE VELOCITY: 350 m/s

Walther 9 mm Model P1 Pistol GERMANY

A double-action trigger mechanism enables the hammer to be cocked and released by a single trigger pull. The hammer can also be cocked manually to produce a single action with a reduced trigger pull. If the weapon is set to 'safe' with the hammer cocked, the hammer will go forward, but the spindle of the change lever locks the firing pin so that it cannot go forward. In addition to the standard 9 mm Parabellum calibre, the P1 was also produced in 0.22 LR (Long Rifle) and 7.65 mm Parabellum calibres.

The Walther 9 mm P1 is the current version of the Walther P38 used by the German Army in the Second World War. After the war, the P38 was produced in a lightweight frame, and this was continued in the P1. The difference in markings on the two weapons is small. Both have 'Walther' and then 'Carl Walther Waffenfabrik Ulm/Do'. The Army pistol has 'P1 Cal 9 mm', and the commercial weapons have 'P38 Cal 9 mm'.

SPECIFICATION:

USED BY:
Chilean, German, Norwegian, Portuguese and other armed forces and government agencies

CONTRACTOR:
Carl Walther Waffenfabrik, Ulm, Germany

FEATURES:
CARTRIDGE: 9 x 19 mm Parabellum
OPERATION: short-recoil; semi-automatic; double-action
LOCKING: hinged locking piece
FEED: box magazine
MAGAZINE CAPACITY: 8 rds
WEIGHT: empty, 772 g
LENGTH: overall, 218 mm; barrel, 124 mm
RIFLING: six grooves, rh, one turn in 254 mm
SIGHTS: fore, blade; rear, u-notch
MUZZLE VELOCITY: 350 m/s

Heckler & Koch 9 mm P7M8 and P&M13 Pistols GERMANY

Heckler & Koch 9 mm P7 pistol

The action of the P7 pistol is self-locked by the gas pressure developed when a round is fired. When the pistol is fired, part of the propellant gas is channelled through a small vent in the barrel ahead of the chamber and into a cylinder lying beneath the barrel. A piston, attached to the front end of the slide, enters the front end of this cylinder, and thus when the slide begins to move rearward under the recoil pressure, the movement of the piston in the cylinder is resisted by the gas pressure. This delays the movement of the slide, which delays the opening of the breech; it also tends to absorb some of the recoil shock. This system gives the advantage of a fixed barrel and does away with the need for a locking mechanism.

SPECIFICATION:

USED BY:
German Special Forces, army and police; US police forces; military and police forces in many other countries, plus wide commercial sales

CONTRACTOR:
Heckler and Koch GmbH, Oberndorf-Neckar, Germany

FEATURES:
P7M8 & P7M13 models respectively:
CARTRIDGE: 9 x 19 mm Parabellum; 9 x 19 mm Parabellum
OPERATION: (both) delayed blowback
FEED: 8-rd box magazine; 13-rd box magazine
WEIGHT: less magazine, 780 g; 850 g
LENGTH: 171 mm; 175 mm
WIDTH: 29 mm; 33 mm
HEIGHT: 128 mm; 135 mm
BARREL: 105 mm; 105 mm
RIFLING: (both) polygonal
SIGHTS: (both) fore, blade; rear, notch
SIGHT RADIUS: 148 mm; 148 mm
MUZZLE VELOCITY: ca. 351 m/s; ca. 351 m/s

P-11 7.62 mm Underwater Pistol GERMANY

Outline drawing of underwater pistol

Attributed to Hechler & Koch although the company has never officially claimed responsibility for its existence. The pistol fires five 7.62 x 36 mm darts which are ignited electrically from a battery pack in the pistol grip. When all five are fired the whole five-barrel fitting is replaced with a new, five-barrel unit. New darts can only be fitted into the empty barrels by the manufacturer.

SPECIFICATION:

USED BY:
Denmark, France, Germany, Israel, Italy, Netherlands, Norway, the UK and USA are believed to have procured this weapon but confirmation of use by Special Forces is unlikely to be forthcoming

CONTRACTOR:
Heckler & Koch (reportedly)

FEATURES:
CARTRIDGE: 7.62 x 36 darts
OPERATION: Electric ignition; single shot
FEED: None – five barrels
WEIGHT: loaded: 1.2 kg; battery pack 700 g
LENGTH: 200 mm
WIDTH: 60 mm
RIFLING: 180 mm; rh
SIGHTS: fore, fixed blade; rear, notch
SIGHT RADIUS: 146 mm
RANGE: 10 – 15 m underwater: 30 m above

EBP 9 mm EP7 Pistol GREECE

SPECIFICATION:

USED BY:
Greek Special Forces

CONTRACTOR:
Hellenic Arms Industry (EBO) SA,
Athens, Greece

FEATURES:
OPERATION: delayed blowback
FEED: 8-rd box magazine
WEIGHT LESS MAGAZINE: 780 mm
LENGTH: 171 mm
WIDTH: 29 mm
HEIGHT: 128 mm
BARREL: 105 mm
RIFLING: polygonal
SIGHTS: fore, blade; rear, notch
SIGHT RADIUS: 148 mm
MUZZLE VELOCITY: ca 351 m/s

IMI 9 x 19 mm/0.40 s&w Jericho Self-loading Pistol

ISRAEL

IMI 9 Jericho pistol

The Jericho pistol is a more conventional type of
locked-breech recoil-operated pistol, relying on the
Browning system of operation to unlock the breech.
The slide moves on internal rails. One feature of this
weapon is its ability to change calibres; it is simply a
matter of field-stripping the pistol and reassembling
it with the appropriate components to make the
conversion. Two calibres are available, 9 x 19 mm
Parabellum and 0.40 s&w (Smith & Wesson).
Optional accessories include a butt-located safety
lock operable by a key, and a silencer kit consisting
of a special barrel and a suppressor assembly.

SPECIFICATION:

USED BY:
Israeli police and police special
anti-terrorist units

CONTRACTOR:
Israel Military Industries Ltd (IMI),
Ramat Hasharon, Israel

FEATURES:
CARTRIDGES: 9 x 19 mm
Parabellum
OPERATION: recoil; semi-automatic;
double-action
BREECH LOCK: cam-operated
dropping barrel
FEED: box magazine
RIFLING: 9 x 19 mm: six polygonal
grooves; rh; one turn in 254 mm;
0.40 s&w: one turn in 407 mm
SIGHTS: (both adjustable laterally)
fore, blade with luminous dot;
rear, square notch with two dots

IMI 9 x 19 mm Uzi Pistol ISRAEL

The Israel Military Industries (IMI) 9 mm Uzi pistol is a shortened and lightened modification of the Uzi sub-machine gun series and of the Micro Uzi in particular, with a mechanism permitting semi-automatic fire only. Although appearing cumbersome by comparison with conventional pistols, it has the advantages of an exceptional magazine capacity for a pistol and a shape and size which allows a very firm two-handed grip; the pistol can accommodate all standard Uzi magazines although a 20-round magazine is standard. The bulk also helps to absorb recoil so that it is easy to control during the firing of a rapid succession of shots. The Uzi pistol was designed for civilian use, but there are obvious applications for military and security forces as examples fitted with suppressors, blank firing attachments and laser pointing devices have been observed.

SPECIFICATION:

USED BY:
Israeli Special Forces

CONTRACTOR:
Israel Military Industries Ltd (IMI),
Ramat Hasharon, Israel

FEATURES:
CARTRIDGE: 9 x 19 mm Parabellum
OPERATION: blowback;
semi-automatic; closed breech
FEED: box magazine
MAGAZINE CAPACITY: 20, 25 or
30 rds
WEIGHT: empty, 1.7 kg; loaded
(25-rd mag), 3.2 kg
LENGTH: overall, 240 mm; barrel,
115 mm
RIFLING: four grooves; rh; one
turn in 254 mm
MUZZLE VELOCITY: approx 345 m/s

Beretta 9 x 19 mm Model 92SB Pistol ITALY

The safety lever is on both sides of the slide, allowing the pistol to be used by left-handers without alteration. The magazine release button is underneath the trigger guard, where it can be pressed without moving the hand from the grip. The button can be switched from the left side to the right side to allow for left-handed firing. The manual safety disengages the trigger from the sear. The firing pin is permanently locked until the last movement of the trigger on firing. The firing pin is inertia operated. There is a half-cock position. The butt is grooved in the front and rear to improve the grip.

SPECIFICATION:

USED BY:
Italian armed forces (special units) and police forces, some foreign armies

CONTRACTOR:
Armi Beretta SpA, Gardone VT (Brescia), Italy

FEATURES:
CARTRIDGE: 9 x 19 mm Parabellum
OPERATION: short recoil; semi-automatic with single- or double-action
LOCKING: falling block
FEED: 15-rd detachable box magazine
WEIGHT: with empty magazine, 950 g
LENGTH: 217 mm
BARREL: 125 mm
RIFLING: six grooves; rh; 250 mm pitch
SIGHTS: fore, blade integral with slide; rear, notched bar dovetailed to slide
SIGHT RADIUS: 155 mm
MUZZLE VELOCITY: nominal, 390 m/s

Beretta 9 x 19mm Model 92FS Self-loading Pistol ITALY

SPECIFICATION:

USED BY:
French Gendarmerie Nationale,
US armed forces and Coast
Guard, law-enforcement agencies
worldwide

CONTRACTOR:
Armi Beretta SpA, Gardone VT
(Brescia), Italy

FEATURES:
CARTRIDGE: 9 x 19 mm Parabellum
OPERATION: short recoil;
semi-automatic with single- or
double-action
LOCKING: falling block
FEED: box magazine
MAGAZINE CAPACITY: 15 rds
(for US civilian use, 10 rds only)
WEIGHT: empty, 975 g
LENGTH: overall, 217 mm; barrel,
125 mm
RIFLING: six grooves; rh; 250 mm
pitch
SIGHTS: fore, blade integral with
slide; rear, notched bar dovetailed
to slide
SIGHT RADIUS: 155 mm
MUZZLE VELOCITY: nominal,
390 m/s

Beretta 9 x 19 mm Model 93R Selective-fire Pistol ITALY

The Beretta 9 x 19 mm Model 93R selective-fire pistol is a modified self-loading pistol which can fire either single shots or three-round bursts and so falls more into the category of a 'machine pistol' in the true sense of the word. However, it can be carried and used in the same way as a single-handed pistol, and as such, it handles as a slightly large 9 mm self-loading pistol of conventional design. It can be used and fired just like any other pistol, but should firers wish to engage a target beyond the normal pistol range, or even to engage a difficult target close at hand, they can quickly fold down the front handgrip and hold the pistol with both hands.

SPECIFICATION:

USED BY:
Italian and other Special Forces

CONTRACTOR:
Armi Beretta SpA, Gardone VT (Brescia), Italy

FEATURES:
CARTRIDGE: 9 x 19 mm Parabellum
OPERATION: short-recoil; single-shot or 3-rd burst
LOCKING: hinged block
FEED: detachable box magazine
MAGAZINE CAPACITY: 15 or 20 rds
WEIGHT: with 15-rd mag, 1.12 kg; with 20-rd mag, 1.17 kg
LENGTH: overall, 240 mm; barrel, including muzzle brake, 156 mm
RIFLING: six grooves; rh; one turn in 250 mm
SIGHTS: fore, blade integral with slide; rear, notched bar dovetailed to slide
SIGHT RADIUS: 160 mm
RATE OF FIRE: cyclic, approx 1100 rds/min
SELECTOR: manual, single self-loading shot or 3-rd bursts
MUZZLE VELOCITY: 375 m/s
METAL STOCK: length folded, 195 mm; length extended, 368 mm; weight, 270 g

9 mm K5 Pistol KOREA, SOUTH

The K5 is a semi-automatic pistol in 9 mm parabellum calibre operating on the delayed blowback system. Designed for military and police use, it has three firing modes: single-, double- and 'fast-action'. The fast-action method of trigger operation allows the firer to have a first-shot trigger pull similar to double-action in length of pull but with the weight of pull very similar to that of a single-action pull. The sights are fitted with luminous dots for operation in poor light conditions.

SPECIFICATION:

USED BY:
South Korean security forces

CONTRACTOR:
Daewoo Telecom Ltd, Pusan, South Korea

FEATURES:
CARTRIDGE: 9 x 19 mm parabellum
OPERATION: delayed blowback; semi-automatic; single-, double- and fast-action
FEED: 12-rd box magazine
WEIGHT: 800 g (empty)
LENGTH: 190 mm
RIFLING: six grooves; rh
SIGHTS: fore, blade with luminous dot; rear, square notch, adjustable for windage, two luminous dots
MUZZLE VELOCITY: 350 m/s

.22LR KP52 Pistol KOREA, SOUTH

.22LR KP52 pistol

The KP52 is a fixed-barrel semi-automatic blowback pistol in .22LR calibre, intended for police and security duties. It has a double-action trigger mechanism and the sights have self-luminous markers inserted for firing at night or in poor visibility.

SPECIFICATION:

USED BY:
South Korean police and security forces

CONTRACTOR:
Daewoo Telecom Ltd, Pusan, South Korea

FEATURES:
CARTRIDGE: .22 LR rimfire
OPERATION: blowback; semi-automatic; double- or single-action
FEED: 10-rd box magazine
LENGTH: 170 mm
BARREL: 97 mm
RIFLING: six grooves; rh
SIGHTS: fore, blade with self-luminous insert; rear, square notch with two self-luminous inserts
MUZZLE VELOCITY: 290 m/s

VANAD P-83 Pistol POLAND

P-83G gas pistol, with four-chamber muzzle attachment

The P-83G gas pistol is basically a blank-firing VANAD P-83 pistol with a muzzle attachment capable of projecting disabling gas pellets. An alternative muzzle attachment can be used to launch up to four flares. If required, the P-83G can fire blanks as a starting or training pistol.

SPECIFICATION:

USED BY:
Polish armed and security forces

CONTRACTOR:
Zaklady Metalowe Lucznik SA,
Radom, Poland

FEATURES:
CARTRIDGE: 9 x 18 mm Makarov;
9 x 17 mm
OPERATION: blowback; self-loading;
single-action or double-action
FEED: detachable box magazine
MAGAZINE CAPACITY: 8 rds
WEIGHT: empty, 730 g
LENGTH: overall, 165 mm; barrel,
90 mm
RIFLING: four grooves; rh
SIGHTS: fore, blade; rear, notch
SIGHT RADIUS: 120 mm
MUZZLE VELOCITY: 9 x 18 mm
Makarov, 312 m/s; 9 x 17 mm,
284 m/s

9 mm Modified Makarov Pistol PMM RUSSIA

At the beginning of the 1990s a group of engineers at the *Izhevsky Mekhanichesky Zavod* (The Izhevsk Mechanical Factory) modified an existing 9 mm Makarov 'pistol and ammunition' system by using a larger load for the standard 9 x 18 mm Makarov cartridge case. Leaving the exterior dimensions of the case intact, the muzzle energy was increased by a factor of 1.7 and the generated gas pressure increased by a factor of 1.25. The modified Makarov pistol features a magazine with an enlarged capacity of twelve rounds instead of the previous eight rounds. The magazine is a double-column, one-position feed construction and the handgrip is of a new improved shape. The inside of the chamber now has threaded grooves to reduce the speed of recoil of the slide and ensures reliable functioning of the system using both standard and modified cartridges.

SPECIFICATION:

USED BY:
Russian Ministry of Interior personnel, police and security services

CONTRACTOR:
IZHMECH, Moscow, Russia

FEATURES:
CARTRIDGE: 9 x 18 mm Makarov standard- and high-impulse
OPERATION: retarded blowback; grooved chamber
OVERALL LENGTH: 169 mm
BARREL LENGTH: 93.5 mm
RIFLING: four grooves; rh; one turn in 260 mm
MAGAZINE CAPACITY: 12 rds
WEIGHT: empty, 760 g
MUZZLE VELOCITY: standard round, 315 m/s; high-impulse round, 430 m/s

7.62 mm PSS Silent Pistol   RUSSIA

7.62 mm PSS silent self-loading pistol

This is a small blowback pistol firing a special cartridge and generating a sound level comparable to that of an air pistol. The trigger mechanism is double-action, with an external hammer and there is a slide-mounted safety catch which lowers the hammer safely on a loaded chamber. There is no conventional Maxim-type silencer in the weapon. Instead, the special cartridge contains a piston between the propelling charge and the bullet. On firing, the propelling charge explodes, driving the piston forward; this impels the bullet forward. The piston is then arrested by the cartridge shoulder, which is securely held by a shoulder in the pistol chamber. The noise and smoke of the explosion is retained inside the cartridge case and the only noise is that of the automatic operation from the muzzle. The bullet has an effective range of 50 m and can penetrate a standard steel helmet at 25 m range.

SPECIFICATION:

USED BY:
Russian security forces

CONTRACTOR:
TSNIITOCHMASH, Moscow, Russia

FEATURES:
CARTRIDGE: 7.62 x 42 mm special (see text)
OPERATION: blowback; semi-automatic; double-action
FEED: 6-rd box magazine
WEIGHT: empty, 700 g
LENGTH: 165 mm

9 mm Star Model 30M & Model 30PK Pistols   SPAIN

9 mm Star Model 30M double-action pistol

The Model 30M is made entirely of forged steel, while the Model 30PK has a light-alloy frame. The pistol is somewhat unusual in having the slide running in internal frame rails, giving excellent support throughout the slide movement with a minimum bearing of over 110 mm. There is an ambidextrous safety catch on the slide which retracts the firing pin into its tunnel, out of reach of the hammer. The trigger and hammer action are quite unaffected by the safety catch action and it is possible to pull the trigger so as to drop the hammer after applying the safety catch. The trigger can also be pulled to raise and drop the hammer for 'dry firing' practice, without needing to unload the weapon. The trigger guard fore-edge is shaped for the two-handed grip and there is a loaded chamber indicator which stands proud of the slide when the weapon is loaded. The sights are clear, the rearsight being adjustable for windage and the gun is very accurate.

SPECIFICATION:

USED BY:
Spanish armed and police forces,
Peruvian police and security
forces

CONTRACTOR:
Star Bonifacio Echeverria SA,
Eibar, Spain

FEATURES:
CARTRIDGE: 9 mm parabellum
OPERATION: short recoil;
semi-automatic
LOCKING: Browning cam
FEED: 15-rd box magazine
WEIGHT: 30M, 1.14 kg; 30PK,
860 g
LENGTH: 30M, 205 mm; 30PK,
193 mm
BARREL: 30M, 119 mm; 30PK,
98 mm
SIGHTS: fore, blade; rear, notch,
adjustable for windage
MUZZLE VELOCITY: ca 380 m/s

MTE 224 V and MTE 224 VA Pistols SWITZERLAND

MTE 224 VA selective fire pistol with foregrip and sound suppressor

The MTE 224 V and MTE 224 VA pistols were designed specifically to fire the 5.56 x 23.5 mm cartridge. This cartridge is one of a group of similar cartridges intended to defeat soft body armour and light armour likely to be encountered in law enforcement and military environments and was developed to meet the NATO Personal Defence Weapon specification. The pistol also meets the US Army Objective Personal Weapon requirement of being capable of carrying in a holster. The intention is that the bullet will penetrate the armour without fragmenting, while retaining sufficient energy to inflict a significant wound once the armour has been defeated. Two magazine capacities are available, 16 or 26 rounds. Combat accessories include tactical lights and laser aiming devices developed by Laser Devices Inc of Monterey, California. Both units fit into accessory rails located in front of the trigger guard. The same rails can also accommodate a forward grip for when the MTE 224 VA is fired on fully automatic. A further accessory is a sound suppressor with a quick-connect device that locates into two interface grooves machined into the end of the barrel. The suppressor is intended for use in the semi-automatic mode only.

SPECIFICATION:

CONTRACTOR:
ASAI AG, Solothurn, Switzerland

FEATURES:
CARTRIDGE: 5.56 x 23.5 mm
OPERATION: blowback; selective fire
FEED: 16- or 26-rd box magazine
WEIGHT: empty, 1.045 kg
LENGTH: 260 mm
HEIGHT: 148 mm
WIDTH: 39 mm
BARREL: 165 mm
SIGHTS: fore, blade; rear, notch
TRIGGER PULL: double-action, 3.9 kg; single-action, 1.6 kg
MUZZLE VELOCITY: nominal, 720 m/s
MUZZLE ENERGY: 750 J

FBP Pistol Silencer SWITZERLAND

The FBP pistol silencer is designed for use on all fixed barrel pistols and most barrel-locked pistols in the calibres 7.65 Browning to 9 mm. Due to construction without a recoil improvement system the FBP silencer design is one of the most compact and lightweight available. The FBP can be improved with a wet-charge which increases sound reduction on the first 15 – 25 shots fired. This silencer is intended for mounting on a threaded barrel.

SPECIFICATION:

USED BY:
Various special forces and police units

CONTRACTOR:
Brugger and Thomet AG, Spiez, Switzerland

FEATURES:
WEIGHT: 190 g
LENGTH: 145 mm
DIAMETER: 35 mm
SUPPRESSION: 24+ dB A (34+ wet)

.45 Model 1911A1 Automatic Pistol USA

Development of this pistol, by John Browning, began in 1896 and culminated in a comprehensive trial by the US Army in 1908. They generally approved of the Colt/Browning design but required some modifications and the perfected design was approved as the M1911, entering US service in that year.

SPECIFICATION:

USED BY:
One of the most widely used pistols in the world

CONTRACTOR:
Colt's Manufacturing Co Inc, Connecticut, USA

FEATURES:
CARTRIDGE: .45 ACP
OPERATION: short recoil; self-loading
LOCKING: projecting lug
FEED: 7-rd box magazine
WEIGHT: 1.13 kg (empty)
LENGTH: 219 mm
BARREL: 127 mm
RIFLING: six grooves; lh; one turn in 406 mm
SIGHTS: fore, blade; rear, u-notch, adjustable for windage
SIGHT RADIUS: 164.6 mm
MUZZLE VELOCITY: 253 m/s

us Marine Corps MEU(SOC) 0.45 ACP Pistol USA

The us Marine Corps Marine Expeditionary Unit (Special Operations Capable) pistol was designed by the Marine Corps Weapons Training Battalion at Quantico, Virginia, to be a back-up weapon for Marines armed with the Heckler & Koch MP5-N 9 mm sub-machine gun or with the M4 carbine.

SPECIFICATION:

USED BY:
us Marine Corps

CONTRACTOR:
us Marine Corps Weapons
Training Battalion Rifle Team
Equipment Shop, Virginia, USA

FEATURES:
CARTRIDGE: 0.45 ACP
OPERATION: short recoil;
self-loading
LOCKING: projecting lugs
FEED: detachable 7-rd box
magazine
WEIGHT: 1.13 kg
LENGTH: 223 mm
BARREL: 127.7 mm
RIFLING: six grooves; rh; one turn
in 406 mm
SIGHTS: fore, high profile blade;
rear, high-profile notch
adjustable for windage
MUZZLE VELOCITY: 253 m/s

Model FBI Special Weapons and Tactics Pistol   USA

Springfield 0.45 ACP Bureau Model FBI Special Weapons and Tactics pistol

The Springfield Armory Bureau Model is a highly modified M1911A1-type pistol of conventional design. It is, however, quite different from standard M1911A1 pistols in that it has many custom features, including a custom-fitted slide and frame, match barrel, polished feed ramp and throated barrel, a specially fitted trigger mechanism tuned to 2.04 kg pull, a lowered and flared ejection port and tuned extractor for positive ejection, a custom-fitted beavertail grip safety and ambidextrous thumb safety, Novak tritium sights, a special magazine well bevelled to fit for positive reloading, and special checkering on the frame. The pistol is finished in proprietary Black T which is highly wear-resistant, virtually impervious to oxidation and is self-lubricating.

SPECIFICATION:

USED BY:
US, FBI, US Marshal's Service, US Marine Corps and many other military and law enforcement agencies

CONTRACTOR:
Springfield Inc, Geneseo, Illinois, USA

FEATURES:
CARTRIDGE: 0.45 ACP
OPERATION: short recoil
LOCKING: projecting lugs
FEED: 8-rd detachable box magazine
WEIGHT: 1.01 kg
LENGTH: 219 mm
BARREL: 127 mm
RIFLING: six grooves; lh; one turn in 406 mm
SIGHTS: fore, blade; rear, low-profile adjustable notch; both with tritium inserts
SIGHT RADIUS: 158 mm

MK23 Suppressor USA

SPECIFICATION:

USED BY:
US Special Forces

CONTRACTOR:
Knight's Armament Company,
Florida, USA

FEATURES:
CONSTRUCTION: stainless steel
TYPE: baffle
WEIGHT: 0.454 kg
LENGTH: 191 mm
DIAMETER: 35 mm
SOUND SUPPRESSION:
38 dB reduction (wet);
28 dB reduction (dry)

Weapons:
Knives

Norinco 0.22RF Type 85 Bayonet Pistol CHINA

Norinco 0.22 Type 85 bayonet pistol, blade extended, shown with sheath

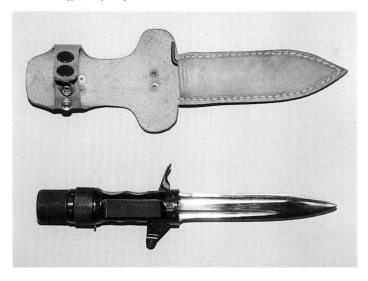

Norinco's Type 85 knife pistol has a folding blade and a magazine that consists of three separate barrels, each chambering its own cartridge. The loaded magazine is inserted into the gun on the right side of the grip, and a vertical trigger at the 12 o'clock position is used to fire the cartridges in succession. No form of sight is provided, and the practical effective range perhaps makes a sight unnecessary. A small safety catch that locks the trigger is located behind the guard. The knife pistol comes complete with a spare magazine, a small screwdriver for removing fired cases from the magazine, and a belt holster for the pistol and accessories. The gun life is given as 600 rounds.

SPECIFICATION:

USED BY:
Chinese Special Forces

CONTRACTOR:
China North Industries Corporation (Norinco), Beijing, China

FEATURES:
CARTRIDGE: 0.22 LR
OPERATION: single-shot
FEED: 3 preloaded barrels
WEIGHT: (unloaded; actual pistol weighed) 330 g
LENGTH OVERALL: blade extended, 265 mm; bladed folded, 150 mm
BARREL LENGTH OVERALL: 51 mm; rifled length: approx 35 mm
RIFLING: six grooves, rh
MUZZLE VELOCITY: approx 140 m/s
EFFECTIVE RANGE: 5-8 m

Eickhorn Solingen Advanced Combat Knife GERMANY

Advanced combat knife

SPECIFICATION:

USED BY:
Special Forces worldwide

CONTRACTOR:
A Eickhorn GmbH and Co,
Germany

FEATURES:
- Universal saw (wood saw can be supplied)
- Screwdriver
- Re-adjustable wire cutter
- Sapphire re-sharpening device
- Bottle opener
- Protection cap allowing knife to be used as a baton
- Tie thongs to secure knife to wearer's leg
- Quick release mechanism to separate scabbard from belt
- Hollow handle for medicaments or water purification tablets

Designed at the request of the German armed forces.

KCB 77 Eickhorn Solingen Bayonets GERMANY

KCB 77 bayonet with its scabbard

SPECIFICATION:

USED BY:
Special Forces worldwide

CONTRACTOR:
A Eickhorn GmbH and Co,
Germany

FEATURES:
- Electronically insulated
- Self-draining scabbard
- Tie thongs
- Wire cutter

Considered by many to be the state-of-the-art bayonet.

Eickhorn Solingen Mark 3 Combat Knife GERMANY

SPECIFICATION:

USED BY:
Special Forces worldwide

CONTRACTOR:
A Eickhorn GmbH and Co,
Germany

FEATURES:
- Electrically insulated
- Length of blade approx 16.7 mm
- Width of blade approx 2.2 cm
- Length of knife approx 29.5 mm
- Weight of knife approx 250 g

This knife has good balance and low weight. A blade sharpening device is built into the scabbard and is thus in use each time the knife is removed and replaced.

Eickhorn Solingen USM 7 Bayonet with USM 8 A1 Scabbard GERMANY

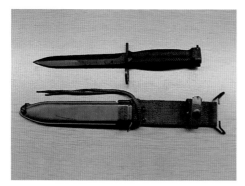

SPECIFICATION:

USED BY:
Special Forces worldwide

CONTRACTOR:
A Eickhorn GmbH and Co,
Germany

FEATURES:
- Can be fitted to most assault rifles
- Electrically insulated
- Length of blade approx 16.7 mm
- Width of blade approx 2.2 cm
- Length of knife approx 29.5 mm
- Weight of knife approx 280 g

Designed for use in the toughest of field conditions. A blade sharpening device is built into the scabbard and is thus in use each time the knife is removed and replaced.

NRS Scouting Knife RUSSIA

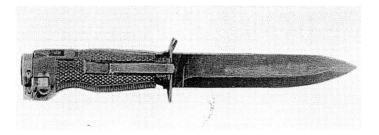

The NRS scouting knife, also known as the NRS-2, is similar to the Chinese Type 85 insofar as it incorporates a firearm in a utility knife. The handle of the knife carries a chamber and short barrel, into which is loaded one 7.62 x 42 mm SP-4 special captive-piston cartridge of the type described under the PSS silent pistol. This captive-piston-type cartridge is virtually silent in use. The muzzle of the pistol is at the end of the knife handle. The knife is reversed in the hand and is fired by pressure in a trigger bar set into the handle. A notch in the crosspiece acts as a rudimentary sight. There is a sliding safety catch to prevent accidental discharges. However, the practical utility of such a device is questionable, as to be used correctly, the blade of the weapon must be held with the blade towards the firer's throat. The knife is a substantial tool which can cut steel rods up to a diameter of 10 mm. The scabbard is insulated to permit the cutting of electrical cables. It also incorporates a screwdriver and can be used for other purposes.

SPECIFICATION:

USED BY:
Russian and other Federation states Special Forces

CONTRACTOR:
Tulsky Oruzheiny Zavod JSC, Tula, Russia

FEATURES:
CARTRIDGE: 7.62 x 42 mm SP-4
OPERATION: single shot
WEIGHT: knife, 350 g; knife with scabbard, 620 g
LENGTH: overall, 284 mm; blade, 162 x 28 x 3.5 mm
MUZZLE VELOCITY: approx 200 m/s
EFFECTIVE FIREARM RANGE: 25 m

Applegate-Fairburn Knife UK

The knife features one-handed opening and closing and can be locked open. It has a double-bevelled blade and is provided with a ballistic cloth sheath.

SPECIFICATION:

USED BY:
Privately purchased by Special Forces

CONTRACTOR:
BCB International Ltd, Cardiff, UK

FEATURES:
Classic:
OPEN LENGTH: 256 mm (10 in)
CLOSED LENGTH: 112 mm (4.4 in)
WEIGHT: 160 g (5.6 oz)

Covert:
OPEN LENGTH: 212 mm (8.3 in)
CLOSED LENGTH: 97 mm (3.8 in)
WEIGHT: 113 g (3.9 oz)

BCB Machetes UK

Spec plus machete (1) and Survival tool machete (2)

The Spec plus machete has a stainless steel black coated single-side blade and a high grip, ribbed moulded handle with a finger guard. It is supplied with a lanyard and leather/Cordura sheath. The Survival tool machete has three different cutting edges: a heavy duty chopping blade; a finer edge for stunning; and a very closely honed edge for food preparation, feathering sticks and so on. The blade is made from carbon steel and has an easy and effective chopping action. It comes in a nylon sheath.

SPECIFICATION:

USED BY:
Privately purchased by Special Forces

CONTRACTOR:
BCB International Ltd, Cardiff, UK

FEATURES:
Spec plus machete:
BLADE LENGTH: 33 cm (12.9 in)
Survival 1201 machete:
BLADE LENGTH: 28 cm (11 in)
LENGTH OVERALL: 40 cm (15.7 in)
WIDTH: 6 cm (2.4 in)
THICKNESS: 6 mm (0.23 in)

Fairburn-Sykes Fighting Knife (Commando Dagger) UK

Fairburn-Sykes fighting knife (1) and correct use of the Fairburn-Sykes fighting knife (2)

This fighting knife has a double-edged blade, sharply pointed tip, hand-guard and ribbed handle. The blade can be unscrewed at the pummel. The knife is kept in a leather sheath with tabs for stitching to the side of a pair of trousers. The blade is kept in place by an elastic strap. It is painted black although presentation models are silver coloured.

SPECIFICATION:

USED BY:
Issued during World War Two to members of Commando Forces, now privately purchased by Special Forces

CONTRACTOR:
Wilkinson Sword Ltd, London, UK

FEATURES:
WEIGHT: 240.9 gms (8.5 ozs)
LENGTH: overall without scabbard, 29.5 cms (11.7 inches)
LENGTH OF BLADE: 17.8 cm (7 in)

S37 SEAL Knife 2000 USA

This knife was the winner of an extensive evaluation programme and was chosen for the US Navy SEALS. The testing covered tip-breaking strength, blade toughness, sharpness and edge retention, handle twist-off limits, two-week salt water immersions, gasoline and acetylene torch resistance, chopping, hammering, prying, penetration performance, cutting ability for six different types of rope and nylon line, low-noise and low-reflection factors and intense hands-on training in the field.

SPECIFICATION:

USED BY:
US Navy SEAL teams

CONTRACTOR:
SOG Speciality Knives and Tools, Inc, Washington, USA

FEATURES:
BLADE LENGTH: 17.8 cms (7 in)
LENGTH OVERALL: 31.4 cms (2.35 in)
WEIGHT: 362.8 gms (12.8 oz)
MATERIALS: AUS6 stainless, powder coated, RC 56-58

SOG RFB81 X-42 Recondo USA

This knife is named after the MACV Recondo School for Special Forces established in 1966. It features a very sharp blade, made from BG-42 stainless steel, with grind lines that focus power on the edge and tip. It has a glass-reinforced Zytel handle. The knife is supplied with a self-draining Kydex sheath.

SPECIFICATION:

USED BY:
US Special Forces

CONTRACTOR:
SOG Speciality Knives and Tools, Inc, Washington, USA

FEATURES:
BLADE: 13.5 cms (5.3 in)
LENGTH OVERALL: 26.7 cms (10.5 in)
WEIGHT: 178.6 gms (6.3 oz)
MATERIALS: BG-42, RC 60-62
HANDLE: Glass-reinforced Zytel

SOG Scuba/Demo SSD99 USA

This is a reproduction of a knife originally made by SOG for the Naval Advisory Detachment for missions on the North Vietnamese coastline in 1964. The knife has a 0.230 in thick double-edged blade with a full serration along the spine. It features a stacked leather washer handle that is epoxied together and secured with a brass pommel. There is also a brass crossguard. The knife is supplied with a dark leather sheath, sharpening stone and leather lanyard.

SPECIFICATION:

USED BY:
US Special Forces

CONTRACTOR:
SOG Specialty Knives and Tools, Inc, Washington, USA

FEATURES:
BLADE: 19.6 cm (7.75 in)
LENGTH OVERALL: 31.4 cm (12.35 in)
WEIGHT: 362.8 gms (12.8 oz)
MATERIALS: AUS8, RC 57-59

Weapons:
Machine
Guns and
Sub-Machine
Guns

F89 Minimi 5.56 mm Light Support Weapon AUSTRALIA

F89 Minimi 5.56 mm machine gun with optical sight and collapsible magazine

The F89 Minimi 5.56 mm light machine gun was adopted by the Australian Army as its light support weapon, with production being undertaken from 1991 onwards at the ADI Ltd Lithgow Facility. The F89 is a multipurpose machine gun capable of sustaining high rates of fire. It can be tripod-mounted and has the same capabilities as heavier weapons. Issued at the rate of two per rifle section, it can also be fired from the bipod or from the hip. The F89 is fitted with the flash suppressor from the Belgian MAG, the optical sight from the F88 rifle, and with a locally developed 200-round collapsible bag magazine. During 1999 the F89 was modified, the optical sight mounting on the feed cover having been replaced by a MIL-STD-1913 Picatinny rail mounting that can accommodate either the F88 optical sight or the Wildcat Enhanced Optical Sight. The rail can also accommodate the Project Ninox Night Weapon Sight.

SPECIFICATION:

USED BY:
Australian armed and Special Forces

CONTRACTOR:
ADI Ltd, Lithgow, New South Wales, Australia (under licence from FN Herstal)

FN Herstal 0.50 Browning M2 HB Machine Gun BELGIUM

FN Herstal 0.50 Browning M3M for helicopter door mounts

The FN Herstal 0.50 M2 Heavy Barrel (HB) Browning machine gun is similar in design and operation to other types of Browning M2 machine guns, being a recoil-operated, air-cooled, belt-fed weapon. The mechanism operates in exactly the same manner as other Browning M2 HBS, so reference should be made to the appropriate separate entry. FN Herstal also produces various mountings for the M2 HB, including the universal M3 tripod and the anti-aircraft M63 mounting. A quantity of these guns has been ordered for British Army and Fleet Air Arm Lynx helicopters. The M3M is also available on a ground service soft mount. The New Zealand Army has ordered 24 examples of this configuration for issue to two motorised infantry battalions. During 2002, the US Marine Corps used a tripod-mounted version of the M2M for trials. It has been reported that a similar model is already in service with British Special Forces.

SPECIFICATION:

USED BY:
Belgium and other nations within Europe, plus countries in South America, the Middle East and the rest of Asia. Often used by Special Forces and mounted on light vehicles or in helicopter doors

CONTRACTOR:
FN Herstal SA, Herstal, Belgium

FEATURES:
CARTRIDGE: 0.50 Browning (12.7 x 99 mm)
OPERATION: short recoil; selective fire
FEED: disintegrating link belt; M2 or M9 links
WEIGHT: empty, 36 kg
LENGTH: 1.656 m
BARREL: 1.143 m
RIFLING: eight grooves; rh; length 1.064 m
MUZZLE VELOCITY: 880 m/s with M33 ball
RATE OF FIRE: cyclic, 450-550 rds/min
RANGE: 6765 m
EFFECTIVE RANGE: 1500 m plus

FN Herstal 0.50 M2 HB/QCB Machine Gun BELGIUM

Since the late 1970s, demand for the 0.50 M2 HB machine gun has been steadily continuing, leading FN Herstal to develop a Quick-Change Barrel (QCB) version. This feature eliminates tedious headspace adjustment, ending the chance of dangerous errors; saves time in training and in operations; and reduces the risk taken in action whilst adjusting headspace. To accompany this machine gun FN Herstal introduced new APEI ammunition. There is also a 0.50 M2 HB/QCB variant for use as a coaxial machine gun on armoured vehicles, firing automatic only.

SPECIFICATION:

USED BY:
Armed and Special Forces in Europe, North America, Middle East, Asia, Africa and Latin America

CONTRACTOR:
FN Herstal SA, Herstal, Belgium

FN Herstal 7.62 mm MAG General-purpose Machine Gun BELGIUM

The FN Herstal MAG is gas operated and belt fed, and it has a quick-change barrel. It is light enough to be carried by infantry and is capable of producing sustained fire over considerable periods when mounted on a tripod. It fires the standard 7.62 x 51 mm NATO cartridge from a disintegrating link belt of the US M13 type; alternatively the 50-round DM 1 continuous articulated belt can be used, but the two types of belt are not interchangeable.

SPECIFICATION:

USED BY:
Known to be in service with the armed forces (and many Special Forces) of Argentina, Australia, Bahrain, Barbados, Belgium, Belize, Bolivia, Botswana, Brazil, Brunei, Burkina Faso, Burundi, Cameroon, Canada, Chad, Colombia, Democratic Republic of Congo (formerly Zaire), Cuba, Cyprus, Djibouti, Dominican Republic, Ecuador, Egypt, Gabon, The Gambia, Ghana, Greece, Guatemala, Haiti, Honduras, India, Indonesia, Iraq, Ireland, Israel, Jamaica, Jordan, Kenya, South Korea, Kuwait, Lebanon, Lesotho, Libya, Luxembourg, Malaysia, Mexico, Morocco, Myanmar (Burma), Netherlands, New Zealand, Nicaragua, Nigeria, Oman, Pakistan, Panama, Peru, Philippines, Portugal, Qatar, Rwanda, Saudi Arabia, Seychelles, Sierra Leone, Singapore, South Africa, Sri Lanka, Sudan, Surinam, Swaziland, Sweden, Switzerland, Tanzania, Thailand, Tunisia, Uganda, United Arab Emirates, the UK, USA, Uruguay, Venezuela and Zimbabwe. This list is probably not complete

CONTRACTOR:
FN Herstal SA, Herstal, Belgium

FEATURES:
Portable infantry version:

CARTRIDGE: 7.62 x 51 mm NATO
OPERATION: gas; automatic
LOCKING: dropping locking lever
FEED: belt
WEIGHT: with butt and bipod, 11.79 kg; spare barrel, 3 kg
LENGTH: 1.263 m
BARREL: rifling, 487.5 mm; with flash hider, 630 mm
RIFLING: four grooves; rh; one turn in 305 mm
SIGHTS: fore, blade; rear, aperture when leaf is lowered, U-notch when leaf is raised
SIGHT RADIUS: sight folded down, 848 mm; sight raised, 785 mm
MUZZLE VELOCITY: 840 m/s
Muzzle energy: 335 kg/m
RATE OF FIRE: cyclic, 650-1000 rds/min
EFFECTIVE RANGE: 1500 m

FN Herstal 5.56 mm Minimi Light Machine Gun BELGIUM

FN Herstal 5.56 mm Minimi light machine gun, standard

The Minimi light machine gun is gas operated, using gas tapped from the forward part of the barrel in conventional fashion. The rotary gas regulator is of a simple design, based on the earlier MAG machine-gun type, and has two basic settings: normal and adverse conditions. Adjustment is by hand, even with a hot barrel.

For users needing a light machine gun shorter than the standard version, there is a para model with a sliding butt-stock and a shorter barrel. The chief advantage of this version is that it is much easier to handle and carry in and out of vehicles, helicopters and similar confined spaces.

SPECIFICATION:

USED BY:
In service in over 30 countries including Australia, Belgium, Canada, France, Greece, Indonesia, Italy, Japan, Netherlands, New Zealand, Sri Lanka, Sweden, United Arab Emirates, UK, USA

CONTRACTOR:
FN Herstal SA, Herstal, Belgium

FEATURES:
Data for standard Minimi; where para differs, in parentheses:

CARTRIDGE: 5.56 x 45 mm (FN SS109 NATO or M193)
OPERATION: gas; firing fully automatic
LOCKING: rotating bolt head
FEED: 200-rd belts or 30-rd M16A1 magazine
WEIGHT: 7.1 kg (7.14 kg)
LENGTH: overall, 1.04 m (stock folded, 736 mm; stock extended, 893 mm)
BARREL: 465 mm (347 mm)
RIFLING: six grooves; rh; one turn in 304 mm (M193) or one turn in 178 mm (SS109)
SIGHTS: fore, semi-fixed hooded post, adjustable for windage and elevation; rear, aperture, adjustable for windage and elevation
SIGHT RADIUS: 495 mm
MUZZLE VELOCITY: M193, 965 m/s SS109, 915 m/s
RATE OF FIRE: cyclic, 700-1000 rds/min
EFFECTIVE RANGE: 1000 m

FN 5.7 x 28 mm P90 Sub-machine Gun BELGIUM

FN 5.7 mm P90 sub-machine gun and magazine pouch (1) and FN 5.7 mm P90 sub-machine gun fitted with suppressor and torch (2)

The P90 is a blowback weapon firing from a closed bolt. The overall design places great reliance on ergonomics, to the extent that the pistol grip, with a thumb-hole stock, is well forward on the receiver so that, when gripped, the bulk of the receiver lies along the firer's forearm. The controls are fully ambidextrous; a cocking handle is provided on each side, and the selector/safety switch is a rotary component located under the trigger. Even the forward sling swivel can be located on either side of the weapon, as required. Two Special Forces variants of the P90 are available, each with a laser target designator. The P90 LV uses an 8 mw visible laser for use in low-light conditions and in indoor situations. The P90 Laser Intercept Receiver (LIR) has a 4.5 mw infra-red laser which can be detected with night-vision devices. It is also possible to mount various forms of night sight.

SPECIFICATION:

USED BY:
Understood to include Cyprus National Guard Special Forces, Netherlands, Peru Special Forces, Saudi Arabia and some Asian nations

CONTRACTOR:
FN Herstal SA, Herstal, Belgium

FEATURES:
CARTRIDGE: 5.7 x 28 mm
FEED: 50-rd magazine located horizontally above barrel
WEIGHT: empty, 2.54 kg; with empty mag, 2.68 kg; with full mag, 3 kg
LENGTH: overall, 500 mm; barrel, 256.5 mm
HEIGHT: 210 mm
WIDTH: 55 mm
SIGHTS: optical reflex x1 magnification, plus emergency iron sights
MUZZLE VELOCITY: SS190, 715 m/s
RATE OF FIRE: 900 rds/min
RANGE: max combat, 200 m; max possible, 1790 m

Diemaco C7 5.56 mm Light Support Weapon CANADA

Diemaco C7 5.56 mm Light Support Weapon (LSW) and accessories

The C7 Light Support Weapon (LSW) is a co-development between Diemaco and Colt Firearms (where the weapon is known as the Colt Model 715 or the M16 light machine gun). The C7 LSW features a select fire mechanism, an hydraulic recoil buffer and an adjustable bipod. The weapon also features a heavy contour Diemaco hammer-forged barrel. The improved life and durability of the barrel during testing has eliminated the need for a quick-change barrel system, greatly simplifying the design and making the LSW accurate to the maximum effective range of the ammunition. The weapon can be supplied in either an open or closed bolt configuration. The C7 LSW is fed from any M16 compatible box magazine, including high-capacity types and it uses the same family of accessories as the C7 rifle. The C7 LSW uses the M16A2 type rear sight as standard but is also available mounting an optical sight as the C7A1 light support weapon – this version has been procured by the Netherlands Marine Corps.

SPECIFICATION:

USED BY:
Netherlands (Marine Corps) and Denmark

CONTRACTOR:
Diemaco, Kitchener, Ontario, Canada

FEATURES:
CARTRIDGE: 5.56 x 45 mm
OPERATION: direct gas; selective fire
LOCKING: rotating bolt
FEED: 30-round box magazine
WEIGHT: 8 kg; loaded, 6.2 kg
LENGTH: normal butt, 1.02 m
BARREL: 510 mm
RIFLING: six grooves; rh; one turn in 178 mm
SIGHTS: fore, post; rear, adjustable aperture, 300-800 m; optical sight optional
MUZZLE VELOCITY: SS109 at 24 m, 920 m/s
RATE OF FIRE: cyclic, 625 rds/min

7.62 mm N AAT mle F1 General Purpose Machine Gun

FRANCE

The principle of operation is delayed blowback but, since rifle calibre ammunition is used, special arrangements have to be made to ensure safe and smooth extraction of the spent case. There are a number of longitudinal grooves in the neck of the chamber running out halfway towards the mouth. Gas enters these grooves and the case floats with equal pressure on each side of the brass wall and can move comparatively freely.

SPECIFICATION:

USED BY:
French armed and Special Forces and those in many other countries

CONTRACTOR:
Originally developed and produced by Manufacture Nationale d'Armes de Chatellerault. Production subsequently transferred to Manufacture Nationale d'Armes de Tulle. Enquiries to Giat Industries, Versailles-Satory, France

FEATURES: COMMON TO BOTH VERSIONS
CARTRIDGE: 7.62 x 51 mm NATO
OPERATION: delayed blowback; automatic
FEED: disintegrating link belt (see text)
SIGHTS: fore, slit blade; rear, leaf graduated 200-2000 m

FEATURES: LIGHT BARREL (HEAVY BARREL)
WEIGHT OF GUN: without bipod, empty, 9.15 kg (10.55 kg); with bipod, empty, 9.97 kg (11.37 kg)
WEIGHT OF BARREL: 2.85 kg (4.25 kg)
WEIGHT OF BIPOD: 0.82 kg (0.82 kg)
WEIGHT OF MONOPOD: 0.685 kg (0.685 kg)
WEIGHT OF MODIFIED US M2 TRIPOD: n/a (10.6 kg)
LENGTH OF GUN: butt extended, 1.145 m (1.245 m); butt retracted, 980 mm (1.08 m)
LENGTH OF BARREL: without flash hider, 500 mm (600 mm)

FEATURES: AAT 52 (7.62 MM N AAT MLE F1)
MUZZLE VELOCITY: 840 m/s (830 m/s)
RATE OF FIRE: cyclic 700 rds/min (900 rds/min)
PRACTICAL RANGE: 800 m (1200 m)
NUMBER OF GROOVES: four (four)

Heckler & Koch 9 mm MP5 Sub-machine Gun GERMANY

The MP5 remains one of the most widely deployed of all current sub-machine guns and has been developed into a family with numerous variants. The Heckler & Koch 9 mm MP5 sub-machine gun usually offers only a choice of single shot or full automatic, but a burst-fire device, allowing two-round or three-round bursts each time the trigger is operated, is offered by the manufacturer to those requiring this facility. This trigger arrangement can be fitted to all automatic weapons in the Heckler & Koch series. With the selector lever placed on 'safe', the selector spindle lies over the trigger lug and prevents sufficient movement of the trigger to disengage the sear from the hammer notch. The position of the safety catch can vary from model to model.

SPECIFICATION:

USED BY:
Afghanistani, Argentinian, Australian Special Forces, Bahrain, Belgian police, Brazilian police, Cameroon, Chile, Colombia, Danish police, El Salvador, France, German police and border police, Ghana, Greece (under licence), Honduras, Icelandic police, Indian Special Forces, Iran (under licence), Ireland, Italian police, Japanese police, Jordan, Kenya, Kuwait, Luxembourg, Malta, Mauritius, Mexico (licence production), Morocco, Netherlands, New Zealand, Niger, Nigeria, Norway, Pakistan (under licence), Peru, Qatar, Saudi Arabia, Singapore, Slovenia, Spain, Sri Lanka, Sudan, Swiss police, Taiwan, Thailand, Turkey (under licence), UAE, UK police and Special Forces, USA Special Forces, Uruguay and Venezuela

CONTRACTOR:
Heckler & Koch GmbH, Oberndorf/Neckar, Germany

FEATURES:
CARTRIDGE: 9 x 19 mm Parabellum
OPERATION: delayed blowback; selective fire
LOCKING: rollers
FEED: 15- or 30-rd curved box magazine
WEIGHT: without magazine, 2.54 kg
LENGTH: overall, 680 mm; barrel, 225 mm
HEIGHT: with magazine, 210 mm
WIDTH: 50 mm
RIFLING: six grooves; rh
SIGHTS: fore, fixed post; rear, apertures for different eye relief, adjustable for windage and elevation; a telescopic or night sight or an aiming projector may be fitted
SIGHT RADIUS: 340 mm
MUZZLE VELOCITY: 400 m/s
Muzzle energy: 650 J
RATE OF FIRE: cyclic, 800 rds/min

Heckler & Koch 9 mm MP5SD Sub-machine Gun GERMANY

Heckler & Koch 9 mm MP5SD sub-machine gun

The Heckler & Koch 9 mm MP5SD is a silenced version of the MP5 sub-machine gun. Its mechanism is the same as that of the MP5, but the weapon differs in having a barrel in which thirty holes are drilled. The silencer on the barrel features two separate chambers, one of which is connected to the holes in the barrel and serves as an expansion chamber for the propulsive gases, thus reducing the gas pressure to slow down the acceleration of the projectile. The second chamber diverts the gases as they exit the muzzle, so muffling the exit report. The bullet leaves the muzzle at subsonic velocity, so it does not generate a sonic shockwave in flight. The silencer requires no maintenance; only rinsing in an oil-free cleaning agent is prescribed. There are six versions of the weapon.

SPECIFICATION:

USED BY:
German Special Forces and numerous military and police forces worldwide. The MP5SD3 is used by UK Special Forces as the L91A1

CONTRACTOR:
Heckler & Koch GmbH, Oberndorf/Neckar, Germany

FEATURES:
CARTRIDGE: 9 x 19 mm Parabellum
OPERATION: delayed blowback; selective fire
DELAY: rollers
FEED: 15- or 30-round curved box magazine
WEIGHT: MP5SD1, 2.8 kg; MP5SD2, 3.1 kg; MP5SD3, 3.46 kg
LENGTH: MP5SD1, 550 mm; MP5SD2, 780 mm; MP5SD3, 652 mm or 804 mm
BARREL: 146 mm
RIFLING: six grooves; rh
SIGHTS: fore, fixed post; rear, apertures for different eye relief, adjustable for windage and elevation; a telescopic or night sight or an aiming projector may be fitted
SIGHT RADIUS: 340 mm
MUZZLE VELOCITY: 285 m/s
Muzzle energy: 380 J
RATE OF FIRE: cyclic, 800 rds/min

Heckler & Koch 9 mm MP5K-series Sub-machine Guns

GERMANY

Heckler & Koch 9 mm MP5KA sub-machine gun

Heckler & Koch introduced its 9 mm MP5K series sub-machine guns for use by special police and anti-terrorist squads. They are extra-short versions of the standard MP5 and are meant for carriage inside clothing, in the glove pocket of a car, or in any other limited space. They offer all the fire options of the MP5.

SPECIFICATION:

USED BY:
German Special Forces and numerous military and police forces worldwide. In UK service, the MP54K is known as the L80A1, and the MP5KA1 is known as the L90A1

CONTRACTOR:
Heckler & Koch GmbH, Oberndorf/Neckar, Germany

FEATURES:
CALIBRE: 9 x 19 mm Parabellum
OPERATION: delayed blowback; selective fire
DELAY: rollers
FEED: 15- or 30-rd detachable box magazine
WEIGHT: without magazine, 2.03 kg
LENGTH: overall, 325 mm; barrel, 115 mm
RIFLING: six grooves; rh
SIGHTS: fore, post; rear, open rotary adjustable for windage and elevation, or x4 telescopic
SIGHT RADIUS: 260 mm
MUZZLE VELOCITY: 375 m/s
Muzzle energy: 570 J
RATE OF FIRE: cyclic, 900 rds/min

OFB INSAS 5.56 mm Light Machine Gun INDIA

OFB INSAS 5.56 mm light machine gun with folding butt

A model with a folding butt is available for use by airborne or other special troops. It is possible to install a shorter barrel (500 mm as opposed to 535 mm) on this model, making the weapon even more compact.

SPECIFICATION:

USED BY:
Indian airborne and Special
Forces

CONTRACTOR:
Ordnance Factory Board,
Government of India, Ministry of
Defence, Kolkata, India

FEATURES:
CARTRIDGE: 5.56 x 45 mm
ss109-based Special
OPERATION: gas; selective fire
LOCKING: rotating bolt
FEED: 30-round plastic box
magazine
WEIGHT: fixed butt, empty,
6.23 kg; loaded, 6.73 kg; folding
butt, empty, 5.87 kg; loaded,
6.37 kg
LENGTH: fixed butt, 1.05 m; butt
folded, 890 mm; butt extended,
1.025 m
BARREL: standard, 535 mm; short,
500 mm
RIFLING: four grooves; rh; one
turn in 200 mm
SIGHTS: fore, blade; rear, flip
aperture, 200-1000 m; optical
sights optional
SIGHT RADIUS: 475 mm
MUZZLE VELOCITY: standard
barrel, 925 m/s; short barrel,
915 m/s
MUZZLE ENERGY: standard barrel,
1780 J; short barrel, 1,740 J
RECOIL ENERGY: standard barrel,
2.75 J; short barrel, 2.85 J
RATE OF FIRE: cyclic, 650 rds/min
RANGE: effective, standard barrel,
700 m; short barrel, 600 m

IMI 5.56 mm Negev Light Machine Gun ISRAEL

IMI 5.56 mm Negev light machine gun with belt feed unit

The IMI 5.56 mm Negev light machine gun is a multipurpose weapon that can be fed from standard belts, drums or magazines and fired from the hip, bipod, tripod, ground/vehicle and helicopter mounts. It is designed to fire standard 5.56 x 45 mm NATO M885/SS109 ammunition. With a replacement barrel it will fire standard M193 rounds. An airborne mount for helicopters is available. This mount includes a link and spent cartridge case sack. Ammunition feed can be a 380-round magazine box or a special 750-round magazine box. The Negev Commando variant is a shorter and lighter version of the standard Negev light machine gun, known as the Assault Negev or Negev Commando. On this model the barrel is shortened to 330 mm, there is no tripod and the butt folds to the side, so that the overall length with the butt folded is only 680 mm. For the assault role a side-mounted forward grip is provided for the user's left hand. Weight of the Assault Negev with a 150-round drum is 6.95 kg. Muzzle velocity is 915 m/s. Vehicle, AFV and helicopter and naval mountings are available.

SPECIFICATION:

USED BY:
Israeli armed and Special Forces

CONTRACTOR:
Israel Military Industries Limited (IMI), Ramat Hasharon, Israel

FEATURES:
CARTRIDGE: 5.56 x 45 mm SS109 or M193
OPERATION: gas; open bolt; selective fire
LOCKING: rotating bolt
FEED: 35- or 30-round box magazine, 150- or 200-round belts in assault drums
WEIGHT: empty with bipod, 7.6 kg; Negev Commando, empty, 6.95 kg; 150-round assault drum, 2.7 kg; 200-round assault drum, 3.4 kg
LENGTH: (long barrel) stock folded, 780 mm; stock extended, 1.02 m; (short barrel) stock folded, 680 mm; stock extended, 890 mm
BARREL: long, 460 mm; short, 330 mm
RIFLING: six grooves; rh; one turn in 178 mm; optional, one turn in 305 mm
SIGHTS: fore, post, adjustable for elevation and windage for zeroing; rear, aperture, 300-1000 m; folding night sight with tritium illumination
SIGHT RADIUS: 440 mm
MUZZLE VELOCITY: 915 m/s
RATE OF FIRE: cyclic, 700-850 or >1000 rds/min

IMI 9 mm Mini-Uzi Sub-machine Gun ISRAEL

IMI 9 mm Mini-Uzi sub-machine gun with stock folded and with two 32-round magazines clipped together

In 1987 Israel Military Industries (IMI) introduced a new smaller version, designated the Mini-Uzi, of the 9 mm Uzi sub-machine gun. In operation it exactly resembles its larger 'parent', differing only in size, weight and firing characteristics. It can be fired either from an open-bolt position or from a closed bolt, using a floating firing pin. The Mini-Uzi will accept a 20-round magazine for its 9 x 19 mm Parabellum pistol ammunition, as well as 25- and 32-round magazines. Since it can be easily concealed under ordinary clothing and can be carried in the minimum of space in vehicles, the Mini-Uzi is particularly intended for security and law-enforcement personnel and for use in commando operations. It can be fired in fully-automatic or semi-automatic mode from the hip or, with stock extended, from the shoulder, and it is said to maintain the high standards of reliability and accuracy set by the Uzi.

SPECIFICATION:

USED BY:
Colombia, Guatemala, Haiti, Israel, Panama, Uruguay and US Special Forces and others

CONTRACTOR:
Israel Military Industries (IMI), Ramat Hasharon, Israel

FEATURES:
CARTRIDGE: 9 x 19 mm Parabellum
OPERATION: blowback; selective fire
FEED: 20-, 25- and 32-rd box magazines
WEIGHT: empty, 2.65 kg; loaded with 25-rd mag, 3.15 kg
LENGTH: butt retracted, 360 mm; butt extended, 600 mm; barrel, 197 mm
RIFLING: four grooves; rh; one turn in 254 mm
SIGHTS: fore, post rear, L-type flip aperture, 50 and 150 m
SIGHT RADIUS: 230 mm
MUZZLE VELOCITY: 375 m/s
RATE OF FIRE: cyclic, closed breech, 1700 rds/min; open breech, 950 rds/min

IMI 9mm Uzi Sub-machine Gun ISRAEL

IMI 9 mm Uzi sub-machine gun with folding stock

The IMI 9 mm Uzi sub-machine gun is a blowback-operated sub-machine gun using advanced primer ignition in which the round is fired while the bolt is still travelling forward. This produces a reduced impulse to the bolt and as a result this component can be designed to weigh less than half the amount that would be required for a static firing breech block.

SPECIFICATION:

USED BY:
Algeria, Angola, Belgium, Bolivia, Central African Republic, Chad, Chile, Colombia, Dominican Republic, Ecuador, Ethiopia, Gabon, Germany, Guatemala, Haiti, Honduras, Ireland, Israel, Kenya, Liberia, Luxembourg, Netherlands, Nicaragua, Niger, Nigeria, Panama, Paraguay, Peru, Philippines, Portugal, Rwanda, Somalia, South Africa, Sudan, Surinam, Swaziland, Taiwan, Thailand, Togo, Uganda, US Special Forces, Uruguay and Venezuela

CONTRACTOR:
Israel Military Industries Limited (IMI), Ramat Hasharon, Israel

FEATURES:
CARTRIDGE: 9 x 19 mm Parabellum
OPERATION: blowback; open bolt; selective fire
FEED: 20-, 25- and 32-round box magazines
WEIGHT: metal stock, 3.5 kg; wood stock, 3.8 kg
LENGTH: metal stock, retracted, 470 mm; metal stock, extended, or wood, 650 mm
BARREL: 260 mm
RIFLING: four grooves; rh; one turn in 254 mm
SIGHTS: fore, post; rear, L-type flip aperture, 100 and 200 m
SIGHT RADIUS: 310 mm
MUZZLE VELOCITY: ca 400 m/s
RATE OF FIRE: cyclic, 600 rds/min

7.62 mm PK Machine-gun Family RUSSIA

7.62 mm PKMSN machine-gun

The PK family of machine guns are gas operated, rotary-bolt locked (Kalashnikov system), open-bolt fired, fully-automatic, belt-fed machine guns firing the 7.62 x 54R cartridge. The ammunition is fed by non-disintegrating metallic belts; current belts are composed of joined 25-round sections, but earlier feed belts were made of one 250-round length. The belts are held either in 250-round ammunition boxes, in special large-capacity boxes on tanks (for the PKT) or in a 100-round assault magazine attached to the bottom of the gun's receiver.

SPECIFICATION:

USED BY:
Russian and allied forces

CONTRACTOR:
Kovrov Mechanical Plant JSC (the PKM), Vladimir region, Russia

FEATURES:
CARTRIDGE: 7.62 x 54R
OPERATION: gas; automatic
LOCKING: rotating bolt
FEED: belt; 100, 200 and 250 rds
WEIGHT: empty, 9 kg; tripod, 7.5 kg; 100-round belt, 2.44 kg
LENGTH: overall, 1.173 m; on tripod, 1.267 m; barrel, 658 mm
RIFLING: length, 550 mm
SIGHTS: fore, cylindrical post; rear, vertical leaf and windage scale adjustable to 1500 m
SIGHT RADIUS: 663 mm
MUZZLE VELOCITY: 825 m/s
RATE OF FIRE: cyclic, 650-720 rds/min: effective, 250 rds/min
EFFECTIVE RANGE: 1000 m

KEDR 9 mm Machine Pistol RUSSIA

KEDR 9 mm machine pistol with stock extended

Safeties include a lock which engages both the trigger and the bolt. A stamped steel butt can be folded up-and-over the receiver with, when folded, the rudimentary butt-plate located close to the muzzle. Ammunition feed is from 20- or 30-round box magazines inserted through a magazine housing in front of the trigger assembly.

SPECIFICATION:

USED BY:
Russian and other RFAS internal security forces

CONTRACTOR:
Rosoboronexport Federal State Unitary Enterprise, Moscow, Russia

FEATURES:
CARTRIDGE: 9 x 18 mm Makarov 57-N-181S; 9 x 18 mm 57-N-181SM; OPERATION: blowback; selective fire
FEED: 20- or 30-rd box magazine
WEIGHT: empty, 30-rd magazine, 1.57 kg; loaded, 1.82 kg
LENGTH: stock folded, 305 mm; stock extended, 530 mm; KEDR-B, 671 mm
BARREL: 120 mm
SIGHTS: fore, blade; rear, notch; sighted for 25 m; laser target designator optional
MUZZLE VELOCITY: V 10 310 m/s
MUZZLE ENERGY: 285 J
RATE OF FIRE: cyclic, 1000 rds/min
EFFECTIVE RANGE: 50 m

9 mm BXP Sub-machine Gun SOUTH AFRICA

This is a conventional blowback weapon, constructed from rectangular steel tubing, steel pressings and precision castings. It is simple to operate and fires from an open bolt. It is extremely compact and can be fired single-handed with the butt folded like a pistol. The bolt is of the 'telescoping' type which envelops the rear end of the barrel, thus allowing the overall length to be short while accommodating the maximum length of barrel. It also helps to keep the centre of gravity over the pistol-grip and thus reduce oscillations caused by the movement of the bolt during automatic fire.

SPECIFICATION:

USED BY:
South African police and security forces

CONTRACTOR:
Tressitu (Pty) Ltd, Verwoerdbury, South Africa

FEATURES:
CARTRIDGE: 9 x 19 mm parabellum
OPERATION: blowback; selective fire
WEIGHT: empty, 2.5 kg
LENGTH: stock extended, 607 mm; stock folded, 387 mm
BARREL: 208 mm
RIFLING: six grooves; rh; one turn in 245 mm
FEED: 22- or 32-rd detachable magazine
SIGHTS: fore, adjustable cone; rear, aperture and v-notch or OEG (collimating) sight
MUZZLE VELOCITY: ca 370 m/s
RATE OF FIRE: 1000-1200 rds/min

Manroy 0.50 M2 HB QCB Heavy Machine Gun   UK

Manroy 0.50 M2 HB QCB heavy machine gun complete with QCB kit, Manroy Softmount and optional flash hider

The Manroy 0.50 M2 HB heavy machine gun is the standard Browning 0.50 M2 HB heavy machine gun, manufactured in the UK by Manroy Engineering. It matches the standard US specification in every respect. In addition to manufacturing the standard 0.50 M2 HB heavy machine gun, Manroy Engineering also produces a Quick-Change Barrel (QCB) version. As with other QCB systems, the barrel can be changed by one person in under 10 seconds and there is no need to adjust headspace at any time. The change is made by rotating the cocking handle rearward and holding it, rotating the barrel, withdrawing it, inserting the new barrel, rotating it to stop and releasing the cocking handle. Examples in service with UK armed forces are known as the L111A1.

SPECIFICATION:

USED BY:
UK, NATO and other forces worldwide, including many Special Forces

CONTRACTOR:
Manroy Engineering Ltd, Beckley, East Sussex, UK

FEATURES:
CARTRIDGE: 12.7 x 99 mm (0.50 Browning)
OPERATION: short recoil; automatic
LOCKING: projecting lug
FEED: disintegrating link belt
WEIGHT: 38.5 kg
LENGTH: 1.651 m
BARREL: 1.143 m
RIFLING: eight grooves; rh; one turn in 381 mm
MUZZLE VELOCITY: 893 m/s
RATE OF FIRE: cyclic, 450–500 rds/min
RANGE: M2 ball, 6766 m; effective, 1850 m

7.62 mm L7A2 General-purpose Machine Gun UK

7.62 mm L7A2 general-purpose machine guns on a vehicle dual mounting

The L7 General-Purpose Machine Gun (GPMG) is based on the FN MAG and was used by UK armed forces for many years both as a Light Machine Gun (LMG) and as a Sustained-Fire Machine Gun (SFMG). For a while, the UK armed forces retained the L7A2 only for the SFMG role, although it is now becoming increasingly employed in the LMG role again, especially for commando and airborne forces. In the LMG role it is fired from the integral bipod mount, while in the SFMG role it is fired from a tripod.

SPECIFICATION:

USED BY:
British (Commando, airborne and Special Forces) and most Commonwealth forces (including many Special Forces) and many other armed forces worldwide

CONTRACTOR:
Royal Small Arms Factory, Enfield Lock (now closed); now manufactured and marketed by Manroy Engineering Ltd, Beckley, East Sussex, UK

FEATURES:
CARTRIDGE: 7.62 x 51 mm NATO
OPERATION: gas; automatic
LOCKING: dropping locking lever
FEED: belt
WEIGHT: LMG role, 10.9 kg
LENGTH: LMG role, 1.232 m; sustained fire role, 1.048 m
BARREL: including 50 mm overhang of carrying handle, with flash hider, 679 mm; without flash hider, 597 mm
SIGHTS: fore, blade; rear, aperture
SIGHT RADIUS: LMG role, sight down, 851 mm; sustained fire role, sight up, 787 mm
MUZZLE VELOCITY: 838 m/s
RATE OF FIRE: cyclic, 750-1000 rds/min

Sterling 9 mm L2A3 Sub-machine Gun UK

The 9 mm L2A3 sub-machine gun consists of a tubular, perforated receiver, a cylindrical bolt and the stock. The magazine fits horizontally into the left-hand side of the receiver and holds 34 9 x 19 mm Parabellum cartridges. The Sterling-Patchett 9 mm L34A1 sub-machine gun is a variant known to be in service in Argentina and Australia.

SPECIFICATION:

USED BY:
The L2A3 is no longer in service with the British armed and Special Forces. The Mark 4 Sterling was sold abroad on a considerable scale, some 90 countries having purchased the gun in varying quantities. The principal purchasers were Canada (licence production), Ghana, India (which still manufactures under licence), Libya, Malaysia, Nigeria and Tunisia. Many are also in service with the Gulf states

CONTRACTOR:
The L2A3 was made by the Sterling Armament Company at Dagenham, Essex, UK. In addition, the L2A3 was manufactured at the Royal Ordnance Factory at Fazackerley. The Mark 4 Sterling and the Patchett/Sterling Mark 5 were manufactured at Dagenham. All rights in Sterling products and designs were purchased by Royal Ordnance plc in 1988

FEATURES:
CARTRIDGE: 9 x 19 mm Parabellum
OPERATION: blowback; selective fire
FEED: 34-round curved box magazine; 10- and 15-round magazine and twin stacked 10 x 2, 15 x 2 and 34 x 2 magazines were also available
WEIGHT: empty, 2.72 kg
LENGTH: butt retracted, 483 mm; butt extended, 690 mm
BARREL: 198 mm
RIFLING: six grooves; rh; one turn in 250 mm
SIGHTS: fore, blade; rear, flip aperture
SIGHT RADIUS: 410 mm
MUZZLE VELOCITY: 390 m/s
RATE OF FIRE: cyclic, 550 rds/min

Browning 0.30 Calibre M1919A4 Machine Gun USA

Browning 0.30 calibre M1919A4 machine gun on tripod M2

The M1919A4 was used as a fixed gun in tanks in the Second World War and on many post-war armoured fighting vehicles. It was also extensively used by infantry as a company-level weapon, mounted on the M2 tripod. Its evolution can be traced back to the 0.30 M1919 Browning tank machine.

SPECIFICATION:

USED BY:
Used by many countries as a vehicle gun. In service with Canada, Denmark, Dominican Republic, Greece, Guatemala, Haiti, Iran, Israel, Italy, South Korea, Liberia, Mexico, South Africa, Spain, Taiwan and Vietnam and in reserve in the US

CONTRACTOR:
No longer in production in the US

FEATURES:
CARTRIDGE: 0.30-06 M1 or M2 (also used in 7.62 x 51 mm NATO form in Canada and South Africa)
OPERATION: short recoil; automatic
LOCKING: projecting lug
FEED: 250-round belt
WEIGHT: 14.06 kg
LENGTH: 1.044 m
BARREL: 610 mm
RIFLING: four grooves; rh; one twist in 254 mm
SIGHTS: fore, blade; rear, leaf aperture; windage scale
SIGHT RADIUS: 354 mm
MUZZLE VELOCITY: 860 m/s
RATE OF FIRE: cyclic, 400-500 rds/min
RANGE: effective, 1000 m

Browning M2 HB 0.50 Calibre Heavy Machine Gun USA

Browning M2 HB 0.50 calibre heavy machine gun on Mount, Machine Gun, Mk 93 Mod 0 developed in response to a US Navy requirement

The air-cooled 0.50 Browning was originally developed for aircraft use and was adopted in 1923 as the Model 1921. In 1933, after developmental changes, it was redesignated the M2, appearing in both water-cooled and air-cooled versions. Combat experience demonstrated that the air-cooled version was eminently suitable for many land-based applications following an increase in the mass of the barrel. It was then renamed the M2 HB and in this form has been used and is still used extensively in the ground role and on vehicles. It is one of the most widespread and successful heavy machine guns in service and will continue as such for many years.

SPECIFICATION:

USED BY:
US armed forces and those from least 30 other countries

CONTRACTOR:
General Dynamics Armament Systems, Vermont, US

FEATURES:
FEED: disintegrating link belt
WEIGHT: 38 kg
LENGTH: 1.651 m
BARREL: 1.143 m
RIFLING: eight grooves; rh; one turn in 381 mm
SIGHTS: fore, blade; rear, leaf aperture
MUZZLE VELOCITY: 930 m/s
RATE OF FIRE: cyclic, 450-600 rds/min
RANGE: 6800 m; effective, 1500 m

US Ordnance 7.62 mm M60 General-purpose Machine Gun System USA

US Ordnance 7.62 mm M60 general-purpose machine gun mounted on light vehicle

The US Ordnance M60 is the US Army's general-purpose machine gun and entered service in the late 1950s. The original design had some interesting features. The straight-line layout allows the operating rod and buffer to run right back into the butt and reduce some of the overall length. The large forehand grip is most convenient for carrying at the hip, and the folded bipod legs continue the hand protection almost up to the muzzle. The gun can be stripped using a live round as a tool. Mountings exist for operating from helicopters, boats and vehicles weapon.

SPECIFICATION:

USED BY:
Australia, South Korea, Taiwan and US forces and Special Forces from many other countries

CONTRACTOR:
US Ordnance Inc, Nevada, USA

FEATURES:
CARTRIDGE: 7.62 x 51 mm NATO
OPERATION: gas; automatic
LOCKING: rotating bolt
FEED: disintegrating link belt
WEIGHT: 11.1 kg
LENGTH: overall, 1.105 m
BARREL: excluding flash hider, 560 mm
RIFLING: four grooves; rh; one twist in 305 mm
SIGHTS: fore, fixed blade; rear, u-notch
SIGHT RADIUS: 540 mm
MUZZLE VELOCITY: 853 m/s
RATE OF FIRE: cyclic, 500-650 rds/min; practical, 200 rds/min
RANGE: 3750 m; (effective) bipod, 1100 m; tripod 1800 m

us Ordnance 7.62 mm m60e3 Light Machine Gun   USA

us Navy SEAL with M60E3 machine gun

The us Ordnance M60E3 light machine gun was developed to provide a lighter, more versatile 7.62 mm machine gun maintaining all the capabilities of the earlier M60, with several additional features of its own. The standard barrel is a lightweight assault barrel. Two optional barrels are available: lightweight/short length for assault and increased manoeuvrability; and heavy barrel for missions demanding sustained fire. A lightweight bipod is mounted on the receiver eliminating the bipod on the spare barrel. An M60E3 conversion kit can be used to convert any serviceable, unwelded, M60 receiver to the lightweight M60E3 version. The kit was procured by the us Marine Corps before their acquisition of complete M60E3 machine guns.

SPECIFICATION:

USED BY:
us Navy (SEALs) and numerous foreign armed and Special Forces

CONTRACTOR:
us Ordnance Inc, Nevada, USA
(no longer in production)

FEATURES:
CARTRIDGE: 7.62 x 51 mm NATO
OPERATION: gas; automatic
LOCKING: rotating bolt
FEED: link belt
WEIGHT: 8.8 kg
LENGTH: 1.077 m
BARREL: 560 mm
MUZZLE VELOCITY: 853 m/s
RATE OF FIRE: cyclic,
500-650 rds/min
RANGE: 3725 m; effective, 1100 m

FNH USA 5.56 mm M249 Squad Automatic Weapon USA

FNH USA 5.56 mm M249 Squad Automatic Weapon (SAW) with short barrel

This weapon is employed as the squad light machine gun in US Army and Marine Corps service. The US Army Rangers use the short (381 mm) barrel; this model is also used with the M5 collapsible butt-stock. Belt feed for the M249 involves 200-round belts using the M27 link, loaded into a plastic container. The M249 Special-Purpose Weapon (SPW) was developed jointly by FN Herstal and FNH USA for US special-operations forces and is a lightened and modified version of the standard M249.

SPECIFICATION:

USED BY:
US Marine Corps, army and various units in Special Operations Command

CONTRACTOR:
FNH USA Inc, South Carolina, USA

FEATURES:
CARTRIDGE: 5.56 x 45 mm
OPERATION: gas; firing fully-automatic
LOCKING: rotating bolt head
FEED: 200-round M27 link belts or 30-round magazine
WEIGHT: 6.85 kg; barrel, 1.7 kg
LENGTH: 1.04 m
BARREL: overall, 523 or 381 mm
RIFLING: six grooves; rh; one turn in 178 mm
SIGHTS: fore, semi-fixed hooded post, adjustable for windage and elevation; rear, aperture, adjustable for windage and elevation
SIGHT RADIUS: 490 mm
MUZZLE VELOCITY: 915 m/s
MUZZLE ENERGY: ca 175 kgm
RATE OF FIRE: cyclic, ca 750 rds/min
RANGE: ca 2000 m; effective, up to 1100 m

FNH USA 7.62 mm M240B & M240G Machine Guns USA

FNH USA 7.62 mm M240B machine gun

The M240 machine gun, designated M240D in its flexible vehicular and helicopter configuration, was originally procured from FN of Belgium (now FN Herstal SA) in 1976. It is a left-hand feed variant of the FN MAG Model 60-40, subsequently licence-produced as a coaxial machine gun for mounting in M60 tanks – the type was later installed in the M1 Abrams tank series. The original M240 was then followed by the M0240C, the main change being that ammunition is fed from the right to suit installations in the M2 and M3 Bradley.

SPECIFICATION:

USED BY:
M240G, US Marine Corps;
M240B, US army

CONTRACTOR:
FNH USA Inc, South Carolina, USA

FEATURES (M240B):
CARTRIDGE: 7.62 x 51 mm NATO
OPERATION: gas; automatic
LOCKING: dropping locking lever
FEED: M13 disintegrating link belt
WEIGHT: 12.25 kg
LENGTH: 1.232 m
BARREL: 627 mm
SIGHTS: fore, blade; rear, aperture
and u-notch; thermal and
optical sight optional
MUZZLE VELOCITY: 853 m/s
RATE OF FIRE: cyclic, 750 rds/min
MAX EFFECTIVE RANGE:
iron sights, 1800 m
RANGE: 3725 m

7.62 mm M134 Minigun Machine Gun USA

The 7.62 mm M134 Minigun machine gun is based on the Gatling gun principle in which a high rate of fire is achieved by having a number of rotating barrels which fire in turn when the 1 o'clock position is reached. The Minigun is driven by a 28 V DC or 115 V AC electric motor and produces a steady rate of fire. This varies according to type, from between 2000 and 6000 rds/min as a top rate, down to 300 rds/min as the slowest rate of fire. At a steady 6000 rds/min the drive motor draws 130 A. The gun itself consists of four groups: the barrel group; gun housin; rotor assembly; and bolt assembly. Six 7.62 mm barrels fit into the rotor assembly with each locked by a 180° turn.

SPECIFICATION:

USED BY:
Australia, UK, US and other armed forces worldwide

CONTRACTOR:
Lockheed Martin Armament Systems (now General Dynamics Armament Systems), Vermont, USA (production complete). Also Aircraft Equipment International Ltd, Ascot, Berkshire, UK

FEATURES:
CARTRIDGE: 7.62 x 51 mm NATO
OPERATION: Gatling action; automatic; six revolving barrels
LOCKING: rotating bolt
FEED: linked belt or linkless
WEIGHT: 16.3 kg; drive motor, 3.4 kg; recoil adaptors (two), 1.36 kg; barrels (six), 1.09 kg; feeder, 4.8 kg
LENGTH: overall, 801.6 mm
BARREL: 559 mm
SIGHTS: vary with employment
POWER REQUIRED: at 6000 rds/min, steady rate, 130 A
STARTING LOAD: 260 A for 100 m/s
GUN LIFE: 1.5 million rounds
MUZZLE VELOCITY: 869 m/s
RATE OF FIRE: up to 6000 rds/min
DISPERSION: 6 mrad max
AVERAGE RECOIL FORCE: 0.5 kN

Colt 9 mm Sub-machine Guns USA

The Colt 9 mm sub-machine gun is a light and compact gas-operated weapon which embodies the same straight-line construction and design as the Colt 5.56 mm M16A2 rifle. This straight-line construction, coupled with the lower recoil impulse of the 9 x 19 mm Parabellum cartridge, provides highly accurate fire with reduced muzzle climb.

SPECIFICATION:

USED BY:
US Marine Corps, US Drug Enforcement Agency and other countries

CONTRACTOR:
Colt's Manufacturing Company Inc, Connecticut, USA

FEATURES:
CARTRIDGE: 9 x 19 mm Parabellum
OPERATION: gas; selective fire
LOCKING: rotating bolt
FEED: 32-rd box magazine
WEIGHT: without magazine, 2.61 kg
LENGTH: stock retracted, 650 mm; stock extended, 730 mm; barrel, 267 mm
SIGHTS: fore, post adjustable for elevation; rear, flip aperture (50 m and 50-100 m), adjustable for windage and elevation
MUZZLE VELOCITY: approx 396 m/s
MUZZLE ENERGY: 584 J
RATE OF FIRE: cyclic, 800-1000 rds/min
EFFECTIVE RANGE: 100 m

Weapons: Rifles, Shotguns and Light Support Weapons

Steyr 5.56 mm AUG Rifle AUSTRIA

Steyr 5.56 mm AUG rifle with accessories

The AUG is a bullpup design of unusual appearance. The intention behind the weapon is to have a light, handy gun with particular emphasis on use in and from vehicles and commonality of parts for the different modes of use. It can be altered for use by a left-handed person by changing the bolt and moving a blanking cap from the left ejection opening to the right.

SPECIFICATION:

USED BY:
Austrian Army as the Stg 77.
Adopted by the armed forces of Australia, Ireland, Malaysia, New Zealand, Oman, Saudi Arabia, Taiwan and other countries, including the UK for the Falkland Islands Defence Force

CONTRACTOR:
Steyr-Mannlicher AG & Co KG, Austria

FEATURES:
CARTRIDGE: 5.56 x 45 mm
OPERATION: gas; selective fire
LOCKING: rotating bolt
Magazine: 30- and 42-rd detachable translucent plastic box
RATE OF FIRE: cyclic, 650 rds/min
SIGHTS: optic sight set in carrying handle, x 1.5 power
ACCESSORIES: bayonet; blank-firing attachment; special receiver for sights; grenade launcher M203 (AUG-8); muzzle cap; carrying sling; cleaning kit; bipod, rifle grenades

FN FNC 5.56 mm Assault Rifle BELGIUM

FN FNC 5.56 mm assault rifle, stripped to its main components

The FN Herstal FNC is a 5.56 mm light assault rifle intended for use by infantry who operate without continuous logistical support or who are in jungle, mountain or other difficult country. The construction is from steel, aluminium alloy and, for non-working parts, plastics, great use being made of stampings and pressings.

There are two versions of the rifle. The first, known as the standard, has a standard-length barrel, together with a folding tubular light-alloy butt-stock encased in a plastic coating and braced by a plastic strut. The second model, the para, is similar but has a shorter barrel.

SPECIFICATION:

USED BY:
Belgium, Indonesia, Latvia, Nigeria, Sweden and others

CONTRACTOR:
FN Herstal SA, Herstal, Belgium

FEATURES:
CARTRIDGE: 5.56 x 45 mm (M193 or SS109)
OPERATION: gas; selective fire with 3-rd burst controller
LOCKING: rotating bolt
FEED: 30-rd box magazine
WEIGHT: (empty magazine) standard 4.01 kg, paratroop 3.81 kg, fixed-butt 4.06 kg; (loaded, 30-rd magazine) standard 4.445 kg, paratroop 4.16 kg, fixed-butt 4.41 kg
LENGTH: (standard) butt extended 1 m, butt folded 756 mm; (paratroop) butt extended 911 mm, butt folded 680 mm, fixed butt 1.012 mm
BARREL: standard, 449 mm; short, 363 mm
RIFLING: six grooves; rh; one turn in 305 mm or 178 mm
SIGHTS: fore, cylindrical post; rear, flip aperture 250 and 400 m
SIGHT RADIUS: 513 mm
RATE OF FIRE: cyclic, 650-750 rds/min
MUZZLE VELOCITY: M193, 965 m/s; SS109, 915 m/s
EFFECTIVE RANGE: 450 m; with optical sight, 600 m

IMBEL Model L and LC 5.56 mm Rifles BRAZIL

IMBEL Model LC 5.56 mm rifle with stock folded

The Model L continues to employ a gas-operated multilug rotating bolt and carries over the STANAG 4179 magazine interface of the MD2 and MD3. A folding stock is standard on both the Model L and Model LC. The Model L can accommodate a 40 mm grenade launcher of the M203 pattern. IMBEL is concentrating its 5.56 mm development on the Model LC (*Leve Curto* – Light Short), also known as the Intermediate model. The photographs illustrate the latest form of this rifle complete with folding stock and foregrip plus an enlarged trigger guard. A sight rail can also act as a carrying handle. The translucent magazines have an M16 interface and can hold 30 rounds.

SPECIFICATION:

USED BY:
Developed to meet the specific requirements of the Brazilian Army and are intended for use in jungle and mountain terrain as well as for issue to police forces

CONTRACTOR:
Industria de Material Belico do Brasil – IMBEL, Piquete-SP, Brazil

FEATURES:
CARTRIDGE: 5.56 x 45 mm M193 or SS109
OPERATION: gas; selective fire
LOCKING: multilug rotating bolt
FEED: 20-rd box magazine or 30-rd US M16 magazine
WEIGHT: (empty) Model L, 3.7 kg; Model LC, 2.9 kg
LENGTH: (Model L) stock extended, 1.01 m, stock folded, 750 mm; (Model LC) stock extended, 811 mm, stock folded, 550 mm
BARREL: Model L, 453 mm; Model LC, 254 mm
MUZZLE VELOCITY: Model L, 960 m/s (M193) or 915 m/s (SS109); Model LC, 806 m/s (M193) or 767 m/s (SS109)
RATE OF FIRE: cyclic, Model LC, 700-750 rds/min
EFFECTIVE RANGE: Model L, 600 m; Model LC, 400 m

Norinco 5.8 mm QBZ Type 95 Assault Rifle CHINA

Carbine variant of Chinese 5.8 mm QBZ rifle

The receiver of the 5.8 mm QBZ bullpup rifle is shrouded in a moulded polymer butt-stock, with the fore-end and pistol grip made from the same dark-coloured material. The cocking lever is protected under a carrying handle which also contains the rearsight; the foresight is on a post protected by a small cylinder. A three-position fire-selector and safety switch is on the right-hand side of the body just above the pistol grip, although this switch is not present on some examples.

The front trigger guard is much larger than usual, as it provides the rear location point for an optional underslung spin-stabilised grenade launcher; it also provides a convenient location for the non-firing hand. The grenade launcher appears to have a calibre of 40 mm and is of the M203 pattern. A flash-eliminator attachment on the muzzle can be used to launch rifle grenades. The top of the carrying handle can also be used to mount optical or night sights.

SPECIFICATION:

USED BY:
Elite formations of the People's Liberation Army

CONTRACTOR:
China North Industries Corporation (Norinco), Beijing, China

FEATURES:
CARTRIDGE: 5.8 x 42 mm
OPERATION: gas; rotating bolt
LOCKING: rotating bolt
FEED: detachable box magazine
WEIGHT: 3.3 kg
LENGTH: 743 mm
BARREL: 490 mm
SIGHTS: fore, post; rear, adjustable aperture
MUZZLE VELOCITY: 930 m/s
RATE OF FIRE: 650 rds/min

FAMAS G2 5.56 mm Assault Rifle FRANCE

A French Marine uses a FAMAS G2 5.56 mm assault rifle to launch a rifle grenade

Mechanically, the FAMAS G2 is the same as the in-service FAMAS F1 and is chambered for the standard 5.56 x 45 mm cartridge. However, the standard rifling is one turn in 228 mm, allowing it to be used with M193 or SS109 types of ammunition. Optionally, the barrel can be rifled one turn in 178 mm or one turn in 305 mm to suit specific requirements. The outline has changed by the adoption of a full-hand trigger guard, allowing the rifle to be fired when wearing NBC or arctic mittens or heavy gloves. The breech-block buffer has been reinforced so as to withstand better the firing of rifle grenades, and the magazine housing now conforms to NATO Stanag 4179 and accepts all M16-type magazines, straight or curved, metal or plastic. The selector lever/safety catch is now placed inside the trigger guard, and the front end of the hand-guard has been given a downwards lip to prevent the hand from sliding forwards onto a hot barrel. Other FAMAS G2 features include the provision of a NATO sight base to allow the fitting of optical day or night sights. A bipod can be fitted, and there is provision for mounting a bayonet.

SPECIFICATION:

USED BY:
French Army and Navy (including the Commandos Marine) and several other armies

CONTRACTOR:
Giat Industries, Versailles Satory, France

FEATURES:
CARTRIDGE: 5.56 x 45 mm
OPERATION: delayed blowback; selective fire; 3-rd burst facility
LOCKING: differential leverage
FEED: 30-rd M16 type magazines
WEIGHT: with empty magazine, 3.8 kg; with loaded 30-rd magazine, 4.17 kg
LENGTH: 757 mm
BARREL: 488 mm
RIFLING: (standard) three grooves; rh; one turn in 228 mm
SIGHTS: fore, blade; rear, aperture to 450 m; provision for optical sights
MUZZLE VELOCITY: 925 m/s
RATE OF FIRE: cyclic, 1100 rds/min
EFFECTIVE RANGE: iron sights, 450 m; optical sight, 600 m

Heckler & Koch 5.56 mm HK53 Short Assault Rifle GERMANY

Heckler & Koch 5.56 mm HK53 short assault rifle with flash hider and three-round burst limiter

The Heckler & Koch HK53 sub-machine gun is chambered for the 5.56 x 45 mm. The method of operation is similar to the other rifles and sub-machine guns made by Heckler & Koch, using a system of rollers which delays the rearward movement of the bolt head until the pressure has dropped sufficiently, allowing the complete bolt unit to be blown back in safety. The HK53 is capable of either single shots or full automatic function, with a selector lever on the left of the receiver above the pistol grip. Optionally, it may be provided with a different grip with burst-fire control and an ambidextrous selector/safety lever. Feed is from 25-round or 30-round magazines which can be coupled together by a clip. The flash suppressor totally eliminates muzzle flash.

Heckler & Koch 5.56 mm G36 Assault Rifles GERMANY

Heckler & Koch 5.56 mm G36E assault rifle

The gas-operated Heckler & Koch 5.56 mm G36 assault rifle is conventional in layout, having a skeleton butt-stock which folds to the right of the receiver to reduce carry and storage length or for firing in confined spaces. Much of the G36 receiver and other components are constructed using high-strength polymer-based plastics. An integral carrying handle over the receiver contains a x3 optical sight with a x1 red-dot combat sight unit mounted on the upper rail of the carrying handle. There are auxiliary iron sights over the handle for use if the optical sight is damaged. The G36 has a x3 optical sight, while the G36E has a x1.5 unit and lacks the red-dot sight.

In addition to the standard G36 in service with the Bundeswehr, a short version, the G36K, is issued to German Special Forces units.

SPECIFICATION:

USED BY:
German army and Special Forces and Spanish armed forces

CONTRACTOR:
Heckler & Koch GmbH, Oberndorf-Neckar, Germany

FEATURES:
CARTRIDGE: 5.56 x 45 mm NATO
OPERATION: gas; selective fire
LOCKING: rotating bolt; six lugs
FEED: 30-rd box magazine
WEIGHT: without magazine, 3.63 kg
LENGTH: butt extended, 998 mm; butt folded, 758 mm
BARREL: 480 mm
RIFLING: six grooves; rh; one turn in 178 mm
SIGHTS: optical, x3; auxiliary iron sights
MUZZLE VELOCITY: approx 920 m/s
MUZZLE ENERGY: approx 1,730 J
RATE OF FIRE: cyclic, 750 rds/min

9 mm AS Special Assault Rifle RUSSIA

9 mm AS special assault rifle with stock extended

This assault rifle is designed for noiseless and flashless firing at ranges up to 400 m and the weapon has the ability to fire armour piercing rounds. The manufacturer claims that these rounds are capable of penetrating armoured vests and soft skinned vehicles. There is a special muzzle silencer that is used to reduce the sound of the weapon which has a folding butt and can be fitted with an optical or night sight.

SPECIFICATION:

USED BY:
Russian Special Forces and Internal Ministry personnel

CONTRACTOR:
TSNIITOCHMASH, Moscow, Russia

FEATURES:
CALIBRE: 9 x 39 mm (SP6)
MUZZLE VELOCITY: 295 m/s
SIGHTING RANGE: with iron and optical sights, 400 m; with night sight, 300 m
MAGAZINE CAPACITY: 20 rds
LENGTH: with night sight, 878 mm; with butt folded, 615 mm
BULLET WEIGHT: 16 g
CARTRIDGE WEIGHT: 23 g
WEIGHT: empty, without sights, 2.5 kg

7.62 mm AK-47 Assault Rifle RUSSIA

7.62 mm AK-47 rifle (1) and 7.62 mm AK-47 rifle (2)

1

2

The AK-47 assault rifle is a compact weapon, capable of selective fire, and is robust and reliable. The former Warsaw Pact countries have now largely replaced it with the AKM, a modernised and improved version, but it is still held in reserve or in second-line use by many former Eastern Bloc countries. The AK-47 may be encountered in two basic configurations: one with a rigid butt (AK-47) and one with a double-strut folding metal butt-stock (AK-47S or ASK) controlled by a simple press-button release above the pistol grip.

SPECIFICATION:

USED BY:
While no longer in general service with Russian forces it is still the most widespread infantry rifle and may well be in service with various special forces. It is certainly in service with numerous guerrilla movements

CONTRACTOR:
Various state factories

FEATURES:
CARTRIDGE: 7.62 x 39 mm M1943
OPERATION: gas; selective fire
LOCKING: rotating bolt
FEED: 30-rd detachable box magazine
WEIGHT: empty, 3.8 kg; loaded, 4.3 kg
LENGTH: overall, 880 mm
BARREL: 415 mm
RIFLING: four grooves; rh; one turn in 235 mm; length, 369 mm
SIGHTS: fore, post, adjustable; rear, u-notch tangent, adjustable to 800 m with battle sight for 200 m
SIGHT RADIUS: 378 mm
MUZZLE VELOCITY: 715 m/s
RATE OF FIRE: cyclic, 600 rds/min

9 mm vss Silent Sniper Rifle RUSSIA

9 mm vss silent sniper rifle equipped with PSO-1 optical sight undergoing tests in the USA

The development of the 9 mm vss (6P29) silent sniper rifle was carried out in parallel with that of the AS silent assault rifle (see separate entry), but whereas the AS is intended for use as a silenced rifle for special forces, the vss (also known as the Vintorez, or 'thread-cutter') was developed for use as a silenced sniper rifle by Spetsnaz undercover or clandestine units, a role made evident by its ability to be stripped down for carriage in a specially fitted briefcase.

The vss fires the armour-penetrating 9 x 39 mm sp-5 cartridge. Sniper fire is normally single shot only, using a 10-round magazine, but it is possible to fit the 20-round AS magazine for fully automatic fire.

SPECIFICATION:

USED BY:
Russian army, Special Forces and Internal Ministry personnel

CONTRACTOR:
TSNIITOCHMASH, Moscow region, Russia

FEATURES:
CARTRIDGE: 9 x 39 mm SP-5, SP-6, PAB-9
OPERATION: gas; selective fire
LOCKING: rotating bolt
FEED: 10- or 20-rd box magazine
WEIGHT: with empty magazine and without sights, 2.6 kg; with PSO-1-1 optical sight, 3.4 kg
LENGTH: 894 mm
BARREL: 200 mm
MUZZLE VELOCITY: 290 m/s
RATE OF FIRE: cyclic, 800-900 rds/min
EFFECTIVE RATE OF FIRE: semi-automatic, 30 rds/min; automatic, 60 rds/min
RANGE: day, >400 m; night, >300 m
OPTICAL SIGHT WEIGHT: 580 g
OPTICAL SIGHT LENGTH: 375 mm

TSNIITOCHMASH KS-23/KS-23M 'Special Carbine' RUSSIA

TSNIITOCHMASH KS-23M combat shotgun with grenade-launching muzzle attachment

The TSNIITOCHMASH KS-23 combat shotgun is termed by its manufacturer as a 'special carbine' but it is essentially a conventional slide-action shotgun on a very large scale. In Western terms, the KS-23 is approximately four gauge. The KS-23 fires a variety of ammunition, including tear gas, rubber bullets, conventional buckshot and an anti-vehicular round, which, it is claimed, can shatter a car engine block. There is also a muzzle adapter for firing grenades and other special munitions.

SPECIFICATION:

USED BY:
RFAS Interior Ministry and Special Forces

CONTRACTOR:
TSNIITOCHMASH, Klimovsk, Russia

FEATURES:
OPERATION: manual, slide action
LOCKING: rotating bolt
FEED: 3-rd tubular magazine
WEIGHT: KS-23, 3.85 kg;
KS-23M, 3.5 kg
LENGTH: KS-23, 1.04 m;
KS-23M, 650 mm
BARREL: KS-23, 500 mm;
KS-23M, 350 mm
SIGHTS: fore, blade; rear, notch

5.66 mm APS Underwater Assault Rifle   RUSSIA

5.55 mm APS underwater assault rifle

Although underwater weapons have been supplied to various maritime Special Forces for some years this is the first of class which has been formally acknowledged and for which detail has been released. Although intended for combat simmers it can be used effectively above the surface. This underwater assault rifle is a selective fire, gas-operated weapon, the mechanism of which appears to be based broadly upon the Kalashnikov rotating belt system. It is of fairly conventional appearance and has a folding butt. The most distinctive feature is the large magazine necessary because of the type of ammunition used. The projectile is a drag-stabilised dart, the rear end of which is held in a conventional cartridge case apparently based on that for the 5.56 x 45 mm NATO. The dart is 120 mm long and the complete round 150 mm long – the reason for the abnormal front-to-back depth of the magazine. Underwater and at the given ranges, the dart will penetrate the usual types of underwater suit and also 5 mm of acrylic plastic face mask to inflict fatal wounds.

SPECIFICATION:

USED BY:
Russian maritime Special Forces

CONTRACTOR:
Institute of Precise Engineering, Izhevsk, Russia

FEATURES:
CARTRIDGE: 5.66 mm Model MPS
OPERATION: gas
FEED: 26-rd box magazine
WEIGHT: empty 2.4 kg; with empty magazine 2.7 kg; loaded 3.4 kg
LENGTH: butt folded 614 mm; butt extended 823 mm
WIDTH: 65 mm
MUZZLE VELOCITY: in air, 365 m/s
LETHAL RANGE: in air, 100 m; in water 5 m deep, 30 m; in water 20 m deep, 20 m; in water 40 m deep, 11 m

SIG 5.56 mm SG550, SG551 (Stgw 90) & SG552 Commando Assault Rifles SWITZERLAND

SIG 5.56 mm SG552 Commando compact assault rifle with butt folded

In designing the 5.56 mm SG550 and SG551, SIG paid particular attention to weight saving, making extensive use of plastics for the butt, handguard and magazine. The magazine is made of transparent plastic, allowing a check to be kept on the ammunition supply even when firing.

SG551 SWAT: This is a Special Forces or law enforcement model virtually identical to the service SG551, apart from a few details such as a revised butt and provision for mounting various models of optical sight. Sights available include the Hensoldt 6 x 42 BL scope (specially developed for this rifle) or the Trijicon ACOG 3.5 x 35 combat scope. The latter scope may be fully integrated with the rifle. Tactical accessories such as a flashlight or a 40 mm M203 or similar grenade launcher are available; as are lightweight transparent magazines holding five, 20 or 30 rounds. The SG552 Commando is a Special Forces compact model.

SPECIFICATION:

USED BY:
Unknown Special Forces

CONTRACTOR:
IG Arms AG, Neuhausen am Rheinfall, Switzerland

FEATURES:
Data for SG550; where SG551 differs, shown in parentheses
CARTRIDGE: 5.56 x 45 mm
OPERATION: gas; selective fire
LOCKING: rotating bolt
FEED: 20- or 30-rd detachable box magazine
WEIGHT: SG550, with empty magazine and bipod, 4.1 kg; SG551 with empty magazine, 3.4 kg
WEIGHT OF LOADED MAGAZINE: 20-rd, 340 g; 30-rd, 475 g
LENGTH: overall, butt folded, 772 mm (601 mm); butt extended, 998 mm (827 mm)
BARREL: 528 mm; (372 mm)
RIFLING: six grooves; rh
SIGHT RADIUS: 540 mm; (466 mm)
MUZZLE ENERGY: 1700 J; (1460 J)
RATE OF FIRE: cyclic, ca 700 rds/min

SOPS Assault-Rifle Suppressor SWITZERLAND

The Brugger & Thomet SOPS Assault-Rifle Suppressor has been developed for interim use on standard 7.62 and 5.56 mm assault rifles. The concept of the SOPS Suppressor is to suppress the sound of the rifle to enable it to be operated without damaging the firer's hearing, and also, to eliminate completely muzzle flash. The SOPS Suppressor is supplied with a weapon specific replacement semi-vortex muzzle flash hider which allows fast and tight mounting of the suppressor to the rifle. The semi-vortex flash hider will allow the use of rifle grenades and all other accessories.

SPECIFICATION:

USED BY:
Various Special Forces and police units

CONTRACTOR:
Brugger and Thomet AG, Spiez, Switzerland

FEATURES:
WEIGHT: 650 g
LENGTH: 250 mm
DIAMETER: 35 mm
SUPPRESSION: 30+ dB

Type 67 Flame-thrower TAIWAN

The Type 67 portable flame-thrower consists of a fuel/pressure unit and a hose/gun unit. The fuel and pressure group comprises a tubular frame with two interconnected fuel tanks, a spherical pressure unit mounted beneath the smaller fuel tank and other accessories. The hose supplies fuel from the tanks to the gun group. Then the fuel is ignited by a replaceable ignition cylinder in the nozzle end of the gun. Sufficient fuel is carried for five to eight flame bursts.

SPECIFICATION:

USED BY:
Taiwanese army and Marine Corps

CONTRACTOR:
CSF Hsing Hua Company Limited, Taipei, Taiwan

FEATURES:
WEIGHT: basic, 11.66 kg; total with fuel, 23.02 kg
HEIGHT: 700 mm
WIDTH: 530 mm
LENGTH: 300 mm
FUEL: gasoline and napalm
FUEL CAPACITY: 17 litres
RANGE: 45-55 m

Accuracy International 7.62 mm PM Sniper Rifle System UK

Accuracy International 7.62 mm suppressed sniper rifle with PM 6 x 42 sight

The Accuracy International 7.62 mm PM sniper rifle was designed from the start as a military sniper rifle, intended to put its first shot on target, in any conditions, from a clean or fouled barrel. Developed by Accuracy International, it was adopted by the British Army and designated L96A1. The counter-terrorist version is fitted with a x10, x2.5 – x10 as well as the infantry 6 x 42 sight. A spring-loaded monopod is usually fitted, which is concealed in the butt. This can be lowered and adjusted so that the rifle can be laid on the target and supported while the firer observes, without having to support the weight of the rifle for long periods. A spiral flash hider is fitted to the muzzle. Iron sights are not normally fitted to this version.

SPECIFICATION:

USED BY:
UK army and several African, Middle Eastern and Asian armies

CONTRACTOR:
Accuracy International, Portsmouth, UK

FEATURES:
CARTRIDGE: 7.62 x 51 mm NATO
OPERATION: bolt action; single shot
FEED: 10-rd box magazine
WEIGHT: 6.5 kg
LENGTH: 1.124-1.194 m
BARREL: 655 mm
TRIGGER: two-stage adjustable, 1-2 kg
SIGHTS: Schmidt & Bender PM 6 x 42

Accuracy International AWM Magnum Sniper Rifles UK

Accuracy International AWM Magnum sniper rifle configured as Gewehr 22 for German Army

The Accuracy International AWM Magnum sniper rifle was designed as a dedicated sniper rifle giving guaranteed accuracy, ease of maintenance, reliability and military robustness. All the lessons learned during the development of the L96A1 sniper rifle, together with many new and innovative ideas, were combined in this weapon. Using the x10 sight and 0.338 Lapua Magnum ammunition, the AWM is able to meet requirements for equipment destruction and light-armour penetration, as well as the normal anti-personnel capability, to ranges well beyond 1000 m. The 16.2 g bullet is still supersonic at 1400 m, at which range there are still over 1000 J of energy remaining. The rifle is supplied in three calibres: 0.338 Lapua Magnum, 0.300 Winchester Magnum and 7 mm Remington Magnum. Special accuracy ammunition is under development to provide a multiprojectile capability. A folding butt-stock is available as an option. This adds 200 g to the overall weight but, when folded, reduces the overall length by 200 mm. Other options include an adjustable cheekpiece, an adjustable butt-plate, a height-adjustable third leg spike for under the butt, and a Picatinny rail interface.

SPECIFICATION:

USED BY:
German, Netherlands and UK armed forces

CONTRACTOR:
Accuracy International, Portsmouth, UK

FEATURES:
CARTRIDGE: 0.338 Lapua Magnum (and see text)
OPERATION: bolt action; single shot
LOCKING: six-lug bolt
FEED: 4- (0.338) or 5- (0.300, 7 mm) rd box magazine
WEIGHT: empty, approx 6.8 kg
LENGTH: approx 1.23 m
BARREL: 0.338, 686 mm; 0.300, 7 mm, 660 mm
MUZZLE VELOCITY: 914 m/s

Accuracy International 7.62 mm AW Sniper Rifle UK

Accuracy International Model AW sniper rifle

The design of the Accuracy International 7.62 mm AW sniper rifle incorporates anti-freeze mechanisms, a different shroud, three-way safety, smooth bolt manipulation, a muzzle brake, simpler and more robust detachable iron sights, an improved bipod, multipoint sling attachments for sling or carrying harness and a 10-round magazine. For the Swedish Army the rifle is fitted with a Hensoldt 10 x 42 Mil Dot Reticle with tritium lighting for night operation. Part of the sniping package used by the Swedish Army is subcalibre saboted ammunition with a muzzle velocity of about 1,340 m/s. This subcalibre ammunition is in service with the Swedish armed forces, along with 7.62 x 51 mm ball, tracer and blank. A folding butt-stock is available as an option. This adds 200 g to the overall weight but, when folded, reduces the overall length by 200 mm. Other options include an adjustable cheekpiece, an adjustable butt-plate, a height-adjustable third leg spike for under the butt, and a Picatinny rail interface. Screw-on muzzle suppressors are available to remove flash and reduce the sound signature. Normal full power ammunition can be used with these suppressors.

SPECIFICATION:

USED BY:
Australian, Italian, Latvian, Swedish and Netherlands armed forces

CONTRACTOR:
Accuracy International, Portsmouth, UK

FEATURES:
CARTRIDGE: 7.62 x 51 mm NATO (see also text)
OPERATION: bolt action; single shot
FEED: 10-rd box magazine
WEIGHT: AW and AWMP, empty, 6.4 kg; AWP, 6.8 kg
LENGTH: AW, approx 1.18 m; AWMP, approx 1.2 m; AWP, approx 1.1 m
BARREL: AW, 660 mm; AWP, 610 mm or 510 mm
RIFLING: AW; rh; one turn in 250 mm
STOCK: chassis with plastic furniture
TRIGGER: 2-stage, 2-3 kg
MUZZLE VELOCITY: Ball, ca 850 m/s; subcalibre, ca 1340 m/s; subsonic, 310 m/s

Accuracy International AW 'Covert' Sniper Rifle System UK

Accuracy International 7.62 mm AW 'Covert' sniper rifle (1) and Accuracy International AW 'Covert' sniper rifle dismantled, with carrying case (2)

One variant of the Accuracy International system is the AW 'Covert'. The system consists of the suppressed AWMP rifle in a take-down version with a folding stock which, together with all its ancillaries, packs into an airline suitcase with fitted wheels and retractable handle. The rifle is the 'Covert' folding AWMP bolt-action repeating rifle fitted with either the PM 6 x 42, 10 x 42 or 3-12 x 50 Schmidt & Bender military sights, two 10-shot magazines, a bipod and one box containing 20 rounds of subsonic ammunition.

SPECIFICATION:

USED BY:
Unnamed units

CONTRACTOR:
Accuracy International,
Portsmouth, UK

FEATURES:
CARTRIDGE: 7.62 x 51 mm subsonic
OPERATION: bolt action; single shot
FEED: 10-rd box magazine
WEIGHT: 6 kg
LENGTH: 1.2 m
TRIGGER: 1-2 kg pull-off, two-stage detachable
MUZZLE VELOCITY: 314-330 m/s
RANGE: 0-300 m
SUPPRESSION: 85 dBA over 125 ms timebase with subsonic ammunition. With full power ammunition, 109 dBA over 125 ms timebase

5.56 mm L85A1/L85A2 Individual Weapon UK

Electronic 5.56 mm L85A1 individual weapon showing electronic interface just above magazine housing

The two 5.56 mm automatic weapons in the Enfield Weapon System (also known as SA-80) are the L85A1/L85A2 IW (Individual Weapon – assault rifle) and the L86A1/L86A2 light support weapon (LSW), which is a light machine gun (refer to entry in machine guns). Both weapons fire the same 5.56 x 45 mm NATO ammunition and also use a majority of common components that give increased flexibility, reduce spares requirements and simplify maintenance in service.

SPECIFICATION:

USED BY:
UK armed forces including the Royal Marines and Parachute Regiment

CONTRACTOR:
BAE Systems, RO Defence, Nottingham, UK

FEATURES:
CARTRIDGE: 5.56 x 45 mm NATO
OPERATION: gas; selective fire
LOCKING: rotary bolt; forward locking
FEED: 30-rd box magazine
WEIGHT: weapon without magazine and optical sight, 3.8 kg; with loaded magazine and optical sight, 4.98 kg
LENGTH: 785 mm
BARREL: 518 mm
RIFLING: six grooves; rh; one turn in 177.8 mm
TRIGGER PULL: 3.12-4.5 kg
MUZZLE VELOCITY: 940 m/s
RATE OF FIRE: cyclic, 610-775 rds/min

Iron Brigade Armoury M40 Series Sniper Rifles USA

Iron Brigade Armoury's Chandler sniper rifles are patterned after the US Marine Corps M40 series sniper rifles but are designed and manufactured to exceed Marine Corps specifications. Chandler M40 Series rifles are guaranteed to achieve 1 minute of angle accuracy to a range of 100 yards/914 m, so every shot will fall within a 254 mm circle at that range. The rifles are built using Remington 700 actions with McMillan stocks, Hart barrels, Leupold military specification telescopic sights with Marine Corps Mil-Dot reticles, Iron Brigade's proprietary sight mount and a one-piece trigger guard. Each rifle is hand-fitted with the bolt squared and aligned to the barrel. The box magazine is welded to the action for durability and the follower and magazine are modified for a five-round capacity. The bolt mainspring is replaced with a Wolfe special spring. The standard Remington trigger mechanism is retained but is rebuilt and tuned for a 1.7 kg trigger pull. Trigger adjustment screws are sealed to prevent loosening under routine use and recoil. The tapered Hart barrel is made of 416R stainless steel. The McMillan epoxy resin stock is available in a variety of styles, including US Marine Corps M40A1 and M40A2 types, or to user specifications.

SPECIFICATION:

USED BY:
Special military and law enforcement organisations worldwide

CONTRACTOR:
Iron Brigade Armoury, North Carolina, USA

FEATURES:
CARTRIDGE: 7.62 x 51 mm; 0.300 Winchester Magnum; 0.30-06; 7.61 S&H, 5.56 x 45 mm
OPERATION: manual; rotating bolt action
FEED: 5-rd internal box magazine
WEIGHT: ca 6.5 kg
LENGTH: ca 1.115 m
BARREL: 660 mm; other lengths available
SIGHTS: Leupold military specification

US Marine Corps 7.62 mm Designated Marksman Rifle (DMR) USA

The 7.62 mm Designated Marksman Rifle is intended to provide the spotter member of US Marine Corps sniper teams with a precision semi-automatic rifle. It should be capable of nearly the same level of accuracy as the standard sniper rifle, while providing the capability to rapidly engage multiple targets with greater effectiveness and at longer ranges than possible with the current spotter rifle. The rifle will also allow both members of the sniper team to carry the same calibre of ammunition, as the spotter is currently armed with the 5.56 mm M16A2 rifle.

SPECIFICATION:

USED BY:
US Navy and Marine Corps

CONTRACTOR:
US Marine Corps Rifle Team Equipment Shop, Quantico, Virginia, USA

FEATURES:
CARTRIDGE: 7.62 x 51 mm
OPERATION: gas; semi-automatic
LOCKING: rotating bolt
FEED: 20-rd detachable box magazine
WEIGHT: 5 kg
LENGTH: 1.112 m
BARREL: 559 mm
RIFLING: five grooves; rh; one turn in 305 mm
SIGHTS: open, fore, protected blade; open, rear, aperture, adjustable for windage and elevation

Colt 5.56 mm AR-15/M16-series Rifles USA

Colt 5.56 mm M16A2 rifle (Colt Model 711)

Upon being type classified as a military weapon in 1962, the AR-15 was designated the M16 and issued initially to the US Air Force. For the US Army the AR-15 rifle was modified as a result of combat experience in Vietnam and, in 1967, became the M16A1. The differences between the M16 and the M16A1 are chiefly that the M16A1 has a bolt with serrations on the right-hand side and a forward assist assembly which protrudes from the upper receiver and can be used to force the bolt home if the return spring for some reason is unable to do so. The forward assist assembly allows the firer to close the bolt when a dirty cartridge or chamber fouling produces a high friction force. The M16A1 then became the main US Army version of the M16 series.

SPECIFICATION:

USED BY:
In all its variations: in service with us forces and also with Australia, Barbados, Belize, Bolivia, Brazil, Brunei, Cambodia, Cameroon, Chile, Democratic Republic of the Congo, Costa Rica, Denmark, Dominican Republic, Ecuador, El Salvador, Fiji, Gabon, Ghana, Greece, Grenada, Guatemala, Haiti, Indonesia, Israel, Jamaica, Jordan, South Korea, Lebanon, Lesotho, Liberia, Malaysia, Mexico, Morocco, New Zealand, Nicaragua, Nigeria, Oman, Panama, Peru, Philippines, Qatar, Somalia, South Africa, Sri Lanka, Thailand, Tunisia, Turkey, Uganda, United Arab Emirates, Uruguay and Vietnam

CONTRACTOR:
Colt's Manufacturing Company Inc, Connecticut, USA

FEATURES (M16A4):
CARTRIDGE: 5.56 x 45 mm
OPERATION: gas; direct-action; selective fire
LOCKING: rotating bolt
FEED: 20- and 30-rd box magazine
WEIGHT: rifle without magazine, 3.4 kg; magazine empty, 30-rd, 110 g; magazine loaded, 30-rd, 450 g
LENGTH: overall, 1 m
BARREL: 510 mm
SIGHT RADIUS: 501 mm
MUZZLE VELOCITY: 948 m/s
RATE OF FIRE: cyclic, 700-950 rds/min
EFFECTIVE RANGE: 800 m
MUZZLE ENERGY: 1765 J

M4A1 Close Quarters Battle (CQB) Weapon USA

M4A1 Close Quarter Battle (CQB) weapon showing reflex sight, AN/PEQ-2 laser pointer, M203 grenade launcher, SOPMOD enhanced stock and back-up iron sight

One of the keys to theSpecial Operations Peculiar Modification M4A1 Accessory Kit (SOPMOD M4A1 Kit) is its adaptability. Three SOPMOD M4A1 Kits are issued to each Army 'A' detachment, four to each 'B' detachment, four to each SEAL platoon, and three per special tactical team. US Army Rangers and other special mission units are issued selected items rather than complete kits to enhance their M4A1 CQB weapons. US Marine Corps units to be equipped with the M4A1 CQB weapon include security force units, direct action platoons, Special Operations Capable Marine Expeditionary Units (MEU-SOC), and military police special reaction teams. The M4A1 (CQB) weapon is a derivative of the M4A1 Carbine intended for use by Special Operations, US Army Ranger and selected Marine Corps units, where it will replace the Heckler and Koch 9 mm MP5 sub-machine gun. The M4A1 CQB weapon incorporates the SOPMOD M4A1 Kit, an accessory suite developed by the Naval Surface Weapons Station.

SPECIFICATION:

USED BY:
US armed forces

CONTRACTOR:
Colt's Manufacturing, Connecticut, USA

FEATURES:
CARTRIDGE: 5.56 x 45 mm
OPERATION: gas; selective fire
LOCKING: rotating bolt
FEED: detachable box magazine
WEIGHT: 3.6kg
LENGTH: stock retracted, 757 mm; stock extended, 838 mm
BARREL: 370 mm
RIFLING: four grooves; rh; one turn in 178 mm
SIGHTS: dependent on mission profile
MUZZLE VELOCITY: 921 m/s
RATE OF FIRE: cyclic, 700-900 rds/min; effective, semi-automatic, 45 rds/min; full automatic, 150 rds/min
EFFECTIVE RANGE: point fire, 500 m; area fire, 800 m

KAC 5.56 mm Modular Weapon System USA

Some of the options involved in the KAC Modular Weapon System

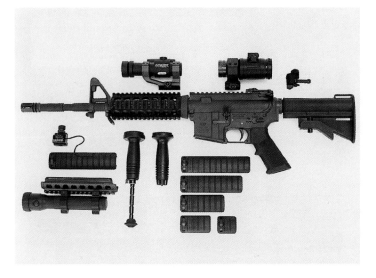

The heart of the 5.56 mm MWS is KAC's aluminium RIS forestock which replaces the standard components and mounts four sections of Picatinny Rail around the barrel to facilitate the attachment of various tactical accessories. The forestock also acts as thermal protection for the user. Tactical accessories that can be used with the RIS include both standard and flip-up iron sights, telescopic sights, reflex sights, starlight telescopic sights, small night-vision devices, visible and infra-red laser aim lights, vertical foregrip, quick-detach mounting for a 40 mm M203 grenade launcher, quick-detach sound suppressor, police flashlights and a KAC Masterkey breaching weapon, the latter being an adaptation of the Remington 870 shotgun. KAC can provide suitable mounts for many types of sighting system. Each RIS rail contains three holes provided for the attachment of camera or video accessories, typically a tripod.

SPECIFICATION:

USED BY:
In production for the US Special Operations Command

CONTRACTOR:
Knight's Armament Company, Florida, USA

ArmaLite 0.243 and 7.62 mm AR-10B Rifles USA

ArmaLite AR-10(T) 7.62 mm match rifle with ArmaLite ST95 telescopic sight and mount

The ArmaLite AR-10B 7.62 mm rifle series is based on the original AR-10 produced during the 1950s, but has been engineered using modern components and manufacturing methods, with an emphasis on reliability and functionality foremost and with commonality of parts with the 5.56 mm M16A2 rifle series as a secondary priority. All AR-10B rifles have several improvements and modifications which differentiate them from similar weapons. All feature forged upper and lower receivers, a firing pin retaining spring to prevent slamfires, and many other modifications to make the AR-10B compatible with 7.62 x 51 mm or 0.243 Winchester ammunition.

SPECIFICATION:

USED BY:
In service with unspecified military special operations organisations

CONTRACTOR:
ArmaLite Inc, Illinoi, USA

FEATURES:
CARTRIDGE: 0.243 Winchester; 7.62 x 51 mm NATO
OPERATION: gas; semi-automatic
LOCKING: rotating bolt
FEED: 10- or 20-rd modified M14 box magazine
WEIGHT: AR-10A4, empty, 4.445 kg
LENGTH: AR-10A4, 1.003 m; AR-10(T), 1.105 m
BARREL: AR-10A2 and AR-10A4, 508 mm; AR-10(T), 609 mm
RIFLING: AR-10A2 and AR-10A4, six grooves; rh; one turn in 305 mm; AR-10(T), six grooves; rh; one turn in 285 mm
SIGHTS: AR-10A2, fore, cylinder on threaded base; rear, flip aperture adjustable for windage and elevation. AR-10A4 and AR-10(T), fore, removable post; rear, removable flip aperture adjustable for windage and elevation
MUZZLE VELOCITY: nominal, 860 m/s

Arms Tech Compak 16 5.56 mm Compact Assault Rifle USA

The Compak 16 was developed to provide a compact and reliable personal defence weapon for military vehicle crew members, Special Operations Forces and police personnel. The Compak 16 is derived from the M16 rifle and the lower receiver of the rifle is identical to that of the standard M16, thereby simplifying logistics support for organisations already equipped with M16-type weapons. The Compak 16 has, however, been engineered to provide a 600 rds/min cyclic rate and reduced muzzle blast while maintaining accuracy out to an effective range of 300 m. Muzzle blast and flash are reduced by a proprietary muzzle device which reduces these effects to a level comparable to that of a standard M16 rifle.

SPECIFICATION:

USED BY:
Unspecified Special Forces

CONTRACTOR:
Arms Tech Ltd, Arizona, USA

FEATURES:
CARTRIDGE: 5.56 x 45 mm
Operation; gas; selective fire; semi- or fully-automatic
LOCKING: rotating bolt
FEED: 20- and 30-rd detachable box magazines
WEIGHT: empty, 2.5 kg
LENGTH: 609 mm
BARREL: 266 mm
RIFLING: six grooves; rh; one turn in 228 mm
RATE OF FIRE: cyclic, 600 rds/min
SIGHTS: optional, to user specification

Arms Tech 0.300 Winchester Magnum Super Match Interdiction Rifle USA

The Arms Tech Super Match Interdiction rifle was developed to fill a need for a precision rifle as accurate as a bolt-action rifle, able to reach targets beyond the range of standard 7.62 x 51 mm weapons, and providing a quick follow-up shot capability, for tactical situations requiring the engagement of multiple targets.

SPECIFICATION:

USED BY:
Unspecified Special Forces

CONTRACTOR:
Arms Tech Ltd, Arizona, USA

FEATURES:
CARTRIDGE: 0.300 Winchester Magnum
OPERATION: gas; semi-automatic
LOCKING: rotating bolt
FEED: 3- or 10-rd detachable box magazine
WEIGHT: empty, 6.3 kg
LENGTH: 1.193 m
BARREL: 660 mm
RIFLING: six grooves; rh; one turn in 304 mm
SIGHTS: optical, to customer specifications
MUZZLE VELOCITY: 971 m/s
RATE OF FIRE: 3-4 rds/min
EFFECTIVE RANGE: 1000 m

Arnold Arms Special Purpose Rifles USA

Arnold Arms Mark II Neutralizer rifle

The Arnold Arms Marks I and II Neutralizer rifles are designed to achieve the highest standard of military and police accuracy. Mark I rifles are built using Remington or Winchester receivers, with chrome molybdenum and stainless steel match grade barrels manufactured by either Douglas, Hart, Kreiger, Lilja or Shilen. Barrels are fully free-floating. Remington actions are optimised, accurised, equipped with a three-position safety and the bolt is fitted with a Sako extractor. A detachable box magazine is installed as standard equipment. Triggers are manufactured by Jewell, Shilen, Remington or Timney. The action is available in short, long and magnum size lengths to accommodate virtually any cartridge. The lower receiver is 7075-T6 aluminium. Neutralizer glass fibre stocks are manufactured by McMillan and are adjustable for length of pull and cheek height. Finish is either black or various camouflage finishes, including desert, woodland and arctic.

SPECIFICATION:

USED BY:
Israel, various US Federal and local law enforcement agencies

CONTRACTOR:
Arnold Arms Inc, Washington, USA

FEATURES:
CARTRIDGE: 5.56 x 45 mm; 7.62 x 51 mm; 0.300 Winchester Magnum
OPERATION: manual; bolt action
LOCKING: rotating bolt
FEED: detachable box magazine
WEIGHT: 3.6 to 8.1 kg, depending on model and configuration
LENGTH: depends on model and configuration
BARREL: 508-660 mm, depending on model
SIGHTS: to customer specifications; rifles are configured for standard optical mounts

H-S Precision Pro Series 2000 Tactical Take Down Rifles USA

The Pro Series 2000 Long-Range Rifle is available in 7.62 x 51 mm/0.300 Winchester Magnum. All H-S Precision rifles are available in either right- or left-hand versions.

SPECIFICATION:

USED BY:
Weapon most preferred by US military and police snipers

CONTRACTOR:
H-S Precision Inc, South Dakota, USA

FEATURES:
CARTRIDGE: 7.62 x 51 mm/ 0.300 Winchester Magnum
OPERATION: manual; bolt action
LOCKING: rotating bolt
FEED: 5- or 10-rd detachable box magazine
WEIGHT: 6.1 kg
BARREL: 597 mm
SIGHTS: none provided; standard Weaver rail accepts most optical mounting hardware

Harris M-89 Multi-barrel Combo Sniper Rifle USA

SPECIFICATION:

USED BY:
Malaysia, US Navy SEAL teams and others

CONTRACTOR:
Harris Gunworks Inc, Arizona, USA

FEATURES:
CARTRIDGE: 7.62 x 51 mm NATO or other calibres
OPERATIONS: bolt-action repeater
FEED: 5-, 10-, or 20-rd box magazine
WEIGHT: with optical sight, 5.2 kg
BARREL: without suppresser, 457 mm; with suppresser 711 mm

This rifle can be fitted with a bipod and will accept a variety of optical, low-light and night-vision sights.

RAD M91 and M91A2 Sniper Rifles USA

RAD M91 sniper rifle

The RAD M91 7.62 mm sniper rifle was developed by Redick Arms Development in co-operation with the US Navy to meet the requirements of US Naval Special Warfare units. It has been procured by the US Navy for SEAL teams and some other US Special Operations units. The RAD M91 7.62 mm sniper rifle is a conventional bolt-action rifle based around a Remington 700 bolt action allied with a match grade 416R stainless-steel cut rifled barrel with a recessed crown. The trigger is also a Remington 700 component reconfigured to meet US Navy specifications with a 1.4 kg pull. Total ammunition capacity is five rounds, four in the box magazine and one in the chamber.

SPECIFICATION:

USED BY:
US Navy Special Operations

CONTRACTOR:
Redick Arms Development, Arkansas, USA

FEATURES:
CARTRIDGE: 7.62 x 51 mm NATO; 0.300 Winchester Magnum; 0.30-06 (optional)
OPERATION: manual bolt
FEED: 4-rd box magazine
WEIGHT: 6.3 kg
LENGTH: 1.143 m
BARREL: 610 mm
RIFLING: six grooves; one turn in 254 mm
SIGHTS: Bausch and Lomb Tactical 62-1040, MIL-Dot reticle

La France 5.56 mm M16K Assault Carbine   USA

La France 5.56 mm M16K assault carbine

Among the smallest and lightest of the M16 variants, the La France 5.56 mm M16K assault carbine can be carried in the confined spaces of aircraft and motor vehicles. It was designed to give special operations units controllable firepower and high lethality in a weapon of minimum size and weight. The specially engineered gas system results in a cyclic rate of fire under 600 rds/min, unusually low for weapons of this calibre. A vortex flash suppresser completely eliminates any trace of muzzle flash.

SPECIFICATION:

USED BY:
Unspecified Special Operations units

CONTRACTOR:
La France Specialties, California, USA

FEATURES:
CARTRIDGE: 5.56 x 45 mm
OPERATION: gas; selective fire
LOCKING: rotating bolt
FEED: 20-, 30- or 90-rd magazine
WEIGHT: empty, 2.5 kg
LENGTH: butt retracted, 610 mm; butt extended, 686 mm
BARREL: 213 mm; with flash suppresser, 254 mm
RIFLING: six grooves; rh; one turn in 177.8 mm
SIGHTS: fore, aperture; rear, flip aperture, adjustable for windage
SIGHT RADIUS: 127 mm
MUZZLE VELOCITY: M193, 732 m/s
RATE OF FIRE: cyclic, 550-600 rds/min

7.62 mm M40A1 (PIP) Sniper Rifle USA

SPECIFICATION:

USED BY:
US Marine Corps

CONTRACTOR:
US Marine Corps Rifle Team Equipment Shop, Quantico, Virginia, USA

FEATURES:
CARTRIDGE: 7.62 x 51 mm NATO
OPERATION: manual bolt action, single shot
FEED: 5-rd box magazine
WEIGHT: 6.1 kg
LENGTH: 1.117 m
BARREL: 610 mm
RIFLING: rh; one turn in 254 mm
SIGHT: telescope, Unertl Special Sniper, x10
MUZZLE VELOCITY: 777 m/s
EFFECTIVE RANGE: 1000 m

The 7.62 mm M40A1 Product Improved (PIP) sniper rifle was originally to have been known as the M40A2. Using the M40A1 as the starting point, every aspect of the original rifle was evaluated to determine if improvement was desirable or necessary. The resultant M40A1 PIP emerged as a completely different rifle.

7.62 mm M40A1 Sniper Rifle USA

The 7.62 mm M40A1 sniper rifle was adopted in the early 1970s to meet the needs of the US Marine Corps for a long range sniper rifle. Each rifle is individually produced by the Marine Corps' Rifle Team Equipment (RTE) Shop located in Virginia.

SPECIFICATION:

USED BY:
US Marine Corps

CONTRACTOR:
US Marine Corps Rifle Team Equipment Shop, Quantico, Virginia, USA

FEATURES:
CARTRIDGE: 7.62 x 51 mm NATO
OPERATION: manual bolt action; single shot
FEED: 5-rd (four plus one) integral box magazine
WEIGHT: 6.59 kg
LENGTH: 1.117 m
BARREL: 610 mm
RIFLING: rh; one turn in 254 mm
SIGHT: telescope, Unertl Special Sniper, x10
MUZZLE VELOCITY: 777 m/s
EFFECTIVE RANGE: 1000 m

Remington 7.62 mm M24 Sniper Weapon System USA

Remington 7.62 mm M24 sniper rifle in issue carrying case complete with accessories

SPECIFICATION:

USED BY:
Egypt, Lebanon, South Africa, UAE
and US Army

CONTRACTOR:
Remington Arms Company Inc,
New York, USA

FEATURES:
CARTRIDGE: 7.62 x 51 mm M118
Special Ball
OPERATION: bolt action; single
shot
FEED: 6-rd integral magazine
WEIGHT: rifle with sling, 5.49 kg;
sight, 794 g; bipod, 318 g
LENGTH: 1.092 m
RIFLING: five grooves; rh; one turn
in 285 mm
SIGHT: Leupold Ultra M3 x10
telescopic
MUZZLE VELOCITY: ca 792 m/s
EFFECTIVE RANGE: 800 m

The Remington 7.62 mm M24 Sniper Weapon
System was the US Army's first complete sniping
system, replacing all other army sniper rifles. First
issues, as a non-developmental item, took place in
November 1988 and the system is issued to infantry
battalions, Special Forces and Ranger units.

Mossberg M9200A1 'Jungle Gun' USA

SPECIFICATION:

USED BY:
US armed forces

CONTRACTOR:
O F Mossberg & Sons,
Connecticut, USA

FEATURES:
CARTRIDGE: 12 gauge, 2.75 in or
3 in Magnum
OPERATION: gas; semi-automatic
LOCKING: projecting lug
WEIGHT: 3.1 kg
LENGTH: 1 m
BARREL: 470 mm
SIGHTS: fore, bead; rear, none.
OPERATIONAL: fore, blade; rear,
'ghost ring' aperture

The Mossberg M9200A1 was derived from the
commercial M9200 shotgun, for use by US Army
Special Operations Forces in Central America on
drug interdiction mission, hence the M9200A1's
nickname of 'Jungle Gun'. The military contract
gun is designated RI-96. The M9200A1 gas system is
significantly modified from that of the sporting
version so that it will accept and function with the
variety of ammunition types used with combat
shotguns.

Barrett 0.50 Model 82A1 and Model 82A1M Rifles USA

The Model 82A1M was designed specially for military operations and Special Forces and, unlike the Model 82A1, will not be sold to private users. It has been adopted by the US Army in preference to the bolt-action Model 95 (XM107) because of its greater potential firepower. One of the main changes on this model is that, by removing a barrel-retaining key, the barrel can be telescoped into the upper receiver to reduce the carry length so that it can be transported inside a hard carry case.

SPECIFICATION:

USED BY:
Bahrain, Belgium, Bhutan, Botswana, Chile, Denmark, Finland, France, Greece, Italy, Kuwait, Jordan, Mexico, the Netherlands, Norway, Oman, the Philippines, Portugal, Qatar, Saudi Arabia, Singapore, Spain, Sweden, Turkey, UAE, UK and US

CONTRACTOR:
Barrett Firearms Manufacturing Inc, Tennessee, USA

FEATURES:
(Model 82A1M)
CARTRIDGE: 12.7 x 99 mm
(0.50 Browning)
OPERATION: short-recoil; semi-automatic
LOCKING: rotating bolt
FEED: 10-rd detachable box magazine
WEIGHT: empty, 14 kg
LENGTH: overall, 1.45 m; reduced, 965 mm
BARREL: 736.6 mm
SIGHTS: x10 telescope; iron sights with rear sight calibrated from 100 to 1500 m
MUZZLE VELOCITY: M33 ball, 853 m/s
EFFECTIVE RANGE: 2000 m

Colt 40 mm M203 Grenade Launcher USA

Colt 40 mm M203 grenade launcher attached to M16A2 rifle

The M203 40 mm grenade launcher is a lightweight, single-shot, breech-loaded, sliding-barrel, shoulder-fired weapon designed especially for attachment to M16 series assault rifles. It allows the grenade launcher to fire a wide range of 40 mm low-velocity high-explosive and special-purpose grenades, in addition to permitting normal use of the 5.56 mm M16 rifle.

SPECIFICATION:

USED BY:
Australia (Special Air Service and Commando units), Brazil, Brunei, Cameroon, Costa Rica, Ecuador, El Salvador, Gabon, Greece, Grenada, Guatemala, Honduras, Indonesia, Israel, Jordan, South Korea, Lebanon, Liberia, Malaysia, Mexico, Myanmar, New Zealand, Oman, Panama, Philippines, Qatar, Singapore, Sri Lanka, Sweden, Thailand, Turkey, United Arab Emirates and the US armed forces

CONTRACTOR:
Colt's Manufacturing Company Inc, Connecticut, USA

FEATURES:
CALIBRE: 40 x 46 mm
OPERATION: single-shot
FEED: breech loading; sliding barrel
WEIGHT: unloaded M16A1 and M203, 5.484 kg; loaded M4 and M203, 4.624 kg
WEIGHT OF LAUNCHER UNIT: empty, 1.36 kg; loaded, 1.63 kg
LENGTH: overall, 380 mm; barrel, 305 mm
WIDTH: 84 mm
MUZZLE VELOCITY: with M406 grenade, 74.7 m/s
RANGE: max: 400 m: max effective: area target, 350 m; point target, 150 m

459

C-MAG 5.56 mm 100-round Magazine USA

Diagram showing the feed system for the C-MAG magazine

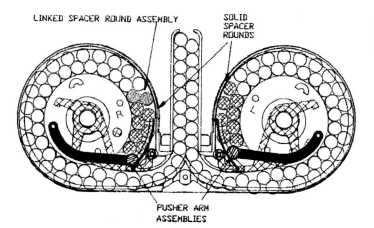

LINKED SPACER ROUND ASSEMBLY

SOLID SPACER ROUNDS

PUSHER ARM ASSEMBLIES

The C-MAG is a twin-drum high-capacity ammunition magazine for rifles, light support weapons, firing port and other specialised weapons in 5.56 mm calibre. It consists of two main components: a double-drum storage housing and a feed-clip assembly. The double-drum storage housing is standard and fits any weapon. The feed-clip assembly is interchangeable and serves as an adapter for various weapon types. The key feature of the C-MAG is the formation of double rows of cartridges in each of the drums. Solid spacer-round strings occupy the feed clip when the magazine is empty. The number required depends on the length and style of the feed clip, which is specific to an individual weapon system.

SPECIFICATION:

USED BY:
German Bundeswehr (Special Forces units employ this magazine with the G36K short assault rifle) and many other military and law-enforcement agencies worldwide, including US armed forces

CONTRACTOR:
The Beta Company, Georgia, USA

FEATURES:

CAPACITY: 100 5.56 mm cartridges
AMMUNITION: ball; tracer; blank rounds
WEIGHT: empty, 1 kg
DIMENSIONS: 251 x 81 x 120 mm
RATE OF FIRE: up to 1300 rds/min
MATERIALS: main components, filled thermoplastic polyester; minor components, non-corrosive steel and alloy materials
SHELF LIFE, LOADED: indefinite

Weapons: Unmanned Aerial Vehicles

STN Atlas Taifun GERMANY

Artist's impression of Taifun combat drone

The Taifun is intended to attack selected tanks,
artillery, radars, command posts and logistics
assets at the rear of the battlefield. An initial
evaluation system is due for delivery in 2004, with
service entry planned for 2006. Short, stubby
fuselage with mid-mounted gull wings, large
dorsal and ventral fins and pusher engine. Outer
wing panels are folded while in container,
unfolding automatically at launch by means of gas
pressure struts which are jettisoned after wings
have locked. Constructed mainly of fibre-
reinforced plastics. Entire fuselage is covered in
radar-absorbent material. De-icing system
standard. Zero-length launch from container by
booster rocket which is jettisoned automatically
after burnout and unfolding of UAV wings. UAVs are
launched sequentially; automatic sequence control
ensures a high rate of launch. Non-recoverable.

SPECIFICATION:

USED BY:
German army

CONTRACTOR:
STN Atlas Elektronik GmbH,
Bremen

FEATURES:
One 32.1 kw (43 hp) Schrick
four-stroke piston engine with
four-blade wooden pusher
propeller
WINGSPAN: 2.26 m (7 ft 5.0 in)
LENGTH: overall excl boosters,
2.08 m (6 ft 9.9 in)
HEIGHT: overall, 1.04 m (3 ft 4.9 in)
WARHEAD: 20 kg (44.4 lb)
PAYLOAD: 50 kg (110.2 lb)
MAX LAUNCHING WEIGHT: 160 kg
(353 lb)
MAX LEVEL SPEED: 108 kts
(200 km/h; 124 mph)
LOITER SPEED: 65 kts (120 km/h;
74 mph)
CEILING: >4000 m (13,120 ft)
TARGET SEARCH AREA: 2000 km^2
(772 sq miles)
TIME ON STATION: at 108 n miles
(200 km; 124 miles) from launch
site, 4 hours

ARMAMENT:
High-resolution K-band (approx
35 GHz) MMW radar seeker with
MTI capability and Doppler beam
sharpening to identify and track
moving or stationary targets; has
range of more than 4000 m
(13,120 ft), resolution of 0.5 m
(1.64 ft), swivel and spot modes,
and weighs 14 kg (31 lb).
Armour-penetrating shaped
charge warhead, delivered in
steep terminal dive

HESA Ababil-T IRAN

Zero-length launch of an Ababil-T (1) and the warhead-carrying Ababil-T attack UAV (2)

Short/medium-range attack UAV distinguishable from the Ababil-s by twin-tailed configuration. Mainly cylindrical fuselage with ogival nosecone, twin, small fins and pusher engine; swept wings at rear, mounted to fuselage underside; swept metal construction foreplanes on top of fuselage near nose. All-composites construction.

SPECIFICATION:

USED BY:
Iranian armed forces. Also available for export

CONTRACTOR:
Iran Aircraft Manufacturing Industries (HESA), Esfahan

FEATURES:
One P 73 rotary piston engine (rating not known), driving two-blade pusher propeller
WINGSPAN: 3.33 m (10 ft 11.1 in)
LENGTH: overall, 2.80 m (9 ft 2.2 in)
HEIGHT: overall, 0.935 m (3 ft 0.8 in)
MAX LAUNCHING WEIGHT: 83 kg (183 lb)
MISSION RADIUS: LOS, 27 n miles (50 km; 31 miles); with GPS, >81 n miles (150 km; 93 miles)

ARMAMENT:
HE warhead; can engage both fixed and mobile targets

IAI **Harpy and Cutlass** ISRAEL

Harpy anti-radar drone with side-force panels deployed

Anti-radar attack UAV. Mid-mounted delta wings with full-span elevons, tip-mounted fins and rudders and retractable side-force panels (two in each wing). Built in two GFRP/CFRP half-shells with integral fittings. Israeli-developed passive radar seeker (recently upgraded to cover a wider range of frequencies) and high-explosive warhead. IAI was reported, in late 2000, to be developing an upgraded version equipped with a dual (electromagnetic and E-O) sensor and datalink, to allow Harpy to receive updates on potential targets and to be directed against a specific emitter. Launch by booster rocket from ground- or truck-mounted 18-round container. Non-recoverable. Development of a ship-launched version has also been reported.

SPECIFICATION:

USED BY:
China, India, South Korea, Spain and Turkey

CONTRACTOR:
Israel Aircraft Industries (MBT Division), Yahud

FEATURES:
One 20.5 kw (27.5 hp) two-cylinder two-stroke engine; two-blade pusher propeller
WINGSPAN: 2.00 m (6 ft 6.7 in)
length: overall, 2.30 m (7 ft 6.5 in)
HEIGHT: overall, 0.36 m (1 ft 2.2 in)
MAX LAUNCHING WEIGHT: Approx 120 kg (264.5 lb)
MAX LEVEL SPEED: 135 kts (250 km/h; 155 mph)
CEILING: 3000 m (9840 ft)
MISSION RADIUS: 216-270 n miles (400-500 km; 248-310 miles)
ENDURANCE AT 400 KM RADIUS: 2 hours

ARMAMENT:
WARHEAD: 32 kg (70.5 lb)

Boeing X-45: Combat UAV for Electronic Attack, Suppression of Enemy Air Defences and Other Missions USA

Boeing model of a production UCAV with six internally stowed small diameter bombs

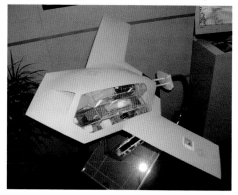

Fully autonomous, including taxi, take-off and landing. This UCAV will be deployable to forward locations, with wings detached, in a storage container. Six X-45A containers could be carried in a C-17A Globemaster III transport aircraft. Conventional and autonomous wheeled take-off and recovery.

This UCAV will exploit real-time, onboard and offboard sensors to detect, identify and locate fixed, relocatable and mobile targets quickly. Secure communications and advanced cognitive decision aids will provide the operator with the situational awareness and positive air vehicle control necessary to authorise munitions release. The air vehicle will carry multiple advanced, precision-guided munitions and relay battle damage assessment information back to the mission control system. Active Electronically Scanned Array SAR (resolution approximately 60 cm; 23.5 in at 43 n miles; 80 km; 50 miles range) and ESM provided by Raytheon.

SPECIFICATION:

USED BY:
US Air Force (interest has been shown by Australia and the UK)

CONTRACTOR:
Boeing Unmanned Systems, Missouri, USA

FEATURES:
POWERPLANT: A, one 28.0 kN (6,300 lb st) Honeywell F124-GA-100 non-afterburning turbofan; B, one 31.1 kN (7,000 lb st) class General Electric F404-GE-102D turbofan. Fuel tankage in fuselage only (A) or fuselage and wings (B). Provision for in-flight refuelling
WINGSPAN: A, 10.31 m (33 ft 10 in); B, 14.93 m (49 ft)
LENGTH: overall, A, 8.03 m (26 ft 4 in); B, 1.89 m (39 ft)
FUSELAGE LENGTH: A, 8.03 m (26 ft 4 in)
FUSELAGE MAX DEPTH: A, 1.09 m (3 ft 7 in)
HEIGHT: overall, A, 2.03 m (6 ft 8 in)
WEAPONS BAY: length, A, 3.73 m (12 ft 3 in); width, A, 0.54 m (1 ft 9.25 in)
DEPTH: A, 0.53 m (1 ft 9 in)
WEIGHT EMPTY: A, 3629 kg (8000 lb)
FUEL WEIGHT: A, 1220 kg (2690 lb); B, 6350 kg (14,000 lb)
ORDNANCE PAYLOAD: A, 680 kg (1500 lb); B, 2041 kg (4500 lb)
MISSION T/O WEIGHT: A, 5529 kg (12,190 lb); B, 16,556 kg (36,500 lb)
MAX CRUISING SPEED: A, M0.80; B, M0.85
TYPICAL OPERATING ALTITUDE: A, 10,670 m (35,000 ft); B, 13,715 m (45,000 ft)
COMBAT RADIUS: B, 1300 n miles (2407 km; 1496 miles)
TIME ON STATION: at 1000 n miles (1852 km; 1151 miles) from base, B, 2 hours

General Atomics MQ-1 and RQ-1 Predator USA

Trials Predator 97-3034, armed with underwing Hellfire missiles

The launch of Operation Enduring Freedom in Afghanistan following the 11 September 2001 terrorist attacks in the USA saw both RQ-1 and MQ-1 Predators deployed to that theatre, the latter reportedly operating under the aegis of the CIA rather than the USAF. According to one unconfirmed source, some 40 operational Hellfire launches had been made by the end of that year. From December 2001, Predators were also tasked with relaying real-time video and targeting information to the crews of AC-130 Spectre gunships operating against Taliban and al-Quaeda forces. On 3 November 2002, a CIA MQ-1, reportedly flying from Djibouti, used its Hellfire missiles to destroy a civilian vehicle containing suspected al-Quaeda terrorists some 161 km (100 miles) east of the Yemeni capital of Sana'a. Conventional wheeled take-off under direct LOS control. Automatic take-off system under development. Wheeled landing recovery under direct LOS control. Butler parachute for emergency recovery in the event of power or command link failure. Automatic landing system under development.

SPECIFICATION:

USED BY:
US navy and air force

CONTRACTOR:
General Atomics Aeronautical Systems Inc, California, USA

FEATURES:
One 84.5 kw (113.3 hp) Rotax 914F four-cylinder, four-stroke turbocharged engine (59.6 kw; 79.9 hp Rotax 912 UL in RQ-1K); two-blade variable-pitch pusher propeller. Fuel capacity 379 litres (100 US gallons; 83.3 Imp gallons)
WINGSPAN: 14.85 m (48 ft 8.6 in)
WING CHORD: at root, 1.10 m (3 ft 7.3 in); at tip 0.40 m (1 ft 3.7 in)
WING AREA: 11.45 m² (123.3 sq ft)
LENGTH: overall, 8.13 m (26 ft 8 in)
FUSELAGE MAX WIDTH: front 1.12 m (3 ft 8.0 in); rear 0.75 m (2 ft 5.5 in)
FUSELAGE MAX DEPTH: front 1.02 m (3 ft 4.0 in); rear 0.60 m (1 ft 11.5 in)
HEIGHT: overall, 2.21 m (7 ft 3.0 in)
TAILPLANE SPAN: 4.38 m (14 ft 4.3 in)
WHEEL TRACK: 2.78 m (9 ft 1.4 in)
WHEELBASE: 2.62 m (8 ft 7.0 in)
PROPELLER DIAMETER: 1.73 m (5 ft 8 in)
WEIGHT: empty, 513 kg (1130 lb)
FUEL WEIGHT: 302 kg (665 lb)
MAX PAYLOAD: 204 kg (450 lb)
MAX T/O WEIGHT: approx 1020 kg (2250 lb)
MAX LEVEL SPEED: 117 kts (217 km/h; 135 mph)
LOITER SPEED: 73 kts (135 km/h; 84 mph)
CEILING: 7620 m (25,000 ft)
T/O & LANDING RUNWAY REQUIREMENT: 1524 x 38 m (5000 x 125 ft)
OPERATIONAL RADIUS: 400 n miles (740 km; 460 miles)
MAX (FERRY) RANGE: >2000 n miles (3704 km; 2302 miles)
ENDURANCE AT OPERATIONAL RADIUS ABOVE: >24 hours
MAX ENDURANCE: >40 hours

Country List of Special and Elite Forces

Special & Elite Forces: who is believed to have what

(This list does not include intelligence, espionage/counter-espionage services nor security agencies – unless these operate as formed units.)

Afghanistan	Presidential Close Protection Team (army)
	Three Special Forces Battalions (army)
Albania	Coastal Defence Command (navy)
	Commando Brigade (army)
Algeria	*Detachment Spécial d'Intervention*: Special Intervention Detachment – DSI (government personnel)
	Brigade Spécial: Special Brigade – Brigade 127 (government personnel)
	Garde Républic: Republican Guard (government personnel)
	Service Action Special Unit: within the Research and Security Directorate – DRS (government personnel)
	Groupe d'Intervention Spécial: Special Intervention Group – GIS: within the DRS (government personnel)
	Unités Republicaines de Sécurité: Republican Security Units – URS (government personnel)
	Marine Fusilier: combat divers (navy)
	Naval Infantry Battalion (marines) *Saajkaa*: commando unit (army)
	18ième Régiment Parachutiste: Special Forces Airborne Commando Division (army)
	Various small, unnamed Special Forces units (army)
	Brigade Mobiles de la Police Judicaire: Judicial Police Mobile Brigades – BMPJ (police)
	Service Central de Répression du Banditisme: Crime-fighting Central Service – SCRB (police)
Argentina	*Prefectura Naval Argentina*: (government personnel)
	Buzo Tacticos: combat divers, swimmer delivery vehicles (navy)
	Infanteria de Marine: Marine Infantry Brigade : includes *La Agrupacion de Commandos Anfibios* – Amphibious Commando Group Special Forces (marines)
	Pagina Anti-Terrorismo: (navy/marines)
	Brigada del Ejercito 601 and 602: includes Special Forces Battalion and Commando/Ranger Battalion (army)
	4th Airborne Brigade (army)
	Two Mountain Brigades (army)
	Batallōn de Ingenieros Anfibios 601: amphibious engineer battalion (army)

	Brigada Especial Operativa Halcon: Falcon Special Operations Brigade, counter-revolutionary warfare (police)
	Federal Police Anti-Terrorist Unit (police)
Armenia	Special Forces Battalion (army)
Australia	Offshore Assault Team: combat divers – OAT (navy)
	Clearance Diver Branch: combat divers (navy)
	Special Air Service Regiment – SASR (army)
	4th Royal Australian Regiment (Commando) – 4RAR (Cdo) (army)
	Tactical Assault Group – TAG (army)
	Tactical Assault Group (East) – TAG(E) (army)
	Three Regional Force Surveillance Units (army)
	Two Commando Reserve Battalions (army)
	Incident Response Regiment – IRR (army)
Austria	Army Marine Wing (army)
	Jagdkommando: commando unit (army)
	Gendarmerieeinsatzkommando – GEK/Cobra: anti-terrorist unit (police)
	Special Operations Group – SOG (police)
	Alpine Police Force (police)
Bahamas	Royal Bahamas Defence Force Naval Squadron includes Marine (marines)
	Drug Enforcement Unit (police)
Bahrain	Special Forces Battalion (army)
	Bahrain Police and Public Security Department: includes counter-terrorist units (police)
Belgium	*Équioes Spécialisées de Reconnaisaince* – ESR: specialised Reconnaissance Teams trains the ESI (army)
	Paracommando Brigade: includes 14th Para-Commando Engineer Company, combat divers (army)
	Escadron Special d'Intervention (Le Group Diane) – ESI: Special Intervention Squadron (police)
Belize	Maritime Wing of the Belize Defence Force (navy)
	Special Force paramilitary unit (police)
Benin	Airborne/Commando Battalion (army)
Bolivia	Bolivian Marine Corps: includes the *Batallón de Infanteria de Marina Almirante Grau* (marines)
	Two Ranger Regiments (army)
	Special Forces Battalion (army)
	Two Regiments of *Carabineros*: rapid intervention force (police)

Bosnia-Herzegovina	Rapid Reaction Brigade: includes the Special Forces/ Ranger Battalion (army)
	Drzavna Granicna Sluzba Bosne I Hercegovine – DGS BiH: State Border Service (police)
Brazil	*Grupo de Mergulhadores de Combat* – GRUMEC: Brazilian Navy Combat Divers Group (navy)
	Corpo de Fuzilieros Navais – CFN; Brazilian Marine Corps: includes the Tonolero Special Operations Battalion – SPECOPS and the *Comandos Anfibios* – COMANFI (marines)
	Antonio Dias Cardoso: 1st Special Forces Battalion (army)
	Parachute Brigade (army)
	Armoured Parachute Squadron (army)
	Destacamento Contra-Terror: Counter-terrorist Detachment (army)
	Comandos de Reconhecimento Terrestre: commando reconnaissance unit (army)
	Federal Police includes anti-terrorist unit (police)
Brunei	Maritime Counter-Terrorism Unit (navy)
	Special Combat Squadron: Special Forces/commando (navy)
	Gurkha Reserve Unit: Royal Guard (army)
	Three Special Forces Companies (army)
Bulgaria	Bulgarian Marine Corps (marines)
	Two Special Commando Companies (army)
	Airborne Regiment (army)
	Two Reconnaissance Battalions (army)
	Red Beret Anti-Terrorist Group (police)
Burkino Faso	Presidential Security Regiment – RSO (government personnel)
	One Airborne Battalion (army)
Burundi	Marine Police Detachment: includes small craft section (police)
Cambodia	Cambodian Marine Corps (marines)
	Three Counter-Guerrilla Brigades (army)
	Special Forces Regiment
Cameroon	Presidential Guard Battalion (government personnel)
	Airborne/Commando Battalion (army)
Canada	Clearance Divers Unit: counter-terrorism (navy)
	Joint Task Force 2 – JTF2: counter-terrorism unit (army)
	Three Parachute Companies (army)
	Royal Canadian Mounted Police: includes Special Emergency Response Team – SERT (police)

Chile	*Parabuzos – Buzos Tacticos*: parachute trained combat divers (navy)
	Infantería de Marina: Chilean Marine Corps (marines)
	1st Battalion Airborne Forces (army)
	Five Commando Battalions (army)
	Four Mountain Infantry Regiments (army)
	Unidad Anti-Terroristes: commando-trained anti-terrorist unit (army)
	Six *Fuerzas Especiales del Ejercito de Chile* (army)
	Carabineros: includes Presidential Guard and Special Forces units (police)
China	Special Anti-Terrorism Troop (government personnel)
	One Marine Corps (marines)
	Three divisions with amphibious training (army)
	6th Special Warfare Group (army)
	8th Special Warfare Group (army)
	12th Special Warfare Special Forces Detachment (army)
	Two Special Forces Brigades (army)
	108 Special Forces Regiments (army)
	Seven Special Forces Battalions (army)
	15th Airborne Army (army)
	Leopard Unit: anti-terrorism unit (army)
	Chinese Special Police Unit (police)
Colombia	*Grupo de Comandos Anfibious* – GCA: combat divers: midget submarines, swimmer delivery vehicles (navy)
	Cuerpo de Infanteria de Marina: Colombian Marine Corps (marines)
	Grupo de Acción Unificado por la Libertad Personal: Unified Action Groups to Rescue Kidnap Victims – Gaulas (government personnel)
	Three *Brigadas de Infanteria Contraguerilla*: include twelve anti-terrorist battalions (army)
	Parachute Battalion (army)
	Lanceros: Ranger Battalion (army)
	Commando Unit (army)
	Counter-Narcotics Brigade (army)
	Fuerza de Despliegue Rápido: Rapid Deployment Force (army)
	Agrupación de Fuerzas Especiales Urbanes – AFEU: urban operations (army)
	Nine Military Police Battalions: counter-terrorism (police)
	Colombian Secret Police – DAS (police)

Côte d'Ivoire	Republican Guard: presidential security force (government personnel)
	Airborne Company (army)
Croatia	Combat Divers: midget submarines, swimmer delivery vehicles (navy)
	4th Guards Brigade: naval infantry unit (navy)
	Croatian Naval Infantry (marines)
	Three Special Forces Brigades (army)
	Anti-teroristicka jedinica – ATJ: anti-terrorist unit (police)
	Postrijba za Sprijecavanje Korupcije I Organiziranog Kriminala – POSKOK: Prevention of Corruption and Organised Crime (police)
Cuba	Two Ministry of the Interior Special Forces Battalions: rapid intervention (government personnel)
	Formación Especial Naval – FEN: combat divers (navy)
	Flotilla de Guardia Desembarco del Granma: Cuban Naval Infantry (marines)
	Comando de Missiones Especiales (navy, army)
	Airborne Brigade (army)
	Two Reserve Battalions of Special Forces (army)
	Department of State Security: secret police force (police)
Cyprus	Special Forces Regiment (army)
	Mobile Immediate Reaction Units (police)
Czech Republic	Rapid Reaction Brigade includes Airborne and Reconnaissance Battalions (army)
	6th Special Forces Counter-Intelligence Unit (army)
Democratic Republic of Congo	Presidential Guard Division (government personnel)
	Congolese Marine Corps (marines)
	31st Parachute Brigade (army)
	3rd Commando Brigade (army)
Denmark	*Frømandskorpsets*: Frogman Corps, Special Warfare Unit (navy)
	Jaegerkorpset: Hunter Corps Special Forces Reconnaissance Company (army)
	Aktions Stryken: Action Force for counter-terrorism (police)
Djibouti	National Security Force (government personnel)
	Airborne Company (army)
	Border Commando Regiment – BCR (army)
Dominican Republic	Combat Divers (navy, marines, army)
	Naval Infantry Battalion (marines)
	Special Forces Battalion (army)
	Special Forces Mountain Rifle Battalion (army)

Ecuador	*Infantería de Marine*: Ecuadorian Marine Corps (marines)
	9th *Patria* Special Forces Brigade (army)
	Four Special Forces Squadrons (army)
	Nine Jungle Infantry Battalions (army)
Egypt	Combat Divers: swimmer delivery vehicles (navy)
	Brigade earmarked for naval infantry role (army)
	Seven Commando Groups (army)
	Task Force 777: counter-terrorism (army)
	Parachute Brigade (army)
El Salvador	Presidential Security Battalion (government personnel)
	Combat Divers (navy)
	Marine Commando Company (marines)
	Marine Infantry Battalion (marines)
	Special Operations Command (army)
	Long Range Desert Patrol Company (army)
	Two Hatchet Strike Commandos (army)
	Naval Commando Company (army)
	Airborne Battalion (army)
	Special Anti-Terrorist Commando Company (army)
	Unidad de Mantenimiento del Orden – UMO: anti-riot unit (police)
	Grupo de Reacción Policial – GRP: SWAT unit (police)
Eritrea	Special Forces Commando Division: possibly twelve Commando Regiments (army)
Estonia	Special Operations Group – SOG (army)
Falkland Islands	Falkland Island Defence Force: non-compliant ship boardings (army)
Fiji	3rd Battalion Fiji Infantry Regiment's Special Forces Company (army)
Finland	*Leivaston Erikoistoimintayksikko*: Naval Special Operations Unit (navy)
	Combat Divers (navy)
	The Nyland Brigade (navy)
	1 *Rannikkojaakarikomppania*: 1st Marine Commando Battalion (marines)
	Sissikoppaniat: ranger unit (army)
	Jaeger Brigade (army)
	Osasto Karhu – Bear Force: counter-terrorism (police)
France	*29ième Service d'Action* – 29SA (government personnel – including combat swimmers)
	Commandant des Opérations Speciales – COS: Special Operations; Command (tri-service)

13ième Regiment de Dragons Parachutists (government personnel)

Groupe de Combat en Milieu Clos – GCMC: maritime counter-terrorism unit (navy)

Fusilier Marine – *Commando Marine*: includes Commando Hubert: Special Force commandos/combat; Divers, swimmer delivery vehicles (navy/marines) and five further *Commandos* – GROUFUMACO (marines)

Nageur de Combat Team: Corsica (navy)

Regiment Parachutiste d'Infanterie de Marine (navy)

Troupes de Marine – TDM (army)

11ième Bataillon Parachutiste de Choc: 11th Airborne Battalion (army)

Groupement Speciale Autonome – GSA (army)

Chasseur Alpines: mountain specialists (army)

Special Operations Army Aviation Brigade – DAOS (army)

27th Mountain Infantry Brigade – 27ième BIM (army)

Légion Étrangère – Foreign Legion: includes one *Demi-brigade* and a *Détachment* plus six Regiments of which the *Deuxième Regiment Etranger de Parachutiste* – 2ième REP – includes the *Commando de Renseignement et d'Action dans le Profendeur* which, in turn, includes *Le Commando de nuit*, *Le Commando de Montagne*, a Combat Diver Company and a Sniper Company. Second Company of the *2ième REP* trained in amphibious reconnaissance: the *6ième REP* includes the *Détachment d'Intervention Opérationelle Subaquatique* – DINOPS: Underwater Special Intervention Detachment (army)

Escadron Parachutistes de la Gendarmerie Nationale – EPGN: anti-hijacking (police)

Groupement d'Intervention de la Gendarmerie National – GIGN: counter-terrorism (police)

Gabon   Airborne Commando Company (army)

Three Brigades of *Gendarmerie National*: paramilitary sea and air force (police)

Gambia   Marine Unit (marines)

Gaza and the West Bank   Palestinian Police Force: four branches with counter-terrorism role (police)

Germany   *Grenzschutzgruppe*: anti-terrorist unit – GSG 9; GSG 9/1, urban terrorism; GSG 9/2, ships, coast installations, oil rigs; GSG 9/3 airborne/aircraft (government police)

	Kampfschwimmerkompanie – KSK: special warfare arm/combat divers/parachutists, swimmer delivery vehicles (navy)
	Kommando Spezialkraft – KSK: Special Forces (army)
	Fernspahkompanien: Special Forces companies (army)
	4th Division Airmobile Forces Command includes three Airborne Brigades (army)
	Alpenjaeger: 1st Mountain Division (army)
Ghana	Two Airborne Special Forces Companies (army)
Greece	*Monada Ypovrixionb Kastrofon* – MYK: combat divers, swimmer delivery vehicles (*Batrahantropos*) (navy)
	32nd Greek Marine Brigade: includes 13th Special Operations Command (army)
	A and C *Amfiva Mira Katadromon*: A and C Amphibious Commando Squadrons (army)
	1st Commando Brigade (army)
	Four Reconnaissance Battalions (army)
	Raider Regiment (army)
	Three ETA Commando Squadrons (army)
	Underwater Missions Squad (customs)
Guatemala	*Caimanes*: Naval Special Forces (navy/marines)
	Two Marine Battalions (marines)
	Kabil: Special Forces (army)
	Two Parachute Battalions
	Special Forces Group: battalion (army)
	Special Forces Platoon (army)
	Tactical Security Group (army)
	Cuerpo Cinco (Batallôn de Reaccion y Operaciones Especiales) – BROE: counter-insurgency (police)
	Cuerpo Seis (Fuerza de ReaccionImmediata) – FRI: rapid response, special operations (police)
Guinea	Presidential Guard (government personnel)
	Commando Battalion (army)
	Special Forces Battalion (army)
Guinea-Bissau	Presidential Protection Unit (government personnel)
	Ranger Battalion (army)
Guyana	Presidential Guard Service (government personnel)
	Special Forces Company (army)
	Anti-Narcotics Unit (customs)
	Target Special Squad: 'The Black Clothes' (customs)
	Berbice: Anti-Smuggling Squad (customs)
Haiti	Counter-insurgency Unit (army/air force)

Honduras	1st *Piranha* Marine Infantry Battalion (marines)
	Agrupacion Tactica Especial: 2nd Infantry Airborne Battalion and Special Forces Battalion (army)
	Military Counter-intelligence Battalion Number 316 (army)
	Fuerza de Seguridad Publica: Special Forces (police)
Hungary	River Flotilla (army)
	3rd Hungarian Division: includes Rapid Reaction Battalion (army)
	RKS: armed response (police)
	Hungarian National Police: anti-terrorist role (police)
India	Aviation Security Force: commandos as sky marshals (government personnel)
	Combat Divers: swimmer delivery vehicles (navy)
	Marine Commando Force – MCF: includes three Quick Reaction Sections – QRS (marines)
	340th Brigade: includes three Para-Commando Battalions; amphibious (army)
	Independent Parachute Brigade (army)
	Rashtriya Rifles: counter-insurgency force – RR (army)
	Special Rangers Group (army)
	Nine Mountain Divisions (army)
	Two Independent Mountain Brigades (army)
	Eight Airborne Battalions (army)
	Thirty-nine Mountain Artillery Battalions (army)
	Unknown number of infantry battalions: counter-insurgency (army)
	Border Security Force (army/paramilitary)
	Rapid Action Force (police)
	National Security Guards: anti-terrorist (police)
	Special Protection Group: VIP security (police)
	National Security Guards – 'The Black Cats': include Special Action Group – SAG and Special Rangers Group – SRG: close protection, anti-terrorism, hostage rescue (police)
	Central Reserve Police Force: augments the RR (police)
Indonesia	*Detachment Jala Mengkara*: maritime counter-terrorism (navy)
	Underwater Demolition Teams – PASKA (navy)
	Kesatuan Gurita: combat swimmers (navy)
	Korps Marinir – KORMAR: Indonesian Marine Corps. Includes *Kommando Intai Para Amphibi* – KIPAM Marine Special Forces (marines)

Special Forces Command – KOPASSUS: includes two
Combat Groups and Detachment 81, counter-terrorism;
Special Operations Group (army)
Paramilitary Mobile Brigade – Brimob (police)

Iran   *Pasdaran Inqilab*: Islamic Revolutionary Guards Corps;
internal security, includes a Marine Brigade and Guards
Special *Qods* Force (government personnel)
Combat Divers, swimmer delivery vehicles (navy)
Three Marine Brigades (navy)
23rd Commando Division (army)
23rd Special Forces Division (army)
55th Parachute Division (army)
SAVAMA: secret police agency, counter-insurgency (police)

Iraq   *Fedayeen Saddam*: Special Republican Guard: believed to
be capable of re-forming (army)
Iraqi Republican Guard: believed to be capable of
re-forming (army)

Ireland   *Sciathan Fianoglach an Airm*: Army Ranger Wing (army)
Gardai Special Branch (police)
Gardai Air Support Unit (police)

Israel   *Mossad Merkazi Le Modin Uletafkidim*: Central Institute
for Intelligence and Special Missions (government
personnel)
Israel Security Agency (*Shin Bet*): counter-espionage/
terrorism (government personnel)
*Shayetet Shlosh-Esrai (13 Commando Yami/Kommando
Yami)*: Flotilla 13/Israeli Naval Commandos, combat
divers (navy)
LOTAR *Eilat*: reserve counter-terrorist unit with Israeli
Naval Commandos (navy)
Givati Brigade: amphibious-trained infantry (army)
Shu'alei Shimson: reconnaissance unit of the Givati
Brigade (Army)
Sayeret Mat'kal: General Staff Deep Reconnaissance Unit
– SM (army)
Sayeret Golani: reconnaissance platoon of the Golani
Infantry Brigade (army)
Sayeret Haruv: reconnaissance unit of the Israeli Defence
Forces Central Command (army)
Sayeret Tzanhanin: commando/parachute/ranger brigade
(army)
Egoz Commando Unit: counter-insurgency (army)

Sayeret Duvdevan: undercover unit in Palestine (army)
Mista'arvin: undercover unit for identifying direct action targets (army)
Sayeret Shaldag (Kingfisher): Air Force Unit 5101, helicopter squadron deployed in support of army Special Forces operations (air force)
Unit 669: search and rescue in enemy territory (air force)
Unit 5707: bombardment intelligence unit (air force)
Matilan: Mobile Warfare Unit in Jerusalem (police)
Latam: works in conjunction with Shin Bet (police)
Yamam: counter-terrorist and hostage rescue unit (police)
Yamas: Border Guard unit, undercover operations in Judea and Samaria (police)
Mishmar-Havgul – MAGAV: paramilitary border police, counter-terrorist operations (police)
Caesarea: hit squad against enemy commanders (police)

Italy
Commando Raggruppamento Subacqui ed Incursori (COMSUBIN): Naval Special Forces; includes two operational groups: *Gruppo Operativo Incursori* – GOI: Attack Divers Operational group; *Gruppo Operativo Subacqui* – GOS: Divers Operational Group: midget submarines, swimmer delivery vehicles (navy and marines)
San Marco Regiment (marines)
Lagunari Serenissima: Amphibious Regiment for Venice, works with the *San Marco* Regiment (army)
Amphibious Brigade (army)
Brigata Paracadutisti Folgore: Parachute Brigade (army)
Alpini Division: Mountain Troops Division: includes one Alpine Parachute Battalion (army)
2nd *Caribinieri* Mobile Brigade: includes the 7th and 13th *Caribinieri* Mobile Regiments and the *Gruppo d'Intervento Speciale* – GIS: Special Intervention Brigade and the *Tuscania Parachute Caribinieri* (police)
Nucleo Operativo Centrale di Sicurezza – NOCS: counter-intelligence, hostage rescue (police)

Jamaica
Maritime Anti-Narcotics Unit (navy)

Japan
Special Guard Unit: combat divers/parachutists (navy)
Special Assault Team: (navy, army)
Airborne Brigade (army)
Police Special Assault Team: counter-terrorism (police)

Jordan
Public Security Directorate: two units – Police and Desert Patrol (government personnel)

	Underwater Swimmer Unit (navy)
	Jordanian Special Operations Command: includes Royal Jordanian Special Forces (RJSF); Nos. 71 and 101 Special Forces Counter Terrorism Battalions; Police Public Security Brigade; Royal Guard (army/police)
	SOU 17: counter-terrorism unit (army)
	Nos. 81 and 91 Parachute Battalions (army)
	Psyops Unit
	Royal Jordanian Air Force Special Operations Squadron – SOS (air force)
Kazakhstan	Republican Guard: VIP protection and anti-terrorist operations (government personnel)
	Alpha Special Force: anti-terrorist unit (government personnel)
	Spetsnaz Brigade (army)
	Attack Helicopter Regiment (army)
	Internal Security Troops (police)
Kenya	Marine Company (marines)
	Airborne Battalion (army)
	Police General Service Unit: uniformed arm of the security and intelligence forces (police)
Korea, North	People's Border Guard: includes security duties at ports and airports (government personnel)
	Combat Divers: midget submarines, swimmer delivery vehicles (navy)
	137th Naval Squadron: sea-borne infiltration (navy)
	Twenty-four Special Forces Brigades: includes eight Sniper Brigades and two Amphibious Sniper (Light Infantry) Brigades; combat swimmers (army)
	Special Operations Corps (army)
	8th Special Purpose Corps; includes airborne and amphibious brigades (army)
Korea, South	Presidential Security Service (government personnel)
	Marine Corps SEALS: combat divers: midget submarines (navy)
	Naval Special Operations Unit: with hovercraft (navy)
	Republic of Korea Marine Corps (marines)
	707th Special Missions Battalion (army)
	Three Counter-Infiltration Special Forces Brigades (army)
	Seven Special Forces Brigades (army)
	Marine Police: incorporates the Coast Guard. Includes anti-smuggling, anti-piracy units (police)

	National Police 868 Unit: counter-terrorism, hostage rescue (police)
Kuwait	National Guard: includes Special Forces unit (government personnel)
	Maritime Special Forces Group (navy)
	Special Forces Commando Group (army)
Latvia	Motor Rifle Brigade (army)
	Constitutional Protection Bureau – SAB: includes Security Police; *Zemessardze's* Internal (counter-intelligence) Section and Military Counter-Intelligence Unit (police)
	Militarised Police Regiment (police)
Lebanon	Lebanese Marine Commando Force (marines)
	101st Parachute Company (army)
	Directorate General des Forces de Securite Interieure: Directorate General of the Internal Security Forces (police)
Libya	Republican Guard: Special Forces Unit (government personnel)
	Combat Divers (navy)
	Naval Infantry Battalion (marines)
	Fifteen Special Forces Groups: commando and paratroop (army)
	People's Security Force (police)
Lithuania	Iron Wolf Motorised Infantry Brigade: includes two airborne battalions – *Rukla Battalion 436* and *Panevezys Battalion 428* (army)
Luxembourg	Two Reconnaissance Platoons (army)
Macedonia	Special Operations Unit (army)
	Falcon Paracommando Unit (army)
	Special Purpose Unit – The Wolves (army)
	Ranger Battalion (army)
	Special Armed *Gendarmerie*: prevention of terrorism and drug-smuggling (police)
Madagascar	Marine Infantry Company (marines)
Malawi	Marine Company (marines)
	Armoured Reconnaissance Squadron (army)
	Parachute Battalion (army)
	Police Mobile Force (police)
Malaysia	Border Scouts: surveillance and intelligence gathering (government personnel)
	PASKAL: Special Sea Unit/Combat Diver Unit: midget submarines, swimmer delivery vehicles (navy)
	Pasukan Khas Laut – *PASKAL*: maritime Special Forces (navy)

	Malaysian Army: all units trained in counter-insurgency (army)
	21st Special Forces Group: three battalions (army)
	10th Parachute Brigade (army)
	Marine Police: includes units for combating illegal fishing, piracy, smuggling, insurgency and terrorism (police)
	Police Air Unit (police)
	Police Field Force: includes five brigades and unit *Vat-69* for counter-terrorist operations (police)
Mali	Special Forces Battalion (army)
	Airborne Battalion (army)
	Two Commando Companies (army)
	Eight *Gendarmerie* Companies: counter-insurgency (police)
Malta	2nd Regiment Armed Forces of Malta (Coast Guard)
Mauritania	Presidential Security Battalion (government personnel)
	Paracommando Battalion (army)
Mauritius	Special Mobile Force (police)
Mexico	Mexican Marine Corps: includes one Paratroop Regiment (marines)
	Two Amphibious Reaction Forces – FRA (navy, marines)
	Security of (Maritime) Strategic Facilities – ASIES: (navy, marines)
	Jose Maria Morelos y Pavon Parachute Rifle Brigade (army)
	Special Forces Airborne – GAFES: counter-insurgency, drug-trafficking (army)
	Special Forces Amphibious – GANFES: counter-insurgency, drug-trafficking (army)
	Kaibiles: anti-guerrilla operations (army)
	Black Needles: high-risk jungle operations (army)
	Green Berets: high-risk parachute operations (army)
	Dirección General de Policia y Transito: paramilitary (police)
	Force F – *Zorros*: Special Police Unit (police)
Moldova	Internal Security Troops (government personnel)
	OMNON riot control (government personnel)
	Spetsnaz Detachment (army)
Mongolia	Internal Security Troops (government personnel)
	Border Troops: counter-espionage (government personnel)
	150th Battalion: rapid reaction (army)
Morocco	Royal Guard: Special Forces (government personnel)
	Moroccan Marine Corps (marines)
	Six Independent Commando Units (army)
	Two Independent Airborne Brigades (army)

	Mountain Battalion (army)
	Corps d'Intervention Mobile: border guards (army)
	Gendarmerie Royale: supports government seal/land/air operations (police)
Mozambique	Mozambique Marine Corps (marines)
	Three Special Forces Battalions (army)
Myanmar	Bureau of Special Operations: controls all Special Forces operations (government)
	Naval Infantry Battalion: counter-insurgency operations (marines)
	Twenty-seven (approximately) Military Intelligence Companies (army)
	Eight Special Police Battalions (police)
Namibia	Namibia Special Field Force: paramilitary, hostage release/anti-terrorist (police)
Nepal	Special Forces Group: includes one Airborne Battalion, two/three Special Operations Companies: counter-insurgency (army)
Netherlands	Combat Divers (navy)
	Royal Netherlands Marine Corps: includes *Amfibisch Verkennings Peloton* – 7 Troop Special Boat Service (Netherlands) (7SBS(NL)); *Bizondere Bijstands Eenheid* – BBE, Special Operations Unit. Within the *Groep Operationele Eenheden Mariniers* – GOEM or Group of Operational Marines – two (plus one reserve) Infantry Battalions and one Amphibious Support Battalion (marines)
	Korps Commandotropen – KCT: Special Forces Regiment (army)
	11th Airmobile Brigade: rapid reaction (army)
	Koninklijke Marechaussee: Royal Military Constabulary (military status): includes civil aviation Security unit (police)
New Zealand	New Zealand Special Air Service Squadron: includes Boat Troop (army)
Nicaragua	*Prefectura de Unidades de Fuerzas Especiales* – PUFA: Special Forces Brigade includes deep reconnaissance and beach reconnaissance commandos (army)
	Regimeiento de Comandancia: includes combat security battalion (army)
	Unidad de Radio-Exploración: SIGINT (army)
Niger	Presidential Guard (government personnel)
	Two Airborne Companies (army)

	Republican Guard: security of state institutions (police)
Nigeria	Presidential Guard Brigade: includes one Commando and one Paratroop Battalion (army)
	82nd Division: includes one Amphibious Brigade and one Airborne Battalion (army)
	Port Security Police: (police)
Norway	*Marinejaegerlag* – Naval Hunter Force: Royal Norwegian Navy Special Forces (navy)
	Coastal Ranger Commando/Battalion: defence of the coastline (navy)
	Finnmark Regiment – Hunter Battalions: includes the *Finnmark 7th Jaeger Company* (army)
	Forsvarets Spesialkommando – FSK: counter-terrorism (army)
	Beredskaptrop: counter-terrorism, hostage rescue (police)
	Police Security Service – PSS: anti-terrorism, counter-intelligence (police)
Oman	Special Forces Battalion (navy)
	Sultan's Special Forces: two regiments each with an amphibious wing (army)
	Sultan's Parachute Regiment (army)
	Royal Guard Brigade: includes two Special Forces Battalions (army)
	Sultan's Special Guard Unit (police)
Pakistan	Federal Investigation Agency: includes anti-terrorist unit (government personnel)
	Naval Special Service Group – SSGN: combat divers: midget submarines, swimmer delivery vehicles (navy)
	Marine Commando Unit (marines)
	Musa Company: combat divers, inland waterways (navy, marines, army)
	Special Services Group (Army) – SSG(A): guerrilla warfare (army)
	Border Rangers (army)
Paraguay	*Cuerpo de Defensa Fluvial*: Paraguay Marine Corps (marines)
	Eight Special Forces Companies (army)
	Anti-terrorist Unit (police)
Peru	*Fuerza de Operaciones Especiales* – FOES: Naval Special Operations Forces (navy)
	Infanteria de Marina del Peru – IMAP: Peruvian Marine Corps (marines)
	Puma Special Forces Group (army)

Airborne Division: includes 19th Commando Battalion, 29th Commando Battalion, 39th Commando Battalion 61st Parachute Battalion and the 10th Airborne Artillery Group (army)

Two Infantry Battalions: jungle warfare specialists (army)

Civil Guard: includes anti-terrorist unit (police)

Philippines Special Warfare Group – SWAG: Philippine Navy Special Forces, combat divers (navy)

Special Reaction Group: combat divers, paratroops (navy)

Philippines Marine Corps (marines)

Special Operations Command – SOC: includes Special Forces Regiment (Airborne) (army)

Alpha Two Zero – A-20: counter-terrorist operations (army)

Philippine National Police Special Action Force – SAF: counter-insurgency (police)

Philippine National Police Aviation Security Command – PASCOM: 710th Special Operations Wing, includes counter-terrorism and parachute operations: Special Operations Group: anti-hijacking (police)

Poland *Grupa Reagowania Operacyjino Mobilnego* – GROM, Thunder: counter-terrorist and hostage rescue special operations unit (navy combat divers and army)

Combat Divers (navy)

Lujcka 7th Naval Assault Brigade (navy)

7th Coastal Defence Brigade (army under naval control)

Special Forces Command (army)

1st Special Commando Regiment (army)

6th Airborne Assault Brigade (army)

Mountain Regiment (army)

Combat Helicopter Regiment (army)

Sea Department (border guards)

Portugal *Fuzileiros*: Portugese Marine Corps: includes *Destacamento do Acções Epeciais* – DAE: Special Forces (marines)

Brigada Aerotransportada Independente: Special Forces (Airborne) Brigade (army)

Airborne Battalion (army)

Grupo de Operacoes Especiais – GOE: Special Operations Group (police)

Qatar Special Forces (Commando) Company (army)

Special Forces Units include Oil Wells Guard Unit (army)

Romania Guard and Protection Service – SPP: presidential protection (government personnel)

	Servicul Roman de Informati – SRI: includes Anti-terrorist Brigade – BA, includes civil aviation protection and anti-hijack duties (government personnel)
	Naval Infantry Force (marines)
	Parachute Brigade (army)
	Special Forces Unit (army)
Russian Federation	*Federalnaya sluzhba okhrany* – FSO: Federal Protection Service, Kremlin's Praetorian Guard (government personnel)
	Border forces: includes Special Forces units (government personnel)
	Glavnoye Upravleniye Ministerstvo Oborony – 12th GUMO: nuclear security and transport (government personnel)
	Spetsialnogo naznacheniya: Three Naval Special Forces – *Spetsnaz* – Brigades: includes one Combat Diver (swimmer delivery vehicles), one Midget Submarine and one Airborne Battalion (navy)
	Morskaya Pekhota – Russian Naval Infantry: includes 103rd Independent Composite Naval Infantry Battalion and two 'elite' companies answering direct to the Commander in Chief of the Navy (marines)
	Alpha and *Beta* Groups: anti-terrorist operations within and without Russia respectively (army)
	Vozdushno Desantniye Voiska – VDV: four Divisions of Russian Airborne Forces (army)
	Thirteen *Spetsnaz* Brigades – SB (army)
	1st Commando Regiment (army)
	Otryad militsii osobennogo naznacheniya – ONON: Special Designation Police Detachment (police)
	Spetsialny otryad bystrogo reagirovaniya – SOBR: Special Rapid Response Detachments (police)
Saudi Arabia	Naval Infantry Regiment: two battalions reported to be commando trained (marines)
	Special Forces Airborne Brigade: two Parachute Companies, three Special Forces Companies (army)
	Special Security Force: SWAT-style force (army)
Senegal	Commando/Airborne Battalion (army)
	COFUMACO *Corps*: counter-insurgency (army)
	Sureté de l'Etat: State Security Force (army)
Serbia and Montenegro	*Resor Drzavne Bezbednost* – RDB: State Security Service (government personnel)
	Kontraobavesajna Sluzba – KOS: Counter-intelligence Service (government personnel)

	82nd Combat Divers Uunit: midget submarines, swimmer delivery vehicles (navy)
	Two Naval Infantry Brigades (navy)
	Special Forces Command: includes 1st (Guards) Brigade, 63rd (Airborne Brigade) and 72nd (Special) Brigade
	Special Anti-terrorist Unit – SAJ (police)
Singapore	Military Security Department – MSD: counter-intelligence (government personnel)
	Coastal Command – COSCOM: regional anti-piracy (navy)
	Two Naval Diving Units – Alpha & Bravo: combat diver (navy)
	Singapore Commando Battalion: includes Underwater and Land Operations Platoons and Special Operations (counter-terrorism) Force (army)
	21st Division: includes one Amphibious Brigade (army)
	Singapore Police Coast Guard: anti-piracy operations (police)
Slovakia	1st Reconnaissance Battalion (army)
Slovenia	*Specialna Enota Ministrstva za Notranje Zadeve* – SA MNZ: Interior Ministry Special Unit: includes *Operativna enota A* – OAE (main operating unit) and *Operativna enota B* – OAB (divers, alpini and cave specialists) (government personnel)
	Special Forces Brigade (army)
	Special Forces Detachment (army)
South Africa	Combat Divers (navy)
	Special Forces Brigade: includes Reconnaissance Commandos: counter-terrorism, long-range reconnaissance, amphibious (army)
	44th Parachute Regiment (army)
	Pathfinder Company (army)
	South African Police Service Special Task Force: hostage rescue, maritime and mountain (police)
Spain	*Unidad Especial de Buceadores de Combate*: Special Naval Divers Unit (navy)
	Infanteria de Marina Española: Spanish Marine Infantry (the oldest in the world) includes the *Tercio de Armada*: Marine Brigade (marines): also includes the *Unidad de Operaciones Especiales* – UOE; parachute and combat divers (marines)
	Brigada Ligera de Infantería: includes Parachute Brigade: *Paracaidist* – BRIPAC (army)
	Three Special Forces Battalions (army)
	Tercio de Extranjeros – Spanish Legion: includes *Bandera*

	de Operaciones Especiales de la Legión – BOEL which includes mountaineering, amphibious and parachuting roles (army)
	Guardia Civil: includes anti-terrorist units (police)
Sri Lanka	Independent Special Forces Group: includes two Commandos (1st and 2nd) and three Special Forces Regiments (army)
Sudan	Airborne Division: includes two Airborne and one Special Forces Brigade (army)
Sweden	*Kurstjaegerskolan*, attack divers: midget submarines, swimmer delivery vehicles (navy)
	Amphibious Corps: includes two Amphibious Brigades (navy)
	Bassäk – Base Security Company: Special Forces (navy)
	Försvarsmaktens Särskilda Skydds Grupp – SSG: Special Protection Group (army)
	Ordningspolisens Nationella Insatsstyrka – ONI: counter-terrorist teams (police)
Switzerland	Maritime Battalion (army)
	Fernspah-Grenadiers – FSK-17: Special Forces unit (air force)
	Kantonspolizei Bern counter-revolutionary warfare team: Stern Unit (police)
Syria	Combat Divers (navy)
	Syrian Marine Corps (marines)
	Special Forces Command: includes 14th Special Forces Division with 1st, 2nd, 3rd and 4th Special Forces Regiments
	Ten Independent Special Forces Regiments: includes Al Sa'iqa: counter-terrorism (army)
	14th Special Forces Division (army)
Taiwan	Taiwanese Marine Corps (marines)
	Airborne and Special Operations Command: includes 1st Special Forces Group: 62nd and 71st Airborne Special Combat Brigades; four Special Operations/Raider Groups (army)
Thailand	Royal Thai Navy SEAL Team: combat divers (navy)
	Royal Thai Marine Corps: includes Recon Battalion (marines)
	Royal Thai Army Special Forces: two divisions (army)
	Task Force 90: counter-terrorism unit (army)
	Thahan Phran Rangers – Hunter Soldiers: thirteen regiments (army)
Togo	Presidential Guard (government personnel)
	Parachute Commando Regiment: one Marine Company, two Infantry Companies (marines/army)
	Commando Group (army)

Trinidad and Tobago	Special Forces Company (army)
	Naval Special Unit (coast guard)
Tunisia	Two Special Forces Brigades (army)
Turkey	*Amfibi Deniz Piyade*: Turkish Marine Corps; includes *Su Alti Savunma* – SAS, underwater defence and *Su Alti Taaruz* – SAT, underwater attack (marines)
	Special Forces Command: four Commando Brigades; 1st Commando Brigade includes two Parachute Battalions; 2nd and 3rd Commando Brigades and 4th Mountain Commando Brigade (army)
	Ozel Hareket Tim – OHT: Police Special Forces: includes commandos and snipers (police)
Ukraine	Directorate of Foreign Intelligence: includes a *Spetsnaz* unit (government personnel)
	Naval Infantry Brigade (marines)
	Border Troops: includes two Sea Brigades (army)
	Spetsnaz Brigade (army)
	Airborne Brigade (army)
	Border Parachute Battalion (army)
United Arab Emirates	Royal Guard Brigade (government personnel)
	UAE Navy Special Operations Group: combat divers, swimmer delivery vehicles (navy)
	Special Operations groups (army)
United Kingdom	Headquarters Special Forces: controls all Special Forces operations (navy/marines/army/air force)
	Three Naval Air Squadrons: 845, 846, 847: Special Forces capable (navy, marines)
	The Royal Marines: includes 3rd Commando Brigade (40, 42, 45 RM Commandos, 29 Commando Regiment, Royal Artillery (army), Armoured Squadron (army), 148 Observation Battery (army), 59 Independent Commando Squadron Royal Engineers (army), Brigade Patrol Troop (marines), 539 Assault Squadron (marines); Fleet Protection Group (marines)
	Special Boat Service (within the Royal Marines): combat divers, swimmer delivery vehicles, beach reconnaissance, advanced force direct action amphibious operations, counter-insurgency (marines, navy)
	Reconnaissance and Surveillance Regiment: world-wide surveillance (all arms)
	Joint Communications Unit, Northern Ireland: surveillance (all arms)

	22 Special Air Service Regiment: includes counter-revolutionary wing (*Pagoda*); four Sabre Squadrons include counter-terrorism, boat, air and mountain troops (army)

22 Special Air Service Regiment: includes counter-revolutionary wing (*Pagoda*); four Sabre Squadrons include counter-terrorism, boat, air and mountain troops (army)

14 Independent Intelligence Company – Northern Ireland (army)

16 Air Assault Brigade: includes 1st, 2nd 3rd Battalion Parachute Regiment including Pathfinder Platoons; 7 Royal Artillery and Royal Armoured Corps support (army)

8 Flight Army Air Corps (army)

47 Squadron Special Forces Flight: Hercules aircraft (air force)

7 Squadron Special Forces Flight: Chinook helicopters (air force)

SO 13: Anti-terrorist Branch (police)

SO 19: Metropolitan Force Firearms Unit (police)

United States
Central Intelligence Agency – CIA (government personnel)

United States Special Operations Command – USSOCOM (all services except USMC Recon)

Naval Special Warfare Command – NAVSPECWARCOM: includes four Naval Special Warfare Groups; seven Sea-Air-Land Teams (SEALS) combat divers, swimmer delivery vehicles (Delivery Vehicle Teams; Special Boat Squadrons, supports counter-insurgency operations (navy)

United States Marine Corps – USMC: Marine Force Pacific and Marine Force Atlantic: include Marine Recon units and full organic armour and air support (marines)

United States Army Special Operations Command – USASOC (army) includes 75th Ranger Regiment; US Army Special Forces Airborne (the Green Berets) unconventional warfare; Delta Force – counter-terrorism (army); Task Force 11 – formed to hunt-down Al Qa'aeda (all arms)

82nd Airborne Division (army)

101st Airborne Division (army)

160th Aviation Regiment: MH 60 and AH-6 helicopters (air force)

Uruguay
Cuerpo de Fusileros Navales: Uruguay Marine Corps, one battalion (marines)

5th Infantry Brigade includes the Airborne Brigade (army)

Montevideo Police includes a quick-reaction, anti-terrorist unit (police)

Uzbekistan
Uzbeck National Security Service – SNB: includes a Special Forces Company (government personnel)

Venezuela
Comando Infantería de Marina: Venezuelan Marine Corps

	(marines) includes Western Amphibious Command and Eastern Amphibious Command; one River Brigade; *Generalissimo Francisco de Miranda* (Special Operations Command) includes Parachute/Commando Unit and Frogman/Commandos: combat divers (marines)
	73rd Ranger Brigade: six battalions (army)
	42nd Paratroop Brigade (army)
	Special Operations Battalion (army)
	1st Infantry Brigade includes *General Jose Ignacio Pulido* (Special Operations Unit 213 (army)
	General de Division Francisco de Paula Alcantara: Air Cavalry Regiment 81 (air force)
Vietnam	Combat Divers: midget submarines (navy)
	Five Naval Infantry Brigades (marines)
	Peoples' Security Force (government personnel)
	Peoples' Security Service (government personnel)
	Peoples' Armed Security Force (government personnel)
Yemen	Battalion Naval Infantry (marines)
	Two Airborne/Commando Brigades (army)
	Special Forces Unit (all arms)
Zimbabwe	Combat Divers (army)
	Commando Battalion (army)
	Parachute Battalion (army)
	Special Air Service Regiment: includes Boat Squadron (army)
	Zimbabwe Republic Police includes a counter-insurgency maritime unit (police)

Photo
Credits

Photo Credits

A. McKascle, USN	302
A. Sharma	280, 332 (both)
ABS Hovercraft	275
Acton	13, 14
Adolfo Ortigueira Gil	323
AE Galarce	340
Aker Finnyards	267
Altama Footwear	55, 56, 57 (top)
Altberg	28 (bottom)
Arktis	28 (top), 31 (bottom), 43, 50 (both)
Armadillo	22 (bottom)
Armor of America	52, 53
Armorshield	27 (bottom)
Arnold Arms	452
Bates	58 (top)
BCB International Ltd	29 (top), 389 (all)
Beaufort Air-Sea Equipment	38 (bottom)
BFA	21 (bottom)
Bill Sweetman	465
BlackHawk Industries	71, 72
Bolivian Navy	344 (both)
Bollé SAS	19, 20
Boston Whaler	341
Browning	12 (top)
C. Cutshaw	433, 445, 453 (top), 456 (top), 457 (top)
Calzaturiera Mastromarco	25 (bottom)
Camil Busqets i Vilanova	333, 345
Chris Sattler	316 (bottom two)
Chris Sorensen/ Messe Berlin	118
Christos J Kourtoglou	23
CMN Cherbourg	308 (bottom)
Colombian Navy	290, 337 (top), 396
CQG	40
Damen	318 (top)
David Boey	320 (both), 321 (both), 334 (bottom)
David Jordan	268
Dessault	113
Divex Ltd	33 (bottom), 34 (both)